Israeli Identity in Transition

Recent Titles in
Praeger Series on Jewish and Israeli Studies

The Hope Fulfilled: The Rise of Modern Israel
Leslie Stein

Continuity, Commitment, and Survival: Jewish Communities in the Diaspora
Sol Encel and Leslie Stein, editors

Critical Issues in Israeli Society
Alan Dowty, editor

Israeli Identity in Transition

Edited by Anita Shapira

Praeger Series on Jewish and Israeli Studies
Leslie Stein, Series Editor

PRAEGER

Westport, Connecticut
London

Library of Congress Cataloging-in-Publication Data

Israeli identity in transition / edited by Anita Shapira.
p. cm. — (Praeger series on Jewish and Israeli studies)
Includes index.
ISBN 0-275-97660-2
1. National characteristics, Israeli. 2. Jews—Israel—Identity. 3. Israel—Social conditions. 4. Israel—Ethnic relations. 5. Social structure—Israel. 6. Social integration—Israel. I. Shapira, Anita. II. Series.
DS113.3.I875 2004
305.8′0095694—dc22 2004012293

British Library Cataloguing in Publication Data is available.

Library of Congress Catalog Card Number: 2004012293
ISBN: 0-275-97660-2

First published in 2004

Praeger Publishers, 88 Post Road West, Westport, CT 06881
An imprint of Greenwood Publishing Group, Inc.
www.praeger.com

Printed in the United States of America

The paper used in this book complies with the Permanent Paper Standard issued by the National Information Standards Organization (Z39.48-1984).

10 9 8 7 6 5 4 3 2 1

Contents

Introduction vii
Anita Shapira

Chapter 1 New Historiography and National Identity: Reflections on Changes in the Self-Perception of Israelis and Recent Israeli Revisionist Historiography 1
Mordechai Bar-On

Chapter 2 Arab–Jewish Relations in Israel: A Deeply Divided Society 31
Sammy Smooha

Chapter 3 Whatever Became of "Negating Exile"? 69
Anita Shapira

Chapter 4 The Diaspora Factor in Israeli Life 109
Eli Lederhendler

Chapter 5 Fifty Years of Israeli Discourse on the Holocaust: Characteristics and Dilemmas 137
Dalia Ofer

Chapter 6 Israeli Identity: The Jewish Component 163
Charles Liebman and Yaacov Yadgar

Chapter 7 Immigrants from the Former Soviet Union: Their Influence and Identity 185
Theodore H. Friedgut

Chapter 8 From Melting Pot to Multiculturalism; or, The Privatization of Israeli Identity 215
Daniel Gutwein

Chapter 9 The Globalization of Israel: Transformations 233
Oz Almog

Index 257

About the Editor and Contributors 267

Introduction

Identity is an ongoing project. The changing zeitgeist, the cultural atmosphere, the impact of a rise or decline in the standard of living, mobility, cultural interchanges, cultural isolation, the rise and decline of social elites—all these and many other factors cause constant changes in the makeup of collective identities. Immigration countries are more prone to such changes than countries with stable populations. Identity-defining components include common ethnicity, religion, ideals and norms, and language and culture and sharing a common past and aspiring to a common future. Immigration countries can hardly boast of any of these. The process through which identity is formed in immigration countries is based on the integration of newcomers into the veteran population. Integration is easier when old-timers and newcomers share a common background and culture. The ratio between immigrants and veterans is also important: the smaller the cohort of immigrants, the quicker the absorption. Eventually, the collective identity is reformulated by a cohesion of the old self and the new elements.

Israeli identity was defined by the generation that established the state, formulating the weltanschauung, the institutions, and the images of the desirable "Israeli." The founding fathers were so-called Ashkenazi Jews, who came mostly from eastern Europe. Infused with a revolutionary fervor and secular worldview, they educated the native-born generation to detest exile and to love and protect their homeland. In the process, they imparted a belief in the basic tenets of Zionism, involving the need of the Jews for their own state in their historic land of Israel. These beliefs were bound by a socialist faith in the emergence of a just, egalitarian society and a "new Jew" who was fit to implement these high ideals. This Israeli identity was put to the test in the 1950s, when the 650,000 old-timers had to absorb twice as many newcomers within the span of a few years. Moreover, many of the new immigrants came from different cultural backgrounds, from countries at different stages of modernity. The unity of language, secularism, beliefs, customs, and norms broke down, never to be regained. In the young state, there remained a substantial Arab minority who preferred not to join their brethren in the refugee camps in the Arab countries. The question of incorporating this minority (whose loyalty to the state was in question) into the evolving Israeli identity was never thought through. Despite everything, the old Israeli identity remained in vogue until the early 1970s.

The Yom Kippur War (1973) brought out all the latent tensions and frustrations. The failure of the leadership to foresee the coming Arab attack and to prepare for that eventuality shattered long-held convictions about the relationship between the government and the public. The realization that the leadership had erred and that its perception of reality had been wrong caused shock waves. It was the end of the Israeli age of innocence. The loss of trust in the Labor Party leadership ushered in a new era in Israeli society and culture. The old social-democratic beliefs that had been accepted by and large by most Israelis since the 1930s lost their hold. In 1977, Labor lost power, and the right-wing Likud Party became the leading force in Israeli politics.

The political upheaval brought to the fore new classes and new cultural milieus: groups that felt excluded from power during the long reign of the Left now demanded their rightful position in politics, in culture, and in the collective memory. Prominent among them were the immigrants who came to the country during the 1950s. The Jews from Arab countries and North Africa felt alienated and discriminated against by the politics of the "melting pot" that were forced on them by the hegemonic Ashkenazi veterans, identified with the Labor Party. The survivors of the Holocaust wished to change the predominant narrative regarding Jewish history, the attitudes toward the Diaspora, and the perception of the Holocaust and its place in the collective memory. Religious groups challenged the traditional role assigned to them at the backseats of the Zionist train and demanded to change places with the secular drivers. The political upheavals and greater openness of Israeli society encouraged the Arab minority, who for many years acquiesced in a second-class citizen status, to press for its rights in Israeli society.

Since the early 1980s, Israeli identity underwent deep changes, resulting in fragmentation of the "old" hegemonic identity into subidentities, so much so that it is questionable whether there exists a single, coherent Israeli identity. The sense of the collective gave way to the emerging individualistic ethos, influenced by trends in the West and by the decline of socialism worldwide. The idea of a comprehensive national society that promotes its basic beliefs and attempts to integrate the different components and traditions of its members into one hegemonic culture was no longer acceptable. A multicultural society emerged that gave legitimacy to different types of Israeliness. Until the 1980s, the Sabra (native-born or locally educated Israeli), considered the epitome of the so-called new Jew, lost his/her primacy. Between the individual and society there appeared mediating bodies. The political parties were no longer organizations guided primarily by opposing worldviews and political agendas. They became the representatives of different sections of society, marked by their ethnic character, special culture, and way of life. The Mizrahi (Oriental Jews), the Haredi (ultra-Orthodox Jews), the Settlers, the immigrants from the former Soviet Union, and the Israeli Palestinians became pressure groups eagerly promoting their own interests.

This splintering of the Israeli identity into subidentities gave the impression of a society in disintegration. In a way, the great debates that raged in the 1990s between so-called Post-Zionist historians, social scientists, and their opponents were the result of this image. Post-Zionist scholars assumed that Israeli society was ripe for a new definition of self, ready to discard the old Zionist, Jewish-centered nationalist creed in favor of a more individualist, cosmopolitan one. The Oslo peace process created an atmosphere of hope—that the age of confrontation and conflict between Jews and Arabs was coming to a close. In the face of the new era, the power of nationalism as a guiding principle seemed to be on the wane. However, in the face of the al-Aqsa intifada that broke out in 2000, the predictions about a society in disintegration proved premature. This does not mean that the fractures were healed: they are still there, waiting for a change in atmosphere that would enable them to be brought to the fore. In the meantime, precedence was given to questions of survival.

This volume attempts to draw a broad picture of the major issues that were on the cultural agenda of Israeli society in the past decade and a half. The divisions of Israeli society—the emergence of political and cultural interest groups that challenged the existence of a national central entity—are reflected in this collection of chapters. Written by leading Israeli scholars, associated with center and left-of-center views, this volume aims at presenting a balanced survey of issues that were in the forefront of the debates on culture, identity, nation-state and multiculturalism, individualism and privatization, Israeliness and Jewishness. These themes impacted public debate, creating a new awareness of Israeli identity and its problems.

The memory of the 1948 war and the way it is being presented in the historical narrative plays a major role in the relations between Israel and the Palestinians. The debate during the past 15 years between "New Historians," Post-Zionist thinkers and scholars, and their opponents began as a discussion about the 1948 war, especially with reference to its results, but soon created a complex of issues, all embedded in the memory of the past. The appropriation of memory served as a tool in the reassessment of past policies and in an overall critique of the very existence of the Jewish state. The attempts to rewrite the past became tied up with the broader issues of postmodernist criticism and the Israeli intellectuals' critique of the policy regarding the occupied territories. In chapter 1, Mordechai Bar-On presents a comprehensive view of the issues involved, including insights relating to the cultural developments and to pressing moral questions.

In chapter 2, Sammy Smooha reviews the current relations between the Jewish majority and the Palestinian minority in Israel. Israel is a Jewish state in the cultural sense and also in the legal sense: certain laws give precedence to Jews over Arabs, notably the Law of Return. To what degree does this kind of discrimination affect the character of Israel as a democracy? The tension between Jews and Arabs in Israel during the past three years was on the rise, leading to the writer's assessment of Israeli society as deeply divided. Smooha charts possible scenarios indicating where this uneasy partnership might be heading.

The perception of Israelis of the Jewish Diaspora is another factor that impacts Israeli identity. Zionist ideology presented Jewish existence in the Diaspora as degenerate and doomed to extinction. This concept, coined "negation of exile," affected strongly the Sabra generation, creating alienation between the young generation raised in Palestine and the Jewish people at large. From the 1940s, following the Holocaust and the mass immigration to Israel, this attitude was in decline. However, despite the obvious anachronism, "negation of exile" became one of the issues in the previously mentioned debate. Post-Zionists questioned the Zionist pretension to protect Jews anywhere, claiming that the concept of negation of exile was the reason behind the alleged abandonment of European Jewry by their brethren in Palestine during World War II. This issue was tied to questions of identity and self-image and also to the incorporation of the memory of the Holocaust in Israeli culture. In chapter 3, Anita Shapira follows the changes in Israeli psyche, from a native-oriented mentality to a Jewish-oriented one, as reflected in Israeli culture and cultural trends.

In chapter 4, Eli Lederhendler offers a different perspective of the relationship between Israel and the Diaspora, with emphasis on American Jewry. The interdependence between the two Jewish communities and their mutual needs are well surveyed. One interesting aspect that appears is the impact on Israeli society and culture of American Jews who immigrated to Israel as agents of westernization in language and as importers of Jewish religious non-Orthodox trends.

The role of the Holocaust in shaping Israeli identity can hardly be overemphasized. The Holocaust became a major issue in Israeli mentality and culture since the Eichmann trial in 1961. As time went by, it gained importance, becoming an educational tool and a cultural focus. Questions of commemoration—of what and how to remember, the appropriation of memory by various political and cultural streams, and the relations between Jews and non-Jews in the wake of the Holocaust—come to light in chapter 5 by Dalia Ofer.

Chapter 6 by the late Charles Liebman and Yaacov Yadgar provides insights into the "civil religion" of Israel and the relationship between religious and nonreligious Jews in Israel. This divide is one of the most important in Israeli society. Much of the enmity and bitterness of the Mizrahi Jews can be explained in terms of the insensitivity and even callousness exhibited by nonreligious Jews in their encounter with traditional, religious communities. In this posthumous chapter, Liebman and Yadgar address the question of the secondary role of Jewish religion in Israeli culture, as they perceive it, despite the fact that most Israelis profess to have a strong affinity to Jewish tradition and practice Jewish rituals. The non-Jewish character of Israeli culture is attributed by them to historical and current reasons. Written by observant Jews, the chapter is evidence of the growing chasm between religious and nonreligious streams in Israeli culture and their mutual misconceptions.

One of the most prominent phenomena in the past decade has been the immigration to Israel of a million Jews from the former Soviet Union, increasing the population by 20 percent. The sheer numbers, the cultural specificity, and the use of the Russian language brought a new element to the mosaic of Israeli society. Since the arrival of the German Jews in the 1930s, no other immigrant group came with such a cultural and professional wealth. In chapter 7, Theodore Friedgut outlines the cultural and sociological characteristics of this substantial group and its impact on Israeli identity. Following the lessons of the "melting pot" policy in the 1950s, this time the newcomers were allowed to follow their cultural preferences. Indeed, "islands" of Russian culture did sprout in literature, the theater, the press, and the media, even special classes for high school students. This notwithstanding, the process of integration into Israeli society is significant, being led by the younger generation. In the meantime, the Russian immigrants form a strong section of the Israeli public, but, contrary to other sections, it seems that this section will be a temporary one.

In chapter 8, Daniel Gutwein brings a neo-Marxist perspective. Analyzing and contextualizing the scholarly and public discussion regarding the melting pot policy, which, Gutwein contends, was intended to consolidate the regulatory powers of the state, enabling the creation of the modern welfare state. Hence, the attempt to deconstruct this policy and ideology was aimed at delegitimizing the Israeli welfare state as part of the privatization revolution that is being implemented in Israel. The erosion of the Zionist ethos, the source of national solidarity, was a precondition for the dismantling of the welfare state, privatization, and extreme individualization. In this chapter, multiculturalism appears as the ideological foundation of the privatization process and the undermining of the welfare state.

Until the Six-Day War, Israel was an isolated country, but since then the country has been increasingly infiltrated by Western customs and lifestyles. The rising standard of living made more Israelis inclined to travel. Israel also became a tourist attraction. The naive provincialism of the early years of statehood gave way to a growing acquaintance with European and, even more so, American culture and ways of life. The media revolution imported to every home the wonders of the postmodern world.

The arrival to Israel of the global village is depicted in chapter 9 by Oz Almog, a cultural sociologist who adds a materialist dimension to the spiritual and mental changes described previously.

Israeli identity is in flux. The most urgent issue on the agenda regards relations with the Palestinians. But as soon as this question is resolved, the fragmentation of Israeli society will come to the fore. The divide between religious and nonreligious, Jew and Arab, and newcomer and veteran and the clash between an overarching Israeli identity and the postmodernist individualist one are here to stay.

Israel is not a cultural island. Processes affecting the West at large are at work in Israel too. Are we witnessing the twilight of a national identity and the emergence of a global village, or is this just a temporary spasm to be soon overshadowed by local cultures and ethnic loyalties?

CHAPTER 1

New Historiography and National Identity: Reflections on Changes in the Self-Perception of Israelis and Recent Israeli Revisionist Historiography

Mordechai Bar-On

THE EMERGENCE OF HISTORIOGRAPHIC REVISIONS

The historiography of Israel's foundation and early years was never uniform. From the very beginning, a myriad of different and at times conflicting narratives appeared in print in an effort to impact the formation of Israel's collective memory.

Moreover, self-conscious and explicit historical revisionism is also not a new phenomenon. Early in the 1960s, a radical critique of Ben-Gurion's policies during the "War of Independence" and his versions of the historical narratives of the war was published by Israel Baer, who was the deputy chief of operation of the Israel Defense Forces (IDF) during the war and a prominent military historian but was later tried for espionage for the Soviets and imprisoned and then wrote his book in jail.

A comprehensive challenge to Israel's dominant narrative was written during the early 1980s by Simha Flapan, a radical leader of the Israeli "Left" and founder and editor of *New Outlook*, a quarterly that promoted dialogue and understanding between Jews and Arab in the 1960s and 1970s.

Yet most of these publications have stirred up only limited controversies, be they in academic circles or in the general public. The debate over the so-called New Historians began to rage only in the late 1980s and more acutely during the 1990s. Three young historians stood at the forefront of this new wave of historical revision: Benny Morris, Ilan Pappe, and Avi Shlaim. But more than their serious studies, which attracted only a limited readership, an article that Benny Morris published in *Tikkun* at the end of the same year sparked off the grand debate.[1]

During the 1990s, scores of angry articles were published from both sides of the controversy in all Israeli newspapers and academic journals. Well-established historians also published critiques of them.

The projection of this supposedly academic debate into the media gave it a deeper and wider dimension. The young sociologist Uri Ram, who experimented with an essay on the sociology of the debate, defined it as "reflecting and elaborating a struggle over the collective memory of Israel, a struggle which may herald expected changes in the definition of Israeli identity."[2]

Those early New Historians were interested primarily in the diplomatic and strategic aspects of the 1948 war and the early years of statehood and focused their studies on Israel's security policy and handling of its conflict with the Arabs. Soon other areas and aspects of Israel's social, cultural, and ideological makeup came under fire. A number of additional historians, sociologists, and anthropologists joined hands with the New Historians in their critique both of Israel's policies and of the traditional perception and narratives of its past. As we shall see later in this chapter, almost every aspect of the Zionist ethos and Israel's dominant ideologies was critically scrutinized. These included the dominant attitude of Israel's establishment and elite toward new immigrants from Islamic countries, perceptions and established interpretations of the meaning of the Holocaust, the status of women in society, the established national mythology, and other central features of Zionist and Israeli culture.

The angry reaction of many Israeli intellectuals and the rejection of the New Historians' narrative by wide sections of the Israeli public, especially among veterans of the 1948 war, suggests that these revisions touched a raw nerve in the Israeli consciousness. In fact, the ongoing heated debate is not just an academic controversy; rather, it seems to be a cultural struggle over identities and self-perceptions with heavy political overtones.

Considering that historical consciousness provides modern societies with a sense of cohesion and existential meaning, Uri Ram sees in the New Historians' debate "an overall challenge to the official and currently popular historic consciousness of the State of Israel."[3] Indeed, the high disciples used by both sides in the public debate clearly pointed to the existence of a crisis of identity, of which this supposedly academic debate is only one expression. Since this crisis went far beyond the narrow confines of academic circles, it may be seen as one aspect of a more comprehensive Kulturkampf. As Baruch Kimmerling articulated, "Social boundaries, which were already there in the past are heightened, while new social boundaries, which support new group identities, are created. These boundaries and identities replicate and reconstruct particularistic collective memories which are retold in modes different from what was customary until then. These memories reestablish the place of these groups in society and thus reshape the history of the state at large."[4]

To gain a better understanding of all this, we shall have to investigate the question, Why did this debate erupt in the 1990s? Is it just a generational advent of young historians and sociologists who were unfettered by the mental constraints under which "Old Historians" (who in most cases personally participated in the events they described and analyzed) worked and which made their work ideologically biased? Or is there a deeper explanation that may also account for the welcome reception of the new revisions by growing sections of the public, albeit still a minority?

One of the explanations that Morris gives in his article in *Tikkun* connects the arrival of the revisionist school in the late 1980s with the customary opening of relevant archives thirty years after the events. This is indeed a normal and quite common process. The opening of archives and the declassification of many documents enable historians to gain a deeper and more precise insight of the events they investigate and therefore facilitate critique of old versions of the story.

This, however, cannot be the central explanation in this case. Most of the revisions by Israel's New Historians have dealt with concepts and interpretations, not with facts. The debate over the "New History" is primarily hermeneutic in its overall tenor. Moreover, many of the Old Historians made ample use of archival materials already in the early years of the state, either because they had privileged access to some archives that were still closed to the general public or because they worked before those archives were properly organized and closed.

Furthermore, many of the facts the New Historians "discovered" in the archives are not new. Thus, for example, the fact that Israeli forces were superior to the Arabs not only in organization and capabilities but also numerically (at least from the end of the first truce at the beginning of June 1948) was known to the IDF History Branch already in 1955. So were most of the details of the secret negotiations between King Abdullah and Zionist/Israeli representatives during 1947–1950.

It seems, therefore, that we must place the revisionist phenomenon within a larger scene concerning wider societal and spiritual developments that unfolded in Israel over the past two decades, focusing less on the "producers" of the New History and more on its "consumers." The key lies, therefore, not in the revisions but in their wide reception and angry rejection.

It had been noted by a number of observers that the objective of the recent historical revisionism is not so much revising what previous academic historians wrote as changing popular images, beliefs, and myths that over the years became dominant in Israeli society. Anita Shapira noted that "the debate on historiography was actually a campaign over the formation of collective memory."[5]

Daniel Gutwein goes further, claiming that the new historiography is altogether an ideological, political, and cultural phenomenon: "The innovation of the new historiography must be found not in the realm of research but in new public and political meanings which were attached to the new data."[6] He posits that the New Historians assail not previous research but extant memories. Rather, they try to suggest alternative memories with the aim of focusing on moral condemnation and guilt.

Thus, the narratives and images against which the New Historians direct their crusade are to be found in school textbooks, commemorative ceremonies, popular journalism, popular songs, and the speeches of politicians rather than in serious historical research.

COLLECTIVE MEMORY AND IDENTITY

The concept of "collective memory" became a popular subject for serious polemic over the past two decades and cannot be dealt with in any detail in the confines of this chapter. Kerwin Lee Klein notes in his detailed survey of the great variety of meanings attached to the term in recent years that "the appearances of the word are so numerous, and its apparent meanings so legion, that it would take the work of a lifetime to begin to disentangle them."[7]

For the purpose of this chapter, it may suffice to focus on the somewhat outdated but still valid meaning of collective memory as a phenomenon that preceded—or must in any case be conceived of as being differentiated from—historiography.

Yosef Yerushalmi considers modern Jewish historiography as positioning itself against the traditional way in which Judaism treated its past, primarily through different devices of "memory."[8] Pierre Nora too thinks of "memory" as essentially an antihistorical archaic discourse that has been corroded by modern rationalism.[9] Along these lines, one may view the Israeli revisionist school as an attempt to pit historical research against false popular or misconceived "collective memory."

Notwithstanding the proclamations of Israeli revisionist historians, we may also conclude that these historians are engaged in a rather ambitious project of reeducating the Israelis. One may assume that what lies behind their motivation is an assumption that the Zionist common ethos and the popular Israeli perception of their past posit psychological obstacles to reconciliation with the Arabs and therefore that it is their charge as historians to correct these deformations.

Michael Schudson noted that memory may characterize groups by revealing their "debt to the past and expressing their moral continuity."[10] However, the term "group identity" is no less vague and confusing than the term "collective memory." Ever since Erik Erikson wrote his first detailed accounts on "identity" and had already noted that "its popular usage has become so varied and its conceptual context so expanded,"[11] a plethora of books and essays made use of and abused this term.

Erikson investigated dimensions of identity primarily as a phenomenon of personal psychic development but also made some seminal observations on the relations of the "self" to one's environment and the position of the individual in "history." He also had some important insights on the notion of "group identity" in general. His basic definition of identity as "a subjective sense of an invigorating sameness and continuity" may serve us well also for a definition of group identity since the terms "sameness" and "continuity" may refer both to the individual's perception of himself and to the joint perception that also defines a group. Erikson, indeed, assured us that "we deal with a process 'located' in the core of the individuals and yet also in the core of its communal culture, a process which establishes, in fact, the identity of those two identities." He views the entire process of identity clarifications as "cultural consolidation."

Social psychologists, especially those who related to the "role" and "reference group" theories, naturally focused their investigations on what Gordon Allport termed "the sense of emotional merging of oneself with others."[12]

One further clarification is necessary. The term "group identity" may be considered from three different points of view:

1. The objective features, which define a group as unique within the wider society
2. The way the group is seen and differentiated by "others"
3. The way members of a group perceive themselves and their position vis-à-vis the "others"

This chapter touches lightly on the first two dimensions but focuses on the third since we shall investigate changes in the self-perception of Israelis. This indeed may be seen as the essence of historiographic and sociological revisionism. It is evident that Israel's society faces today an identity crisis in which individuals are challenged to decide where they stand with respect to traditional values, beliefs, and conflicting interpretations of their past. The New Historians enter this "battleground" with an attempt to leave their own mark. As part of this struggle, historians lend their craft to that effort to reveal their debt to the past, especially to the most formative events of that past.

THE SALIENCE OF 1948'S MEMORIES

It seems safe to assume that very wide sections of the Israeli public hold similar notions about what happened in 1948. These included images of "Little David" (the Jews) who slew "Giant Goliath" (the Arabs) or of the "Perfidious Albion," which did not intend to leave Palestine at all and did everything in its capacity to foil the attempts of the Jews to create a Jewish state. The widespread anger unleashed against the New History is a good indication of the depth of these convictions since it can be understood only as a reaction born out of fear of losing some of the basic beliefs that were upheld for many years by most Israelis and constituted the way they perceived themselves and their position in the world. These notions of perennial Jewish quantitative inferiority and the essential enmity of the outer world are also ways many Israelis see their fate in the present and their odds for the future and constitute a basic dimension of the way they conceive of their collective identity.

Besides common language, common territory, and common cultural traditions that tend to demarcate the boundaries of human groups, a sense of common history—whether past sufferings and defeats or past victories and successes—tends to define the collective identity of groups, especially of nations. Much of this is a spontaneous growth out of what Erikson defines as "affiliative loyalty," which includes "a passion of excluding others, that is of knowing against what and whom one will stand and fall together." However, to be sure, leaders too know that it is necessary "to offer the youth, as well as the perennial adolescent in adults, some over defined enemies against whom to maintain a sense of identity."[13]

It is no accident that the angriest attack against the New Historians was launched not by an academic historian but by Aharon Megged, a noted novelist who charged that the New History may lead to national suicide.[14]

Over the past few years, I have encountered angry reactions and loud heckling during lectures in which I explained the realities of the shifting balance of power that occurred during the 1948 war. I was accused of being a New Historian, a title that was not meant to be a compliment.

It seems, therefore, that the interesting question to be investigated is not the normal and common appearance of a new generation of young historians who understandably want to tell a story of their own and refuse to uncritically accept established truths. Rather, it is the fact that a growing segment of the Israeli public is impressed by and tends to adhere to most of the interpretations that the New Historians have enunciated. This debate is only one aspect of a general "crisis of identity" to which we have been witness over the past two decades. Before proceeding to analyze the more specialized debate on the military and political narrative of the 1948 war and its aftermath, a few comments need to be made about this crisis in general.

PROLIFERATION OF IDENTITIES

Over the past decade, a new perception of the collective identity of Israel has gained wide currency. It is widely held that during the early days of statehood, a high level of homogeneity prevailed. One particular ideology and certain cultural patterns gained total dominance as a result of the unchallenged political and cultural hegemony of the labor movement over the Israeli political arena and Israeli society.

However, since the mid-1970s, a growing plurality has gained the upper hand. It seems that Israeli collective identity is becoming increasingly segmented into a variety of cultural and ideological subgroups that coexist side by side and struggle for their independence, positive valence, and public conspicuity. A struggle for political, economic, and social preferences is also constantly being waged among the different groups, though none of them gain dominance. According to this perception, the old, pioneering, socialist-oriented culture lost its power to impact the entire society and was relegated to the status of just one more minority subgroup. Baruch Kimmerling describes this process succinctly: "A cluster of sub-groups is being formed, in which every group defines itself differently."[15] He believes that "in front of our eyes a new Israeli identity is created, both as a structural formation as well as a potential of a new collective meta-identity." This new identity, he posits, "is a belated result of the decay of the cultural-political hegemony of the secular, quasi-western, Ashkenazi 'Israeliness.'"

Moreover, the very idea of dominance now comes under attack, and plurality is considered not only as normal but also as a preferred pattern. Obviously, this new trend is influenced by the general vogue in Western societies in which preference is given to the discourses of plurality. In Israel, too much of current historiography and social science tends to highlight divergence rather then uniformity. In Israel too, loyalty to subidentities wins precedence over loyalty to overarching identities. The collective national memory has dimmed, weakened, and splintered into different varieties of discourse.

David Ohana goes so far as to doubt "whether in principle, a positive collective identity may be sustained in a culturally multiple, post-ideological society, which is torn over basic issues, devoid of any national consensus and became imprisoned in a coalition of minorities."[16] He defines the new Israeli identity as "a mosaic of dreams, a stage of different longings, a crisscross of memories."

In addition to the mostly urban veteran middle-class Ashkenazi groups who lost their dominance, the main subgroups that constitute Israeli society today are the "Mizrahi" community, Jews who immigrated in the 1950s from Islamic countries, the growing Orthodox communities, Russian-speaking immigrants from the former Soviet Union, and the Arab Palestinian minority.

The Palestinization of the Arab minority as a result of their renewed contacts with their brethren in the territories occupied in 1967, the qualitative and quantitative preponderance of the Russian immigrants, and the overwhelming identification of modern Orthodoxy with the extreme and belligerent settlers all resulted in each group's self-assertion. They feel that the doctrine and policies of the "melting pot" that was promoted by Ben-Gurion and the Labor movement during the first two decades of statehood was only a guise for maintaining the dominance of the veteran, secular, Ashkenazi elite. In the process, their own unique cultures were undermined. They now demand full recognition of the value of their separate cultural heritages and a more central position in society and the political community.

This new perception of Israeli identity gave birth to a flood of books, articles, and films that describe it and try to analyze it, thus fortifying the new images. However, its seems to me that the new plurality reflects a diversification of self-perceptions and self-assertion rather than a growing plurality of actual lifestyles and cultural behavior. Wide exposure to a common media, compulsory universal military service, the overwhelming perception of common dangers and sacrifices, and the growing use of Hebrew and other such factors draw the immigrant and the veteran Israelis toward a syncretic Hebrew culture. Even in the Arab and ultra-Orthodox communities, the use of Hebrew as the everyday language makes communication with the rest of the population easier and intergroup dialogue more frequent and intensive. The growing number of ultra-Orthodox young men who volunteer to serve in the special units recently organized by the army may also be an indication of this process.

It seems to me that the process that is depicted as growing pluralism and fragmentation did not occur in the "objective identity" but rather in the way the different groups, especially their spokespersons, began to perceive themselves. Simon Herman, in his seminal study on the identity of Israelis, differentiated between the "central" features of identity and the "salience" of certain aspects of the same identity.[17] By "centrality" he meant all features that actually fill the everyday life of an individual and constitute his or her "actual identity." Salient are those features, whether central or not, that are considered by the individual as being most important, valent, and worthy of attention, nourishment, and exposure. To use Herman's terms, what we observe is the growing intensity of the "salience and positive valence" attached to the unique facets of the sectorial subidentities and at the same time a growing "centrality" of more uniform features of the common identity in the "life-space" of most Israelis. Nevertheless, for the purpose of our study, the dimensions of group identities that seem to be salient for members of the group are the most relevant here since we investigate the historiographic representation and reception, and these are important aspects of mental consciousness and perception.

The term "New History" at first called public attention to suggested revisions in the narratives concerning primarily the 1948 war and the Arab–Israeli conflict in general. Yet revisionist historiography spread out to many other narratives and fields of interest: the origins of tensions between secular and religious circles, the status of women and gender problems in general, and the formation of ideological and political dichotomies and problems of ethnicity.

Before investigating further the revision in its original sense, we shall look at a short survey of those sectorial dimensions and then proceed to the deal with struggle over Israeli identity and with aspects of the common collective memory of the nation. The following section focuses on the specialized narrative of Mizrahi immigrants and their offspring.

MIZRAHI SELF-ASSERTION

Despite the growing social, economic, and political participation of Jews from Islamic countries who immigrated during the 1950s and of their children and grandchildren in the Israeli public space, the expressed alienation of Mizrahi spokespersons from what they perceive as the suppressing veteran Israeli homogenizing identity is intense. This may explain the surprising success of Shas, the Mizrahi ultra-Orthodox party, during the past decade and the popularity of some of the old Mizrahi rabbis. The widespread veneration of the deceased Baba Sali, a popular Moroccan Jewish "saint," may be explained against the background of traditions imported from the "old country." Yoram Bilu noted that "folk veneration of Saints was a major (if not the major) constituent in the collective identity of the Jews in North Africa."[18] Indeed, since Morocco opened its gates to the visits of expatriates, many Israelis of Moroccan extraction, including those of the second and third generations, visited old graves of venerated Jewish saints buried in Morocco. Issachar Ben-Ami terms this "an exemplary model of a past lost and idealized."[19] These are correct observations, but it seems that they fall short of explaining the success of the younger Baba Baruch, an ex-convict and a shallow individual, in inheriting the veneration of his father. One has to understand this phenomenon as based not so much on old traditions as on the background of new struggles for self-assertion inside Israeli society. To be sure, already back in Morocco these traditions should be explained as defenses against the inroads of modernity but here, in the "new country," modernity is closely linked with social stratification and ethnic differentiation.

Among more secularized and modernized Mizrahi intellectuals, a group known as "Hakeshet ha-Mizrahit" (The Oriental Bow) has recently emerged. This is another indication of the general trend. The group's declared goal is to struggle for the correction of old grievances and to highlight the value of their unique culture. We may therefore turn once more to Erikson, who defined this process as "pride of gaining strong identity [which signifies] an inner emancipation from a more dominant identity, such as that of the 'compact majority.'"[20] Furthermore, there is likely to be a strong link between communities with insecure identities and a passion to delve into the past. This may explain the recent preoccupation with "roots" among second- and third-generation Mizrahi Israelis, who should now be well integrated into Israeli society.

Some New Historians, especially proponents of the "New Sociology," deal directly with these matters and dedicate some of their work to a sharp critique of the old dominant culture and try to expose the suppression of different minorities in Israeli society. In a groundbreaking compilation of critical essays published in 1993, Uri Ram included some strident assaults on the dominant Zionist ethos and its alleged hypocrisy.[21] In the process, he uncovered great contradictions between the declared pious aims and the actual practices of inequality and suppression in the areas of ethnicity, gender, and preferential distribution of society's goods and assets. For example, three articles expose the low status of women, who were relegated by the Zionist macho ethos to a secondary role even in the kibbutz movement, which always claimed to be an example of social equality between the genders. Another indicates that already in the early formative period of Zionist settlement in Palestine, social and economic stratification followed ethnic lines.

Cognizant of the intimate connection between identity and memory, intellectual elites of the disadvantaged groups try to reassert themselves as unique and important segments of Israeli society and attempt to run their own "politics of identity" by reconstructing the collective memory of their groups. Immigrant communities typically try to focus on narratives from the "old country" while re-creating the story of their plights and the discriminations they had to suffer in the "new country." Writers who have followed this path include Yehuda Nini, Esther Meir, and Yaron Tzur.

In addition, a growing number of belletristic and poetic expressions of the life of Jews in Morocco, Iraq, and other Muslim countries, on the one hand, and reminiscences of experiences during the early years in Israel, on the other, fill Israel's bookshelves. A good example of this are two novels by Eli Amir: *Farewell to Baghdad*, which describes the life of Jews in Iraq, and *Scapegoat*, the autobiographical story of Amir's early years in Israel.

All this literary harvest may well exemplify Nora's observation that "what is called memory may become a form of counter-history that challenges the false generalizations in exclusionary 'History.'"[22] Memory becomes a device to redeem the "other within" from the oppressive exclusion of "the totalizing variety of historicism" and to redefine the boundaries of his or her regained identity and thus paradoxically push it into the center of the multicultural Israeli stage. A special form of the same syndrome is noticeable among scholars and political activists who try to preserve the European heritage and combine it with the new Mizrahi self-assertion. The solution for this duality was found in the promotion of a new "identity" that may be termed "Mediterraneanism." David Ohana, one of the promoters of this "identity," wrote, "The Mediterranean option is offered as a cultural possibility in which Israel does not alienate itself from the space in which it exists yet does not disconnect itself from the West."[23]

One cannot help but sense a certain escapism in this approach. Ohana himself admits that they aspire to "spread a broader cultural framework in which we shall not remain alone with our immediate neighbors, the Arabs and the Palestinians, in which we shall find ourselves sharing with them a wider partnership."

This new yearning may also be found in popular music. Over the past two decades, a concerted effort was visible to legitimate "Oriental music" as a dignified form of art, yet real popularity was found in Greek music. It seems indeed that Israelis may feel at home, as Amos Oz has put it, in Piraeus, Naples, or Barcelona rather than in Damascus or Baghdad.

All these ventures may serve as examples for the statement by Richard Handler, who wrote, "Cultures get constructed, deconstructed, and reconstructed as people pursue their identities."[24]

A concomitant feature of the same phenomenon of self-assertion is a recently popular trend of iconoclasm among the same promoters of Mizrahi identity. It is claimed that in the process of their assimilation, in an attempt to build "a new nation," the dominant "white" elite imposed on the new immigrants a "Zionist collective memory." This involved highlighting memories connected with the Land of Israel (in particular, biblical memories) and the narrative of the struggle for the country in the past hundred years (which was actually the narrative of the old elite). Such a narrative, which was aired primarily in the state schools and the media, downgraded and even defamed Jewish existence in the diaspora and suppressed the particular memories of the absorbed groups. It imposed on them a "collective amnesia" of their own past. Therefore, as a supplement to the rediscovery of their unique culture and retrieved collective memory, the new elites try to downgrade the old Zionist narrative by exposing all its pitfalls and sins and restructuring the history of the Jews in Palestine and Israel in less flattering colors.

In 1991, a group of young intellectuals based at the Van Leer Institute in Jerusalem began to publish a quarterly under the title *Teoria u-Vikoret* (Theory and Critique). Over the past 10 years, this journal became the home of most postmodern, postcolonial, and Post-Zionist scholars and critics of Israeli society. As the founders specified in the introduction to the first issue, they have decided to concentrate on "the modes in which [Israeli] reality is represented in various cultural fields and want to expose the ways in which cultural agencies which deal with representational work. We shall investigate the patterns of participation of those representational agencies in the construction of the social order and its replication. or in the formation of power relations within society."[25]

REVISION OF THE NARRATIVE ABOUT THE ARAB–ISRAELI CONFLICT

The limited scope of this chapter does not allow me to continue investigating in greater detail all these important dimensions of the new search for identity and the full scope of recent intellectual revisionism. This chapter proceeds to identify the significance of the particular revision that focuses on the foreign and security policies of Israel in the early years and the attempts to reconstruct the narratives about the Arab–Israeli conflict in general. While this revisionist school coincided with and sometimes overlaps the critique of the previously mentioned sectorial reconstructors of the collective memory and reinforces the general trend of deconstruction of the old Zionist, dominant narrative, they are not similarly motivated since they come mostly from within the dominant elite, and their efforts are an attempt not to construct a new sectorial memory but rather to correct the memory of the entire Israeli collectivity.

The diminishing respect for the old elites that results from the new wave of ethnic self-assertion as described earlier in this chapter may well have also inspired those young historians who dealt with issues of war and peace, though they, for their part, may well have contributed to the same iconoclastic trend. Both are reflections of the new critical ethos that has developed in Israel over the past two decades. The debate over the New History in the narrower sense cuts across all other social rifts. It should rather be understood as a generational leap. There is also a clear political and ideological dimension to this debate, one that also cuts across other rifts. This debate crosses the entire community, setting apart only the two contending sides to the conflict: Jews and Arabs.

Before we turn to a closer discussion of this debate, it seems necessary to clarify that despite the observable intensity and conspicuousness of this debate in the Israeli press and media, the entire discourse is actually rather limited to narrow segments of the public. It is a controversy that touches primarily on more educated sections of society, while important sectors of the population are mostly left out of it. These include the million or so new immigrants from the former Soviet Union, many if them still unable to read Hebrew; half a million members of the ultra-Orthodox circles who do not often read secular scripts; and many other social and economic groups on the periphery of society. Nevertheless, it is an important discourse since centrally positioned agents who have the capacity to impact public opinion and future public images are deftly involved and, according to some assessments, have already made significant inroads into Israeli education. An interesting indication to that effect is the massive counterattack recently launched by Yoram Hazoni and his Shalem Institute, a bastion of conservative intellectual activity, that centered around the inroads that New History has made, according to their claims, into many recently published school textbooks.

Hazoni sees in this debate a "struggle for Israel's soul."[26] Nevertheless, it should be stated at this point that the debate Hazon initiated is being waged primarily among limited academic and intellectual circles and that, while it may coincide with and reflect some political and ideological delineation, it does not represent a specific social group or strata.

THE MAIN ISSUES REVISED

Academic revisions are limited mostly to the period for which most of the relevant documents have already been declassified and made available to scholars. Therefore, they deal mainly with the early years of the State of Israel (up to and including the 1956 Sinai campaign). More recently, some research was completed on the 1960s and the Six-Day War.

However, the major offensive was launched on the narrative of the war of 1948 and its immediate results. It has focused on six main tenets held dearly by Israel's popular perception, tenets that the New Historians consider to be fallacious or—as they often love to call them—false myths:

1. The war of 1948 was initiated by the Arabs who rejected the UN decision to partition Palestine and establish a Jewish state alongside an Arab state. The war was therefore a desperate attempt by the Jews to defend themselves against the Arab onslaughts.
2. Israeli forces throughout the war were inferior in numbers and weapons to the Arab attackers. It was a struggle between "little but clever David" and "giant but inefficient Goliath."
3. The British sided with the Arabs, increasing the heavy burden laid on the Jewish forces. Moreover, the British never really intended to relinquish control of Palestine, but they now decided to do this via their Arab stooges.
4. The war ended in a stunning victory gained as a result of Jewish superiority in moral and combat capabilities. The Israelis put in the field a glamorous force with distinguished commanders and fighters superior in their courage, endurance, and wisdom.
5. Full responsibility for the creation of the Palestinian refugee problem lies with the Arab leadership. It was a result of the flight of the Palestinians who fled despite the pleading of Israeli authorities who asked them to stay put.
6. The war ended only in fragile armistice agreements, not in full peace, since the Arabs declined to accept the verdict of the war and refused to recognize the very existence of the Jewish state in their midst.

VARIETIES OF REVISIONS

The revisionists of Israel's political history may be divided into three groups with three different motivations. The first represents an attempt to revive old controversies that raged at the time of the events. Participants in these controversies—whose analysis and prognosis were defeated and the policies they advocated never tested—and their younger disciples tried to vindicate those alternative policies and claim that they were not only feasible but also preferable since they could have avoided the escalation of the conflict or ended it peacefully once it erupted. This approach views the "road taken" as a mistaken and lamentable policy and tries to convince the reader that the "road not taken" would have been preferable for all parties involved. They lean on the obvious fact that the "road not taken" will always remain pristine since it was never tried, while the "road taken" is marred by bloodshed and costly mistakes.

The main protagonist of this group was Simha Flapan, who during the 1948 war was a leader of the left-wing faction of Mapam. He believed at the time that the creation of a binational state was preferable and feasible. Forty years later, he blamed the Zionist leadership for not taking the road he and his colleagues had recommended and of violently extinguishing all prospects for its realization.

This group of historians deals primarily with the first and fifth assumed fallacies of the traditional Israeli perceptions. They believe that the 1948 war was avoidable and became inevitable mainly as a result of the uncompromising stance adopted by Ben-Gurion and his tendency to escalate violence and unnecessarily expand the territorial gains of the Israeli forces as much as possible.

This group gained very little attention in Israel. It did not even invite much angry response. This may be explained in two ways. On the one hand, the deep and lasting enmity and quite understandable hatred of the Arabs against the Zionist endeavor a hatred that began long before the war of 1948, makes this thesis totally incredible to most Israelis. It may be assumed that the war and the dispossession of the Palestinians from their land contributed to this enmity, but it did not initiate it. Israelis find it difficult to believe that the Arabs would accept the founding of a Jewish state in their midst if only Israel would have adopted a more appeasing strategy. There are many indications that even at the time, the vast majority of his own party members did not accept the theories of Simha Flapan and his friends. They stood too much in stark contradiction to the realities that people experienced.

On the other hand, we may assume that the rejection of this approach also failed since it challenged one of the deepest and most salient facets of Israeli identity. The repetitive violent attempts of the Palestinians to disrupt the Zionist project in 1920, 1921, and 1929—and especially in their Great Revolt of 1936–1939—became a central feature of the socialization of young Israelis and new immigrants alike. The personal experiences of many Israelis during the 1948 war reinforced the conviction of many Israelis that the overarching story can be narrated only as a Jewish defensive response to the total rejection by the Arabs of Jewish aspiration for independence.

The self-positioning as victims also feeds on the traditional Jewish ethos that perceives the Gentiles as perennial enemies who are always set on harassing the Jews and, if possible, on exterminating them. The experience of the Holocaust, only five years earlier, fortifies this self-righteous ethos of the Israelis. Erik Erikson warns us that "we should be prepared for the fact that such resistance joins other defensive reactions against insights which seem to rob us of our self-made certainty."[27] Therefore, it is not surprising that a thesis that tries to put the blame for the conflict mostly on the Israeli side is doomed to be rejected or at best not taken seriously.

NOT SO HEROIC, NOT SO FEW

The second group is interested primarily in refuting the second and fourth assumed fallacies. They attempt to prove that throughout the war, the Jewish side was superior not only in organization and motivation but also in the number of fighting men and formations put on the battlefield. They also claim that in most phases of the war, the Jews were better equipped, while the Arabs not only were ill prepared and lacked unity of purpose and organization but also did not bring to the field adequate forces. Moreover, some go further to claim that the Israeli army was not so heroic, its commanders were mostly amateurs, and the number of their failures and defeats exceeded their successes and victories.

This group may be described as "iconoclasts for iconoclasm's sake." Wistrich and Ohana explain the motivation of such iconoclasm on the assumption that "Israel has no further need for larger-than-life heroes, least of all role models of reckless bravery or military prowess."[28] Some of these iconoclasts are politically motivated, while others seem to believe that the time has come to educate the public not to yield to uncritical admiration of the Israeli army and its leadership and to increase the understanding of the limitation imposed on the use of force in general.

This tendency to look more critically and less laudatory at the Israeli military elite may have well been impressed by the failures of the Israeli forces in the "War of Attrition" during 1968–1970 and in a more acute way in the debacle of the 1973 war. The massive protest movement that in the winter of 1974 successfully brought into the streets tens of thousand Israelis—mainly young demobilized reserve soldiers, aimed primarily at deposing General Moshe Dayan, an icon of Israeli bravery and prowess, from his position as minister of defense—helped corrode the image of other Israeli generals and the security establishment. This must be viewed as a real revolution in the traditional Israeli self-perception and collective identity of which the heroic and victorious Israeli army was always a central theme.

A peculiar dimension of the same trend was represented in a wave of deconstruction and demystifying of the three main symbols of heroism that were sanctified and ritualized by the Zionist movement. At issue here are the myth of Masada, the bravery of Bar-Kochba, and the battle of Tel Hai and its main martyr, Joseph Trumpeldor. The suicide committed in the year 73 A.D. by the Zealots—remnants of the defeated rebellion of Judaea who were besieged in Masada and chose to die rather then fall into the hands of the Roman legionnaires—was sanctified by the Zionist movement since the 1930s under the slogan "Masada will never fall again!" The futile, disastrous rebellion of Shimon Bar-Kochba in the years 133–135 A.D. was also ritualized by the Zionists as an example of personal and military bravery in the struggle for freedom. Tel Hai, a small Jewish settlement in the Galilee, also became a sort of secular shrine, commemorating the heroic though useless death of Trumpeldor and a few of his comrades who fell in an attempt to defend the settlement in the spring of 1920.

During the past two decades, a number of studies and essays—academic, polemic, and popular—were published in Israel in a conscious attempt to demythologize these events and deflate their meaning. Despite the impressive project of Masada's excavation and reconstruction performed by archaeologist Yigael Yadin and the declaration of Masada as a universal treasure by UNESCO, the place lost much of its glamour as a national symbol. The adoration of death by suicide came under severe attack from a number of writers.

Trumpeldor became a popular theme for satire and cynical commentary by Israeli cartoonists and comedians for some years. The wisdom and worth of the defense of Tel Hai was also questioned by academic research, and though the Zionist ritual continues as before, it too has lost a much of its previous shine.

An explicit ideological assault on the myth of Bar-Kochba was presented by Yehoshafat Harkabi, head of Israel's military intelligence in the 1950s, who after 1967 became one of the most active and articulate peace activists. He explicitly considered this myth as tilting the Israelis' psyche against a much-needed realistic perception of their position in their conflict with the Arabs. In his view Bar-Kochba was foolhardy and vainglorious, launching his rebellion without any chance of success and as a result bringing about the death of hundreds of thousands of Jews and the total destruction of the Judaean community that survived the first revolt in the year 70 A.D.

NOT SO RIGHTEOUS

The third group of revisionists are academic historians who dedicate their research to different specific aspects of the Arab–Israeli conflict. Benny Morris revisited the creation of the Palestinian refugee problem and the border wars in the early 1950s, Avi Shlaim focused on the relations between King Abdullah and the Zionists, and Ilan Pappe looked into the role played by Great Britain in the war.

At the same time, other scholars who do not necessarily consider themselves New Historians or even some who position themselves as critics of the critique produced new works that reinvestigated these and other aspects of the period. The most outstanding among these is Yoav Gelber, who completed two volumes of an exhaustive history of Israel's intelligence agencies during the 1948 war and recently published his version of the way the Palestinian refugees were dispossessed. Avraham Sela wrote a new version on the relations of the Zionist movement and the State of Israel with Abdullah of Jordan, and Alon Kadish revisited the case of Ramle and Lod.

Some younger historians began to dedicate their work to local histories. Most of these historians try to distance themselves from the traditional ideologically loaded Israeli narrative and do not hesitate to uncover facts and episodes that are less flattering to the Israelis. The main thrust of this school is to tell the story not as a conflict between the righteous Jews and the evil Arabs but rather as a complex situation in which both sides found themselves engaged in a bloody conflict from which they were unable to disentangle themselves. Many Israelis find it difficult to face such narratives, but to the degree that these historians did not take on the role of supreme judges and focused on a better understanding of the intricate threads of the tragedy, they made an important contribution to our understanding of the past.

CULTURAL DECONSTRUCTION

A special kind of historiographic and sociological critique has surfaced over the past few years. This critique, which is inspired by recent Western cultural criticism, aims not at the revision of a particular set of "distorted" narratives but rather at the Zionist ethos and Israeli identity proper. Its implicit ambition is to revise some basic traits of Israeli culture that are viewed by these authors negatively. Adi Ophir defines well the ambition of this intellectual project as an attempt to "question both the Jewish-Israeli identity as well as the way by which this identity is acquired, since it subverts the capability of the Zionist ideology to continue to construct and spread this identity and deconstructs its last grain of efficacy."[29]

While none of these authors admit explicitly that their motivation was triggered by the contemporary Israeli grand debate on war and peace, one may guess that the new trend is a reflection of a deep sense of frustration stemming from the inability of the Israeli peace camp to transcend its marginal position in Israeli society. These authors seem to assume that the reason for that failure can be found not on the level of political argument or on the ideological level but in the very structure of the Israeli Zionist culture as it evolved over the past century. This new version of revisionism must be seen as a total assault on the Zionist ethos and on the common identity of Israelis.

This section takes a look at three scholars who published their books almost simultaneously in 2002, well into the second year of the second intifada ("Intifadat al Aqsa"), in which almost 2,000 Arabs and more then 600 Jews were killed and tens of thousands wounded. The hot political debate in Israel ever since the violence erupted in October 2000 rages between the Israeli "Right," which maintains that no political or diplomatic avenues are to be followed until Palestinian violence is extinguished by the use of force, and the Israeli "Left," which agrees that the suppression of Palestinian terror requires the use of force but demands a simultaneous political effort to ensure what is termed a "political horizon." At present, it seems that the "Right" has gained a clear majority among the Jews, many of whom lost faith in the ability or readiness of the Palestinians to come to an honest conciliation, while only few challenge the heavy hand that the IDF has put on the Palestinians for many months. All the authors discussed in this section seem to believe that this situation is anchored in deeper cultural roots that are the evil fruits of the Zionist endeavor itself and must be challenged and corrected.

Motti Golani of Haifa University, a positivist historian, published an autobiographical and reflective book under the title *Wars Don't Just Happen.*[30] The main thesis of the book is that from its earliest days, the Zionist movement had chosen power as the preferred way to fulfill its aspirations. This choice was transformed over the years into a comprehensive ethos that corrupted the culture into which young Israelis were framed. This is true also for the Arabs; therefore, "more than the two sides of the conflict react to what the other side does or abstains from doing, they react to their own conceptions and fears."[31] In his book, Golani undertook to expose this corruption and confront it. As Golani readily admits, he was not the first scholar to investigate the role of force, violence, and aggression in the march of Zionism. Anita Shapira analyzed the gradual transformation of the initial Zionist "defensive ethos" into an overwhelmingly "offensive ethos," which, in her opinion, came as a reaction to the growing violent opposition of the Palestinians.[32] Her research ends with the 1948 war, and Golani decided to continue this line of argument and bring it up to date. The bitter controversy between David Ben-Gurion and his minister of foreign affairs, Moshe Sharett (who served during 1954–1955 also as prime minister) over the use of force in combating Arab infiltration during the first half of the 1950s was dealt with by every researcher who studied the story of Israeli security issues in those days. According to the writers who try to vindicate Sharett's position, he was dismissed in June 1956 because he objected to the way Ben-Gurion and his generals used excessive power. In 1995, Uri Ben-Eliezer, a young sociologist, published his study on the militarization of the Zionist movement.[33] His main thesis is that the growing use of military power in the management of the conflict with the Arabs caused a thorough militarization of Israeli society.

Golani take this approach further. He suggests that "the use of violence was an integral part of the Zionist choice . . . this fact became clear already in the 1930s. The establishment of the State of Israel only intensified the use of violence."[34] In his opinion, the Zionist movement used violence at the beginning somewhat hesitatingly, while "Israel uses it with relish." According to Golani, the use of force, ever since 1948, was not necessarily functional and rational. It became a basic feature of the Israeli ethos and collective identity.

Yona Hadari, in her book *Messiah Rides a Tank,*[35] surveyed an immense volume of representations of what she terms "the public thought" (i.e., texts written by scholars, novelists, poets, journalists, and political personalities over a span of 20 years between 1955 and 1975) and discovered a clear pattern. In between the major wars (1956, 1967, and 1973), Israeli society became saturated with a malaise that indicated a loss of idealism, a lack of positive motivation, and general pessimism, but war brought about a wave of euphoria and messianic exhilaration. The public ethos of Israel replaced the initial "realist utopia" of the pioneering prestate period with a militaristic ethos in which the normative figure is a "messianic soldier" who represents a new "messianic, secular, but pious utopia." Moreover, Hadari detects a continuous process of "erotization of war" in which the dominant figure is the "fighting soldier as the lover of the land." This "fighting masculine romanticism" connects the concept of "manhood" with "nationalism." "The masculine ideal becomes the symbol of a national renaissance." Hadari does not grace her work with an explicit theory, but her entire style and use of terms turns her book into a strident, sweeping critique of Israeli identity in which war became a central theme of the Israeli anima.

The third assault on Israeli culture came from a declared postmodernist, Idith Zertal, who drew some public attention by her blatant criticism of the way Israelis in general and the Zionist leadership in particular dealt with the horrors of the Holocaust. Her book *Death and the Nation*[36] continues to analyze the attitude of Israelis to the Holocaust but expands the discussion to a general investigation of the way the Zionist movement and, later, the State of Israel made death and the fallen victims of the struggle into a central feature of its collective identity and self-perception. Drawing on Benedict Anderson, Zertal admits that the use of "holy victims" accompanied all nations in the process of "imagining themselves" but points to the unique Israeli experience in which "from the establishment of the State, the Holocaust and its dead are constantly present in it . . . in its laws, speeches, ceremonies, courts, newspapers, poetry, monuments, and memorial books."[37] She surveys the way Israelis inextricably connected the Holocaust with the creation and justification of the Jewish state but also shows how the Holocaust discourse serves as the rationale for the building of its military power and the justification of its employment. "It gave birth to an old-new myth of an enormous scope that enjoined disaster and redemption, powerlessness and power, a myth which was extricated from history and its political dimensions."[38]

The fact that Golani, Hadari, and Zertal chose to assail not just one particular facet or chapter of the collective memory, as did the original New Historians, but rather the collective identity in its totality means that their prospects of wielding a significant influence on public images are rather scant. Some narrow circles on the left of the Israeli political spectrum may applaud their courage, but it is unlikely that any significant sector of the intellectual elite will negate perceptions that they held dear for so long. All three, we must admit, expose facets of Israeli culture that exist and can be observed in real terms, but their reductionist approach turns their critique into a radical negation of some basic features of the common Israeli collective identity. Their project is bound to fail.

We should clarify that despite their strident critique, Golani and Hadari do not challenge the Zionist project itself but merely question some of the cultural and moral characteristics that afflicted it. Zertal, on the other hand, seems to question the very moral justification and wisdom of the Zionist enterprise in its totality. She was admittedly impressed by Hannah Arendt's critique of the Zionist idea and dedicates large parts of her book to Arendt's thinking on these matters.

NEW HISTORY AND POST-ZIONISM

The controversy over the New History soon became intertwined with another heated controversy between those who may be termed "loyal Zionists" and a group of writers who are often called "Post-Zionists." This last term remains quite nebulous and conceals a great variety of ideological concepts and precepts. It essentially indicates that Zionism is a phenomenon that outlived its purpose and therefore that the time has come to forge a new set of ideas and policies that have to be pursued today and tomorrow. Eric Cohen explained the new trend by the "inability of the established [Zionist] ideology to respond creatively to the problems posed by Israel's occupation of the territories [which caused] a decline of its relevance to the formation of Israeli public opinion."[39] He opines that "the Post-Zionist predicament is thus one of anomie."

As the debate intensified, two different and even contradictory versions evolved. On the one hand, there are people who identify, albeit critically, with the Zionist past and accept favorably in principle the new reality that the Zionist process generated, especially the establishment of Israel as a "Jewish state." They believe, however, that the changing circumstances require a deep redirection of the road taken previously. On the other hand, there are writers who believe that from the outset Zionism was a faulty ideology and that its praxis was very often unjust to many "others": Arabs, Mizrahi Jews, women, and new immigrants in general. Echoing some of the postcolonial theories that became popular in Western academic circles, some of these critics of Zionism describe it as just another example of Western colonialism and highlight the domineering and exclusionary characteristics of the unfolding Zionist project in Palestine.

This group accepts Israel as an irreversible fact. But since with regard to the Arabs it was born in sin, it must at least now remove the evils perpetrated against the Palestinian people. This involves a retreat from all territories conquered in 1967, the facilitation of the creation of a Palestinian state alongside Israel, the ending of all discrimination against the Arab citizens of Israel, and annulling the particular Jewish character of the state, reconstituting it as a "state of all its citizens."

While the first version concentrates on issues of future policies, the latter goes much deeper and challenges the basic concept that, even amidst the proliferation of identities described previously, remains a common denominator of the overwhelming majority of the Jewish citizens of the state, namely, the right of the Jews to a state of their own. This also explains why so many Israelis deeply resent the different expressions of Post-Zionism. It also explains why every attempt at the revision of the common Zionist narrative is labeled "Post-Zionist" with a strong negative implication. In fact, there is no intrinsic connection between the New History and Post-Zionism, but many do not differentiate between the two since in the popular perception any assault on the Zionist narrative is motivated by anti-Zionism. The angry response indicates indeed that many Zionists still feel threatened.

THE END OF IDEOLOGY?

To be sure, at least in one respect the two different versions of Post-Zionism, as well as the New Historians, share an underlying conviction: the declining need of or even the negative role that Zionist ideology may play in the future. The motivating force of the Zionist idea in shaping realities in Palestine over the past hundred years is a well-known dimension of the story. Every Israeli child is exposed at an early age to the famous Herzlian slogan: "If thou wish it is not a fairy tale."

The implication of this aphorism is that the Zionist dream is actually a fairy tale, but the power of will, the power of the idea, can turn it—and actually turned it—into reality. This indeed remained an important mental legacy and a main trait of the way Israelis perceive themselves vis-à-vis the realities they have to confront. Many Israelis still believe that Zionism can and should march on. A large banner was recently hung in the streets and roads of the country by the Israeli Zionist Council reading, "We shall continue to dream the Dream!"

Yet on the Israeli Left, many believe that there are limits to what the Zionist dream can achieve. The thought that in many ways Zionism had already achieved its optimal aims began to permeate growing sections of public opinion. The conviction that, at least in its territorial dimension, Zionism may even have to retract from some of these achievements is already accepted today, according to recurrent public opinion polls by a majority of Israelis. Moreover, Israel has reached, according to this approach, a high level of normalcy, affluence, and stability. This makes Zionist ideology superfluous and redundant. It should indeed be replaced by modern, Western, and humanistic values.

This approach is, of course, not acceptable to the Israeli Right, especially to those who still dream of the "Greater Israel" and espouse the settling of all occupied territories. According to this school of thought, Zionism did not complete its mission and must march on; therefore, Zionist ideology must be upheld as the main motivating force behind Israel's policies. Right-wing propaganda often insinuates that the Left has betrayed and deserted the Zionist idea. The settlers and their protagonists in the political establishment tend to utilize the very word "Zionism" to vindicate their expansionist policies. After the murder of Jews in the occupied areas, settlers often try to establish a new settlement on the spot of the incident and term it "an appropriate Zionist response." A similar manipulation of well-entrenched stereotypes is the use of the terms "National Camp" or "National Action" to define all right-wing groups who adhere to expansionist policies by excluding all the others.

It seems that this co-optation of the Zionism by the Right has motivated many intellectuals on the Left to claim that Zionism had outlived its purpose and now serves only conservative and reactionary forces. Among the many schisms that rip Israeli society apart, this seems today to be one of the most bitter. The schism between Right and Left is above all a crisis of identity: does Israel today embody Zionism on its march toward yet greater achievements, or is it a ripe fruit of the Zionist project that does not have to continue its march and should prefer to stabilize its achievements and adjust them to new realities?

Among the New Historians, the desire to liberate their work from the excesses of Zionist ideology is expressed by a harsh criticism of the ideological bias that tainted, in their opinion, the writings of "old historians" and by a pedantic cleansing of any vestige of ideological bias from their own writing. Thus, for example, any "loaded" term is avoided: "immigrant," not "olim"; "The War of '48," not "The War of Independence"; and even "Palestine," not "The Land of Israel." This new terminology became a sort of "shibboleth" to detect a New Historian. However, those old, loaded terms become over many decades capsules of identity and serve as hinges on which to turn Israel's collective memory. As Pierre Nora taught us, they became sanctioned "lieux de memoire."[40] However, if not taken to excess, this cleansing may help historians write better histories, provided that one does not lean over backward and become a protagonist of the other extreme and an ideologue in his own merits. Thus, for example, it seems that a strong pro-Abdullah and anti–Ben-Gurion bias spoils the otherwise excellent research of Avi Shlaim and that the obsessive urge of Benny Morris to discover every case of cruelty and inhuman behavior perpetrated by Israeli soldiers does not improve his otherwise convincing work. Ilan Pappe extricates himself from this dilemma by following postmodern doctrines. He readily admits that for political reasons, he adopts the Palestinian narrative since no one narrative has any advantage over another. This is an honest statement indeed, but good history it cannot yield.

IMAGES OF THE IMPORTANT "OTHER"

An important aspect of the work of many young Israeli historians that has a strong bearing on questions of identity is the recent attempt by some to reconsider the role the Palestinians played in the conflict. The Arabs in general and the Palestinian Arabs in particular were always the important "other" in Israeli society, especially since many Israelis originated in Arab countries and share some cultural traits with the indigenous societies and wished to draw sharp lines of demarcation to establish clear boundaries of their national and/or religious Jewish self. The continuous and often violent enmity of the Palestinian Arabs against Jews tended to help demarcate those boundaries by sustaining the images of the "other" as belligerent, evil, wild, and uncivilized.

Until 1948, many Jews in Palestine maintained intensive and often friendly relations with Arabs and often strove to exonerate the Palestinian "simple people" from the guilt of violence and hatred. The popular explanation had put the blame either on the Arab "effendi" (i.e., the rich landowners who exploited the Palestinian masses and incited them against the Jews in order to divert their attention away from their own plight) or on the British government, which adopted, according to this view, a policy of "divide and rule." But the bloody and very violent war of 1948 destroyed most of these rationalizations. The image of the naive but essentially well-intentioned Palestinian fellah could not be sustained any more. Facilitating the new image of the Arab as an unrelenting, cruel, and primitive enemy was the fact that between 1948 and 1967, Jews had only limited contact with the few Palestinians who stayed behind and became citizens of Israel and a total absence of any ties with Arabs across the armistice lines.

During this period, Israeli national solidarity, the phenomenon that Erik Erikson terms "affiliative loyalty," was in full power among the Israelis who also developed "the passion of excluding others, that is, of knowing against what and whom one will stand and fall together." Israeli leaders too "found it necessary," as Erikson tells us, "to offer youth, as well as to the perennial adolescent in adults, some over defined enemies against whom to maintain a sense of identity."[41]

In the aftermath of the 1967 war, Israelis came once more in contact with Palestinians in the occupied territories. The abolition in 1964 of the military administration over the Israeli Arabs also facilitated greater contact between Jews and Arabs inside Israeli society. Furthermore, by the end of the 1970s and during the 1980s, a growing number of Israeli Jews became involved in the peace movement and participated in dialogues with Palestinians, including leaders of the Palestine Liberation Organization (PLO). Coexistence projects, organized by diverse peace groups, proliferated.

Many of these new contacts were widely covered by the media, and though negative images of the "Arab enemy" continued to prevail and were further fed by continuing Palestinian violence, a slow change of the negative stereotypes could be observed among the circles from which most young historians came. Articles that portray Palestinians in human terms and bring their plight to the attention of the Hebrew reader are regularly published in the press. Palestinian spokespersons are more regularly invited to take part in public affairs and in the media. A number of documentary and feature films included "positive" Palestinian personae and works of Palestinian writers, and both novels and memoirs of political leaders were translated into Hebrew and had a wide readership.

These changes could not help but influence young historians who felt impelled to take another look at the Arab role in the conflict in the past as well. Besides translations of works written by Arab historians, a few Israeli scholars started to publish more balanced descriptions and analyses of what transpired on "the other side of the hill." Unlike the popular press, historians use less defaming terms in their writings. Thus, for example, the Hebrew words *knu-*

fiot (gangs) and *por'im* (marauders), which were amply used in the past to describe groups of Palestinian fighters, are being replaced in academic scripts by more neutral terms, such as "fighting units" or "guerillas."

THE INFLUENCE OF WESTERN CRITICAL THOUGHT

This chapter began by asking why the new historiography surfaced in full force specifically in the late 1980s and during the 1990s. To be sure, these new tendencies in Israeli historiography and social research were greatly influenced by trends in the intellectual discourse in Western universities that became highly conspicuous in the 1970s and 1980s. The poststructuralist theories of Michel Foucault and the neo-Marxist thinking of Antonio Gramsci and Jürgen Habermas are well known by Israeli intellectuals. So are the postmodern writings of Jacques Derrida and Jean Baudrillard and the postcolonial writing of Edward Said, Homi Baba, and many others. Despite the strident criticism that Said hoists against Zionism and the State of Israel, his influential conceptual insights—spelled out mainly in his book *Orientalism*, which was translated into Hebrew and became popular among students and scholars—did not escape the attention of historians as well. Above all, these influences induced these writers to be aware of the subjectivity of their approach.

In 1991, responding to recent critical theory and the expansion of cultural studies in general, a group of young academics established the previously mentioned scholarly journal *Theoria u-Vikoret* (Theory and Critique). Around this journal, in fact, an ideological, Post-Zionist intellectual "Fabian Club" was informally established. This group represents a wide spectrum of criticism of policies and revisions of old narratives concerning problems of gender, the Arab minority, nationalism, and, of course, the ethnic rifts. On the occasion of the jubilee of Israel (1998), the founder of this group, Adi Ophir, edited a compendium of 50 articles written mostly by Post-Zionists. Each article focused on a theme that has preoccupied public attention in each of these 50 years. Most of the articles were written in a way that can be subsumed under the term "New History" and thus became the best ideological concentration of the revisionist movement. Some of the New Historians were also incorporated into this group, and its influence may be easily detected among many younger historians and the new generation of the behavioral studies in Israel's universities.

The pronounced anti-Zionist inclination of many of the outstanding leaders of this group, however, deterred many others. Among these leaders, a clear tendency may be observed to criticize not only the way Zionist scholars represented in the past the realities that Zionism created in Palestine but also those realities in and of themselves. Zionism is portrayed as a "nationalistic" (meant in the negative sense of the word), colonialist, and intrinsically exclusive suppressing movement. Only a handful of Israeli historians were ready to go as far as adopting the extreme relativistic approach of Hayden White, an approach that blurs the customary boundaries between fiction and historiography and is quite popular with the cultural analysts of *Theoria u-Vikoret.* On the other hand, the writings of Erik Hobsbawm and in particular Benedict Anderson greatly influenced scholars in Israeli universities. They are cited regularly by young historians who share at least in some measure the view that "nationalism" is basically an evil phenomenon and inspire some historians to look hard for any defect in the performances and policies of the Zionist movement and of Israel.

These self-negating tendencies of *Theoria u-Vikoret* not surprisingly limited the influence of the group to some parts of the academic sphere but generated much opposition elsewhere since it threatens to deconstruct important facets and features of Israeli identity with all its diverse varieties. Nevertheless, the influence of this group has doubtlessly fortified skepticism and critical thinking among Israeli scholars and irreversibly undermined their readiness to accept uncritically popular narratives and well-entrenched perceptions as well as the value of authority in general. It must be recognized that, on the whole, this new mood may yield better and more interesting historiography. The new approaches that train young historians to problematize every event and every process they investigate is obviously an important starting point for deeper research.

THE IMPACT OF WARS AND THE PEACE PROCESS

Besides those external influences, it seems to me that the main explanation for the advent of the critical-revisionist mood in Israel's academia must be sought in those internal cultural developments analyzed in this chapter as well as in the impact of dramatic developments in the Arab–Israeli conflict. Most of the New Historians came to adulthood a full generation after Israel's War of Independence. They may have some personal memories of the Six-Day War and probably took part in the October 1973 war but matured academically only during the 1970s or later. They seem to be free of the highly consensual notions that prevailed in Israel before 1967 with regard to the essential nature of the Arab–Israeli conflict. Only few Israelis at the time had questioned the basic assumption that the roots of the conflict are to be found in the Arab refusal to accept a Jewish state in their midst. Therefore, all the wars Israel had to wage, no matter who opened fire first, were imposed on Israel. This left Israel with no alternative but to defend itself, whether through defensive means or by initiating a preemptive offensive. The wars of 1956 and 1967, certainly the war of 1948, were considered as "wars of no choice" (in Hebrew, *Milhamot Ein Breira*).

This unanimous perception began to crack in the late 1960s against the background of the growing political controversy around Israel's policies in the territories occupied during the Six-Day War. A growing minority segment of Israel's intellectuals began to doubt the piously declared intentions of the government to achieve peace with the Arabs. Some began to doubt whether the renewal of warfare along the Suez Canal and the Jordan River, the so-called War of Attrition, could not have been avoided. On April 4, 1970, a group of high school seniors about to be drafted into military service wrote in a letter to Prime Minister Golda Meir: "Until now we believed that we must serve three years and be ready to fight because there is no other choice . . . [now] we and many others are wondering how can we fight a permanent, futureless war, while our government's policy is to ignore any chance for peace."[42]

As mentioned previously, the great shock of the October 1973 war brought home to many more Israelis, who came back from the front frustrated and disappointed, severe doubts about the wisdom and integrity of the government and about the competence of the military elite. The Israeli press too was awakened to realize that by its customary docile and disciplined acceptance of every piece of information handed out by government agencies, it had betrayed its own avocation and became an accomplice to the disaster. Since 1974, the Israeli media became much more critical and skeptical. The Israeli invasion of Lebanon in 1982 hastened this process. The majority of Israelis believed not only that this war was superfluous and misconceived but also that it involved conscious manipulation, disinformation, and deception of the public—and even of the government itself.

All this disillusionment and growing criticism of policies pursued by the political and military leadership became fertile ground for growing doubts concerning policies pursued by the dominant elite during earlier periods. Question marks were now also placed against the interpretation and narration of events during the most constitutive war of 1948.

The beginning of the peace process in the Middle East, first with Egypt in 1977 and then with the Palestinians in the 1990s, a process that led to the Oslo Accords and the famous handshake between Yasser Arafat and Yitzhak Rabin on the lawn of the White House in Washington, D.C., in 1993, gave many Israelis a new hope. But the escalation of Palestinian violence and internal political obstacles in Israel have proven that not all Israelis are ready for the sacrifices and concessions that seemed necessary to successfully complete the process. The minds of a large section of the Israeli public remained burdened by mental and ideological preconceptions and negative images of the "others" that were born out of a hundred years of cruel and bloody conflict and that became an integral part of Israel's collective identity. Intellectuals on the left side of the political spectrum came to realize that there is a dire need to reeducate Israelis and make them also relearn and reinterpret their perceptions of their past.

Few historians will admit that they have an agenda beyond their desire to write "good history," but, whether intentionally or not, much of the work in which young historians in Israel are now engaged may have a lasting impact on the way future Israelis will identify themselves and define the meaning of their relation with the Arabs and the "others" among whom and with whom they are bound to live forever.

In a speech delivered at a UNESCO roundtable in Paris, Menahem Ya'ari, a prominent economist from Jerusalem, asserted that the "a-historicity" that characterizes scientific research may help create a culture more conducive for peace. "In science we must learn early on to let bygones be bygones and not to allow accumulated emotive deposits to affect ongoing work," the professor told his audience.[43] Ya'ari went on to assert that a similar approach should guide peace efforts: "Parties in conflict should seek to achieve fair reconciliation rather than demand an uncompromising historical justice."

As a peace activist, I fully endorse these words, but as a historian, I must find them improbable and unrealistic. Historicity and collective memories are always a central dimension of the conflict. They shape the way the parties perceive not only the conflict, its origins and nature, and the enemy but also their own collective identity. Therefore, they are bound to remain alive and kicking even after political reconciliation has been achieved.

Thus, it is mistaken to make peace contingent on the transformation of collective memories and identities. On the contrary, peace can and should be achieved despite the fact that narratives of the past will continue to conflict. Nevertheless, a more sober and less self-centered and self-laudatory perception of the behavior of one's own side in handling the conflict and a less demonized perception of the way in which one's enemy handled it over the years may help conciliatory leaders gain the popular support of their respective constituencies. Beyond the professional aspiration to produce a better history, this may well be another important role that historical revisionism can play in reshaping the political culture of the peoples or at least of their intellectual elites.

Indeed, we may join Erikson's call for a "new identity" that will requires a new awareness of the "interrelatedness between the repression of inner conflict in those who over adjust to power, the suppression of adversary opinions, and the ready oppression of foreign people . . . [and] recognize the potential of hubris in an expansive initiative which by its very material success seemed to be its own best justification." Erikson concludes, "Liberation can come only from insights into the relevance of past guilt and into the place of ethical choice in the reformation of identity."[44]

NOTES

1. B. Morris, "The New Historiography," *Tikkun* 3, no. 3 (1988).

2. U. Ram, "Memory and Identity: The Sociology of the Historian's Debate in Israel," *Theoria u-Vikoret* 8 (summer 1996): 9–32 (in Hebrew).

3. Ram, "Memory and Identity," 12.

4. B. Kimmerling, *The End of Ashkenazi Hegemony* (Jerusalem, 2001; in Hebrew), 31.

5. A. Shapira, "Politics and Collective Memory: The Debate over 'New Historians' in Israel," *History and Memory* 7 (winter and spring 1995): 9–40.

6. D. Gutwein, "The 'New Historiography' and the Privatization of Memory," in *Vision and Revision*, ed. Y. Weitz (Jerusalem, 1997), 316, 324.

7. K. L. Klein, "On the Emergence of Memory in Historical Discourse," *Representations* (winter 2000).

8. Y. Yerushalmi, *Zahor: Jewish History and Jewish Memory* (New York: University of Washington Press, 1982).

9. Pierre Nora, "Between Memory and History," *Representations* (spring 1989).

10. M. Schudson, *Watergate in American Memory: How We Remember, Forget and Reconstruct the Past* (New York: Perseus, 1992), 51.

11. E. H. Erikson, *Identity: Youth and Crisis* (New York: Norton, 1968), 15.

12. G. W. Allport, *The Nature of Prejudice* (Reading, Mass.: Addison-Wesley, 1954), 293–94.

13. E. H. Erikson, *Dimensions of a New Identity* (New York: Norton, 1974), 95–96.

14. A. Megged, "The Drive for Suicide," *Ha'aretz*, June 17, 1994.

15. Kimmerling, *The End of Ashkenazi Hegemony*, 30–31.

16. D. Ohana, *The Last Israelis* (Tel Aviv, 1998), 25.

17. S. Herman, *Israelis and Jews* (Philadelphia: Random House, 1971).

18. Y. Nilu and E. Ben-Ari, "Modernity and Charisma in Contemporary Israel," *Israel Affairs* 1, no. 3 (spring 1995): 204–36.

19. I. Ben-Ami, *Folk Veneration of Saints among the Jews of Morocco* (Jerusalem, 1984).

20. Erikson, *Identity*, 22.

21. U. Ram, *Israel Society: Critical Perspectives* (Tel Aviv, 1993).

22. Nora, "Between Memory and History."

23. Ohana, *The Last Israelis*, 276.

24. R. Handler, "Is Identity a Useful Cross-Cultural Concept?" In *The Politics of National Identity*, ed. J. Gillis (Princeton, N.J.: Princeton University Press, 1994).

25. *Theoria u-Vikoret* 1, no. 1 (1991).

26. Y. Hazoni, *The Struggle for Israel's Soul* (New York: Basic Books, 2000).

27. Erikson, *Dimensions of a New Identity*, 102–3.

28. R. Wistrich and D. Ohana, eds., *The Shaping of Israeli Identity: Myth, Memory and Trauma* (special issue of *Israel Affairs* 1, no. 3 [spring 1995]: vii).

29. A. Ophir, *Working for the Present: Essays on Contemporary Israeli Culture* (Tel Aviv, 2001).

30. M. Golani, *Wars Don't Just Happen* (Tel Aviv, 2002).

31. Golani, *Wars Don't Just Happen*, 11.

32. A. Shapira, *Land and Power* (Tel Aviv, 1992).

33. U. Ben-Eliezer, *The Emergence of Israeli Militarism 1936–1956* (Tel Aviv, 1995).

34. Golani, *Wars Don't Just Happen*, 102.

35. Y. Hadari, *Messiah Rides a Tank: Public Thought between the Sinai Campaign and the Yom Kippur War, 1955–1975* (Jerusalem, 2002).

36. I. Zartal, *Death and the Nation: History, Memory and Politics* (Tel Aviv, 2002).

37. Zartal, *Death and the Nation*, 16.

38. Zartal, *Death and the Nation*, 229.

39. E. Cohen, "Israel as a Post-Zionist Society," in Wistrich and Ohana, *The Shaping of Israeli Identity*, 210–11.

40. Nora, "Between Memory and History."
41. Erikson, *Dimensions of a New Identity*, 95–96.
42. See *Yediot Ahronot*, 2 October 1992.
43. Speech delivered at the UNESCO roundtable, Paris, 12 November 2002.
44. Erikson, *Dimensions of a New Identity*, 111.

CHAPTER 2

Arab–Jewish Relations in Israel: A Deeply Divided Society

Sammy Smooha

In mid-2003, the Arab citizens of Israel numbered over one million, 16 percent of Israel's population and over one-tenth of the Palestinian people.[1] They stood out also for being an integral part of the enormous regional majority of 270 million Arabs and for being under the cross-fire between the Palestinian al-Aqsa intifada and the state of Israel.

These Arab citizens have been living in Israel within its pre-1967 borders since 1948.[2] They are scattered in the Galilee, the Little Triangle, Northern Negev, and the mixed towns, split into 82 percent Muslims, 9 percent Christians, and 9 percent Druze, and internally divided along lines of social class, kinship, religion, religious observance, and political stream.

I analyze the relations between the Arab minority and Jewish majority. The emphasis is on intergroup relations rather than on either group, and in order to keep a sharp focus, the internal divisions within both sides are not discussed. Being part of Israeli society, the attitudes, behavior, and status of the Arab minority will be seen in comparison with the Jewish majority and be placed in the wider context of life in the Jewish state.[3]

THEORETICAL FRAMEWORK

Societies may be classified according to the degree of severity of their internal ethnonational division that can roughly be measured by two criteria: the nature of the minority and the depth of the divide. A mobilized minority of over one-tenth of the population would pose a much greater problem than a disorganized and smaller minority. A divide is deep when the minority and majority diverge in culture, maintain separate institutions, and disagree sharply on basic ideology.

Societies can be classified into three categories of divisiveness: "undivided" if none of the previous two criteria prevails, "divided" if only one is met, and "deeply divided" if both are present. Most contemporary societies are divided, indicating the universality and significance of ethnonational divisions. A small number of societies are undivided, including the Scandinavian countries, the two Koreas, and Japan. The number of deeply divided societies is also small but very important. These include Iraq, Sudan, Rwanda, Sri Lanka, Northern Ireland, Serbia, and Latvia, among others. Countries in this special category have to cope with enormous disunity and intense conflicts and are susceptible to political instability and mass violence.

The study and comparative study of deeply divided societies began in the 1960s in response to decolonization. Called "plural societies," "segmented societies," "communally fragmented societies," and the like, they were originally described by J. S. Furnivall as composed of "a medley of peoples" who meet only in the marketplace and are held together by the colonial administration. The comparativists M.G. Smith, Leo Kuper, Pierre van den Berghe, R. A. Schermerhorn, and John Rex developed a "theory of pluralism" to account for the structure and dynamics of these societies, revealing considerable variations among them, synthesizing perspectives of conflict and integration, and pointing to nonviolent modes for managing intense internal conflicts.[4]

The central question that preoccupies students of deeply divided societies is the type of regime that can secure ethnic and political stability. Many question whether the classical type of liberal democracy is suitable and workable in this type of society. Found in most Western countries, such as the United States and France, liberal democracy is a political system that extends individual rights to all but denies recognition and collective rights to ethnic groups and national minorities. The state protects citizens against discrimination and encourages them to mix and assimilate. All citizens, regardless of their descent and religion, are treated as members of a single civic nation, sharing a common language, a common culture, and a common identity.

In his book *Democracy in Plural Societies*, Lijphart (1977) generalizes that the deeper the divisions in society, the less the chances for any kind of democracy to persist. He identifies a nonliberal type of democracy that he calls "consociational democracy" as more capable of surviving and regulating the internal divisions in plural societies. Consociational democracy is found in Belgium, Switzerland, and Canada but is rather rare. This kind of system is built on the institutionalization of ethnonational differences. The state takes a neutral position toward the constituent groups and provides the minority with all the necessary arrangements, including separate education, for keeping its language, culture, and identity. Conflict management is achieved through the mechanisms of ethnic autonomy, proportionality in resource allocation, power sharing, veto power on vital decisions, and politics of consensus, compromise, and indecision.

Another theoretical contribution is made by Lustick (1979), who formulates "control" as a viable alternative to both liberal and consociational democracy for keeping law and order in deeply divided societies. While the two types of democracy achieve stability through equality, cooperation, and building of overarching identity and civic institutions, control operates through unilateral conflict regulation. The group in control takes over the state, imposes its culture, and promotes its own interests without considering the other groups. Minority acquiescence is secured by containing the resistance capability of the minority through segmentation (dividing the minority internally and isolating it from the majority), dependence (making the minority dependent on the majority for employment and other benefits), and co-optation (capturing minority elites and leaders). Since control is conceptualized more as a set of mechanisms that can be applied in both democratic and nondemocratic regimes, it cannot be seen as a type of democracy.

Another democratic regime, nicknamed "ethnic democracy," is delineated by Smooha (2002b). It is found in some deeply divided societies, such as pre-1972 Northern Ireland and Slovakia. The state in ethnic democracy is declared to belong exclusively to the majority ethnic nation. The regime is based on two contradictory principles: extension of rights for all and institutionalized dominance of the majority. The minority is perceived as a major threat, put under control, but allowed to wage an intense struggle for change and to effect piecemeal improvement. The political system suffers from an endemic deficit of legitimacy because the minority does not identify itself with the state.

It is not clear which type of democracy can best manage deep conflicts. Lijphart's contention that consociational democracy works best in deeply divided societies is questioned because its effectiveness is limited to cases where the intergroup differences in views and interests are moderate and the gaps in socioeconomic status small (van den Berghe 2002). Smooha's argument that ethnic democracy can be stable under certain conditions is also highly criticized (Yiftachel 1993), and the eventual collapse of the ethnic regimes in Northern Ireland and Macedonia can be cited as evidence.

It is the central thesis of this chapter that Israel is a case of a deeply divided society in which ethnic democracy is effectively used to obtain political stability and ethnonational calm. Israel's features as a deeply divided society and as an ethnic democracy and the mechanisms employed to stabilize the system will be the thrust of the ensuing analysis of Arab–Jewish relations.

SETTING

An overview of the setting in which Arab–Jewish relations is anchored can provide a general understanding of the status of the Arab minority in the Jewish state.

The classification of Israel into the special type of a deeply divided society is incontestable. The Arab minority is a numerically significant and politically mobilized minority. It is sharply separated from the Jews in culture, institutions, power, socioeconomic status, and fundamental ideology.[5] Scholars also agree that while Israel is similar to other deeply divided societies in its high potential for disruption, it has a remarkable record of success in preserving ethnic tranquillity and political stability. They disagree, however, on whether the relative quiet is temporary and whether the long-term trend in Arab–Jewish relations is escalation of the conflict and violent confrontation.

Arab–Jewish relations are shaped by the following factors that best divulge Israel's character as a deeply divided society:

National security. The Arabs are considered by the state and by the Jews as part of the enemy and as a result suspected of likely disloyalty and put under surveillance.

Zionism. It is Israel's raison d'être and de facto ideology that makes Israel Jewish in demography, language, culture, national goals, and policies, thereby preferring Jews to Arabs and splitting the two communities.

Democracy. Israel is a democracy that grants Arabs citizenship and certain collective rights and allows them to conduct an intensive struggle for equality and peace. Democracy is the source of legitimacy for the Arab demands for equality.

All-round Jewish dominance. Jews are dominant in all respects: numerically, politically, culturally, ideologically, and socioeconomically. Suffering from structural subordination, Arabs cannot fairly compete with Jews over resources and national goal setting.

Palestinian people and Arab nation. Israeli Arabs are one of the three segments of the Palestinian people and part of the greater Arab nation.[6] Committed to Palestinian and pan-Arab nationalisms, they constitute a nonassimilating Palestinian Arab national minority in Israel.

Islam. Islam as a religion and a culture as well as Islamic awakening and fundamentalism are strong forces that keep Israeli Arabs apart from Jews and the Jewish state.

The balance sheet of these factors is quite negative. With the exception of democracy, all of them adversely affect Arab–Jewish relations.

What is the type of political regime prevalent in Israel for coping with the deep division between Arabs and Jews and the forces that keep them apart and in conflict? Israel does not qualify as a liberal democracy. It proclaims itself and actually is the state of and for the Jews, not of and for its citizens. In addition to civil rights, it grants some collective rights to the Arabs. It retains two official languages, fails to forge its citizens into a united civic nation, and favors Jews in its policies and practices. Neither does Israel fit the other type of consociational democracy. Although it recognizes Arabs as a community and allows them to preserve their distinct culture and identity, it does not apply any consociational mechanism of conflict regulation. Rather than being a binational state, Israel is a Jewish and a democratic state.

Precisely because Israel is neither liberal nor consociational democracy, some scholars argue that Israel is a nondemocracy or ethnocracy. It is an ethnic state that denies its minority complete membership and full equality and a state that is constituted and run on the undemocratic principle of the "tyranny of the majority" (Ghanem 1998; Yiftachel 1999). This view is untenable because Israel is a democracy for Jews and Arabs.

It is, therefore, best to regard Israel as an "ethnic democracy" (Smooha 2002a). There is an inherent contradiction between two principles of organization the Israeli system is based on: democracy for its Arab and Jewish citizens and structural dominance of the Jewish majority. The protection and promotion of the Jewish ethnic nation, rather than equal treatment of all citizens, are the main mission of the Jewish state. Although differentially treated, the Arab minority is bestowed individual and collective rights and permitted to wage a struggle for improving its status. While it violates the tenet of equality, Israel's ethnic political regime meets the procedural minimum definition of democracy. It is a second-rate democracy in which the Arabs pay a high price in terms of discrimination, exclusion, and alienation.[7]

In view of the nature of Israel as a deeply divided society, its non-Western type of democracy (and for some even a nondemocracy) and the major forces shaping Arab–Jewish relations, the question is, What is the long-range trend of change of Arab–Jewish relations? It is possible to discern three different theses on this issue. The dominant thesis is "mutual rejection." It is popular in academia and the media, among policymakers, and with the Jewish public. Represented by Israeli (1993, 2002), Kedar (2003), Landau (1993), Rekhess (2002), Schueftan (2001, 2002), and Soffer (1993, 1997, 2001), among others, it posits that Arabs and Jews are becoming increasingly radical, estranged to each other and marching toward confrontation. It puts the emphasis and blame on the radicalizing processes that the Arabs are undergoing. Modernization underscores the inferior achievements of the semi-modern Arabs in comparison to the advanced Jews. Palestinization makes Arabs Palestinian in identity and more loyal to Palestinian than to Israeli causes. Islamization transforms a growing proportion of Arabs into politicized and fundamentalist Muslims who repudiate the Jewish state for being an illegitimate and repressive body. The rejection of Israel by the Arab and Muslim worlds drives a wedge between Israeli Arabs and Jews. Radicalized Arabs alienate Jews, who in turn reject Arabs, and rejected Arabs become more radicalized, resulting in a vicious circle of mutually reinforcing hostility between the two sides.

The second thesis is "mutual resistance." It is popular among Arab scholars, media, and public as well as among Jewish non-Zionists and anti-Zionists. Espoused by Ghanem (2000), Lustick (1980), Rabinowitz (2001), Rouhana and Ghanem (1998), Yiftachel (2000, 2002), and Zureik (1979), among others, it presumes that Arabs are becoming increasingly resistant to the exclusionary and discriminatory nature of the Jewish ethnic state, and since the state and Jews remain intransigent, violent conflict and widespread disruption are in store. These scholars place the stress and fault on the Jewish state, which is castigated as nondemocratic despite the misleading facade of democratic procedures. To mention just the main line taken by some analysts, Zureik regards Israel as a colonial society in which Arabs are an internal colony, Lustick portrays it as a generator of anti-Arab discriminations and controls, and Yiftachel presents it as an ethnocracy (a nondemocratic ethnic state) engaged in a repressive project of "Judaization." All adherents to the resistance thesis stress the role of the oppressive occupation of the West Bank and Gaza Strip since 1967 as a crucial factor that stimulates Israeli Arab resistance. While the Arabs are the victims and Jews are the aggressors, the true villain is the Jewish nature of the state that Arabs understandably and justifiably resist and Jews selfishly and shortsightedly buttress.

I have rejected these two widespread and seemingly plausible theses and formulated the "mutual rapprochement thesis" (Smooha 1992). It assumes that the overall trend in Arab–Jewish relations since 1948 is of mutual accommodation. The trend is not linear and straightforward but rather laden with ups and downs. The Arabs are enduring a process of Israelization that makes them bilingual and bicultural and installs an Israeli component into their ways of living and thinking. Arabs appreciate Israel as a modern, welfare, and democratic state and realize that they do not have any better option. The growing Arab pragmatism is matched by a parallel Jewish realization that Arabs are here to stay and that fair treatment and integration are more effective means to handle them. Israel as a state has been democratizing since the mid-1960s. Democratization brings to the fore the value and protection of individual rights for all and enhances the status of nondominant groups, thereby benefiting the Arabs.

All these favorable processes sustain relative quiet and stability in Israel. They counterbalance the forces of frustrating modernization, Palestinization, and Islamization that engulf the Arabs and offset the right-wing drift that sweeps the Jews. Israel's ethnic democracy is resilient, robust, and capable of producing piecemeal improvements. While violent clashes between minority and majority are frequent in deeply divided societies, the moderating conditions prevalent in Israel make Arab–Jewish confrontation less likely.

HISTORY AND COLLECTIVE MEMORY

A brief review of the history of Arab–Jewish relations is essential for understanding not only their origin and development but also the unresolved issues that are still splitting the two communities. The conflictual history ignites and fuels antagonistic collective memories.

History

In 1882, at the inception of the new Jewish settlement of Palestine, Jews numbered only 24,000 (5% of the total population), but because of their steady immigration, they reached 630,000 (33%) on the eve of Israel's proclamation in 1948. During the first half of the twentieth century, a new society, called the new Yishuv, was created by immigrants from Eastern and central Europe, who were inspired and backed by the Zionist movement. Mandatory Palestine was "a dual society," in which Palestinian Arab and Jewish communities lived side by side, held separate institutions, maintained minimal economic contacts, and shared only the administration of the British Mandate (Horowitz and Lissak 1978). The indigenous Palestinians opposed the British Mandate, Jewish immigration, and land sale to Jews and insisted on the instant formation of an Arab state in the entire area (Nevo 1983). The Jewish settlers were engaged in intensive nation building, believing in their exclusive rights to Eretz Israel, but also ready to compromise on partition.

The Palestinian efforts to stop the Jews failed. The Palestinian revolt of 1936–39 was crushed by the British, and in consequence the Palestinian society began to disintegrate. Backed by the Arab states, the Palestinians waged all-out war to prevent the implementation of the UN resolution on November 29, 1947, to divide Palestine into two national states, but they were defeated. The defeat, known as "Al-Nakbah" (disaster), was catastrophic, yielding painful humiliation, loss of Palestine, a sticky refugee problem, a diaspora, the destruction of hundreds of villages and towns, and Jewish confiscation of large Palestinian property.[8]

Another fateful upshot of the Al-Nakbah is the formation of a Palestinian Arab minority in the new Jewish state. At the end of the war, only 180,000 Arabs remained in Israel.[9] As part of a vanquished enemy who continued to fight the very existence of Israel, the Arabs were put under military government until December 1966 (Bauml 2002; Ozacky-Lazar 2002). They were a weak minority, consisting of mostly uneducated and traditional farmers and lacking political leadership and an urban elite. A high proportion of their lands was expropriated. A fifth of them became internal refugees who were forced to resettle in other Arab places because their villages were demolished (Cohen 2002). The Arabs had to adapt to a minority status in a new modern, Jewish state that occupied and ruled them. To expedite their adjustment, Israel extended automatic citizenship to them, launched programs of development and modernization, and practiced a policy of integration along with separation of cultures, communities, and identities. During the 1950s and 1960s, the Arabs underwent appreciable social transformation, a pivotal component of which was proletarization (Haider 1995).

Two turning points in Arab–Jewish relations can be discerned in the 1948–2003 period. The first "fault line" was the first Land Day strike of March 30, 1976. The way to this historical signpost was cleared by the 1967 war, which terminated the isolation of Israeli Arabs from the Arab world. They were reunited with their Palestinian brethren and reopened to the influence of Palestinian nationalism and Islamic fundamentalism. Freed from the military administration, they began to form independent voluntary associations and protest movements. Their emerging leadership declared a general strike in protest of a government plan to take over lands, of which only 6,000 *dunams* (1,200 acres) were owned by Arabs. The strike ended with violent confrontation with the police, six Arabs dead, and scores wounded. It ushered in a new phase marked by intense Arab protest and a show of solidarity with the first 1987–93 intifada. The 1992–95 term of the Rabin government was a golden age for the Arabs. They regarded the Oslo Accord with the Palestine Liberation Organization (PLO) as a prelude to the end of the Palestinian–Israeli conflict and as a transition to a new Middle East. Furthermore, the Rabin government, depending on the parliamentary support of the Arab parties, paid attention to them and initiated a fresh policy of civic equality.

The October 2000 Arab uprising was the second turning point. It was an offshoot of the deterioration of the Arab situation in the aftermath of Yitzhak Rabin's assassination in 1995. After the ascendance of the right wing to power in 1996, the peace process and the corrective policies toward the Arab minority were stopped. The Arabs were further hard hit by the economic recession. Their hope that the new Labor government that took over in 1999 would renew the benevolent dispensation of the Rabin government was shattered quickly. The collapse of the Camp David talks with the Palestinians in July 2000 deepened Arab disaffection. The Israeli Arab demonstrators who took to the streets in solidarity with the Palestinian protest over the al-Aqsa mosque met violent police counteractions, ending with 13 Arabs dead and many wounded. For a week, many Arab localities became restive, public facilities were damaged, highways were blocked, and apprehension on both sides skyrocketed. In response to the Arab indignation and pressure, an official public inquiry commission, the first of its kind in the history of Arab–Jewish relations, was appointed to investigate the causes of the unrest and to look into its mishandling by the authorities and into suspicions of a foul play by Arab leaders.

The legacy of a century of animosity, violence, and privations left each side with bitter ill feelings as well as with a number of pending issues among which the land dispute is the gravest. The Arabs have not resigned themselves to the land takeovers and to the petty compensations offered to them. The internal refugees have not given up on the option of reconstructing their ruined villages. The residents of unrecognized villages demand ownership of the land and a permanent municipal status. Many Arabs wish the state to admit its guilt and to compensate them for the suffering it inflicted. Israel and the Jewish majority are afraid of this awesome package of issues, which has become known as the "dossiers of 1948" (Rekhess 2002).

Collective Memory

The conflict-laden history of Arab–Jewish relations is the origin of conflicting narratives: the Zionist narrative of the Jews and the Palestinian narrative of Israeli Arabs. The Zionist narrative holds that the Jews returned to their homeland after centuries of exile and persecution. They developed the backward country for all its inhabitants, Jews and Arabs. Unlike the big Arab nation with its numerous states, the tiny Jewish nation has only one state that is absolutely necessary for its continued survival and normalization. Jewish rights to Eretz Israel are widely recognized as reflected in the Balfour Declaration of 1917, the Mandate for Palestine confirmed by the League of Nations in 1922, and the UN partition resolution of 1947. The Holocaust has given enormous credence to these international proclamations.

According to the Zionist narrative, Palestinian Arabs behaved maliciously and irrationally. They totally repudiated Jewish rights and did their utmost to thwart the rebuilding of a Jewish homeland. They refused to compromise even on a partition that the Jews reluctantly accepted. Arab belligerency failed to expel the Jews and to topple their state, causing catastrophes on the Arabs themselves who are guilty of the Al-Nakbah and the continued predicament of refugees. They resort to wars and terrorism against the Jews, who continue to be victims, much like Diaspora Jews. The Jews cannot endanger their security and cannot trust Arabs, not even Arab citizens who remain loyal to Israel as long as it is strong. The retention of Israeli Arabs' loyalty requires ongoing state control over them. Like all minorities in nation-states, Israeli Arabs are obliged to accommodate themselves to Israel as a Jewish nation-state They should respect the Jewish majority's desire to keep Israel Jewish and the international recognition of Israel as Jewish. Israel grants Arabs civil rights, welfare services, and the advantages of modernity that none of the Arab states bestows on their citizens.[10]

By contrast, the Palestinian Arab narrative portrays the Jew as the aggressor and the Arab as the victim. However, the real scoundrel is Zionism, which viciously uprooted the Jews from their countries of origin and disseminated the myth that Palestine belongs to them. The Arabs are the true owners and the centuries-old residents of Palestine. The Jews invaded Palestine as European settlers and dispossessed its Palestinian inhabitants. The Arabs failed to liberate the country from Jewish colonization because of Arab disorganization, Western treachery, and Jewish settlers' shiftiness and capital.

In the struggle over the rule of the country, the Jews exhibited wrongdoing and viciousness. They terrorized and slaughtered Arabs, demolished Arab localities, dislodged Arab farmers from their land, and, when they obtained state power, expropriated Arab lands, expelled hundreds of thousands of Palestinians, occupied a territory earmarked for a Palestinian state, and disobeyed the UN resolutions to retreat from Arab areas and to let the refugees return to their homes. The Jews are racist, contemptuous of Arabs and Arab culture, and foreign to the region. Their expansionist drive is insatiable, and their collusion with Western powers is perilous. Despite their formidable military strength, they pretend to be an insecure and helpless victim in order to gain world sympathy and to extract political concessions from the Arabs. The Jews do not acknowledge the Palestinian rights, do not admit the injustices they perpetrated, do not feel any guilt, and do not seek reconciliation. They do not really want peace, refuse to withdraw from Arab territory, and present exaggerated demands for security and normalization of ties with the Arab world.[11]

According to the Palestinian narrative, "the 1948 Arabs," or "the Arabs of the Interior" (these are the common appellations used by Palestinians to name Israeli Arabs), are objects of exploitation and dispossession by Zionist racism. They are deprived of their lands, discriminated against in all walks of life, and subjected to failing Jewish attempts to cut them off from their Palestinian people and Arab nation.

The espousal of the Zionist narrative by the Jews and the Palestinian narrative by Israeli Arabs reveals the abyss that keeps them apart. They conceive of their history and destiny in opposite terms, speak antagonistic discourses, place the blame on the other side, and reject each other's narrative. These rival narratives were, nevertheless, moderated a bit in the 1990s. Under the Post-Zionist attacks and the Oslo Accords, the Zionist narrative has become less diametrical and more understanding of the Palestinians and Israeli Arabs. Continuous life in Israel and the peace process have taught Arab citizens to distinguish between different streams of Zionism, different Israeli governments, and different kinds of Jews and to refine their own narrative accordingly. They have also learned that they cannot afford to freely act on their narrative because of Jewish backlash. For instance, in its appeals to the Supreme Court, Adalah, the Legal Center for Arab Minority Rights in Israel, avoids the Palestinian narrative and uses a liberal discourse of civil rights that is acceptable to the court (Jabareen 1999).

PLURALISM

Pluralism in divided societies has two meanings. "Empirical pluralism" refers to the range and stability of the cultural diversity and institutional separation between the constituent groups, whereas "normative pluralism" means legitimacy of the personal and collective choice between diversity and separation on the one hand and cultural and social assimilation on the other without paying a price for either choice made.

CULTURAL DIVERSITY

Arabs and Jews diverge on all core elements of culture. They have different languages, religions, nationalities, family patterns, and ways of life. Each of these cultural components contains many values, norms, symbols, beliefs, preferences, feelings, heritages, and memories, turning the Arab and Jewish cultures into genuinely distinct and separate cultures and making the ethnic boundaries between the two communities clear, rigid, and hardly passable. A person who passes from group to another through the standard procedure of religious conversion has also to change language, nationality, identity, name, family norms, and lifestyles.

The culture and heritage of the Arabs are Arab Muslim, whereas those of the Jews are Hebrew-Jewish. The Arabs are more traditional, more religious, and less Western than the Jews. In 2001, the fertility rate of Muslims was 4.71, while that of the Jews was 2.59.[12] The participation of Arab women in the labor force was 23.8 percent, much lower than the Jewish rate of 55.9 percent. The proportion of the religious among Muslim Arabs is twice the Jewish proportion. Social control over the behavior of Arab women is strict as compared to the freedom enjoyed by Jewish women. Arabs are obliged to their extended family, while Jews usually do not. Individualism, privacy, self-fulfillment, competition, achievement, nonconformity, materialism, and permissiveness, to mention only a few important Western core values, are much more widespread and rooted among Jews than among Arabs. Not less marked are the differences in human relations. The Arab is less willing than a Jew to conduct impersonal relations. Respect of adults, family honor, and neighborliness are central values among Arabs but much less so among Jews. Arabs are also much better mannered. They speak politely, indirectly, cautiously, and patiently, whereas Jews speak spontaneously, directly, assertively, and impatiently. The two communities differ in their pastimes. Arabs listen mostly to Arabic music, to which only few Jews do. Fewer Arabs than Jews read books, go to the theater and museums, and engage in sports.

Over the years, a cultural rapprochement between the two communities took place as a result of Arab Israelization that transpired without Jewish Arabization. The Arabs have acquired the Hebrew language and the Hebrew culture as a second language and a subculture, respectively. Their traditional culture has also continually been softened by modernization. This cultural change prompts their adaptation to Israeli life and relations with Jews. Most Arabs communicate with Jews in Hebrew and behave in encounters with Jews according to the dominant Jewish standards and expectations. Since 1948, the Arabs have proved to be a nonassimilating minority, in correspondence with their own goals and tenets of Palestinian nationalism and with the approval of the Jews, Israel, and Zionism.

The fact that Arabs and Jews successfully retain their different languages and cultures does not necessarily imply that Israel is a pluralistic society in the normative sense. In fact, multiculturalism as an ideology does not prevail in Israel (Yonah 1999). According to Zionism, Israel should have a single language, a single culture, and a single nation. Arab culture is considered inferior, a culture from which Jews should keep away and of which Jews from Arab countries should rid themselves. An Israeli Arab or Jew does not have a real choice between the two cultures since it is ideologically illegitimate and highly costly to cross over.

SOCIAL SEPARATION

Separation between Arabs and Jews is substantial. Legally, the Israeli population is divided into *millets* (religious communities) entrusted with the administration of personal status. There is no provision in the law for interfaith marriages, although they are not illegal. Arabs are geographically separated from Jews in all levels. Nine-tenths of them live in all-out Arab communities and one-tenth in separate Arab neighborhoods in Jewish towns. Residential isolation reinforces institutional separation. The two bulwarks of integration of Jews in Israeli society, namely, schools and army, sharply divide Arabs and Jews. Arabs attend separate Arabic-speaking schools, except at the higher-education level, because of the absence of separate Arab colleges and universities. They are excluded from the army and other security services on grounds of distrust. They are also organized in separate national political parties that received about 70 percent of the Arab vote in the 2003 Knesset elections. Most voluntary associations are separate for Arabs and Jews.

This vast communal separation is further consolidated by isolation in informal contacts. Mixed marriages are rare and regarded as deviant. Next-door-neighborly relations are infrequent. Only a minority of Arabs and Jews maintain personal friendships and mutual home visits.

Separation declined over the years, however. Before 1948 and during the 1950s, it was nearly complete. Thereafter, Arabs were allowed to enter Jewish institutions, such as the Histadrut (General Federation of Labor) and political parties. They mix with Jews in workplaces and public facilities, such as government offices, bus stations, hospitals, shopping centers, parks, beaches, theaters, and soccer fields.

This considerable separation has several effects for Arabs. It enables the government to discriminate Arab communities and institutions by applying double standards. Yet it shields Arabs against assimilation and creates protected Arab niches, such as schools and economic enclaves. The Arab "invasion" of Jewish communal villages and kindergartens in mixed cities triggers Jewish resistance but also causes keener awareness among Jews of the inferior services rendered to Arabs and hence increases Jewish support for improving Arab conditions in order to avoid integration (Gavison 1999a). Separation is a mixed blessing also for social change. It slows down modernization among Arabs because they continue to live in their own conservative communities and exercise a high degree of social control. On the other hand, the in situ urbanization that the Arabs experience saves them the terrible ills of the Third World, where millions of villagers migrate to the large cities, becoming homeless, jobless, and deprived of basic facilities and living on the margins of society. Separation has also mixed repercussions for autonomy for Arabs. So far, Arab institutional separation has not developed into autonomy. Arab schools, religious courts, Muslim religious endowments (Waqf), and other institutions are controlled by the state (Smooha 1999). It provides them, however, with a solid institutional infrastructure that the government can devolve powers to when it deems fit. It also serves as a power base for Arabs. The Islamic movement aims to harness separation for building a completely separate Arab society for Arabs only and ruled by Arabs.

It is a moot question whether Arab–Jewish separation is involuntary segregation. Arabs and Jews are ideologically and consensually nonassimilating groups, and the retention of their linguistic and cultural differences necessitates institutional separation. At the same time, Arabs are devoid of a real option of integration into Jewish communities and institutions. Although they do not intend to assimilate, most Arabs insist on having the option of integration in order to experience separation as voluntary, and some of them would integrate if given the choice.[13]

DIFFERENCES IN IDENTITY

Arab–Jewish pluralism is well evident in the differences of identity. Jewish identity is less problematic than Arab identity. Since Israel is a Jewish state with a large Jewish majority, Jews can see themselves as both Jewish and Israeli without being overwhelmed by strains and contradictions. In fact, many Arabs and Jews use the term "Israeli" to refer to Israeli Jews. Although Jews adhere to both identities, they differ in their choice between the two. Secular and left-wing Jews prefer Israeli identity, whereas religious and right-wing Jews prefer Jewish identity. These identity choices express different orientations toward Zionism, Diaspora Jewry, democracy, secular Jewish and religious Jewish characters of the state, Israeli–Arab conflict, and Arab minority.

As members of a minority, Arabs have more components to their identity and have to work harder to balance them. For most Arabs, being a Muslim, a Christian, or a Druze is salient in their lives, and they highly appreciate their ethnoreligious identity. With the minor exception of the Druze, Arabs take it for granted that they are Arab by language, culture, and affiliation to the wider Arab nation. While these religious, ethnic, linguistic, cultural, and pan-Arab national ingredients in Arab identity are common and consensual, even from a Jewish viewpoint, the real problem lies in the Israeli versus Palestinian identity (Rouhana 1997; Suleiman 2002). Arabs are Israeli by citizenship and Palestinian by nationality, but both memberships are problematic. Israeli identity is not very significant because civic identity per se is weak in Israel. As an ethnic state with an ethnic democracy, Israel cannot extend full membership to its Arab citizens, who in turn cannot be fully equal to Jews and cannot fully identify themselves with the state. Equally conflict laden is Palestinian identity. Arabs in Israel are the smallest and least important of the three segments of the Palestinian people—the Palestinians on the West Bank and Gaza Strip are the dominant part and Diaspora Palestinians the largest and most unsettled section. For this reason, Arabs feel neglected and a bit exploited by the Palestinian leadership. More important, many Arabs do not feel at ease with Palestinian identity for fear of the Jews and authorities who castigate it as subversive and incompatible with Israeli citizenship. In the Jewish mind, it is tightly associated with Palestinian hate, belligerence, and terrorism. These difficulties with both the Israeli and the Palestinian identities urge some scholars to speak of Arabs in Israel as constituting "a double periphery," that is, being marginal both to Israeli Jews and to the Palestinian people (Al-Haj 1997).

Despite the tensions and hardships involved in forming a meaningful and gratifying identity, most Arabs are attached to both the civic and the national components in their identity. They can hardly escape or relinquish either one. It is difficult for them to conceive of themselves without the Israeli dimension in their lives and to disown their Palestinian affinity, nationality, and heritage. They try to mold a synthesis between these identities. The hybrid identity that is slowly emerging and spreading among them is the self-identification as "Palestinians in Israel." It properly conveys the primacy of Palestinian affiliation and orientation without renouncing Israeli connections.[14]

Inequality

The striking inequality between Arabs and Jews in the distribution of resources is an ongoing concern to the Arabs, the Jews, and the state because they concur that equal opportunity and access to power should be extended to all in Israel as a democratic and Jewish state.

Socioeconomic Gaps

Various indicators unravel the considerable socioeconomic gaps between Arabs and Jews. The policy of free education from the ages of 5 to 17 and the existence of a separate educational system enable Arabs to acquire a substantial degree of education. For this reason, Arabs have only 1.4 years of schooling less than Jews (11.2 versus 12.6). Their real disadvantage is in the higher levels, where education is neither free nor separate. The rate of Arabs who continue postsecondary education is half the Jewish rate (22.1% versus 42.2%). Their chances to obtain a matriculation diploma and to attend institutions of higher learning are much lower (of all twelfth graders in 1991–92, 28.0 percent of the Arabs versus 48.8% of the Jews began postsecondary or higher education by 1999–2000). They are highly underrepresented among graduates from Israeli universities (in 2001–01, they constituted 6.7% of the recipients of a bachelor's degree and 2.6% of the recipients of a master's degree). These discrepancies in education contribute to the Arab lower achievement in the labor market. For instance, 20.3 percent of Arabs as compared to 38.2 percent of Jews in 2001 were employed in the three top occupational categories (academic/professional, semiprofessional/technical, and managerial).

Arabs are at a marked disadvantage in standards of living. Their wage earnings and per capita incomes are lower. An official classification of all 210 local authorities in Israel in 2001, according to multiple indicators of their population's socioeconomic characteristics, assigns 52 percent of the Arab local authorities to the two lowest clusters and 96 percent to the four lowest clusters. These villages and towns maintain poor infrastructures and provide substandard services. About 80,000 Bedouin live in unrecognized settlements without basic facilities, such as access roads, running water, electricity, schools, and clinics. The incidence of families living in poverty in 2001 was 41.3 percent among Arabs as compared to the national average of 17.7 percent. These material disparities stem from cumulative Arab weaknesses, including a low female participation rate in the labor force, large families, less skilled employment, and discrimination in the labor market and in public funding.

Arabs have remained a working-class minority in a predominantly middle-class Jewish society. Their share in the middle and higher strata is limited. Although their standards of education, employment, income, housing, and health have steadily risen over the years and the enormous initial gaps with the Jews have narrowed, inequality is still appreciable (Kraus and Yonay 2000). Since Arabs take the Jews as their comparative group, they feel an acute sense of relative deprivation, especially because of continued discrimination and the government's unpreparedness to launch a crash program to bring them to a par with the Jews. Both as individuals and as a collectivity, the Arabs cannot compete equally and fairly with Jews for opportunities because of untrustworthy status, incomplete command of Hebrew, exclusion from powerful Jewish social networks, and interpersonal and institutional discrimination.

Power Disparities

At the local level, Arabs enjoy power and influence. They staff all power and elite positions in their separate communities, serving as heads of local governments, councilors, officials, school principals, lawyers, doctors, businessmen, owners of small plants, and the like. These highly coveted roles are toughly contested by individuals and *hamulas* (extended kinship groups). Another area of influence is the growing Arab civil society that is composed of over 1,000 local and statewide voluntary associations providing cultural and welfare services and promoting advocacy and protest. Another sphere of activity is launched by the Islamic movement, which has formed numerous organizations through which it serves, educates, and remolds the Arab community. It is building "a separate Islamic society" that aspires to be self-sufficient and independent of the state.

While Arabs wield effective control of their communities, their penetration of the national power structure is meager with one notable exception: the parliament. Since the mid-1990s, the Arabs are equally represented in the Knesset because they are elected through both Arab and Jewish parties. But hardly any Arabs are found in the government, in high-ranking administration and military positions, and in the Supreme Court, nor do many serve as directors of state corporations and regulatory agencies, on planning and zoning committees, on the Israel Lands Authority, and in other governing bodies.

Despite the impressive headway that Arabs have made since the mid-1970s, they are still far from sharing power with Jews. Their separate educational system, notwithstanding the significant reforms it underwent in the 1990s, is still under Jewish control (Al-Haj 2002). The Arabs are not extended cultural autonomy, and their local governments, like all local authorities in Israel, depend on the central government for funding and approval of bylaws and policies. Being permanent opposition parties, Arab parties are not eligible for participation in government coalitions, and unlike Jewish religious parties, they cannot convert their parliamentary representation into effective protection and promotion of the views and interests of their constituents. Their exercise of power beyond the voicing of protest is considered illegitimate by Jews. Without the external support of the Arab parties, the Rabin government would not have a parliamentary majority and the Oslo Accords would not have been ratified. But this was precisely one of the major reasons why the right-wing political bloc denied legitimacy to the Rabin government and to its peace process. Most Jews believe that a Jewish political majority is necessary for installing a government in power and for taking fateful decisions, such as Israel's withdrawal from the Golan Heights and the West Bank and Gaza Strip.

Conflict

The history of Arab–Jewish relations is marred by severe events: the mass expulsion of Arabs and the destruction of hundreds of Arab villages during the 1948 war, the military rule over Arab areas during 1948–66, the massacre of villagers from Kfar al-Kassem in 1956, and the bloody clashes during the first Land Day strike in 1976 and during the Arab uprising in 2000. However, vis-à-vis its Arab citizens, Israel lacks a record of recurrent patterns of mass population transfer, genocidal attempts, pogroms, riots, biological racism, a quasi-apartheid legislation, state terrorism, denial of human rights, and other grave phenomena that are widespread in deeply divided societies. The common manifestations of the ethnonational conflict in Israel are rather ethnocentrism, distress, controversial issues, and protest.

Ethnocentrism

Ethnocentrism is reflected in excesses of stereotyping, distrust, rejection, and discriminatory attitudes and practices. Many Arabs stereotype Jews as persons ready to give up self-dignity for convenience, career, and money and as being racist, exploitative, and indifferent to Arab life. They see Hebrew culture as materialistic, permissive, and immoral. Many Jews, on the other hand, stereotype Arabs as traditional, backward, violent, and indifferent to Jewish life. Jews regard the Arab as the "other," an inferior "Oriental" figure that demonstrates the superiority of the new Israeli Jew (Jamal 2002b; Moore 2000; Soen 2002).

Most Arabs and Jews deeply distrust each other. Arab basic distrust is continuously nourished by the widespread Jewish suspicions and long-standing discriminatory policies against Arabs. The equally profound Jewish distrust is reinforced by Arabs' belonging to the enemy, their exclusion from the security forces, and the state control imposed over them. Furthermore, Jewish mistrust is persistently strengthened by the Arab public identification with the hostile Palestinians through demonstrations, pronouncements, and occasional acts of terrorism.

Representative surveys of Arabs and Jews show that rejection is mutual but clearly asymmetric. While two-thirds of the Arabs report having Jewish friends, only a third of the Jews claim having Arab friends, and by the same token most Arabs but only a minority of Jews are willing to have friends from the other group. Most Jews are not willing to have Arabs as neighbors, and both sides strongly oppose intermarriage. As the weaker party, Arabs are naturally more predisposed to mix with Jews than vice versa because they have more to gain by intergroup contacts (such as connections and better services).

The stickiest question is discrimination. For most Jews, the idea of a Jewish state is not limited to a Jewish majority, Jewish symbols, the Hebrew language, and ties with Diaspora Jewry but extends to a favored Jewish status. Public opinion surveys show that a minority to a majority of Jews, depending on the question asked, expect preference in employment in the civil service, admission to universities, entitlements to social security benefits, access to land, and even better protection against being dismissed from jobs. To illustrate, in a survey taken in October 2001, 56.9 percent of the Jews said that the state should prefer Jews to Arabs, 92.6 percent supported the Galilee Judaization Program, and 33.4 percent expressed unwillingness to have an Arab as their superior in a job. Jews see the Jewish Zionist nature of the state and threats to national security as justifications for restricting Arab rights. In the same survey, 26.6 percent of the Jews were in favor of denying Arabs the right to vote in Knesset elections, and 41.7 percent agreed that the state should seize on any opportunity to encourage Arab citizens to leave the country.[15]

Discrimination against Arabs takes many forms (Kretzmer 1990). From an Arab viewpoint, the very nature of Israel as a Jewish state is discriminatory because it dispossesses Arab land and disregards Arab culture, symbols, and needs. Israel grants special status to the Jewish Agency and to the Jewish National Fund and delegates to them certain state functions, such as provision of some welfare and social services, planning of settlements, forestation, and land cultivation. Since these bodies are Zionist and geared to serve Jews only, they ipso facto discriminate against Arabs. The state also applies double standards in its budgets, appointments, and contracts (Fares 2002). For instance, the per capita development budget of Arab local councils is much smaller than that of comparable Jewish local councils because of lower allocations from the Ministry of the Interior and other offices. Arabs are discriminated against in public lands. The Arab municipal area has become too dense because of past land expropriations, the government's reluctance to assign lands to Arab local authorities, and the Arabs' rapid natural population increase. Arabs are discriminated against in the administration of justice, from police maltreatment to conviction to punishment (Rattner and Fishman 1998). Discrimination in the labor market is another major problem (Lewin-Epstein and Semyonov 1993; Wilkinson 1991). Three-fifths of the Arabs work in the Jewish economy, but very few can get better-paid white-collar jobs. Although discrimination is legally forbidden, deficient law enforcement cannot tackle its diverse informal and indirect forms (e.g., publicity of jobs in Hebrew only, irrelevant job requirements, and recruitment through interpersonal referrals).

Jews are ambivalent about discrimination against Arabs. They are increasingly aware of and ready to admit it, especially as a result of the frequent Arab complaints and protest. Yet they tend to dismiss Arab grievances because they expect preferential treatment for being Jews living in a Jewish state and for being citizens defending and contributing to their country. In Jewish eyes, the Arabs who fought against the creation of the state and remain a burden on it do not deserve equal treatment.

DISTRESS

Arabs in Israel endure distress in various spheres of life. They share the hard living conditions along with Jews in the lower strata. Like all Israelis using public conveniences and spending time in Jewish towns, they are exposed to terrorism, although their own communities are not targeted. They are afraid of Jewish maltreatment when passing through security checkpoints and when by chance they happen to be in a place hit by terrorism. But as a national minority, they have their own deprivations, including a high incidence of poverty, a population explosion, the repression of women, underdeveloped residential areas, a shortage of housing and land, discrimination in employment, and a high rate of unemployment. These deficiencies are augmented by the wider tribulations of the chronic budget deficits that cripple local authorities, land takeovers, and the predicament of Bedouin in unrecognized villages.

The deep distress that Arabs feel is evident in the findings of a public opinion poll taken in the fall of 2002, two years after the outbreak of the al-Aqsa intifada. They agreed that Arabs in Israel face the dangers of a serious restriction of civil liberties (78.5%), a loss of citizenship by Arabs who perpetrate severe security offenses (62.2%), massive land expropriations (61.9%), state violence (59.6%), ceding the Arab Triangle to a Palestinian state (44.1%), and a population transfer (37.2%). Half (50.1%) felt being alien and rejected citizens of Israel. A large majority (79.4%) censured the Zionist movement of racism. They perceived the government as treating Arabs as second-class citizens or handling them with hostility (86.7%) and assessed Arab–Jewish relations as not good (62.6%).

This gloomy picture should be counterbalanced by the advantages accrued to Arabs, disclosing the complexities and contradictions in their status. Negatively stated, they are protected against miserable refugee life, subjection to prolonged and illiberal military occupation, and displacement from the homeland and other dislocations that their Palestinian brethren endure. Positively stated, they enjoy employment in a high-income economy, a steady rise of standards of living, many precious welfare state benefits, advanced medicine, the rule of law, democratic freedoms, political stability, and modernity. To cite several findings from the 2002 Arab survey, 53.9 percent were satisfied with their lives as Arab citizens in Israel, and only 5.8 percent reported political harassment or economic deprivation as a result of protesting against the government. They do not contemplate to move to a new Palestinian state and define the proposal that the Triangle will be ceded to it as a Zionist ploy and a hazard to their being part of Israel.

CONTROVERSIAL ISSUES

The emergence of an Arab minority in Israeli society was a tragic event for both Arabs and Jews. Israeli Arabs were part of the defeated enemy that went to war in order to liquidate the fledgling Jewish state. During the 1950s, the two sides came to realize that they were stuck with each other, and over the years they have resigned themselves to the fact of Arab–Jewish coexistence. Arabs respect the territorial and political integrity of Israel and tie their lives and futures with it, and the Jews reconcile themselves with an Arab minority entitled to civil rights in their midst. Coexistence per se is not an issue. There is also agreement that Arabs are entitled to civic equality and protection against discrimination and that the state should act to raise Arab communities to Jewish standards.

Beyond the sheer mutual acceptance of each other, Arabs and Jews disagree sharply and ideologically on several interrelated issues. Following are the key disputes:

Land. The state considers the area under its jurisdiction as the "land of Israel," designated for Jewish settlement and use. The Arabs lost much land, and their continued deprivation is reflected in a small municipal area per capita, a shortage of lands for public development and housing, a lack of new Arab settlements, exclusion from government bodies in charge of land allocation and urban planning, and restricted access to residence in Jewish communities (Yiftachel and Kedar 2000). The state frustrates Arab desires and needs for the return, allocation, and control of land.

Unrecognized villages. About half the Negev Bedouin live in 45 unrecognized villages, as do several thousand Galilee Bedouin. Since these settlements are considered squatter areas, they are denied infrastructure and basic amenities. Around a million *dunam* are in dispute between the state and the Bedouin who lack official deeds to the land. The government aims to concentrate these Bedouin on new urban townships, whereas they demand recognition of their villages and land claims.

Internal refugees. These consist of about 200,000 Arabs of refugee origin whose villages were smashed in 1948 and whose property was confiscated. Although resettled in other villages, they are not yet fully adjusted, and they maintain emotional ties with their original villages and harbor hopes of return. The state regards its uprooted Arab citizens as well settled and rejects their demands.

The nature of the state. As part of the Palestinian homeland people, the Arabs wish to transform Israel from a Jewish to a binational state and to equalize their civic and national status with that of the Jews. They reject the idea that Israel is a state of and for the Jews, doing its utmost to guarantee and to increase its Jewish majority. They oppose the Law of Return, the lavish state support for Jewish immigrants ("absorption basket"), the exclusivity of the Jewish state symbols, the domination of the Hebrew language, the ramified ties with the Jewish Diaspora, the central role of the Holocaust in the state, the official status of the institutions of the World Zionist Organization, the exclusion of Arabs from settlement projects, and the preferential treatment accorded to Jews. Basic laws cast Israel as a Jewish and democratic state, barring the formation of a political party and disallowing the participation in Knesset elections to a group or a person that denies this principle. Although all attempts to harness these laws to block Arab parties and candidates from contesting Knesset elections have so far failed, they serve as a threat, a deterrent, and a restraint.[16]

The Palestinian–Jewish conflict. Israel's Arabs subscribe to the Palestinian perspective according to which European Jews invaded Palestine, dislodged the Palestinians from their land, expelled them, founded an expansionist and a racist state, maintained a repressive occupation, and have been pursuing intransigent policies. Israeli Arabs endorse the mainstream Palestinian view that in order to end the protracted dispute, Israel should withdraw totally to the pre-1967 borders, divide Jerusalem, dismantle all Jewish settlements, respect the Palestinian refugees' right of return to Israel proper, allow the establishment of an independent and militarized Palestinian state, and maintain open borders with the new state of Palestine. While the Jews differ in their stands on the conflict, they clearly reject all these Arab views. They blame the Palestinians for the continued strife and for their reluctance to reach fair, pragmatic compromises. They see Zionism as a national liberation movement of the Jewish people, Israel as an equal and legitimate member of the family of nations, and their position on the conflict as just and realistic. What Israeli Arabs condone as a legitimate Palestinian resistance to occupation Jews censure as reckless violence and terrorism against innocent victims.

Israel's international orientation. Immediately after its independence, Israel joined the Western instead of the nonaligned bloc. It regards itself as a Western state, firmly linked and committed to Diaspora Jews, most of whom are concentrated in the West. It tries hard to integrate militarily, politically, economically, and culturally into the powerful, affluent, and prestigious West. It intends to use the end of the conflict with the Arab world as a means to disengage from the region and to deepen its incorporation into the West. Israeli Arabs reject Israel's staunch Western orientation. They have reservations about and objections to the West in general and to the United States in particular for its allegedly indecent cultural patterns and unfriendly position toward the Palestinian people, the Arab nation, and global Islam. They prefer Israel to integrate into the Middle East and the Arab world rather than to remain a foreign body in this area.[17]

Compensations. Most Arabs feel victimized by the state. They were placed under military rule for 18 years, over half their land was confiscated, a fifth of them became internal refugees, some of their close relatives reluctantly left or were driven out of the country, they have been subject to institutional discrimination as individuals and communities, and they continue to suffer additional privations and humiliations. These past and present deprivations serve as a basis for a nascent approach that regards the Arab minority as an ex-colonial native people, such as indigenous populations in Australia and some other settler societies. A population in this category, it is claimed, is entitled to a special status, to the return of its lost lands and villages, to the restoration of its historical national rights, to a proper compensation for past injustices and suffering, and to preferential treatment in funding and hiring. These arguments also underpin the nationalist Arab demand for turning Israel into a binational state.[18] They are obviously dismissed by the state and the Jewish majority.

From a Jewish perspective, the insistence of Israeli Arabs on both the transformation of Israel into a binational state and the formation of a new Palestinian state in the West Bank and Gaza Strip is an untenable position. The Jews hold that justice and wisdom are done by the partition of the disputed land into two national states, that in the exchange for their renunciation of Greater Israel they deserve Arab legitimacy of their right to a Jewish state, and that Palestinian citizens of Israel should fulfill their national desires by the very existence of a Palestinian Arab and Muslim state and could move there if dissatisfied. Israeli Arabs disagree sharply with this Jewish view. For them, a Palestinian state alongside Israel is only a partial rectification of the enormous injustice done to their people, who are the true owners of the land of Palestine, and that such a state would leave them forever an excluded and discriminated minority in an ethnic Jewish state. They regard themselves as paying the highest price because the final division of Palestine into two states would consolidate their status as a permanent and unequal minority in Israel and make them a victim of continued Judaization and Zionization of the state. In the eyes of Israeli Arabs, the Palestinian question can be resolved by establishing a new state for non-Israeli Palestinians and turning Israel into binational state for Israeli Palestinians.[19]

These controversial issues are not bones of contention that are common in divided societies but rather ideological disputes that typify deeply divided societies and dissident minorities.

PROTEST

The strategy of the authorities for dealing with the intense Arab struggle for equality and peace is based on several principles. First, the Arabs are allowed to freely employ any legal means. Second, they are put under selective, clandestine, and sophisticated surveillance in order to prevent illegal or nondemocratic activities, such as subversion, terrorism, sabotage, provocation, instigation, civil disobedience, riot, long-term general strikes, and severe damage to the state's international reputation. Third, Arabs are protected against Jewish and state violence, harassments by Jewish extremists, racist statements, and blatant discrimination. For instance, Knesset member Rabbi Kahana was barred from Arab localities in order to stop his pestering of Arabs, his party was banned from taking part in Knesset elections on grounds of incitement to racism, and the anti-Arab successor Kach movement was outlawed. Finally, the authorities practice a pragmatic policy to avert confrontations and to effect piecemeal improvements. The police negotiate with Arab leaders terms of conduct of demonstrations, processions, and rallies and deploy their forces afar in order to forestall clashes with Arab protesters. The authorities do not take action against thousands of instances of illegal Arab construction projects, and they stopped the massive land expropriations after 1976. Furthermore, they accept the charge that Arabs are discriminated against and promise to rectify the past injustices step by step. To illustrate, heads of Arab local councils often shut down municipal services and stage sit-ins in front of the prime minister's office in protest of discrimination in funding. In response, they receive extra funds, and in fact over the years the policy has shifted from malign to benign discrimination of Arab localities with regard to the provision of supplementary budgets. Arab protest continues, however, because of the chronic budget deficits of local Arab governments.

Protest on behalf of Arabs can be characterized by several features. First, the protest is conducted by and for Arabs. The Jews play a minor or no role in Arab protest. Even the Communist-backed Democratic Front for Peace and Equality, which stands for a joint Arab–Jewish struggle, is clearly Arabized and has scant Jewish participation.[20] Second, the Arab protest is recurrent and even more common than the highly frequent Jewish protest. The high incidence of Arab protest is due to the Arab belief in the efficacy of protest, the partial remedies gained, and the need to continue protesting in order to exact further concessions. Third, Arab protest is militant but not radical. The Arab community and leadership have made a strategic commitment to intense, lawful, and nonviolent struggle. The goals of the struggle are not rejectionist but rather "two states to two peoples" and civil and national equality within Israel. The measures used are parliamentary and extraparliamentary but not extralegal politics. They include participation in the elections to the Knesset, Histadrut, and local governments, as well as petitions, propaganda, litigation, demonstrations, and general strikes. Finally, Arab protest has been internationalized. Arab advocacy associations appeal to UN committees for the protection of minority or human rights, to international or European nongovernmental organizations, to foreign embassies, and to foreign media. Some of them even file shadow reports to international bodies in criticism of official Israeli reports and manage to get favorable responses (Adalah 2001; Arab Association for Human Rights 1998; State of Israel 1997; United Nations 2003).

The mutual Arab–Jewish restraint diminished after Rabin's assassination in 1995. The combination of Arab disaffection because of the setbacks in foreign and domestic policies and the entry of the Islamic movement and the secular nationalist Balad Party into Arab politics radicalized the Arabs. In October 2000, Arab protesters marched in solidarity with the al-Aqsa intifada and clashed with the impatient police. Thirteen protesters were shot to death, and scores were wounded. For a week, the Arab sector was restive, blocking highways and damaging public facilities. Under strong Arab pressure and for the first time in Israel's history, a public inquiry commission was appointed to look into Arab grievances—the causes of the unrest and police violence. Hundreds of Arab protesters were criminalized, being arrested, interrogated, brought to court, and punished (Rosenberg 2002). The Jewish backlash was expressed in boycotts of Arab businesses, heightening fears of Arabs, and legislative and political countermeasures against what was interpreted as Israeli Arab backing of the Palestinian armed resistance. The Arabs got more disillusioned with the Jews and the state, boycotted the elections for the prime minister in 2001, and stepped up their protest.[21] The number of Arabs involved in terrorism increased significantly during the first two and half years of the al-Aqsa intifada, but the Arab community as a whole did not join the Palestinian armed uprising.

CHANGE

Although each of the three theses regarding the trend of change in Arab–Jewish relations—mutual rejection, mutual resistance, and mutual rapprochement—can marshal plausible supporting evidence, it is the last thesis that fits best the complex and ostensibly inconsistent reality. Let me examine the pertinent facts bearing on the following two questions: What is the trend of change in Arab behavior and attitudes over the years—an increase of radicalism, resistance, or rather politicization? What is the trend of change in Jewish behavior and attitudes—an increase of indifference, intransigence, or rather openness?

The evidence usually cited for the radicalism and resistance of Arabs is numerous and impressive. It includes an increase in voting for Arab nationalist parties, the support of radical movements such as the Islamic movement, the popularity of nationalist symbols and narratives (the Palestinian flag, the collective memory, and commemoration of al-Nakbah), tremendous public solidarity with the first and second intifada, some involvement in terrorism, the

Palestinization of identity, intense extraparliamentary and to some extent extralegal politics, and public opposition to the Jewish Zionist character of the state.

These facts are weighty, but their interpretation as lending credence to Arab radicalism and resistance is not unequivocal. Most of these developments can be interpreted as indicating legitimate "protest" in a democratic state rather than as "rejectionism." For instance, Arab citizens have a "protest" right to oppose the Jewish Zionist nature of the state and a "protest" right to adopt a Palestinian identity, but they have neither a "rejectionist" right to deny Israel's right to exist nor a "rejectionist" right to abet and perpetrate terrorism. The two kinds of rights should not be equated and mixed up. The attitudes and behavior of a majority of Arabs fall in the "protest" rather than the "rejectionist" category. Furthermore, the theses of radicalism and resistance also underplay strong "pragmatist" forces that impel Arabs to accommodate themselves with life as a minority in Israel, including bilingualism, biculturalism, attraction to modernity, dependence on the benefits of a welfare state, appreciation of democratic freedoms, and "Israelization" in the existential sense of becoming accustomed to life in Israel.

The Arab politicization thesis that raises these objections emphasizes the importance of government policy in shaping Arab attitudes and behavior. Politicization means that the Arabs acquire a political consciousness as Israeli citizens and Palestinians, become less tolerant of discrimination, struggle more intensely for equality, and see Israel as their state. This process gained momentum during the Rabin government in 1992–95 thanks to its unprecedented domestic and foreign policies in favor of the Palestinians on both sides of the Green Line. But since 1996, these favorable policies have been discontinued, shifting the trend from politicization to radicalization among Arabs in Israel. The reversal in the historical trend was also prompted by the entry of the Balad Party and the Islamic movement into Arab politics, pushing Arabs to nationalist and to some extent even to rejectionist discourse. The post-1995 radicalization phase was evident in the Arab uprising of October 2000.

The shifts in the trend in Arab orientation are reflected in Arab attitudes. Table 2.1 presents rates of endorsement of unambiguously *rejectionist* attitudes found in comparable, representative public opinion surveys of the adult Arab population in Israel that I conducted during the years from 1976 to 2002. Three conclusions can be deduced from the figures. First, the overall rate of rejectionism is restricted to a minority of Arabs. Second, rejectionism was clearly on the decline over time or at least not on the rise. Finally, the 1995 survey figures are clearly exceptional. They are found in the survey taken a short while before Rabin's assassination, gauging the considerable impact of the beneficial policy of his government on the Arabs. After 1995, the rejectionist rates reverted to the pre-1992 period. To illustrate, the rate of Arabs denying Israel's right to exist without any reservation was 20.5 percent in 1976,

Table 2.1
Selected Rejectionist Attitudes, Arabs in Israel, 1976–2002

	1976	1980	1985	1988	1995	2001	2002
Deny Israel's right to exist	20.5	11.0	17.6	13.5	6.8	15.6	15.8
Do not believe in the use of democratic procedures for improving the Arab situation	16.3	17.6	8.9	10.6	4.4	6.4	8.2
Support the use of unlicensed demonstrations	17.1	7.0	10.8	13.1	6.0	9.5	8.3
Support the use of violence	17.9	7.5	8.1	8.0	6.0	4.5	5.4
Define oneself as a (non-Israeli) Palestinian	32.9	25.7	29.2	27.1	10.3	20.0	11.5
Support the formation of a Palestinian state in all of Palestine instead of Israel	58.7	38.1	32.3	29.5	16.6	29.1	17.9
Not willing to have Jewish friends	21.2	13.6	15.5	14.2	10.3	7.1	9.3

Source: Sammy Smooha's continuing survey of Arab–Jewish relations.

dropping to 13.5 percent in 1988, reaching a record low of 6.8 percent in 1995, and bouncing back to 15.8 percent in 2002.[22]

The mutual rejection and resistance theses make parallel arguments about the Jewish orientation. They portray Jews as having been increasingly indifferent and intransigent in their relation to Arab citizens and base this assessment on the facts that since 1967 the Jews have shifted to the right and become more hawkish and intolerant of Palestinians. The additional pieces of supporting evidence are the emergence of a Jewish radical right that calls for restricting the rights of Arabs, the implementation of state policies that blurred the Green Line and consequently equated citizen and noncitizen Palestinians in Jewish minds, and the coming to power of anti-Arab groups—Revisionists, Jews from Muslim countries, religious Zionists, ultra-Orthodox Jews, and Russian immigrants of the 1990s.

This interpretation of the Jewish orientation, like the interpretation of the Arab orientation, is one-sided and oblivious of processes that mitigate Jewish attitudes toward Israeli Arabs. Despite the drift toward the political right, the Jews have remained divided between the political right and left, which differ markedly in their stance on the Arab minority. A comprehensive process of democratization has swept Israeli society and state, evident in a greater freedom of the media, the judicial activism of the Supreme Court, public criticism of the security forces, the changeover of governments, and the enactment of quasi-constitutional basic laws regarding rights and freedoms. All Israeli governments, including the most nationalist ones, have practiced policies that clearly distinguish between Arab citizens and Palestinian aliens even if they disregard the Green Line in other respects. They also have respected the Israeli Arab right to wage an intense struggle, have not repressed Arab protest, and have responded favorably though partially to Arab demands. Furthermore, the history of the Israeli–Arab conflict since 1979 is marked with keystones that have contributed to Jewish pragmatism: the peace treaties with Egypt and Jordan, Israel's recognition of the Palestinian people and the rights embedded in the Oslo Accords, and the Jewish acceptance of a two-state solution. These developments have made Jews cognizant of Arab citizens as evidently marked off from the Palestinians on the West Bank and Gaza Strip and recognizing Arab entitlement to equal rights. As a result, the Jews have increasingly opened up to the Arabs and come to terms with their integration into hitherto pure Jewish institutions.

The alternative Jewish accessibility thesis raises these criticisms and stresses the growing openness and pragmatism of the Jews and the Jewish state over the years. The Jews have become increasingly aware of discriminatory and exclusionary practices against Arab citizens, more willing to let them enter Jewish institutions, and more tolerant of their strong protest. On the other hand, the October 2000 Arab uprising marks a change in the position of the Jewish majority and the state. The killing of 13 Arab protesters by the police and the attendant Arab unrest altered the behavior and attitudes of both sides. It was a turn toward greater mutual alienation, apprehension, and isolation. Despite this deterioration, public opinion surveys taken since 1980 do not reveal any hardening of Jewish attitudes. As shown in Table 2.2, despite the Israeli Arab support of the two intifadas, there is no evidence for a historical trend of a toughening Jewish intransigence.

Taken together, the trends in Arab and Jewish behavior and attitudes square better with the mutual rapprochement thesis than with the mutual rejection and mutual resistance theses. The trends are nevertheless neither unilinear nor overdetermined, and after 1995 a turn for the worse took place among

Table 2.2
Selected Intransigent Attitudes, Jews in Israel, 1980–2001

	1980	1985	1988	1995	2001
Deny Arabs' right to live as a minority in Israel	—	15.9	19.4	9.8	11.3
Deny Arabs' right to vote in Knesset elections	—	24.1	42.8	30.9	26.6
Think that Israel should encourage Arab citizens to leave the country	50.3	42.4	39.9	36.7	41.7
Think that Israel does too much for the Arabs in Israel	36.4	32.9	37.4	20.7	22.9
Unwilling to have Arab friends	39.1	37.4	40.5	32.2	27.0

Source: Sammy Smooha's continuing survey of Arab–Jewish relations.

both sides. If state policy toward the Arab minority will improve and the peace process with the Palestinians will proceed, another turn for the better is expected in Arab–Jewish relations.

SUMMARY AND CONCLUSIONS

This review of the main areas of Arab–Jewish relations discloses numerous tensions and dilemmas. Let me conclude by discussing the questions of how Israel manages the threat posed to its stability by the Arab minority and what it can do to reduce this threat more effectively without losing its Jewish character.

The Arabs are categorically separated from the Jews in nationality, language, religion, culture, history, and collective memory. As an integral segment of the indigenous Palestinian people, they are a national minority. Originating as a remnant of a vanquished people, they have remained part of the enemy and have been placed under control in order to hinder their subversive potential. They are a nonassimilating minority, living in separate communities. Despite their ramified Israelization and integration, the Arabs are still an ideologically dissident minority, being concentrated in the lower strata, excluded from the national power structure, and subjected to severe discriminations and restrictions.

The Arab–Jewish divide places Israel among the special type of deeply divided societies whose propensities and experiences are relevant to Israel, such as Northern Ireland, Sri Lanka, and the former Yugoslavia. These countries suffer from the endemic problems of lack of legitimacy on the part of the minority and vulnerability to large-scale violence and political instability. On the other hand, Israel has so far preserved ethnonational tranquillity. The question is how Israel will succeed in managing its deep conflict and whether this success will be sustainable.

The belief that Arab acquiescence is apparent and transient is widespread among policymakers, the Jewish public, advocates of the Arab cause, and critics of the Jewish state. Some point to the collapse of many deeply divided societies as a clearly bad omen for Israel. Others argue that the settlement of the Palestinian question will not bring about acceptance and legitimacy to Israel by the restive Arab and Muslim worlds. Many assume that no minority with self-dignity will ever reconcile itself with a subordinate minority status in an ethnic state such as Israel. These external and internal forces are a constant sources of conflict that will continue to block Israeli Arab accommodation to the Jewish majority and state.

Relative Arab calm and Israel's stability are, however, solid for various reasons. Israel preserves a large and permanent Jewish majority thanks to a continuing influx of immigrants who offset the high rate of Arab natural growth. It is a very strong and centralized state that imposes an effective machinery of control over minorities and dissidents. The Jews are a firm and resolute majority, convinced in their inalienable right to a Jewish and democratic state. While the Arabs deny legitimacy to Israel, the international community unreservedly accepts it as a Jewish state. Despite the Muslim, Arab, and Palestinian influences, the views, behavior, and fate of Israeli Arabs are shaped primarily by Israel. They realize that they cannot count on outside forces to alter their situation and that they have to come to grips with Israel. They are accustomed to life in Israel and appreciative of the benefits it offers: modernity, democracy, and extended welfare services. Understanding that they do not have a better alternative to a minority life in a Jewish state, they reject the possibility of moving to a future Palestinian state or having their adjacent villages and towns annexed to it. Their experience has confirmed their belief that by an active struggle they can advance their status and life conditions even without turning Israel into a binational state as they would prefer.

Israel meets all the conditions specified for the stability of ethnic democracies (Smooha 2002a). These are a large and stable majority, a majority that feels threatened and needs control of the state to contain perceived and real threats, a strong state that does not allow external interference in minority affairs, and a state that enjoys international legitimacy to be an ethnic nation-state. The continuity of these conditions explains the persistence of ethnic democracy in Israel, whereas their absence or diminution accounted for the breakdown of ethnic democracy in Northern Ireland in 1972 (Smooha 1997) and in Macedonia in 2001 (Berg and Meurs 2002; Daftary 2001).

Whether or not Arab–Jewish relations are stable, reason and justice call for a significant change. Since the Jews wish to retain Israel as a Jewish state and have the power to do so, the alternative liberal or consociational democracy is not realistic.[23] At the same time, the current formula of a Jewish and democratic state has run its course. It is possible to conceive of an infinite number of versions of a Jewish and democratic state that can be more fair and more effective than the present one. In order for the new dispensation to be acceptable and workable, it has to emerge from negotiation and dialogue between the two sides.

Following is a reform package that can appreciably meet Arab needs without undermining the Jewish and democratic character of the state:

1. The establishment of a Palestinian state to fulfill the national aspirations of the Palestinian people and the Palestinian Arab minority
2. The launch of a Marshall-type plan to narrow the Arab–Jewish gaps in socioeconomic resources and level of services
3. The enactment of a state constitution to guarantee civil equality and protection of individual and minority rights
4. The use of legal and educational means to reduce discrimination and exclusion of Arabs
5. The adoption of a policy of affirmative action to boost Arab social mobility and to rectify past discrimination

6. The implementation of power sharing by appointing Arabs to top positions, allowing Arab political parties to join government coalitions, and letting the Arab minority apply the sectorial model, used by religious and ultra-Orthodox Jews, to promote its particular collective interests
7. The encouragement of Arabs to serve in the army or to render a civil service instead to reach equality of duties
8. The recognition of the Arabs as a national Palestinian Arab minority with legitimate ties to Palestinian nationalism, culture, and identity and legislating their right to a proportional share of budgets and appointments
9. The granting of cultural, educational, and religious autonomy to Arabs.

Although these reforms would stretch the hegemonic Zionist paradigm, they would remain within its limits. The remolded Israel will retain its Jewish Zionist identity, Jewish majority, symbols, calendar, heroes, Law of Return, denial of the right of return to Arab refugees, ramified relations with the Jewish Diaspora, and domination by the Jews. At the same time, Israel will become much less discriminatory and more acceptable to its empowered Arab citizens. The Palestinian Arab minority could rest assured that the new Palestinian state will guarantee the survival of the Palestinian people and the promotion of Palestinian culture and interests in the same way that Israel acts on behalf of the Jewish people.[24]

NOTES

1. According to official figures, Israel's population numbered 6.7 million in May 2003 and was divided into 5.4 million Jews and others (240,000 non-Jews related to Jewish immigrants), 1.04 million Arab citizens, and 0.25 million non-Jewish permanent residents (234,000 Palestinians from East Jerusalem and 18,000 Druzes from the Golan Heights, who are, by and large, not Israeli citizens, although Israeli law applies to them and counts them as part of Israel proper). If noncitizens are excluded, Arabs make up only 16 percent of the total population. See the press communiqué and the figures in the Statistical Abstract of Israel in the Web site of Israel's Central Bureau of Statistics (http://www.cbs.org.il). Unless indicated otherwise, figures are quoted from this official source throughout this chapter.

2. It is hard to choose the proper term for naming the Arabs in Israel. They are interchangeably called Palestinians in Israel, Arab citizens, Israeli Arabs, Arabs in Israel, and the like. For the sake of clarity, I avoid the use of the word "Palestinian" in order not to confuse Arab citizens with noncitizen Palestinians on the West Bank and Gaza Strip.

3. A more detailed analysis of Arab–Jewish relations and an extensive bibliography appears in Smooha (2001). For other general discussions of the political and ideological issues involved, see Gavison and Abu-Raya (1999), Gavison and Hacker (2000), Ghanem (2001), and Rekhess (1978).

4. The emergent approach to the study of "pluralistic societies" appeared in the collection edited by Kuper and Smith (1969). For a summary of the approach and an analysis scheme to be applied also in this chapter, see chapter 2 in Smooha (1978).

5. Israel qualifies as a deeply divided society also for the profound division between ultra-Orthodox and non-Orthodox Jews.

6. The Palestinian population is estimated to reach over 9 million in 2003, divided roughly into 3.5 million in the West Bank and Gaza Strip, 4.5 million in the Diaspora, and 1 million in Israel. For details, see http://www.passia.org.

7. There is an ongoing heated debate on the nature of the Israeli political system, focusing on ethnic democracy. The controversy lies at the core of the status of Arabs in the Jewish state. For the main positions, see Dowty (1999), Gavison (1999b, 2002), Jamal (2002a), Neuberger (1999), Sa'di (2000, 2002a), Smooha (2000, 2002a), and Yiftachel, Ghanem, and Rouhana (2000).

8. The data on the number of the destroyed Arab localities are not consistent. Morris (1989, map 1) enumerates 369 settlements that were evacuated by either desertion or expulsion, Kaiman (1984, table 1, p. 9) speaks of 350 settlements, and Khalidi (1992) counts 430 villages. The villages were toppled in order to prevent the return of refugees. It was also resolved to ruin them instead of settling them by Jews because of their backwardness and Arab facade. During the first two years of statehood, about 200 new Jewish settlements were established, most of them on the lands of the demolished villages.

9. They were composed of three parts: 156,000 Arabs who did not leave, 30,000 inhabitants of the Little Triangle that was ceded to Israel in April 1949 according to the cease-fire agreement with Jordan, and several thousand Arabs who returned illegally.

10. The Zionist narrative underpins the Zionist historiography, which has come under attack in the 1980s and 1990s by the so-called Post-Zionists. For the stances of both sides, see Friling (2003), Gerber (2002), and Silberstein (2002).

11. The Palestinian narrative underlies Palestinian and Post-Zionist Jewish historiography. See, for instance, Gur-Ze'ev and Pappe (2003), Sa'di (2002b), and Said (1979).

12. The fertility rate of the Druze was 3.03 and that of the Christians 2.46. The Christians differ widely from Moslems and Druzes in all indicators of modernization and well-being. For an account of Israel's Christian Arabs, see Tsimhoni (2002).

13. The Ka'adans case well demonstrates the complexity of the issue. The Ka'adans, a Muslim couple from an Arab town in the Triangle, applied for residence in Katzir, a nearby new Jewish locality, in order to improve their living conditions. The selection committee disqualified them, and they appealed to the Supreme Court in 1995. The appeal was filed by the Jewish-led liberal Association for Civil Rights on grounds of the individual right for open occupancy. After five years of intentional delay of judgment, the Supreme Court ruled in favor of the Ka'adans, declaring illegal the public policy of establishing new settlements for Jews only and ordering the pertinent bodies to reconsider the application. The ruling was framed as case specific, without implications for past policies and for future "special" Jewish settlements (such as Kibbutzim, Moshavim, communal villages, and ultra-Orthodox towns). While Jews on the far right interpreted the ruling as the end of Jewish settlement and Zionism, the Arab community was quite indifferent. Even more reserved was Adalah, the Legal Center for Arab Minority Rights in Israel, which refused to take the case in the first place. It feared that the protection of the Arab right to integrate into Jewish communities would be counterproductive because it would make redundant the Arab struggle for national

collective rights and autonomous institutions. Despite the ruling, the Ka'adans were unable to move to Katzir. For the court ruling, see Supreme Court (2000).

14. In a survey taken in October 2002, Arab citizens were asked to choose the most appropriate category out of nine to define their self-identity. Collapsing the answers into three broad categories, 41.8 percent of the Arab respondents defined themselves as non-Palestinian Israelis (Israelis, Arabs, Israeli Arabs, or Arabs in Israel), 46.8 percent as Israeli Palestinians (Israeli Palestinians, Palestinians in Israel, or Palestinian Arabs in Israel), and 11.5 percent as non-Israeli Palestinians (Palestinian Arabs or Palestinians). The leading identity was Palestinians in Israel, and this was the identity that grew steadily over the years. These and additional findings quoted in this chapter are taken from surveys conducted by the author during the 1976–2002 period. All the surveys of both Arabs and Jews were based on representative and statewide samples of 1,200 persons (the sampling error is 3.5%). The surveys contain a common core of questions and are comparable over time. For a full report of the early surveys, see Smooha (1992).

15. According to a representative survey taken in April 2003 by the Israel Democracy Institute, 53 percent of the Jews opposed full equality of rights between Arabs and Jews, 77 percent thought that there should be a Jewish majority in fateful state decisions, 69 percent objected to the inclusion of Arab political parties in government coalitions, and 57 percent held that the government should encourage Arabs to leave the country (Arian et al. 2003, 18).

16. The Supreme Court overturned in January 2003 the decisions of the Central Elections Committee to bar Knesset members Tibi and Bishara and the Balad Party from participation in the January 2003 elections to the Knesset. It interpreted very narrowly the legal grounds for disqualification, namely, denial of Israel as a Jewish and democratic state and support of armed struggle against Israel, to the extent that some critics charged that these causes are worthless and ineffective for disallowing any militant Arab candidate or party from taking part in parliamentary politics. The justices who ruled against disqualification insisted on the fulfillment of two conditions: that the violation is explicit and extreme and that it is very feasible. It is hard to meet both conditions. For the full text of the ruling, see Supreme Court (2003).

17. The Arab stance toward the West is, however, quite ambivalent and inconsistent. It is more positive toward the European Union, which supports the Arab cause, and is more negative toward the United States for its alleged biases in favor of Israel and against the Arabs and Islam. When asked in the 2002 survey where Israel should integrate culturally, Israeli Arabs were divided between 56.5 percent who preferred the Middle East and 43.5 percent who favored Europe-America. Even more favorable Arab attitudes toward the West are found in a comparative survey of Arabs in seven Arab states and Israel, taken in 2002 by Zogby International. It was found that contrary to "the long-held stereotypes about the Arab world and its supposed anti-Western sentiment, France, Canada and Germany receive among the highest approval ratings, demonstrating that low approval ratings for the United States and the United Kingdom stem from those countries' foreign policies" (Zogby 2002). Another global survey taken in mid-2003 in the aftermath of the war against Iraq shows reserved to negative Muslim attitudes toward the United States and Western culture (Pew Research Center 2003).

18. This line of reasoning can be found in the thinking of Adalah's lawyers, such as Jabareen (1999, 2001), although they are cautious for tactical reasons not to inject it

into their appeals to the Supreme Court. Hints of this line of reasoning can be found also in Post-Zionist writings and proposals for radical change in the status of the Palestinian Arab minority (Rabinowitz, Ghanem, and Yiftachel 2000).

19. These conflicting views are well reflected in the telling debate between the leftist, Zionist, Jewish writer A. B. Yehoshua and the Israeli Palestinian Arab writer Anton Shamas. For details, see Silberstein (2002).

20. In 2003 and for the first time in its history, the delegation to the Knesset of the Communist-based Democratic Front for Peace and Equality does not include a Jew. Its Jewish candidate, who was fourth on the list, did not make it because the party received only three seats. The bitter preelection infighting within the party to place the Jewish candidate in a secure slot failed.

21. The Arab participation rate in the 2003 Knesset elections dropped to a record low of 62 percent as compared to the national rate of 68 percent.

22. In their book, Rabinowitz and Abu Baker (2002) concretize their Arab radicalization thesis by the progression of three Arab generations during the 1948–2002 period. The first generation, nicknamed "the surviving generation" and shaped by Al-Nakbah, was disoriented and compliant. The second generation, called "the worn-out generation," was molded by the 1967 war and the 1976 Land Day strike. It waged a struggle for civic and national equality by parliamentary and extraparliamentary democratic means but reached an impasse. The third generation, named "the stand-tall generation," is emerging in reaction to the somber experience of the October 2000 Arab uprising, which exposed the evil face of Israeli "democracy" and state. This new generation has grave doubts about participation in Israeli politics and integration into Israeli society. Its identification with the Palestinian people is overwhelming, and its strategy is apparently to develop a separate Arab civil society instead of Arab–Jewish coexistence.

23. One of the many signs for the hegemonic idea of a Jewish state is the attempt of Israeli elites to hammer out a new national covenant in order to bridge the deep divisions among Jews and to inspire Israel with a new ethos. From its inception, the forum included representatives of all Jewish political streams, including the non-Zionist ultra-Orthodox, but excluded Post-Zionists and all the Arabs. The total exclusion of the Arab citizens stemmed from the assumption that it is impossible to reach an agreement with them. For the text of the charta, see Forum for National Responsibility (2001).

24. For a more radical transformation of Israel and Arab status, see Ozacky-Lazar, Ghanem, and Pappe (1999), Rabinowitz et al. (2000), and Shafir and Peled (2002).

REFERENCES

Adalah. 2001. *Institutionalized Discrimination against Palestinian Citizens of Israel.* Adalah's Report to the World Conference against Racism, Racial Discrimination, Xenophobia, and Related Intolerance, Durban, South Africa, August/September.

Al-Haj Majid. 1997. "Identity and Orientation among Arabs in Israel: A Situation of Double Periphery." *Medina Mimshal Veyehasim Benleumiyim* 41–42: 103–22. (in Hebrew)

———. 2002. "Multiculturalism in Deeply Divided Societies: The Israeli Case." *International Journal Of Intercultural Relations* 26, no. 2: 169–83.

Arab Association for Human Rights. 1998. *The Palestinian Arab Minority in Israel: Economic, Social and Cultural Rights* (a report presented by Arab Association for Human Rights to the UN CESCR Committee on Israel's implementation of the international covenant on economic, social and cultural rights). Nazareth: Arab Association for Human Rights.

Arian, Asher, David Nachmias, Doron Navot, and Daniel Shani. 2003. *Israeli Democracy Index 2003*. Jerusalem: Israeli Democracy Institute. (in Hebrew; for an English summary, see http://www.idi.org.il)

Bauml, Yair. 2002. "The Military Government and the Process of Its Revocation, 1958–1968." *Hamizrah Hehadash* 43: 133–56. (in Hebrew)

Berg, Eiki, and Wim Meurs. 2002. "Borders and Orders in Europe: Limits of Nation- and State-Building in Estonia, Macedonia and Moldova." *Journal of Communist Studies and Transition Politics* 18, no. 4 (December): 51–74.

Cohen, Hillel. 2002. "The Internal Refugees in the State of Israel: The Struggle for Identity." *Hamizrah Hehadash* 43: 83–101. (in Hebrew)

Daftary, Farimah. 2001. "Conflict Resolution in FYR Macedonia: Power-Sharing or the 'Civic Approach.'" *Helsinki Monitor* 4: 291–312.

Dowty, Alan. 1999. "Is Israel Democratic? Substance and Semantics in the 'Ethnic Democracy' Debate." *Israel Studies* 4, no. 3 (fall): 1–15.

Fares, Amin. 2002. *The State Budget for the Year 2002 and the Share of the Arab Population*. Position paper. Haifa: Mossawa Center. (in Hebrew)

Forum for National Responsibility. 2001. "The Kineret Declaration." http://www.achrayutleumit.org.il/content/amanatkineret-eng.htm.

Friling, Tuvia, ed. 2003. *A Response to a Post-Zionist Colleague*. Tel Aviv: Yedioth Acharonot. (in Hebrew)

Gavison, Ruth. 1999a. *Does Equality Require Integration? The Case of the State Educational System in Jaffa*. Beit Berl: Institute for Israeli Arab Studies. (in Hebrew)

———. 1999b. "Jewish and Democratic? A Rejoinder to the Ethnic Democracy Debate." *Israel Studies* 4, no. 1: 44–72.

———. 2002. "The Jewish State: Principled Justification and Its Desirable Character." *Tkhelet* 13: 50–88. (in Hebrew)

Gavison, Ruth, and Isam Abu-Raya. 1999. *The Jewish-Arab Cleavage in Israel: Characteristics and Challenges*. Jerusalem: Israel Democracy Institute. (in Hebrew)

Gavison, Ruth, and Dafna Hacker, eds. 2000. *The Jewish-Arab Rift in Israel: A Reader*. Jerusalem: Israel Democracy Institute. (in Hebrew)

Gerber, Haim. 2002. "Orientalism, Zionism and the Palestinians." *Hamizrah Hehadash* 43: 27–48. (in Hebrew)

Ghanem, As'ad. 1998. "State and Minority in Israel: The Case of Ethnic State and the Predicament of Its Minority." *Ethnic and Racial Studies* 29, no. 1 (May): 428–48.

———. 2000. "The Palestinian Minority in Israel: The 'Challenge' of the Jewish State and Its Implications." *Third World Quarterly* 21, no. 1: 87–104.

———. 2001. *The Palestinian-Arab Minority in Israel, 1948–2000: A Political Study*. Albany: State University of New York Press.

Gur-Ze'ev, Ilan, and Ilan Pappe. 2003. "Beyond the Destruction of the Other's Collective Memory: Blueprints for a Palestinian/Israeli Dialogue." *Theory, Culture and Society* 20, no. 1 (February): 93–108.

Haider, Aziz. 1995. *On the Margins: The Arab Population in the Israeli Economy.* New York: St. Martin's Press.
Horowitz, Dan, and Moshe Lissak. 1978. *Origins of the Israeli Polity: Palestine under the Mandate.* Chicago: University of Chicago Press.
Israeli, Raphael. 1993. *Muslim Fundamentalism in Israel.* London: Brassey's.
———. 2002. *Arabs in Israel: Friends or Foes?* Jerusalem: Eliyahu Gabbai Publisher. (in Hebrew)
Jabareen, Hassan. 1999. "On the Oppression of Identities in the Name of Civil Equality." *Adalah's Review* 1 (fall): 26–27.
———. 2001. "'Future-Looking' Israeliness of the Arabs according to Jewish-Zionist Time, in a Space without Palestinian Time." *Mishpat Vemimshal* 6, no. 1 (July): 53–86. (in Hebrew)
Jamal, Amal. 2002a. "Beyond 'Ethnic Democracy': State Structure, Multicultural Conflict and Differentiated Citizenship in Israel." *New Political Science* 24, no. 3 (September): 411–31.
———. 2002b. "The Dialectics of 'Othering' in Zionist Thought Arabs and Oriental Jews in Israel." *Tel Aviver Jahrbuch für Deutsche Geschichte* 30: 283–231.
Kaiman, Charles. 1984. "After the Catastrophe: The Arabs in the State of Israel 1948–1950." *Mahvarot Lemehkar Velebikoret* 10 (December): 5–91. (in Hebrew)
Kedar, Mordechai. 2003. "Reluctant Israelis: Arabs for Each Other." *Nekuda* 259 (January): 42–45. (in Hebrew)
Khalidi, Walid, ed. 1992. *All That Remains: The Palestinian Villages Occupied and Depopulated by Israel in 1948.* Washington, D.C: Institute for Palestine Studies.
Kraus, Vered, and Yuval Yonay. 2000. "The Power and Limits of Ethnonationalism: Palestinians and Eastern Jews in Israel, 1974–1991." *British Journal of Sociology* 51, no. 3: 525–51.
Kretzmer, David. 1990. *The Legal Status of the Arab Minority in Israel.* Boulder, Colo.: Westview Press.
Kuper, Leo, and M. G. Smith, eds. 1969. *Pluralism in Africa.* Berkeley: University of California Press.
Landau, Jacob M. 1993. *The Arab Minority in Israel, 1967–1991: Political Aspects.* Oxford: Clarendon Press.
Lewin-Epstein, Noah, and Moshe Semyonov. 1993. *The Arab Minority in Israel's Economy: Patterns of Ethnic Inequality.* Boulder, Colo.: Westview Press.
Lijphart, Arend. 1977. *Democracy in Plural Societies: A Comparative Exploration.* New Haven, Conn.: Yale University Press.
Lustick, Ian 1979. "Deeply Divided Societies: Consociationalism versus Control." *World Politics* 31, no. 3 (April): 325–44.
———. 1980. *Arabs in the Jewish State: Israel's Control of a National Minority.* Austin: University of Texas Press.
Moore, Dalia. 2000. "Intolerance of 'Others' among Palestinian and Jewish Students in Israel." *Sociological Inquiry* 70, no. 3: 280–312.
Morris, Benny. 1989. *The Birth of the Palestinian Refugee Problem, 1947–1949.* Cambridge: Cambridge University Press.
Neuberger, Benjamin. 1999. "Democracy with Four 'Stains.'" *Panim* 9: 104–8. (in Hebrew)
Nevo, Joseph. 1983. "The Palestine Arabs' Attitude towards the Yishuv and the Zionist

Movement." In *Zionism and the Arab Question*, ed. Shmuel Almog. Jerusalem: Zalman Shazar Center.

Ozacky-Lazar, Sarah. 2002. "The Military Government as an Apparatus of Control of the Arab Citizens in Israel: The First Decade, 1948–1958." *Hamizrah Hehadash* 43: 103–32. (in Hebrew)

Ozacky-Lazar, Sarah, As'ad Ghanem, and Ilan Pappe, eds. 1999. *Seven Roads: Theoretical Options for the Status of the Arabs in Israel.* Givat Haviva: Jewish-Arab Center for Peace. (in Hebrew)

Pew Research Center. 2003. *Views of a Changing World June 2003.* Washington, D.C.: Pew Research Center for the People and the Press. http://people-press.org/.

Rabinowitz, Dan. 2001. "The Palestinian Citizens of Israel, the Concept of Trapped Minority and the Discourse of Transnationalism in Anthropology." *Ethnic and Racial Studies* 24, no. 1 (January): 64–85.

Rabinowitz, Dan, and Khawla Abu Baker. 2002. *The Stand-Tall Generation: The Palestinian Citizens of Israel Today.* Jerusalem: Keter. (in Hebrew)

Rabinowitz, Dan, As'ad Ghanem, and Oren Yiftachel, eds. 2000. *After the Rift: New Directions for Government Policy toward the Arabs in Israel.* An emergency report submitted to Prime Minister Ehud Barak by an interuniversity team of researchers. November 2000. (in Hebrew)

Rattner, Arye, and Gideon Fishman. 1998. *Justice for All? Jews and Arabs in the Israeli Criminal Justice System.* Westport, Conn.: Praeger.

Rekhess, Elie, ed. 1978. *The Arabs in Israeli Politics: Dilemmas of Identity.* Tel Aviv: Tel Aviv University, Dayan Center. (in Hebrew)

———. 2002. "The Arabs of Israel after Oslo: Localization of the National Struggle." *Israel Studies* 7, no. 3 (fall): 1–44.

Rosenberg, Rina. 2002. "On the Collective Criminalization of Political Protesters." *Adalah's Review* 3: 8–23.

Rouhana, Nadim. 1997. *Identities in Conflict: Palestinian Citizens in an Ethnic Jewish State.* New Haven, Conn.: Yale University Press.

Rouhana, Nadim, and As'ad Ghanem. 1998. "The Crisis of Minorities in Ethnic States: The Case of the Palestinian Citizens in Israel." *International Journal of Middle East Studies* 30: 321–46.

Sa'di, Ahmad H. 2000. "Israel as Ethnic Democracy: What Are the Implications for the Palestinian Minority?" *Arab Studies Quarterly* 22, no. 1: 25–37.

———. 2002a. "Catastrophe, Memory and Identity: Al-Nakbah as a Component of Palestinian Identity." *Israel Studies* 7, no. 2 (summer): 175–98.

———. 2002b. "The Peculiarities of Israel's Democracy: Some Theoretical and Practical Implications for Jewish-Arab Relations." *International Journal of Intercultural Relations* 26, no. 2 (April): 119–33.

Said, Edward. 1979. *The Question of Palestine.* London: Routledge and Kegan Paul.

Schueftan, Dan. 2001. "Arab-Jewish Relations in Israel: From the Illusion of 'Solution' to Damage Control." *Iyunim Bebitahon Leumi* 1, no. 1 (June): 128–63. (in Hebrew)

———. 2002. "The New Identity of the Arab Knesset Members." *Tkhelet* 13: 23–49. (in Hebrew)

Shafir, Gershon, and Yoav Peled. 2002. *Being Israeli: The Dynamics of Multiple Citizenship.* Cambridge: Cambridge University Press.

Silberstein, Laurence J. 2002. *The Postzionism Debates: Knowledge and Power in Israeli Culture*. New York: Routledge.

Smooha, Sammy. 1978. *Israel: Pluralism and Conflict*. Berkeley: University of California Press.

———. 1992. *Arabs and Jews in Israel: Change and Continuity in Mutual Intolerance*. Vol. 2. Boulder, Colo.: Westview Press.

———. 1997. "The Viability of Ethnic Democracy as a Mode of Conflict-Management: Comparing Israel and Northern Ireland." In *Comparing Jewish Societies*, ed. Todd Endelman. Ann Arbor: University of Michigan Press.

———. 1999. *Autonomy for Arabs in Israel?* Beit Berl: Institute for Israeli Arab Studies. (in Hebrew)

———. 2000. "The Regime of the State of Israel: Civil Democracy, Non-Democracy, or Ethnic Democracy?" *Sociologia Yisraelit* 2, no. 2: 565–630. (in Hebrew)

———. 2001. "Arab-Jewish Relations in Israel as a Jewish and Democratic State." In *Trends in Israeli Society, Volume 1*, ed. Ephraim Yaar and Zeev Shavit. Tel Aviv: Open University. (in Hebrew)

———. 2002a. "The Model of Ethnic Democracy: Israel as a Jewish and Democratic State." *Nations and Nationalism* 8, no. 4 (October): 475–503.

———. 2002b. "Types of Democracy and Modes of Conflict-Management in Ethnically Divided Societies." *Nations and Nationalism* 8, no. 4 (October): 423–31.

Soen, Dan. 2002 "Democracy, the Jewish-Arab Cleavage and Tolerance Education in Israel." *International Journal of Intercultural Relations* 26, no. 2: 215–32.

Soffer, Arnon. 1993. "Full Equality of Rights to Arabs—Is It Possible?" *Nativ* 31, no. 2: 50–53. (in Hebrew)

———. 1997. "The Affiliation of Arabs in Israel to a Palestinian State." *Nativ* 10, no. 1–2 (January–April): 77–81. (in Hebrew)

———. 2001. *Israel, Demography 2000–2020: Dangers and Opportunities*. Haifa: University of Haifa, Center for National Security Studies.

State of Israel. 1997. *Combined Initial and Second Report of the State of Israel concerning the Implementation of the United Nations Covenant on Economic, Social and Cultural Rights (CESCR), Submitted in 1997 to the United Nations Committee on Economic, Social and Cultural Rights*, comp. and ed. Michael Altan. Jerusalem: Ministry of Foreign Affairs, Ministry of Justice, and Ministry of Labor and Social Affairs.

Suleiman, Ramzi. 2002. "Perception of the Minority's Collective Identity and Voting Behavior: The Case of the Palestinians in Israel." *Journal of Social Psychology* 142, no. 6 (December): 753–66.

Supreme Court. 2000. "Appeal to the Court of Justice 6698/95: A'adel and Iman Ka'adan against Israel Lands Authority, Ministry of Construction and Housing, Local Council Tal-Eron, the Jewish Agency, Katzir-Cooperative for Communal Settlement in Samaria, and the Farmers' Union of Israel." *Piske Din* 54, 1, no. 258. (in Hebrew)

———. 2003. "Appeal to the Court of Justice 11280/02: Decisions of the Central Elections Committee to the Sixteenth Knesset" (ruled on January 7, 2003, and published on May 15, 2003). http://www.court.gov.il.

Tsimhoni, Daphne. 2002. "The Christians in Israel: Aspects of Integration and the Search for Identity of a Minority within a Minority." In *Middle Eastern Minorities and Diasporas*, ed. Moshe Ma'oz and Gabriel Sheffer. Brighton: Sussex Academic Press.

United Nations. 2003. "Concluding Observations of the Committee on Economic, Social and Cultural Rights on Israel's Second Report." May 23.

van den Berghe, Pierre. 2002. "Multicultural Democracy: Can It Work?" *Nations and Nationalism* 8, no. 4 (October): 433–49.

Wilkinson, Benjamin W. 1991. "Ethnic Discrimination in Employment: The Israeli Experience." *Journal of Ethnic Studies* 17: 260–81.

Yiftachel, Oren. 1993. "The Concept of 'Ethnic Democracy' and Its Applicability to the Case of Israel." *Ethnic and Racial Studies* 15, no. 1: 125–36.

———. 1999. "'Ethnocracy': The Politics of Judaizing Israel/Palestine." *Constellations* 6, no. 3 (September): 364–90.

———. 2000. "Ethnocracy and Its Discontents: Minorities, Protests and the Israeli Polity." *Critical Inquiry* 26, no. 4: 725–56.

———. 2002. "The Shrinking Space of Citizenship: Ethnocratic Politics in Israel." *Middle East Report* 223 (summer).

Yiftachel, Oren, As'ad Ghanem, and Nadim Rouhana. 2000. "Is 'Ethnic Democracy' Really Possible? Jews, Arabs and the Israeli Regime." *Jama'a* 6: 58–78. (in Hebrew) (For a shorter English version, see As'ad Ghanem, Nadim Rouhana, and Oren Yiftachel, "Questioning 'Ethnic Democracy': A Response to Sammy Smooha," *Israel Studies* 3, no. 2 [fall 1998]: 253–67.)

Yiftachel, Oren, and Alexander Kedar. 2000. "Power and Land: the Israeli Land Regime." *Theoria Vebikoret* 16 (spring): 67–100. (in Hebrew)

Yonah, Yossi. 1999. "Fifty Years Later: The Scope and Limits of Liberal Democracy in Israel." *Constellations* 6, no. 3 (September): 411–28.

Zogby, James J. 2002. *What Arabs Think: Values, Beliefs and Concerns.* Washington, D.C.: Zogby International.

Zureik, Elia T. 1979. *The Palestinians in Israel: A Study in Internal Colonialism.* London: Routledge and Kegan Paul.

CHAPTER 3

Whatever Became of "Negating Exile"?

Anita Shapira

Of all the concepts upheld by the Zionist movement, the idea of "negating exile" seems to have enjoyed the most lingering popularization, as if Israel and the Jewish Diaspora were constantly at odds with one another. Since the publication of Sh. Beit Zvi's book in 1997,[1] the concept has become a buzzword for Zionism's whole- or halfhearted detractors: it serves as a meta-explanation, so to speak, for the limited attempts of Palestine's prestate Jewish leadership to rescue European Jewry during World War II, for the political use made by Yishuv leader David Ben-Gurion of Holocaust survivors in the struggle to establish a Jewish state in the land of Israel, and for the problematic encounter between the survivors and Palestine's prestate Jewish community—the veteran Yishuv. Claims to this effect have appeared in the works of Tom Segev, Idith Zertal, Yosef Grodzinsky, Moshe Zuckerman, and others,[2] who related to what they saw as the ramifications of "negating exile" for the relationship between the Jewish community in the land of Israel and the Jewish people outside of it. At the same time, Amnon Raz-Krakotzkin attacked the concept on different grounds: to his mind, it led to the establishment of the State of Israel—an unfeeling, inhumane, militaristic entity, diametrically opposed to the "exilic" Jewish experience. Krakotzkin presented the latter as the natural Jewish way of life, which was usurped by Zionism.[3] The concept thus became an important lever in contemporary political debates aimed at debunking one of the generative myths of the State of Israel, namely, its role as defender and savior of Diaspora Jewry. The controversy posited a constant dichotomy between general Jewish interests and particularistic Israeli (or Zionist) interests, as if the two had come into the world mutually hostile and were found to be mutually contradictory.

This chapter attempts to trace the changing concept of "negating exile" since the establishment of the State of Israel. The topic deserves a book-length study, and this chapter does not purport to do more than introduce it. The working hypothesis is that, since the 1960s and especially the 1970s, Israeli society has gradually retreated from the idea of negating exile, to the point of rendering it an anachronism. The harbingers of the process, in my view, are the revised attitudes to Holocaust memory, to Jewish history, and to Israel's "archaeological" identity. Another way of looking at it is by generation. In respect of negating exile, clear lines single out the first generation raised in the country (what poet Saul Tchernichowsky named "the generation in the land") from both the generation of the founding fathers, which preceded it, and the first generation raised in statehood, which succeeded it. The term "generation" is used here loosely. Only the middle generation has relatively clear hallmarks: born or bred in the Yishuv prior to statehood, they were the "native sons," the "*sabras*," the "Palmah̲ generation" who fought in the 1948 War of Independence. The other two generations serve merely to delineate its chronological and thematic boundaries.

THE FOUNDING FATHERS AND THE "NEGATION OF EXILE"

The concept of "negating exile" was built into Zionism from the very start. Political Zionism, as formulated by Leon Pinsker or Theodor Herzl, held that if Jews wished to survive, they had to diverge from the ways of their forefathers who had dwelt among other nations and establish a state of their own. This repudiation of a minority status within a majority nation was defined as shedding exile. In principle, political Zionists were not opposed to the continued existence of Jewish communities outside the boundaries of a Jewish state. On the contrary, Pinsker expected that on the disappearance of the "living dead" (as he defined the Jewish people), that is, the dissolution of the Jewish anomaly of being everywhere a "guest people" and nowhere a "host," the Jews would be able to live safely also among Gentiles. Herzl made it clear at the outset that the Jewish state was meant only for such Jews as would not or could not assimilate, and he hoped that the state's establishment would facilitate the assimilation of Jews who did not wish to throw in their lot with it.

The term "negating exile" was born in the heat of the controversy between the Zionists and the Autonomists, who rallied around historian Simon Dubnow. It was an internal dispute in the Jewish national movement between those who thought it possible to ensure the Jewish minority national, cultural autonomy among nation-states and those who demanded a separate Jewish territory. The opponents of "national autonomy" (i.e., the Zionists and territorialists) were dubbed by their rivals "negators of exile." Zionist thinker Ah̲ad Ha-Am (Asher Zvi Ginsberg) distinguished between subjective and objective negation: subjectively, he asserted, all Jews "negated exile"; that is, they were conscious of the Jewish people's woeful condition among the Gentiles as "a lamb among wolves," and they longed to change this. Were the Messiah to come and gather up all of Israel's scattered exiles, all would follow him eagerly. This was the "subjective negation" of exile. "Objective negation" meant acknowledging that, in view of the circumstances that had emerged, Jews could not survive as a scattered people. This was the root of the disagreement between the Zionists and the Autonomists: the former claimed that the Jews had no future as a national entity in the Diaspora; the latter claimed that, under the right conditions, they did.[4]

At this stage, "negating exile" was conceived as negating the possibility of exilic Jewry's continued existence as a people because of objective circumstances. It was the basis of what, in time, was to be called "catastrophic Zionism": the forecast of impending disaster for European Jewry, which made it necessary to urgently create a haven in the land of Israel. Although Herzl explicitly spoke of a disaster involving bodily harm,[5] no one, of course, could foresee the Holocaust; the thinking was in terms of pogroms, loss of income, the forfeiting of equal rights, and a bleak future. A typical example can be found in the poem by Uri Z̲vi Greenberg, "*Ha-Hekhrah̲*" (The Imperative), published in his first book of poetry in the land of Israel, *Ema Gdola Ve-Yare'ah̲* (Dread and the Moon, 1924). It was an ode of love and longing for the life left behind in Poland: the landscape, the climate, the customs of the Ukrainian village, and the big bustling cities and their rich cultural offerings. It expressed the rootless immigrant's yearning for an existence he had forsaken. The land of Israel was sketched as a "land that devours its inhabitants" (Numbers 13:32), and yet he and his friends had joined the "the army of the barefoot on the shores of the Mediterranean," for "we had to go. The earth cried out beneath our soles, the ground shook." The phrase "we had to go" recurs up to the stanza that prophetically reads, "We had to go in pain from towns and look again at homes through fiery tears— / Knowing that they would be lapped in flame one day. / We kissed no threshold dear, we kissed no walls, nor stroked in pain well-loved panoply / —for beyond the brow, the past was now burnt to ash—with many-colored coats, snow-white beds and canopies / And along came the years and stretched out at our feet howling like loyal dogs in Gentile fields."[6]

A similar view was voiced by Berl Katznelson when eulogizing his friend, educator Eliezer Schein, "*Le-Lo Hitgalut*" (Without Revelation): "I do not know whether our elders, who would rise at midnight for prayers and lament the hardships of bondage and the bitterness of exile, felt our people's foundering and our people's shame as painfully as we, the young, tempestuous revolutionaries. . . . Awake and asleep, we saw the flash of a knife, the wasting of the body and cremation of the soul of the Jewish masses. We saw bad omens in all: atrophy in 'rebirth,' surrender in revolution, alienation in liberation. In the dark alleyways of Jewish Vilna, in the hunger, the squalor and the drone of their penny existence, we breathed the air of extinction." The feeling that they were witnesses to the final days of Jewish existence in the Diaspora was accompanied by a sense of responsibility for the fate of the Jewish people. The sense of imminent doom galvanized and was the life force of the young "tempestuous revolutionaries."[7]

At the same time, however, the concept of "negating exile" came to be conceived as the rejection of the exilic Jewish way of life. In this sense, the Zionist movement was a true daughter of the Enlightenment: criticism of Jewish traditional life was a key component of the public agenda of all the movements that sought to modernize the Jews and open them up to currents in the non-Jewish world, even prior to the appearance of Zionism. Abraham Mapu, Judah Leib Gordon, David Frischmann, and Mendele Mokher Seforim (Shalom Jacob Abramowitsch) depicted a Jewish world rotten through and through and called for productivity, secularization, and education, without drawing Zionist conclusions. Unlike the thriving Yiddish literature at the time, which treated Jewish society compassionately, humorously, and indulgently (Isaac Leib Peretz and Shalom Aleichem [Sholem Rabinovitz]), Hebrew literature flew the flag of social and cultural protest, objecting to the status quo. Micha Yosef Berdyczewski and Joseph Hayyim Brenner condemned the norms of Jewish society, demanding a complete makeover of the value system: instead of the spiritual, the earthly; instead of alienation from the land, agriculture; instead of individual materialism, mobilization for pioneering tasks for the common good, the building of a country for the Jews. Censure of Jewish society and the call to create an alternative society in the land of Israel went hand in hand: the more the critics were fired by a utopian vision of a new, model society, the harsher and stronger their criticism of the society from which they came. The greater the sacrifice demanded of the pioneer by the new society, the greater the tendency to denigrate the old society: the heart of every pioneer was stamped with a picture of the past, and the longings, at times, were unbearable. The pull of home, to parents, beloved family, childhood scenes, and a familiar climate, was overpowering. These had been years of cultural blossoming, intellectual storm, and even economic and social progress among eastern European Jewry. To counter this pull, the exilic Jewish society from which they had come was portrayed as suffering from every possible social malaise. To this end, the pioneers could call on an inexhaustible repertoire of Enlightenment literature that demanded modernization, of socialist literature that chastised capitalism, and of anti-Semitic literature, some of whose claims seeped into Zionist thought. Above all, however, it was the criticism of the revolutionary who strove to build a new world order from scratch and create a "new man (and woman)," worthy of that world and able to sustain it. For those who wished to resettle in the land of Israel and preserve their old way of life, there was little or no need to criticize Jewish society. But for those who sought to change society's norms, criticism was a vital psychological weapon to justify the new course and put brakes on all thoughts of regret.

The "new Jew" was supposed to be different from his elders in worldview, in the approach to Jewish and non-Jewish interaction, in the attitude to manual labor, and in the ability to defend himself. He had to be prepared to subordinate his own interests to the common good (the collective or the nation), be well versed in Hebrew culture, and love his people and his land, umbilically tied to that strip of Mediterranean coast to which the Jewish people had bound their fate and their history. Distant horizons were not to beckon him or arouse his senses. Of his own free will, he was to renounce worldly pleasures. Whereas for the pioneers of the founding generation who had come to the country out of Zionist consciousness or a sense of "the imperative," the "negation of exile" was meant to dam up desire for the way home. For the generation reared in the country, it was meant primarily as an antidote to wanderlust (a quality listed by their fathers as one of the ailments of the Jews). The negative depiction of Jewish life in the Diaspora was to "add value" to the sparsity and dangers that marked the existence of the small Jewish Yishuv in Palestine, lending it an advantage over the life led by Jews in the countries of Europe. Until the rise of Nazi Germany and the weakening of the Jewish middle class in Poland, the Yishuv was the lesser value in the equation of relations with exilic Jewry: the latter provided funds, manpower, and political pressure. The Yishuv was small, feeble, and leaning for sustenance on its mother communities in Europe. This equation and interdependence were reversed only in the mid-1930s. Thus, the need to equip Yishuv youth with a zealousness for the land of Israel is understandable. Experience had shown, as in the case of the old *moshavot* (colonies), many of whose members had upped and left the country during and after the Uganda crisis, that being raised in the country was in itself not enough to ensure a deep bond to it.

The "negation of exile" was instilled by both formal and informal education. In school, its principles were transmitted through the study of, among others, J. L. Gordon ("*Kutzo shel Yod*" [The Dot on the "i"], "*Zidkiyahu Be-Veit Ha-Pekudot*: [Zedekiah in Prison]), and Hayyim Nahman Bialik ("*Be-Ir Ha-Haregah*" [In the City of Slaughter] and "*Yatmut*" [Orphanhood]). Rising from these works was a picture of exilic Jewish society as fanatically religious and narrow-minded or as assimilationist and losing its Jewish moorings. Jews were portrayed as spineless cowards holing up before rioters and not daring to emerge even to protect their wives and daughters. They engaged in contemptible occupations, were poor and miserable, and were unable to cope with reality. Mendele's hefty addition to the "negation of exile" was a grotesque characterization of Jewish society. Shalom Aleichem and I. L. Peretz, it is true, furnished a softer, more indulgent portrait, but though these works were also part of the curriculum, their protagonists did not suit the activist spirit of youth in the land of Israel. They were attracted to Saul Tchernichowsky's tempestuous poetry. "The raging blood of Canaan's conquerors" is what appealed to them. They admired King Saul galloping on his horse to En Dor to conjure up Samuel before falling on his sword in the hills of Gilboa.

In the Labor youth movements, two of Brenner's works exerted a great influence: "*Haarakhat Atzmenu Bi-Shloshet Ha-Krakhim*" (Self-Appraisal in Three Volumes), a review of Mendele's work, and "*Hu Amar La*" (He Told Her). The former included some of Mendele's most grotesque deliveries, a mock of Russian Jews and their traditional way of life; some of the statements might have been lifted straight from an anti-Semitic lampoon.[8] The latter was a monologue by a young Jew bent on joining a self-defense unit in Russia and arguing with his mother, who is opposed to the idea. The main theme is that, while the older generation meekly accepted persecution, the younger generation would not resign themselves to so despicable a death.[9]

In the transition from the generation of the fathers to the generation of native sons, the understanding of the codes used by the authors, codes that until then had been part of the unwritten agreement between writer and reader, became impaired. When the fathers read Bialik's "In the City of Slaughter" or Brenner's "He Told Her," they were overcome by rage and fury that found release in adopting the principle of self-defense as a hallowed tenet of the Jewish national liberation movement. When the sons read the same works, they were struck most of all by Jewish impotence. To them, self-defense was no longer an existential or intellectual revolution but a fact of life. The need to protect Jewish life and honor was no longer up for discussion. They found it strange that exilic Jews put up with being persecuted. The same was true of "Self-Appraisal": Brenner, for all his censure of Jewish society, just like Mendele, ultimately made peace with the object of his reproof, for, despite all their failings, these were his people, and he cherished them. The fathers knew that Mendele's and Brenner's portrayals were grotesque and, as such, deliberately distorted. For all their criticism of the Jewish *shtetl* (town), they were its children, sharing a close knowledge of the life depicted in the literature, in all its lights and all its shadows. They identified intimately with traditional Jewish society, and even though they had turned their backs on it, it remained a part of them. Their criticism was a lover's criticism. Solidarity with the Jewish people and a commitment to act for their deliverance—this, to them, was the essence of Zionism and the project of statehood in the land of Israel. In contrast, the native sons read Mendele and Brenner at face value: the condemnation they internalized was not tempered by a shared life experience and knowledge of flesh-and-blood people or by the realization that the literary portrayals did not reflect reality but a warped flip side. To them, the idlers of Kisalon represented the Jewish *shtetl* that once was, in all its misery and airy-fairy trades of *luftgescheft*, its cringing meekness before Gentiles and its disconnection from a natural life.

There were two aspects to the censure of exilic Jewish society: criticism of traditional society in the name of modernization and criticism of assimilation in the name of nationalism. The very concept of "assimilation" was, in Zionist terms, blatantly negative, symbolizing a renunciation of national identity, an attempt to borrow a false identity, pretense, and fraud. The struggle against would-be assimilationists into non-Jewish society was no less fierce than that against traditional society. Most of the literary images, however, alluded to traditional Jewish society in eastern Europe, from which most of the Yishuv population stemmed at the time.

THE "NATIVE GENERATION" AND "NEGATION OF EXILE"

Kibbutz members were to gaze on their children, growing up splendidly, and agonize over the "new Hebrews" sprouting in their fields. The disquiet about the new type of person rising in the land of Israel was aroused as early as the 1930s. In considering the contrast between his sons and his forefathers, Shelomo Lavi, a member of En Harod (and of the second Aliyah immigration wave), said, "We cast off the excessive spirituality that we believed to be the legacy of exile. Our forefathers in exile had been concerned mainly with the soul; we, who shed the yoke of exile, concerned ourselves mainly with the body, with practicality, pride, pluck. All this, it seems to me, we have achieved. We have obtained a generation of *shkotzim* [non-Jewish boorish louts]. And having won it, we stand and wonder: is this what we hoped for?" He tried to put his finger on what was lacking in the generation of native sons: "A little thought about their place in the world, their place in Judaism, our past and our future and, in general, a little self-consciousness and emotional depth."[10] His fellow kibbutz member David Maletz (who had come in the third Aliyah) feared that kibbutz children were becoming people of action and organization, "matter," like the golem who had turned on his creator. They lacked the spiritual sense of the human condition, the "eternal sorrow that attends man through life," the "moan, the moan of eternal human suffering." And he added, "These rudiments we absorbed there, after all, in the *shtetls* of exile. In the hovels of poverty and in the air of woe and suffering. There, we were suckled on rebelliousness, empathy, a great, profound compassion, and love, the love that comes with compassion. From there, too, comes the thirst for Israeli soil. And yet our children amongst us, amidst our own creation that suckles on these spiritual impulses, they, of all people, are so very removed from all these impulses."[11]

The distance between the emotional worlds of the founding generation and the native sons astounded the fathers. As is typical of revolutionaries, they viewed the gulf that separated them from their elders as a matter of fact, but they assumed that their own children would follow in their footsteps, dispensing with a generation gap. Lyova Levite, one of the intellectuals of the Kibbutz Ha-Me'uhad movement (Mapai's left-wing faction), defined the gap at the kibbutz conference in October 1941 thus: "We and our children are not mere categories—different age groups. We and are children are the sons of two very different worlds." The bitterness was evident in the sense of estrangement between parents and children—so close to one another and yet so very far apart. The youth sprouting up on the soil of the land of Israel took their childhood environment for granted: "What for our generation (and for numerous generations of the Jewish people) had been a tremendous revolution—manual labor, land, language, commune—for our children were givens." As a result, they related to these realities simply and naturally, and this was responsible for their simplistic outlooks. Unlike their fathers, *sabras* reared in the land of Israel did not share the pain of the human condition, did not try to fight for world reform, and did not show either human or Jewish sensitivity. Levite summed up with the attitude of kibbutz youth to the Jewish people: "It is hard to say—our children need more of a 'love of Israel.'" He compared their perspective to Brenner's critical approach to his people: "Behind the scalpel of a merciless 'self-appraisal'—beat a conscious, hurting Jewish heart, devotion to this folk corpus, Jewish solidarity and an infinite love for the Jewish masses." In contrast, "our children's love for their people and loyalty to the vision of their [the people's] redemption is no doubt intact. But the people appear as an abstract at times, and [our youth's] love for them may be accompanied by a sense of strangeness towards and disparagement of the concrete Jews of exile. Love is sometimes replaced by pity." Levite raised reservations about the validity of local education toward "negation of exile": it is doubtful that what was necessary in exile was called for in the land of Israel, where freedom is taken for granted, requiring no additional corroboration. On the other hand, as a result of this form of education, the image of exilic Jewry is distorted. Levite sounded the alarm on the young's paltry knowledge of Jewish history and took issue with the way in which Jewish history was taught, as a sequence of "pogroms [and submissiveness, going] like sheep to the slaughter" (the term apparently pre-dated the Holocaust). He demanded that the teaching of Jewish history include also its elements of rebellion, valor, and upheaval. Touching on the alienation of the young from exilic Jews, he raised the matter of the absorption of Jewish refugees in the country after the war, people sapped and broken whose world had been devastated (he was not referring to the Holocaust, of course, which had not yet taken place). "With what measure of love, of respect, of tact, of brotherly warmth . . . will we be able to root them among ourselves?"[12] Levite was speaking at a discussion on the kibbutz's second generation, within the framework of the Kibbutz Me'uhad movement conference. There were no dissenters. "Our second generation see the exilic Jewish prototype as a miserable soul," Baruch Eisenstadt (Azaniya) concurred, adding that "we must ensure that our children do not regard the Jewish people as strangers, as is the case today."[13]

This, then, is how the native generation educated in Palestine appear to have interpreted the concept of "negating exile" bequeathed to them by their parents. Their distance from flesh-and-blood people—their inability to translate the abstract concepts of Jewish Diaspora life into tangible situations and actual faces, character, and vitality—in their eyes transformed the criticism into objective portrayals and the caricatures into mirror images. A limited worldview, a narrow cultural horizon, lack of education, and anti-intellectualism—all faults that were attributed to *sabra* youth—contributed to their two-dimensional, intolerant picture of Diaspora Jews as "others."

The discussion on the second generation in the Kibbutz Me'uhad movement took place early in World War II and before the Holocaust. It exposed the prevalent attitudes of the country's youth in the 1930s, attitudes that were to grow stronger as a result of the halt in immigration during the war years. The constant tension between the consolidation of a local, native identity and the process of immigration dated back to the first Aliyah and the budding "nativeness" in the colonies during World War I: every wave of immigration "diluted" the local identity and reinforced Jewish identity, drawing on varied sources, whether traditional or revolutionary, Yiddish or German culture, and so forth. The halt of immigration in World War II provided an incubation period for a new identity and dovetailed with the coming of age of a significant number of young people either born or bred in the country. Thus, for the first time, it was possible to speak in terms of a generational cohort in the land of Israel (according to Karl Mannheim's definition).

Levite's warning against portraying Jewish history as a chronicle of weakness was soon borne out. In 1943, Hayyim Hazaz published his story "*Ha-Drasha*" (The Homily), in which the protagonist declared himself divorced from Jewish history.[14] Although it remains a moot point whether the hero marked the author's own position or his intent to shed critical light on a perturbing phenomenon, it makes little difference for the purpose at hand. So enthusiastically was the story received that Hazaz might have issued a political statement rather than having sketched a literary figure. His main character removed the long period of exile from the continuum of Jewish history and established an ostensible link between ancient Jewish history in the land and contemporary history.[15] In so doing, he simply took to the extreme existing Yishuv phenomena, among them the profound affinity for biblical tales as representing the bond between the people and the land. The mythology of the nation's birth and its covenant with the land came to replace actual Jewish history. The ancient past, swathed in mists of legend, the glowing grandeur of King David's reign, and the valor of the Hasmonean dynasty were to be the bedrock of an alternative identity, different from the exilic/ Jewish identity and lending historical legitimacy to Jewish belonging and Jewish right to the land of Israel.

Labor leader Berl Katznelson, addressing Mapai's young guard at a seminar on Mount Carmel in the summer of 1944, was highly conscious of the signs of alienation of local youth from both exilic Jewish history and the concrete Jewish people. He detected the emergence of a peculiarly Israeli tribe, ready to identify with the heroic exploits of the native sons, perhaps even with Bar Kokhba, but detached from other types of Jews beyond their cultural orbit. He attributed this estrangement to Zionism's right wing: "Spiritual Revisionism, actually, and [Ze'ev] Jabotinsky, personally, had no need for the continuity of Jewish culture. He sought something noble, of the ancient Jewish race that connects us to the race of Joshua Bin Nun, Bar Kokhba and Judah Halevi. But Jewish history in sequence, the continuity of its human type—this he had no need for."[16] In contrast, he presented the Jewish Labor movement emerging in Palestine as a blend of "the extension of a spiritual world no longer intact, as it had been in the Second Temple [period], but having absorbed some of the elements of Jewish exile."[17]

Berl's was not the only legitimate outlook in the Labor movement: on more than one occasion, David Ben-Gurion expressed opinions negating both exile and the Jews of exile, in the very same vein that Katznelson ascribed to Jabotinsky. After the establishment of the State of Israel, Ben-Gurion went even further, describing contemporary Jewry's rebirth in their land as the extension of the First Temple period and crowning Joshua as his favorite biblical character. The assertion that Zionism was a clean break in the sequence of Jewish history was a key element in his worldview. The detachment from the Jewish *shtetl* as a metaphor for the exilic experience was a basic pillar of his thinking. His aversion to Yiddish was an outward expression of that basic stance that sought to loosen the cord between the Jewish tribe dwelling in Zion and their exilic parentage.[18] Yizhak Tabenkin (the leader of Kibbutz Me'uhad), on the other hand, though he defined the "new Jew" as having "hoe in hand and a rifle on the shoulder," nonetheless felt a great affection for Jewish folkways outside Palestine and the display of Jewish courage and genius there. He was sympathetic toward the Jewish workers' movement and revolutionary trends in the Diaspora and viewed them as the spiritual comrades of the Jewish Labor movement in Palestine. He rejected historical discontinuity. And while he saw the Bible as one of the founts from which he had imbibed, he never lionized it as Ben-Gurion did toward the end of his life.[19] Katznelson's attitude was similar to Tabenkin's. Tabenkin, however, limited his identification to the Jewish working class or masses, while Katznelson identified with the Jewish people down the generations, feeling Jewish martyrdom as a palpable experience. They both loved Yiddish and did not regard it as rivaling or inimical to Hebrew. All three believed in "catastrophic Zionism" and foresaw disaster looming for European Jewry. But for each of them, the notion of "negating exile" donned a different form and was reflected by a different attitude toward Diaspora Jews.

This variegation, illustrated by Katznelson's total identification with Jewish fate down the generations, Tabenkin's identification with the Jewish masses and, Ben-Gurion's more radical approach that excised portions of Jewish history, indicates that as far as the "founding fathers" were concerned, the concept of "negating exile" meant different things to different people at different times. U. Z. Greenberg wrote some of the harshest things imaginable about Polish Jewry after his poem "*Ha-Hekhrah*," which was filled with longing for the life he had left behind, and before his return to Poland for a number of years. Authors and poets wrote alternately in Hebrew and in Yiddish (Mendele, Shalom Aleichem, Bialik, Greenberg, Itzhak Katznelson, and so on), and there was no impregnable wall between the two cultures. All this was prior to the Holocaust. One might say that, despite its prominence as an ideological and cultural component, the concept of "negating exile" was not the only or the dominant trend. There were contrary currents that strove rather to emphasize the bond to Jewish tradition, to Judaism as a culture and mind-set pervaded by social sensitivities and aspirations of world reform. These currents sought to preserve the emotional ties to the Jewish *shtetl.*

One of the criteria whereby Berl Katznelson tried to gauge the growing estrangement between the Jewish "tribe" in Palestine and the Jewish people outside of it was the attitude of the young to the Holocaust. He saw local youth distancing themselves from Jewish suffering in Europe and diagnosed the cause in the inability of the young to identify with Jewish powerlessness; they could identify with the ghetto rebels in whom they recognized a common spirit of valor. Katznelson, on the other hand, was not ashamed of Jewish impotence. He told the youngsters that "even if there had been no uprising in the ghetto, I would not say a single word against the Jews of the ghetto," for he understood their impossible plight. Against the physical bravery of the rebels, Katznelson held up the conduct of the brother of the rabbi of Gur, who, in going to his death, had asked for some water so that he and his fellow Jews could purify themselves. "To me—this is an incredible demonstration on one's day of death. And I know that it is the Jewish death of *kiddush hashem* [martyrdom]."[20] One can discern here the first glimmer of later attitudes to the Holocaust: opposition to the preeminence of rebellion or physical resistance in collective memory, empathy for Jewish helplessness, and esteem for the efforts to preserve one's human image.

Katznelson exposed the alienation of native youth from the Jewish tragedy. The absence of a "love for Israel"—which Levite had mentioned three years earlier—had become more extreme as a result of the closure of Yishuv society during the war years. It is impossible to determine the impact of deliberate and nondeliberate education toward "negating exile" on the young or the extent to which their attitudes were dictated by the realities of life. The first generation to grow up in a land of colonization naturally develops a "native" consciousness, viewing their fathers and their fathers' culture as "other" and resisting it in order to mold, in the course of this contest, an identity of their own. The "native generation" rejects the past that does not belong to their territory. "The old country," which for the fathers is an object of yearning, for the young is a sentimental anachronism. The 1940s saw the first emergence of the cultural and political phenomenon of "Canaanism." A group of young people, reared in Palestine though not necessarily born there, rallied around Uriel Shelah, known as the poet Yonathan Ratosh, and the Committee to Consolidate Hebrew Youth, a body he set up in 1940. It comprised people from both Left and Right. Ratosh, himself, was a right-wing extremist. He published his views in a modest pamphlet, *Ktav el Ha-No'ar Ha-Ivri* (Essay to Hebrew Youth), essentially advocating that the new Hebrew entity in the land of Israel sever itself completely from any attachment or affiliation to the Jewish people. The latter was a religious, ethnic worldwide group (a *milet* in Ottoman terms). The former was the Hebrew nation, bound by territory, history, and language to the early peoples of the Fertile Crescent. Hebrew youth were connected to their Canaanite ancestry: the daring seafarers of Tyre and Sidon, the glorious peoples who spawned the civilization of Baal and Ashtoreth (Astarte), and the goddess Anath and other early gods unearthed in the archaeology of Syria in particular and the Fertile Crescent in general. Hebrew youth were a product of their natural birthplace and had nothing to do with the religious Jewish group. The picture of the future, according to Ratosh, was as splendid as that of the archaeological past: the Fertile Crescent was the cradle of the Semitic peoples. Their language was Hebrew. The current Hebrews were destined to rule the entire Crescent, unifying it through the Hebrew language. Arab nationalism was an artificial creation of British imperialism and doomed to oblivion in the face of the reemerging alliance of the Semitic minorities.[21] Ratosh's thesis had a certain magic to it, depicting a glorious past unfettered by religion; wedded to national, creative, and cultural eminence; and promising a no less glorious future, bright and harmonious: a vast Hebrew land.

The construction of a new Hebrew national identity based on territory, language, and history matched the emotional needs of "native" youth who, consciously or not, felt not only different from the generation of the fathers but also disconnected from all foregoing generations. The encounter with Ratosh's ideas was bewitching, as described years later by poet Haim Gouri, whom Ratosh had made a special effort to win over: "The effect of my meeting with him at first—I, a young man at the time—was that of the fascination of adultery with another possibility and the fear that accompanies the alternative, much like religious conversion. I was searching for a true identity in those days. My soul was often at war with itself. Sometimes it was like a deviant prowling amid [different] faiths and arrested at dawn for vagrancy. My route to the Jewish people was not simple."[22] Ratosh captivated young *sabra* intellectuals, his ideas opening before them an avenue to a local identity, stripped of religion and tradition, unburdened by Jewish history, leading to the big wide world and offering an all-embracing answer for past, present, and future. Aharon Amir, Benjamin Tammuz, Moshe Atar, Moshe Vaadia, Alex Keinan, Ezra Zohar, Matti Peled, and numerous others followed Ratosh like disciples after a rabbi. He lent concrete expression to their vague stirrings about belonging to the local geographical space, having links to a glorious Hebrew past and no connection with anything that smacked of exile. The flight from history to archaeology was immeasurably spellbinding: history, as Hazaz had said, was humiliating, oppressive, and boring. Archaeology was inspiring, riveting, and mysterious. It opened a window into political greatness, cultural flowering, and spatial blending. It was anchored in this soil, in this ancient landscape, where Arab villages looked like living remnants of a rooted entity that belonged, that had sprouted from the crevices in the rocks and the ravines of the Judaean Hills. Archaeology was deemed more contemporary and real than the Jewish *shtetl*, which represented all that was foreign to local youth: language and culture, lifestyle and tradition, climate and scenery, and dependence, humiliation, and impotence. It lent legitimacy to Hebrew existence in the land of Israel, independent of the train of 2,000 years of exile, the return to Zion and redemption—major Zionist concepts that on the one hand juxtaposed exile with redemption but on the other also connected them irrevocably. In "*Massa Ha-Ptiḇa*" (Opening Essay), his key document published in 1944, Ratosh cut the Gordian knot with the Jewish people: an immigrant nation had arisen in the land of Israel, distinct from its biological fathers, just as American immigrants were distinct from their British parentage.

Organizationally and politically, "Canaanism" (as poet Abraham Shlonsky derisively designated the new Hebrew nationalism), was never more than a small cult of faithful clinging to a guru.[23] Culturally, however, it was highly influential, reaching far beyond the circles that had joined up with Ratosh. Thus, for instance, in 1947, Uri Avneri published a series of pamphlets titled *Ba-Maavak* (The Struggle) on behalf of a group he called Eretz Israel Ha-Ẕe'ira (The Young Land of Israel). With the arrogance and condescension of youth, the pamphlets gave voice to the upcoming generation, and central to Avneri's thinking was the call to hand over the regime to the young. The essential difference between him and Ratosh lay in their attitude to the "Arab masses." Avneri, too, had aspirations of the Hebrews dominating the Semitic expanse "through a Semitic revolution—reunifying the country on behalf of all its residents, and unifying the Semitic space on behalf of all its countries, a true partnership in which the Hebrew nation would win its destined place as leader of the Semitic world."[24] But he explicitly sought a Hebrew-Arabic blend in common local education, where Hebrew and Arabic enjoyed equal status, as opposed to Ratosh's Hebrew dominance.

In terms of attitude to the Jewish people, there was no real difference between the articles in *Ba-Maavak* and Ratosh's doctrine. The dividing line between Jewish and Hebrew, however, was more obscure in *Ba-Maavak*, for, in Avneri's opinion, the affiliation to the new nation depended on a totally different psychological state and mind-set; a local breeding ground was not enough. Avneri did not sever the connection to exilic Jewry, maintaining it for political rather than emotional or moral reasons: the editors of *Ba-Maavak* apparently could not ignore the increasing sensibilities of the young about exterminated Jewry. Given Ratosh's advocacy of complete severance from the Jewish people, the "Canaanites" and proto-"Canaanites" were accused of turning their backs on the Jewish Diaspora, which desperately needed assistance. They replied, "This is a vile lie concocted by sick demagogues. We have turned our backs on the exilic way of life and traditions—traditions that are so decisively to blame for the ghastly destruction of exilic Jewry. We will not permit such traditions to insinuate themselves into the land of Israel and turn the Yishuv into a new ghetto. However, we have not abandoned the people of the Diaspora to their fate. The 'generation in the land' has fought and will fight for its gates to be opened to these Jews. They know that this is a matter of life for the Yishuv, itself, for it will not be able to endure and develop without a hefty supplement of manpower."[25] This was hardly a statement of human warmth. To be sure, "exilic Jews" were needed as human potential for the Yishuv's growth, but they lacked the right spirit, which is why they had been unable to save themselves in the Holocaust. For the same reason, "the exilic Jews ruling the Yishuv" had been unable to save their fellow Jews abroad in the Diaspora. Only rule by the "native" generation can ensure the rescue of exilic Jewry, "serve as their guardian."[26] Uri Avneri and the newspaper he bought and edited after the State of Israel was established, *Ha-Olam Ha-Zeh* (This World), played an important part in Israeli society of the 1950s in fostering ideas that negated exilic Jews.

The "Canaanite" periphery encompassed broad elements of the Palmah generation (the young strike force in the 1948 war). Wrote Haim Gouri, "Perhaps it was an early 'Canaanism,' rooted in the secular humanist education of the free-thinking schools of Labor Israel that diverged from the accepted national line involved in true religious experience . . . there they loved Esau rather than Jacob, Saul rather than Samuel"—thus, in retrospect, he tried to explain his own and his peers' attraction to the "Canaanite" idea.[27] When critic Baruch Kurzweil entered the fray against the "Canaanites," he situated them in the linear development of the new Hebrew literature. "This movement is no more than the logical, consistent conclusion of aesthetic, intellectual aspirations that have inspired our literature for almost a hundred years now," he declared, on the one hand robbing the "Canaanites" of their pretension to originality and on the other blaming its Zionist detractors for its very growth. "The poetry of Ratosh and A. Amir is inconceivable without the poems of Tchernichowsky and [Zalman] Shneour," he further charged; "from the point of view of literary continuity, the 'Canaanites,' as a literary-intellectual phenomenon, are the consistent extension of the 'anti-mission' line in our literature since the 19th century."[28] This portrayal of "Canaanism" as an extreme but "built-in" conclusion of cultural potentials latent in the criticism of traditional Jewish society embodies a determinism that a priori rejects any possible opposition to that society. It also rejects the potential growth of a strain of religious "Canaanism" that is highly pertinent today among settler groups across the Green Line. For our purposes, Kurzweil presented "Canaanism" as the steady evolution of an "exile-negating" concept that stemmed from the Diaspora and had been applied locally via education. As for the "Canaanites" themselves, they saw themselves not as disciples of Zionism's negation of exile, which they despised, but rather as a new shoot bred in homeland soil, nourished on its air, and fed of its waters, as a consequence of which they had developed as they had. Contrary to Kurzweil, who ostensibly forced them into an essentially Jewish, Zionist mold, they cast off all ties to any cultural tradition, seeing themselves as a local, spontaneous outgrowth, as is common in countries of immigration.[29] Ratosh acknowledged no debt to Hebrew literature, merely to Adiya Gur-Horon, a scholar of ancient civilizations who had initiated him into the secrets of the faraway Semitic past of the peoples of the Fertile Crescent. Gouri believed that Kurzweil had not plumbed the "Canaanite" experience, confining it to the literary realm, and that he had failed to appreciate the politics of identity it embodied, which was bound up with the essential question of Israeli identity.[30]

STATEHOOD AT THE CROSSROADS

The watershed of "Canaanism" was the establishment of the State of Israel, although many years were to pass before this was recognized. Thousands of years after distant stars die and vanish, their light continues its journey in space, as if they still lived on. Something similar happens in history: the awareness of social or cultural change lags behind the transforming event itself. Occasionally, on the verge of extinction, a late blooming occurs, seemingly a sign of vitality; in truth, however, it is the light of a bygone star. In the early 1950s, the journal *Aleph* ("A") appeared, edited by Ratosh and marking the refinement of the cultural impact of "Canaanism." The literary corpus attributed to the "Canaanites" was produced largely at the start of the 1950s.[31] "Canaanite" literature was a quasi-counterpoint to the literature of the "Palmah generation," which, according to critics such as Mordekhai Shalev and Baruch Kurzweil, lacked authenticity and inner truth. "Canaanite" literature was also antiestablishment in the sense that it rebelled against the socialist ideological accoutrements that characterized the Palmah generation. It was the maiden outburst of an individualism that, within a few years, was to find mature expression in the appearance of the *Likrat* (Towards) circle. The fact that in this period Kurzweil found it necessary to declare war on the "Canaanites," while expressing admiration for their literary talents, points to an anxiety about the emergence of a new elite, cut off from its Jewish sources.[32]

From the perspective of time, the appearance of the "Canaanite" phenomenon seems to have been a late blooming of a process already on the wane. The mass immigration that arrived in Israel in the first few years after its establishment spelled its decline. Even as *Aleph* appeared and Ratosh and his coterie enjoyed a momentary sense of power, processes were afoot that already heralded their decline. The new immigrants very soon became the majority in the young state and felt no kinship with the "native *sabra*" mentality and its hallmarks. Some of them were rooted in Jewish culture and saw no reason to hack off their traditional roots in order to be transplanted in Israeli soil. They "negated exile" as generations of Jews had done, praying for "next year in Jerusalem" and lamenting exile much like Ahad Ha-Am's subjective negation. They had not come to Israel because they "negated exile," nor did they seek to create a "new Jew" but rather to continue traditional Jewish life in Zion and under Jewish rule. This definition was particularly valid for Jews from the countries of Islam. As for the European immigrants, the great majority of them were Holocaust survivors, their bond to the Jewish people cardinal. To them, the dichotomy between Jews and non-Jews defined their identity. They wished to live among Jews, in the state of the Jews. Both types of immigrants found the *sabra* experience foreign, an experience that, overnight, became the province of a small minority of Israelis.

Years later, the "Canaanites" were able to recognize the radical transformation that had taken place in the 1950s, a change they had not realized at the time. Twenty years after the state's establishment, one year after the Six-Day War, which reignited Ratosh's nationalist fervor, he wrote, "Today . . . nearly 20 years after the sudden change in the first two years of statehood in Israel's population composition, a change that briefly obscured the process of consolidation and self-definition, we return, quite naturally, to a natural coalescence."[33] Amos Keinan defined it thus: "More and more I share the view I once heard from Uri Avneri. I did not hear it as an opinion. But as a question. Can it be that a geological rift opened up in Israeli society in '48, and we simply are not the same people that were here before '48?" He went on to note, "The people that were here in '48—are gone. A different people are here now. And, in fact, there is no people here. It is a motley crowd."[34] Apparently, the *sabra* arrogance toward "exilic Jewish newcomers" has not dissolved with time.

Mostly, "Canaanism" was the hallmark of the 1948 generation. The state's establishment had been a terrible trauma for them—the war, the casualties, the ensuing sense of missed opportunities, and bitterness. No real study has as yet been done on the attitude of the 1948 generation toward the state that arose. My remarks are consequently impressionistic, being based on reading material written by that generation. The sense of having "missed out" was lodged in political, cultural, and psychological causes. Politically, many of them found themselves in the desert along with the left-wing Mapam Party. The dismantling of the Palmah̲ and "resignation" of some of the officers who had featured prominently in the war left many feeling that a debt was owed them. The state's establishment did not bring about the change in regime that Uri Avneri and his comrades had hoped for: the "old" (who were not so elderly) remained in office. No one gave up a place to make room for the young. The formation of the Israeli bureaucracy and the decreasing need for volunteers engendered disappointment: this was not the ideal state they had dreamed of. The numerous casualties among the young created a sense of crisis, with no catharsis to follow—there was a feeling that there was no recompense for the dead. The state appeared in a poor light considering the price that had been paid. The disappointment of soldiers returning home to find that the world goes on unappreciative of the depth of their pain and suffering, of the emotional revolution they underwent, has historical precedence in post–World War I Europe. "Canaanist" circles were connected to the young state's disillusioned on both sides of the political divide. Yonatan Ratosh, Benjamin Tammuz, Aharon Amir, Uri Avneri, Amos Keinan, Bo'az Evron, and a whole series of young intellectuals adopted an extreme stance against Ben-Gurion and Mapai rule. It was not an opposition identified with either Right or Left; mostly, it was just "anti."

On the whole, changes in awareness become noticeable only after they have ripened and taken on a clear direction. In early statehood, schools continued to educate toward "negating exile" by force of inertia. Hazaz's "*Ha-Drasha*" (The Homily) was part of the high school literature syllabus. Prime Minister Ben-Gurion elevated the Bible to the focus of national education. The Bible circle that met at his home may not have resulted in revelations of any scholarly value, but they occupied a place in public consciousness, and Ben-Gurion, by acquitting himself of controversial pronouncements on "burning" issues (i.e., the Exodus), turned the Bible into a media event. Moreover, Bible quizzes vied for popularity with military parades on Independence Day. The Bible was also the link between the generation of the fathers and the Palmah̲ generation and, to a more limited extent, the following generation that was raised in statehood. Archaeology was the national hobby of the 1948 generation. The most famous dilettante to dabble in antiquity was General Moshe Dayan, who increasingly came to symbolize the daring youth of the 1950s. Dayan defined *sabras* as Hebrew-speaking peasants who knew how to hold a gun—a definition that had nothing to do with Jews or Judaism.[35] The interest in the archaeology and antiquity of the land of Israel represented a bond to territory, patrimony, and the land of the Hebrews to which they were now returning. Every archaeological find that corroborated the connection between Jews and the land of Israel was greeted with much publicity. The tour de force of all this activity was Yigal Yadin's exploits. Yadin, the son of archaeologist E. L. Sukenik, who had obtained for the Jewish people the Dead Sea Scrolls, was chief of operations at the General Staff during the War of Independence and, later, the Israel Defense Forces (IDF) chief of staff. After his military service, he, too, became a professor of archaeology, discovering remains dating back to Bar Kokhba's warriors in the Judaean Desert and conducting excavations at Massada. In his own person, he embodied a bridge between past heroics and present valor. Archaeological discoveries earned headlines far beyond public interest in cultural developments. The finds were treated not as something belonging to the distant past but as a supporting layer for the myths of the Jewish people's return to their ancestral land. In the decision to erect the Israel Museum in Jerusalem, the Dead Sea Scrolls and other finds excavated in the area were earmarked as the salient hub of the complex.[36]

The territorial-archaeological ethos, however, was accompanied by a slow, almost furtive process of return to the Jewish people. In 1956, the Committee of Israeli-Jewish Consciousness was appointed to reexamine school curricula, prompted by reports of Israeli youth's alienation from all things Jewish.[37] The government's basic guidelines, approved by the Knesset in the autumn of 1956, included a commitment to foster among youth Jewish consciousness and the bond to Jewish history and Diaspora Jewry.[38] The commitment had been promoted by Education Minister Zalman Aran. The very definition "Israel-Jewish consciousness" was a novelty in that it recognized the need to nurture such awareness. Committee discussions were full of self-flagellation at having inculcated in youth a negation of exile: local education had been most successful in instilling Hebrew language and a sense of homeland. In contrast, it had utterly failed to instill identification with the Jewish people in the present. "Anyone involved in children's education will admit that when we talk to our youngsters about exilic Jewry, we find their hearts shut," said educator Barukh Ben Yehudah.[39] The children did not distinguish between "negating exile," which is one of the tenets of Zionism, and negating the Jewish world abroad or, in particular, the Jews themselves.

Among the examples cited by the speakers was the scathing criticism of Jewish conduct in the Holocaust: "The first thing to come out of their mouths when we talk about Diaspora Jewry is: 'What do they have to do with us? We have nothing in common.' The children dare to say this plainly, dare to censure the ghetto: 'Why did they go to their deaths without lifting a finger, we would have acted differently . . .' Their obtuseness is total. This is why they dislike this [Shoah] literature and these Jews."[40] While this attitude was discerned among children raised in Labor settlements, it was not restricted to them. Ben-Yehudah reported on a seminar he had conducted with the Young WIZO (Women's International Zionist Organization) during the Holocaust itself at which the girls had rejected all association with the Jews in Europe. "'What do they have to do with us? We don't understand them, they don't understand us. Jews from there will be coming with their kaftans, dealers and black market trade.' I had a heated argument with them, and I found that neither talk nor persuasion have any effect."[41] Elimelekh Rimalt reported on the failure of spontaneous attempts by teachers to impart empathy for European Jewry during and subsequent to the Holocaust. Why had the Jews not immigrated to Palestine in time? the pupils countered.[42] Their alienation from Jews outside of Israel led many young Palmah̲ graduates who studied abroad to feel greater identification there with non-Jews than with Jews, integrating into an environment that had only the flimsiest connection to Jews and Judaism.[43] This was a recurring theme in the encounter between *sabras* and non-Jews abroad: the latter were often surprised to learn that *sabras* were Jews, noting that Israelis were "different." The *sabras*, for their part, proud of the distinction, were oblivious to its anti-Semitic undertones. Yet aversion and condescension for exilic Jewry were no guarantee that Israelis would remain in Israel: many of the students did not come back. Ephraim Urbach, a scholar of the Mishnaic period, arrived at a paradoxical conclusion: negation of exile had led *sabras* to negate exilic Jewry. Now they commended exile but negated its Jews.

The discussions of the Committee for Israeli-Jewish Consciousness were symptomatic in detecting the *sabra* attitude to the Jewish world. They also revealed the difficulties in dealing with the problem: how to instill in the young the relative advantages of life in Israel without negating the Jewish world abroad. There was, between the lines, a concern that youth would draw anti-Zionist conclusions: if life outside of Israel were not disqualified but, indeed, safe and offering existential rewards free of the anxieties attendant on the Israeli situation, what was to stop Israelis choosing to live there rather than here?[44] On the other hand, in general the Committee hoped to mend the *sabra*'s negative image of Diaspora Jewry. Particularly painful was the *sabra* attitude toward Jews who had perished in the Holocaust and, implicitly, toward survivors. Their introduction to the Jewish people in the present, particularly to the Jewish center in the United States, was put forth as an important goal. The top priority, however, was to inject into schools traditional Jewish content to familiarize children with basic Jewish rites and not just the Bible. Ultimately, in 1959, a pamphlet appeared on the deepening of Jewish consciousness, based on the circulars of the Education Ministry's director general. The recommendations revolved around three elements: the study of traditional texts, emphasis on the continuity of Jewish history and the bond between the Jewish people and the land of Israel, and study of contemporary Jewry with the accent on the common fate and mutual responsibility of Israeli Jews and world Jewry.[45] The use of the new term "*Yehudei Ha-Tefutzot*" (Diaspora Jewry) rather than the negative concept of "*Yehudei Ha-Golah*" (exilic Jewry) was telling. Whereas the Jewish exilic world had been seen as being on the brink of destruction (see the previous discussion), the Jewish Diaspora was considered a permanent fixture that would continue to accompany the existence of the Jewish state. The Holocaust, astonishingly enough, even though it featured prominently in Committee discussions, was not mentioned in Ministry circulars. It was referred to indirectly in the curriculum of teaching seminaries for 1958, where the one and only allusion was, "The vengeance of exile, which in our generation extirpated a third of our people."[46] It is hard to say that this mention, which blames exile (in the existential sense) for the Holocaust, helped equip youth with an antidote to the "negation of exile" as they conceived of it.

HOLOCAUST MEMORY AND NEGATION OF EXILE

Yet, apart from the mass immigration, no other topic seems to have so shaken and dented the concept of negating exile as did the Holocaust. Back in 1944, Ratosh, in his "*Massa Ha-Ptiḇa*," included the unforgivable phrase of "rabbit courage" prepared to do battle only when pressed to the wall. He was speaking of the fighters of the Warsaw Ghetto uprising,[47] and his haste to blacken them was no accident: he had spotted a nascent, potentially dangerous trend of empathy and compassion—if not yet identification—for the Jews exterminated in the Holocaust. His assessment—that the tendency to nurture a new Hebrew nation in the land of Israel was threatened by the tendency to identify with the Jewish tragedy—showed a keen intuition for national psychology.

The exposure to the Holocaust and the lessons drawn from it for the negation of exile was a gradual process initially shared by very few young people. Following an evening at the Kibbutz Ha-Me'uẖad conference, devoted to two of the first survivors of the He-H̱alutz pioneering movement to reach Palestine, a young counselor of the Maẖanot Ha-Olim youth movement noted that of those present, thousands of adult kibbutz members had grieved in loss—for relatives, for townspeople, for an entire existence that had gone up in flames—whereas for she herself, her whole world was here in the land of Israel, here was all that she held dear. "And suddenly," she added, "I did not feel good with this wholeness, there was a sense of 'first Hebrews,' though not of 'last Jews,' the bridge was missing . . . and numerous thoughts about the way we had been educated surfaced in a hard, glaring clarity."[48] In the same article, she advocated a change in attitude toward the Jews "from there," from pity mixed with contempt to true identification and brotherhood, flesh of our flesh, with the accent on the interrelation and interdependence of Palestine and the Jewish world. The distinction she made between "first Hebrews" and "last Jews" is worth noting. Here was an exceptionally astute young woman. In 1945, differences of opinion within Maẖanot Ha-Olim ended in a movement split between Left (Aẖdut Ha-Avoda) and Right (Mapai). One of the bones of contention between the two streams was the centrality of the Holocaust as an educational factor. But even the stream that sought to emphasize the recent Jewish calamity in youth movement education regarded this not yet as an emotional need but rather as an expression of national precedence over the Left's Marxist education.[49]

The place of the Holocaust in the literature of the 1948 generation is vague and fuzzy. It generally comes across in the figure of overseas volunteers who joined the War of Independence military effort (GAHAL). The antithesis of *sabras*—authentic, rooted, good-looking, and brave—the newcomers were presented as carrying bygone anxieties on their shoulders and cherishing survival at all costs, which translated into badgering, soldierly ineptness, and signs of timidity. In the memorial literature of the 1948 fighting forces, such as the volumes of *Gvilei Esh* (Scrolls of Fire), the Holocaust barely features. The same is true of *Sefer Ha-Palmaẖ* (The Palmaẖ Book).[50] The "canonic" works of the 1948 generation did not internalize the Holocaust, relating to it and to the survivors as some sort of seam between those who "belonged" and those who did not: both mine and not mine at one and the same time. Yet, even before the State of Israel arose, Uri Avneri found it necessary to defend himself against charges of aloofness from the calamity of the European Jewry, and he did so by blaming the "old" leadership for having proved unable to succor exilic Jewry (a claim taken from the accusations in the 1940s of the right-wing, military underground, Irgun Z̲eva'i Le'umi [IZL], against Mapai for its failure to save the Jewish people in the Holocaust). The young had been prepared to embark on rescue operations (Avneri protested), but the leadership, composed of the fathers, had not. Now they were trying to save traditional Jewish culture because of pangs of conscience.[51] Avneri's aggressive defense hints at the gravity of the question of Shoah memory for the Yishuv and its young people, at whom his response was aimed. The great trauma of the War of Independence, it may be assumed, obliterated the preliminary attempts to internalize the Holocaust among the young.

The 1950s, in many respects, was an incubation period for processes that matured in the following decade. Left and Right banded together against Ben-Gurion and the policy of reconciliation he adopted toward West Germany (a policy symbolized by the term he coined of the "other Germany") and the reparations agreement. Left and Right joined forces also in the (Malkiel) Gruenwald trial, which went down in history as the (Israel) Kasztner Trial and, to a certain extent, marked a climax in the estrangement from the existential Jewish experience under Nazi rule and the unheroic Jewish efforts at survival. Shmuel Tamir, a former IZL member and sworn foe of Ben-Gurion, turned the trial into a confrontation between the proud worldview of *sabra* fighters and ghetto fighters in the face of the ostensibly exilic worldview of Kasztner, who, though he tried to save Jews, did so at the cost of collaborating with the Nazis and forfeiting both self- and national respect. *Ha-Olam Ha-Zeh* made the trial its cause célèbre, cultivating the image of Shmuel Tamir, the young militant *sabra* of the IZL versus the exilic Kasztner of Mapai. So whipped up was public opinion against Kastner that even those who identified with him and felt that they owed him their lives dared not come to his defense. For the Left, this extreme position derived from the key place accorded the leaders of the ghetto uprisings in the myth of Ha-Shomer Ha-Z̲a'ir and the Kibbutz Ha-Me'uh̲ad and the association of West Germany with the camp of Western imperialism. For the Right, it was an extension of the oppositionist stance to Ben-Gurion and the Zionist leadership of the 1940s that was bound up with the alienation felt by "Canaanite" and proto-"Canaanite" circles toward "Jews of exile." Kasztner became the symbol of this Jewry.[52]

But even in this period, there were signs of contrary trends brewing beneath the surface. In 1950, Amir Gilboa published his poem "*Yiz̲h̲ak*" (Isaac): "The sun strolled through the forest at dawn / With Father and me / My right hand in his left. // Like the flash of a knife amid the trees. / And I dreading so my fearful eyes on blood-stained leaves. // Quick, Father, quick, rush to save Isaac / And none shall be absent from the midday feast. // It is I, my son, who am slaughtered, / My blood now on the leaves. / His voice was smothered. / His face, colorless // And I sought to cry out, flailing, incredulous / Eyes wide open. / And I awoke. // My right hand, bloodless."[53] The poem is the obverse of the biblical story of Isaac's binding: in place of the son, the father is offered on the altar. In Israel's imagery, the War of Independence was perceived as the (voluntary) binding of the sons—they made the ultimate sacrifice, like the young girl and boy in Nathan Alterman's poem "The Silver Platter." In Gilboa's poem, it is the father's blood that is shed and the stunned son who is incapable of helping him. Also in the imagery of the State of Israel, the young Yishuv was perceived as the right hand of the Jewish people, and yet, at the critical moment, that hand was found to be wanting—the Yishuv was unable to help its people. At the start, the relationship between father and son is filled with intimacy, trust, and the child's dependence on his elder. This is followed by love, the pain of loss, and a sense of guilt. Gilboa was one of thousands of young people who enlisted during the war in the British army in the latent hope of somehow helping his family who had remained "there." He symbolized the other cultural trend among the *sabra* generation, the "generation in the land." The same was true of Hanokh Bartov (*Shesh Knafayim La-Ehad* [Six Wings to One][54]), Yehudit Hendel (*Anashim Aherim Hem* [Those People Are Different][55]), and others. While not marginal, the current they represented was not central.

THE EICHMANN TRIAL AND NEGATING EXILE

The trial of captured Nazi Adolf Eichmann in 1961 rewound the clock to zero in terms of the attitude to the Holocaust and to survivors. It was the start of a long, slow process that was to fully ripen only in the 1980s. In the spring of 1970, Gad Ufaz wrote in the kibbutz organ *Shdemot:* "The sense of power and of powerlessness are counterpoised, both drawing on a single formative experience—Holocaust awareness and identification with the fate of the Jewish people. Many of us came up against our Judaism in the course of our lives; as for myself, I began to be 'Jewish' in my 20s, during the Eichmann trial. It is a long process, and it climaxed in May-June on the eve of the Six Day War. Since then, it has extended through all the days of tribulation we have known."[56] Just as in 1948 historical and generational changes coalesced, so too did they in 1961 and 1967. The generation that identified with the Jewish people and the Holocaust was the generation reared in statehood. But change was perceptible also among older people, the generation of 1948, who embarked on a long journey toward the real Jewish people.

In the prime minister's Independence Day address in 1961, a few days after the Eichmann trial began in a Jerusalem public hall, Ben-Gurion noted "two highly significant events" that had taken place in this, the *bar-mizvah* year of the State of Israel. They were "the encounter between the heroes of the War of Independence in our own times and those who fought for their people's sovereignty and homeland 1,830 years ago in the Judean Desert . . . [and] the Hebrew trial in Israel's capital against the exterminator of European Jewry."[57] The address tied together the State of Israel's archaeological myth, which was dominant at the time, and the Holocaust myth. It is a fine example of the limits of human understanding. Contrary to the claims that Eichmann's capture and trial had been deliberately orchestrated and used by Ben-Gurion,[58] this anecdote plainly shows that Ben-Gurion did not understand and appreciate the import of Eichmann's apprehension.[59] Even then, almost a year after the public and international furor over Eichmann's capture, he presented the two events—the discovery of the Bar Kokhba scrolls and Eichmann's trial—as equivalent. But while Yigal Yadin's Judaean Desert finds have meanwhile largely been forgotten, interesting only a relatively small public, the Eichmann trial has become a decisive juncture: it was responsible for Holocaust memory penetrating Israeli consciousness and becoming a national myth as well as a point of contact between world Jewry and the Jews of the State of Israel.

The Eichmann trial "dropped" into an Israel where Bible and archaeology formed the chief layers in the construction of a national identity. "For years now, I have been searching by the light of a clay lamp [*menorah*] for a Major whose desk is not bedecked with a Second Temple clay lamp," journalist Yiz̲hak Tishler quipped, "let alone for Major-Generals and their NCOs who make do with less than an [ancient] pot in their gardens."[60] The myth was spun around sweeping Negev and Judaean Desert plains, grand imposing cliffs, a freedom fight to the death, and military valor. Like Ben-Gurion's address, Tishler's article unveiled a level of association between the archaeology myth and the Holocaust myth. It dealt with archaeological finds, the preoccupation with the Bible and the Eichmann trial. Tishler objected to the attempt to historicize phenomena, a process that, in his view, sapped them of their mythical element and stripped them of effect. He much preferred El'azar Ben Ya'ir's talk on Massada, the fruit of Josephus's imagination, to the fragmented quotations from the authentic writings of Bar Kokhba found in the Judaean Desert or Yiz̲hak Sadeh's "*Ah̲oti al Ha-H̲of*" (My Sister on the Shore) to the mounds of documents collected in advent of the Eichmann trial. He predicted that "the minute details of Europe's Holocaust would not tug at a single young heartstring, with or without Eichmann," and called for "imparting the symbolic and, thus, the true, meaning of the new history."

Tishler stood on the archaeology-Holocaust mythical divide: he was critical of the way in which the ancient myth had been passed down, but he identified with it and related it to youthful experience, to grueling treks and awesome landscapes—the tools that engender a love for one's country. In contrast, with regard to the Holocaust myth, he said that the books published (community memorials, ghetto uprising chronicles, the stories of the Partisans) and gracing the libraries of thousands of people had not managed to pave a path to the public heart; "unfortunately, I do not know of even a handful of people, either they themselves or their children, who know what is in those books. Which is only natural." Yiz̲hak Sadeh's article, on the other hand, "My Sister on the Shore," in his opinion created true identification with the Holocaust. The

Holocaust myth lacked a local component, and for this reason Tishler and his peers found it difficult to identify with it. Historical details could not make up for the gaping void of consciousness between Holocaust experience and local experience, and this is why he suggested using "My Sister on the Shore" as an educational device to bridge the gulf. Yizhak Sadeh was part and parcel of the local experience, and his empathetic encounter with a survivor on Palestine's shores seemed to "transpose" the Holocaust experience from "there" to "here," setting up a mental connection between the two.

Ben-Gurion, indeed, was late in recognizing the import of the Eichmann trial. Not so, however, the circles affiliated with the "nationalist Hebrews," who were concerned that the pendulum was swinging from the territorial myth to the Jewish-people myth. Bo'az Evron supplied the ideological direction in an article that appeared in the summer of 1960, some two months after Eichmann's capture. Evron did not disclaim the relationship between the Jews destroyed and the Jews of Israel as Ratosh had. But he wanted to universalize the trial: the problem was not the slaughter of Jews at the hands of Germans in World War II. In a quasi introduction to Hannah Arendt (well before she committed these thoughts to paper), he stated that "the massacre of the Jews is not to be separated from the general framework of Nazism and modern totalitarianism. Not only Germans were capable of killing, and not only Jews were victims." He argued that there had been Nazi plans to pursue additional genocides (the Slavic peoples) and presented the Holocaust as a dress rehearsal, so to speak, for the murder of other peoples.[61]

It is doubtful that historical documentation corroborates this claim: as far as is known, apart from the Jews, the policy of genocide was waged only against the Polish intelligentsia and itinerant Gypsy tribes. Nevertheless, the argument won a following and was carefully cultivated. Ratosh soon endorsed it and took it to extremes. In a press interview to *Ha-Boker*, he railed against the seeming attempt, grounded in a baseless Judeo-centric approach, to situate the Eichmann trial on the anti-Jewish historical continuum. He demanded that the prosecution at the Eichmann trial deal with Nazism's extermination of races. "Their explicit goal was to the destroy all the Slavic peoples . . . the number of people that the Nazis killed was double the number of Jews they killed." The presentation of future Nazi plans for the extermination of other peoples was meant to melt down the uniqueness of the Jewish Holocaust in a worldwide context: the problem was not the Jews but totalitarianism, and the logical conclusion had nothing to do with Jewish identity but with the struggle against racism the world over. Ratosh took exception to the wave of Jewish identification that washed over Israel: "The Holocaust dealt cruelly with the Jewish religious community. But the Hebrew nation that rose in the land of Israel has no connection with the Jewish religious community. The Jewish government of the Hebrew nation took it upon itself to hold a trial on behalf of the Jewish religious community and thereby criminally diminished the image of Nazism."[62]

Uri Avneri's coverage of the Eichmann trial provided a fascinating weave of different frames of reference. Avneri was attuned to the earthquake rumbles in Israeli society: "A profound change of values is taking place, its first signs already visible, now in the fifth week of the trial." He described the emotional resistance of Israeli youth over the previous 16 years to hearing or learning anything about the Holocaust. "It may very well be that the main reason was a sense of shame. The 'Israeli person' did not wish to identify with the abject Jews who went to the gas chambers." "The Hebrew person" did not wish to identify with the millions who "died as martyrs, rather than a hero's death." And now, the Eichmann trial suddenly depicted the Nazi regime as abject, the master killers—as cowards—and Eichmann himself a wretched specimen in body and soul. All the myths about the tall handsome Nazis were shattered. Juxtaposed with Eichmann in his compartmentalized defense seat stood Yizhak Zukerman in the witness stand, tall and handsome, courageous and valiant. Everything was reversed. As a result of the trial testimony, the "Israeli person" learned that the conduct of Jews under Nazi rule and their resignation to their fate had been no different from the reaction of other peoples in their own lands to Nazi terror. He learned about the admirable fortitude of the members of the Jewish underground, young women who had performed incredible deeds. Avneri summed up: "The Nazis were far from being heroes, and many Jews were far from being cowards—the evaporation of the resistance to hearing about the Holocaust was conditional on this realization. The emotional windows opened up—and once they did, it was virtually impossible to shut them." He described how hundreds of thousands of people were glued to the radio, read the press, and wept. "It is a catharsis in the true, original sense of the word—the purging of the personal and national soul by a storm of emotion."

Underlying Avneri's description were stereotypes about Jews and Nazis that had been widespread in his group of The Young Land of Israel. Now, too, Avneri did not identify with the Jewish masses who had gone to their deaths. But he had come to understand their passivity. His heart, however, was with the fighters, the underground, and he likened them to the members of the Yishuv undergrounds. He also took the opportunity to blame Zionist propaganda for the disgust he and his peers had felt for exilic Jewry: "It taught that the ghetto Jew was a sub-human, unproductive parasite, pale and hunched up. The more it preached 'Jewish values,' the more it taught contempt for the Jews themselves." The portrayal was the image of the Nazi profile on Jews (although the author cannot recall any such descriptions in Zionist sources). At the same time, by means of a deft ruse, he accused Zionist propaganda of fostering Jewish values. Zionism was now doubly guilty—of both holding Jews in contempt and seemingly returning to Jewish values. Avneri's distinction between Jews, Zionism, and Judaism amid his adoption of Jews and rejection of the latter two was a result of the Eichmann trial, which aroused empathy for the Jews and eroded the popularity of "Canaanite" and proto-"Canaanite" circles. But even then, Avneri found it difficult to make his peace with the Jews: throughout the article, he stressed the difference between "the Israeli Hebrew person" and the Jews—that is, they were not the same: yes, there was a kinship, much like the qualified kinship between the "Hebrew nation" and the Jewish people. After mentioning the catharsis engendered by the trial, he added, "This emotional crisis—can hardly be overestimated. It will help construct a normal attitude to yesteryear, to banish complexes that, to date, have precluded a healthy relationship between the new Hebrew nation, the Jewish past and the Jewish present."[63] This statement appears to have aimed at delineating the differing attitudes to Jews of Avneri's group and Ratosh's group. Otherwise, it is hard to understand a position that supports absorbing the Holocaust into "Hebrew" national memory while carefully erecting a barrier between Hebrew and Jewish identity.

But it was not long before Avneri adopted another perspective on the Holocaust: instead of the cathartic national experience, there was a stab at situating the Holocaust within the world context. After reading an article by Hannah Arendt in *The New Yorker*, Avneri was pleased to discover that she too, like *Ha-Olam Ha-Zeh* and *Etgar*, his two magazines, could not be counted among Ben-Gurion's fans and believed that the trial had missed an opportunity to lay bare the Nazi regime before the whole world. The crucial point, which Avneri found worthy of emphasizing, was that Zionist Jewish leaders everywhere had been unable to cope with the realities of Nazism because they had understood it as part of the age-old anti-Semitism rather than as a new phenomenon. They had thus not understood total genocide (and if they had, how would they have coped?). Here he diverged from Arendt to return to Ratosh and Evron: "The Jews (and Gypsies) were mere guinea pigs of genocides. Auschwitz continued to expand as the number of Jews dwindled. After the Jews was to come the turn of the Poles, the Russians, and who knows who else."[64] The ritual spouting of this unfounded contention about an overall Nazi plan of genocides in which Jews merely served as the first round was meant to remove the Holocaust from the context of Jewish/non-Jewish relations, the context of Jewish history, and instate it in the context of twentieth-century totalitarian regimes. This made it possible to connect to the Holocaust while drawing universal conclusions and ignore the fact that the actual victims were the Jewish people.

Many other people, however, drew entirely different lessons from the catharsis of the Eichmann trial. As will be recalled, the negation of exile stemmed from a rejection of the Jewish existential condition; in practical terms, it resulted in disengagement from the Jewish *shtetl*, from the history of the Jewish people and the image of exilic Jewry. This conception now began to change, as reflected by two forms of expression: (1) an identification with Jewish history and an attempt to reconnect with Jewish sources and (2) a desire to study the history of the Jewish people in the Holocaust and to understand it in personal terms, as something that had happened to oneself.

The process was most evident among the "statehood generation," though it did not skip over the "native" generation. Foremost among the latter was Ḫaim Gouri, who covered the trial for *La-Merḇav*, his articles later appearing as a collection, *Mul Ta Ha-Zkhukhit* (The Glass Cage).[65] The book enables readers to follow the *sabra*'s maturation and reconciliation with his people. Gouri begins with a new insight into Jewish life under Nazi rule—how powerless people were caught in a trap with no way out. He moves on to the realization that neither as an individual nor as a representative of a collective did he have the right to judge the Jews who were there. His heart drew him to the rebels, yet he refrained from demanding rebellion from the Jewish people. This humility, this suspension of judgment, was an outcome of the Eichmann trial: an understanding of what had happened "there" and sheer horror at the events recounted. In the 1950s, the concepts of "Holocaust and heroism" were virtually an inseparable couplet, so much so that the tale of a handful of rebels was the dominant Holocaust story. Gouri undercut the accepted narrative, juxtaposing active combat with the nonmartial courage expressed in day-to-day survival, in preserving one's human image. His words were reminiscent of Berl Katznelson's: "We know now more than ever that we had not known the main thing: the compassion and succor, the Hebrew and arithmetic exercise books on the edge of the grave, the light of prayer, the hand on the shoulder, the lips on the forehead, the parting of lovers."[66] Gouri's complete identification with the debased and murdered Jews aroused a sense of guilt. Now he asked if the Yishuv had indeed done all that it might have to help save its fellow Jews. This question shifted the burden of guilt from the Jews who went "as sheep to the slaughter" to their fellow Jews in Palestine. It was a role reversal—from prosecutor to defendant. From Israeli superciliousness toward the survivors—to a stance that may be summed up as awe: "put off thy shoes from off thy feet, for the place whereon thou standest is holy" (Exodus 3:5).[67]

The Holocaust became a permanent motif in Gouri's work. Several years after the trial, he published *Iskat Ha-Shokolada* (The Chocolate Deal), which depicts the complexities of the survivors' return to life.[68] At the end of the 1970s, he devoted several years to producing a film trilogy: "*Ha-Maka Ha-81*," "*Ha-Yam Ha-Aharon*," and "*Pnei Ha-Mered*" (The 81st Blow, The Last Sea, and The Face of Revolt). The trilogy brushes the fringes of the Holocaust: the survivors' encounter with the Israeli experience, the epos of illegal immigration, and the part played by the Jews in anti-Nazi resistance organizations. Recently, Gouri published a new edition of *Ad Alot Ha-Shahar* (By Daybreak), which deals with the War of Independence. He added a preface and epilogue to the book, which first appeared in 1950. The epilogue is his reckoning with the idea of Greater Israel—his romance with the old land of Israel and its political implications. The preface is titled "*El Ha-Aḇ Ha-Bilti Yadua*" (To the Unknown Brother) and deals with his encounter with young survivors from Czechoslovakia and Hungary who were his charges. To these youngsters in his care, he dedicated the new addition.[69] Gouri's journey from Ratosh's "Canaanite" ideas to his dedication to young survivors of a book written at the height of the Palmah generation's defining experience can stand as an example of the route traveled by many of his generation, the *sabra* native sons.

NEGATING EXILE: THE ROAD BACK

When the process first began, there was no clear distinction between the desire to return to Jewish sources, to learn about Jewish tradition, and the attempt to connect with the Holocaust experience. Nurit Orhan, of Kibbutz Ein Ha-Horesh, gave a talk at a party celebrating the issue of a new edition of *Lehavot Ba-Efer* (Flames in the Ashes) by partisan fighter Ruzhka Korczak. Her talk, reported in the editorial of the kibbutz magazine *Ha-Shavua* (The Week), provides an indication of how unconscious the process still was. Her words were crowned as testimony "of the cogent, radiating force triggered in Jewish history's most glorious episode of a 'few against many'—the ghetto uprisings." Actually, however, Orhan had questioned the attempt to understand the Holocaust in terms of heroism: Vilna ghetto commander and poet Abba Kovner, along with his comrades who had included Ruzhka Korczak, were Jews requiring neither explanations nor proof. They had identified not with Jewish physical valor but with Jewish helplessness. And from this identification with weakness, the decision to fight was born. Orhan objected to the tendency to sketch a continuum of Jewish courage down the generations. The typical Jewish trait, she contended, was weakness, and true identification with the people made it necessary to recognize this weakness and accept it. "National identification is indivisible. I can't pick out the raisins, and throw away the rest. This sort of 'heroic' identification is, in fact, 'Canaanite,' not Jewish."[70] Her somewhat faltering words revealed a search not only for a way to assimilate Holocaust memory but also for a path toward understanding Diaspora Jewry while accepting them as they were, with all their faults and all their virtues.[71]

The 1960s saw the emergence of the Shdemot group, kibbutz offspring, largely of the generation that had come of age after the state's establishment. They sought avenues to Jewish identity via a return to tradition and a link with Jewish history. A pamphlet of articles expressing longing for new ties to religion and tradition closed with a quotation attributed to author Shmuel Yosef Agnon: "The profound connection with the past comes with age. The day will come that you—the native-born generation who pretend that you have started everything anew—will suddenly feel an irresistible compulsion to expose and discover your roots."[72] The Shdemot group's quest for Jewish roots was more intellectual than existential. More than it quested after the Jewish people, it quested after spiritual content to counter the materialistic emptiness that pervaded the kibbutzim. The search for Jewish identity was a form of rebellion on the part of some of the younger generation against the meager spiritual diet that their parents had fed them on, in the face of the crisis of faith in socialism and amid a deep yearning for meaning. It was living proof of the aphorism that grandchildren take renewed interest in roots rent by children.[73]

The Six-Day War was a watershed. The three-week waiting period between the Egyptian army's incursion into Sinai and the IDF assault on it was traumatic both in Israel and for the Jewish people as a whole. The danger of war, brandished on the other side of the boundary as a war to destroy Israel, along with the absence of any real reaction by the international community to Nasser's unilateral moves (violating Sinai's demilitarization, evacuating the UN forces, and closing the Straits of Tiran), gave rise to growing feelings in Israel of isolation and abandonment. The press began to adopt the discourse of World War II: desertion of a weak ally and a dictator who grew brasher as his interlocutors showed weakness and shirked confrontation. The army was secure in the conviction that if Israel attacked first, it would gain superiority. The general public felt no such confidence. The government, along with every last citizen, was caught up in anxiety. Ben-Gurion, who was widely regarded as a feisty statesman ready to take on the whole world, advised digging in rather than embarking on a campaign without the support of an allied power. Military personnel, though itching for battle, estimated the number of casualties at tens of thousands. The government's indecision emitted a message of weakness and loss of control. Nor were Israelis alone in their anxiety: the Jewish community in the United States felt that Israel's very existence was under threat and, for the first time since the War of Independence, rallied to help the state of the Jews. In retrospect, Muki Tsur wrote, "We tend to forget that pre-war period, and perhaps justifiably. But at the time, we came closer than ever to the Jewish fate which, for years, we had shunned as if burnt. Suddenly everyone was talking about Munich, the Holocaust, and the Jewish people left to their fate."[74] Suddenly, there was a feeling that Jewish fate had reached the shores of the Mediterranean, that the distinction between Jewish fate in exile and the fate of the Jewish people in their own land had not withstood the test of history, that the state was no guarantee against annihilation, and that in its time of trial, Israel's only ally was Diaspora Jewry.

During the War of Independence, when the existential dangers had perhaps been greater, there had been no talk of annihilation. People had believed that there would be hardship and heavy losses, but there had been no doubt as to the war's outcome. This is the attitude that comes across from contemporary literature, memoirs, and the press.[75] Now, however, the fear of destruction was part of the public and especially the private discourse, accompanied by the Holocaust's growing invasion of general consciousness. "It is no accident that the smoke of the Holocaust began its sad, slow drift over our country's shores only in the 1950s," said poet Yehuda Amichai at the Hebrew Writers conference on the state's twentieth anniversary (1968). Juxtaposing the uniqueness of the "native generation" ("its name alone, in the singular, conveys pride, a single instance, a single occurrence, the first generation and the last generation, a departure, with a pinch of peculiarly 'Canaanite' aloofness") with the pluralism of successive generations, he added, "The generation of the War of Independence was detached from the Diaspora . . . [whereas] the generation of the Six-Day War, I would venture even now, lived with a greater consciousness of the Holocaust, of an emotional tie to the entire Jewish people wherever they dwelt."[76]

This assessment by Amichai, who chronologically belonged to the generation of the War of Independence but emotionally to the generation of the 1950s, was corroborated by *Siah̲ Loh̲amim* (The Seventh Day), a collective work based on interviews and discussions with combatants, mostly from the kibbutz sector. The hand of the editor (Avraham Shapira of Kvuz̲at Yizrael) was evident in the choice of interviewers and interviewees, the topics discussed, and the editorial decisions. Not a spontaneous collection, it nevertheless expressed the mind-set of a particular elite that, in the previous generation, had been attracted to "Canaanite" ideas, far removed from any emotional identification with the Jewish people. Now the winds blew in the opposite direction: phrases such as "Jewish fate" and "Jewish tragedy" cropped up again and again in the words of the young people. Said one, Yariv Ben Aharon, "We believed that we would be annihilated if we did not win. This concept was delivered or bequeathed by the Holocaust. It was a concrete concept for anyone who had grown up in Israel, even if they had not lived through the Holocaust themselves, but had only heard or read about it."[77] H̲aim Gouri's explanation of *Siah̲ Loh̲amim* was, "The Holocaust exists as a certainty in the hearts of this generation, who knew the unbelievable and could conceive of the possibility of recurrence."[78]

The Holocaust surfaced in the soldiers' memory when they came up against Arab refugees or acts of cruelty against Arab civilians. It served as a rein against inhumane behavior but also as a spur to stand firm, for "here it will not happen." It lodged in the consciousness as a historical experience that taught the need for Jewish force to make sure that there would be no more annihilation and to ward off the humiliation and powerlessness of a people stripped of all defense. For some, the element of extermination was the decisive factor; for others, it was the ignominy. The two were occasionally intertwined—as in the letter Ofer Feniger wrote to his girlfriend in 1963 after reading K. Z̲etnick's *Beit Ha-Bubot* (The Dolls House): he identified with the victims going to their death and, out of this identification with impotent Jews, concluded that strength was an imperative. "When I see a frightened Jew, a picture or word which recalls all that, I regret every moment that I wasted in the army by not trying to be better, more lethal."[79] A recurring motif in *Siah̲ Loh̲amim*, these components attest to the change that had transpired since the native generation, the Palmah̲ generation, had fought in the 1948 war: like the latter, the participants of the volume accorded the country a major place (even though the highly charged term "homeland" was rarely used); now, however, alongside the land, there was also the Jewish people, not as an abstract concept but as a real corpus, translated into names, figures, flesh, and blood.[80]

From the perspective of time, rapprochement and familiarization with the Jewish people appears to have been the decisive process of the 1960s. Yet at the time, the direction seemed unsettled, and the "Canaanite" option still seemed valid. The Six-Day War contributed to the changing mood, challenging the "negation of exile," as did the Yom Kippur War, which Uzi Ornan (Ratosh's brother), in an important article in the 1970s, described thus: "It was as if the Yom Kippur War thoroughly routed the concept of the Jewish *milet* versus the Israeli nation. As if the Jews had snickered: Look, even 'beautiful Israeli' was led off into captivity. No more will Jews be ridiculed for having been crushed by the Nazi boot. 'Jewish fate' threatens both Israelis and the Jewish people. In various articles, one could discern a vindictive joy, the joy of those who identified with the Jewish *milet*, at the fact that the Israelis had not succeeded this time as in the past."[81] The vindictive joy that ostensibly marked the attitude of the Jews toward Israelis was, of course, in the eye of the beholder. It is true, however, that the shock of the Yom Kippur War reinforced the sense of a tenuous Jewish existence, this time in Israel, a sense that has always accompanied the Jewish lot. It also highlighted the fact that when vulnerable, Israelis do not behave differently from their fellow Jews.

The processes by which systems of ideas change from relevant to anachronistic are elusive and difficult to map. Social and cultural processes may be likened to mild but steady earth tremors, hard for a seismograph to measure. In addition, there are always exceptions that do not conform to the processes described. Decades have passed since school curricula in literature or history contained works that might instill a "negation of exile." For the past 20 years, Holocaust memory has been one of the chief topics in education out of empathy with the weakness and powerlessness of exterminated Jewry. The encounter between youth and young people with survivor witnesses has become the accepted mode of marking Holocaust Day, focusing on human experience and ordinary people. If in the 1960s one wondered that so few young people wrote about the Holocaust and the establishment of the State of Israel, the two big topics of the period, in the past two decades this question was no longer relevant: the Holocaust has become one of the most prevalent topics in literature, theater, and art.[82] The search of Israeli youth for their Jewish roots in eastern Europe is reflected by annual group trips to Poland.[83]

Sabra-hood became unfashionable, "exile" fashionable: it was okay to identify with "Polish-ness."[84] The macho Israeli, the tough, strong-armed native son, fell from glory. One of the distinguishing characteristics between native sons and "Jews of exile" had been the former's aversion to displays of emotion, self-exposure, and signs of weakness. Dan Ben Amotz described his envy of the self-contained native son who never showed his feelings in public: "I wanted to be like Kobi. I wanted to be tough, strong, aloof, self-contained."[85] Now public tears and compassion became legitimate even for seasoned soldiers. A popular tune speaks of men weeping by night when, in truth, they weep also by day.

Israeli society lost its distinctiveness. Israeli Jewish society is multicultural, not by intent or desire but in fact. The same processes that impeded the consolidation of a clear local identity throughout the twentieth century still come into play. Every wave of immigration brings with it new elements that disrupt the attempts to fuse a local identity. Since the 1960s, the baggage of immigrants arriving in Israel has omitted a negation of their countries of origin. Moroccan Jews did not look back in anger or hostility or transmit to their children rebellious messages against "exile." The immigration from the former Soviet Union in the 1990s had a variety of motives—idealistic, materialistic, and political—but it, too, did not internalize a negation of "exile": the attempts of the newcomers to preserve their Russian culture indicate that they do not regard their immigration as a divorce from their original society. The same is true of Ethiopian immigrants and especially of Western immigrants, who certainly did not cultivate an ethos of contempt for the states from which they came. Israeli identity is a project in constant motion. In this respect, it is no different from other countries of immigration: nor was British primacy in the United States—a favorite analogy of Ratosh's—carried forward in that great land of immigration.

The "exile" that was negated at the time inhered in the conditions of Jewish life in Europe before World War II both in traditional society and in assimilating Jewish society in eastern and central Europe. The two societies, each out of different motives, sang the praises of "the eternity of exile" and clashed with conceptions that sought a territorial solution to the "Jewish Problem." The Holocaust did not answer the question of whether Jewish national existence is possible in the land of Israel or even the question whether it is possible in the Diaspora, but it did put an end to the way of life and realities of Zionism's opponents. The "negation of exile" became irrelevant because the "exile" in question vanished from the world. "One cannot . . . speak today of a Jewish community in terms of Poland or Russia prior to WWII," noted an article in *Ha-Hinukh* (Education) in 1967 (before the Six-Day War) under the title "Fostering the Bond to Diaspora Jewry as a Tenet of Our Education." "And one hardly needs to add that nowhere in the world today is there any longer a Jewish town of the sort described by Shalom Aleichem, Mendele and others."[86] The picture of Jewish life and the image of Jews portrayed by the "negators of exile" no longer rested on anything real, only on the ghosts of past images.

Among its other aims, the "negation of exile" was meant to deter native sons from leaving the country. Its disappearance has been accompanied by a "creeping" legitimacy for emigration. The terms *aliyah* and *yeridah* (ascent to and descent from the land) reflected a system of beliefs and views about the country, "exile," and their interrelation. This system was important as long as the world was divided into ideological boundaries. The waning of the twentieth century's significant ideologies sapped also Zionism of its vigor. As stated, "exile" no longer conjures up the traditional images depicted in art and literature. The term "Diaspora" (*tefuzot*) stopped being a more positive buzzword for "exile" (*golah*). Its usage connotes a new type of Jewish life and Jewish interaction with a non-Jewish environment. Proud and influential American Jews do not constitute a modern version of the Jewish *shtetl* but another form of Jewish life, unprecedented in Jewish history. On the other hand, Israel no longer has the status of a land attracting immigrants from trouble spots by default. It is part of the developed world, drawing Jews and non-Jews from less developed countries. The world of the twenty-first century is open to Jews. As a result, the decision to immigrate to Israel is primarily a matter of free choice, not of survival. In these new circumstances, anti-"exilic" zealousness, for fear of its magnetism, has naturally been curtailed. The barb flung by Prime Minister Yitzhak Rabin, in his first reign of office, at Israeli emigrants whom he called "the fallout of the weaklings" reflected the education that he had received growing up in the Yishuv; in the 1970s, emigration aroused criticism. Today there is an air of sheepish conciliation between Israelis and *yordim* (emigrants): there are large communities of *yordim* on both the West Coast and the East Coast of the United States, and many of them maintain strong ties with Israel. Their children occasionally even reverse the trend and return to Israel. The term *yeridah* has thus lost its stigma.

Furthermore, as the number of Israelis raised in the country increases, the natural bond to one's native environment takes on added dimension. While this bond may never have posed a barrier against *yeridah*, it is a powerful force, far more so than ideology in a postideological age. Israeli Jews remain in the country because this is their birthplace and their home, and this is where their cultural milieu is, where their language is spoken, and where their families live. It is a "localness" no longer accompanied by hostility and arrogance toward Jews who do not live in Israel. Again, this statement need not apply to everyone or every situation: no doubt there are still "pockets" of local haughtiness vis-à-vis new immigrants. It stems, however, no longer from "negating exile" but from the mind-set of a land of immigration, where every set of immigrants has its sights on those who preceded them and tramples those who followed them. This, rather than the "negation of exile" of old, is behind the incessant complaints by "newcomers" about the treatment they receive at the hands of "old-timers." Israeli identity maintains a constant dialogue with the Jewish past, with religion and tradition, with Jewish identity. Sometimes the dialogue is conducted amid confrontation, other times amid identification, but it always remains within the boundaries of Israeli Jewish identity, with no attempt to step outside this framework or invent an alternative identity.

As a cultural movement and political option, the phenomenon of "Canaanism" appears to have been confined to a specific generation—the "native generation," with, here and there, early forerunners and late throwbacks. It was essentially an Ashkenazi phenomenon—few members of other communities got caught up in it. It may be seen equally as an extension of "negating exile" and an independent, spontaneous, local-native phenomenon. It was a movement that shattered conventions that, like other ideological movements, pretended to reorganize the world on the basis of pure rationalism. There was something violent about it, something destructive and strident, that came to the fore in the public writings of Ratosh, Avneri, Keinan, and others. Not by chance was it a movement of men; women occupied only a marginal position in it.

The fascination with toughness and fierceness seems to be related to both generation and age: with the exception of a hard core, most of the people associated with "Canaanism" began, after the flush of youth and the approach of middle age, to try to redefine Jewish identity. On the other hand, in every generation, teens and young people in their twenties are given to spontaneous expressions that attest to the hubris of youth, manifested in a swaggering arrogance toward anyone unlike them. True, "negation of exile" as an ideological, political, or educational concept has dissolved with the mists of time. But the disdain for anyone who is not "one of us" or for Diaspora Jewry remains age specific, and as such it recurs spontaneously in youth only to vanish again in maturity.

Two other questions related to the "negation of exile" warrant separate study: one is the paradoxical appearance of a religious Jewish strain of "Canaanism" among the settlers in Judaea and Samaria. In their case, the pendulum between love of the Jewish people and love of the land of Israel seems to favor the territorial pole. For them, love of place, soil, and ancient myth is the decisive factor. This subject requires further investigation. The second question concerns the attitude of Israelis toward Jewish communities, especially in the United States. The diminution of the "negation of exile" has not improved the rapport between Israelis and Diaspora Jewry. The spontaneous drifting apart of the two poles of contemporary Jewish existence may be likened to continental drift and is unconnected with past images. Nevertheless, the practical result is the existence of distinct Jewish tribes. This, too, is a separate issue deserving of discussion.

Gabriela Avigur-Rotem's *Heatwave and Crazy Birds* gives current literary expression to the cultural battlefield that began with the Eichmann trial.[87] Ben-Gurion, at the time, saw the trend to connect with the archaeological past of the Jewish people in their own land and the desire to retain Jewish consciousness and solidarity with the Jewish people wiped out in the Holocaust as complementary rather than contradictory processes. The ostensible encounter between the two identities in his address on Israel's thirteenth anniversary reflected his limited cultural imagination: as a true representative of the generation of the founding fathers, he saw no clash between "negating exile," which he clothed in rather extreme form, and complete identification with the Jewish people along with a sense of responsibility for their fate and future. Ben-Gurion was no "Canaanite" despite the animosity he showed for historical Jewry. He did not appreciate the danger of severance from concrete Jewry that was inherent in his admiration for ancient Jewry, for the archaeological essence as against the historical essence.[88] *Heatwave and Crazy Birds* depicts the penetration of the archaeological-historical contest into the Israeli national psyche. It is the story of the protagonist's journey to herself via her introduction to the fate of her family in the Holocaust. It describes the Israeli experience in a remote housing complex built in the 1950s that is home to many survivors. The search for roots in their new country leads them to dig for archaeological roots and to strive to bury the Holocaust experience. The attempt to create a grand, local picture of a distant past becomes an intellectual exercise, meant to bury a recent past that is too difficult to bear. Ultimately, the self-searching leads to the provinces of lost Europe. Excavations in Israeli soil, clay shards, idolatrous statues, and associations with the ancient past did not yield existential answers. Archaeology, though neither spurned nor abandoned, retreated before history.

NOTES

Key to Notes: Titles in italics denote books, journals, newspapers, etc., as opposed to articles, poems, etc., which are in quotation marks. H/h is the guttural eighth letter of the Hebrew alphabet. Z/z is to be read as tz/ts.

I would like to thank Bo'az Levtov for his help in collecting material for this chapter.

1. Sh. Beit Zvi, *Ha-Zionut Ha-Post-Ugandit Be-Mivhan Ha-Shoah* (Post-Ugandan Zionism in Light of the Holocaust) (Tel Aviv, 1977).

2. Tom Segev, *Ha-Milyon Ha-Shevii: Ha-Yisre'elim Ve-Ha-Shoah* (Jerusalem: Keter Publishing House and Domino Press, 1991) (English ed.: *The Seventh Million: The Israelis and the Holocaust* [New York: Hill and Wang, 1993]); Idith Zertal, *Zehavam shel Yehudim* (Jewish Gold) (Tel Aviv, 1996); Yosef Grodzinsky, *Homer Yehudi Tov* (Good Jewish Human Material) (Or Yehuda, 1997); Moshe Zuckerman, *Haroshet Ha-Yisre'eliyut, Mitosim Ve-Ideologgia Be-Hevra Mesukhsekhet* (The Production of Israeliness, Myths and Ideology in a Society in Conflict) (Tel Aviv, 2001).

3. Amnon Raz-Krakotzkin, "*Galut Be-Tokh Ribonut: Le-Bikoret 'Shlilat Ha-Golah' Be-Tarbut Yisre'elit*" (Exile in Sovereignty: A Critique of "Negating Exile" in Israeli Culture), *Teorya u-Vikoret* (Theory and Criticism) 4 (fall 1993).

4. Ahad Ha-Am, "*Shlilat Ha-Golah*" (Negating Exile), in *Al Parashat Drakhim* (At the Crossroads) (Berlin, 1930), 4:106–9.

5. Theodor Herzl, diary entry of June 13, 1895, in *Ktavim* (Tel Aviv, 1960), 1:102.

6. Uri Zvi Greenberg, "*Ha-Hekhr'ah*" (The Imperative), in *Ba-Emza Ha-Olam U-be-Emza Ha-Zmanim* (Mid-World and Mid-Time) (Tel Aviv, 1979), 30–31.

7. Berl Katznelson, "*Le-Lo Hitgalut*" (Without Revelation), in *Ktavim* (Tel Aviv, 1946), 4:246–47.

8. J. H. Brenner, "*Ha-Arakhat Atzmenu Bi-Shloshet Ha-Krakhim*" (Self-Appraisal in the Three Volumes), in *Kol Kitvei* (Complete Works) (Tel Aviv, 1937), 7:219–67.

9. J. Ḥ. Brenner, "*Hu Amar La*" (He Told Her), in *Kol Kitvei* (Complete Works) (Tel Aviv, 1937), 6:29–33.

10. Shelomo Lavi, "*Be-Vikuaḥ al Kitot Ha-Hemshekh*" (The Debate on High School Classes), in *Ktavim Nivḥarim* (Selected Writings) (Tel Aviv, 1954), 109.

11. David Maletz, "*Aleinu Ve-al Yeladeinu*" (About Us and Our Children), in *Mi-Saviv La-Ikar* (Around the Main Thing) (Tel Aviv, 1970), 39–40.

12. Lyova Levite, "*Anaḥnu Ve-Yeladeine*" (We and Our Children), 13th Conference of the United Kibbutz Movement, Ashdot Yaacov, 3–8 October 1941, cited in *Mi-Bifnim*, January 1942, 70–83.

13. Baruch Eisenstadt, *Thirteenth Conference of Ha-Kibbutz Ha-Me'uḥad*, Ashdot Yaacov, 3–8 October 1941 (En Ḥarod, n.d.).

14. Ḥayyim Hazaz, "*Ha-Drasha*" (The Homily), in *Avanim Rot'ḥot* (Steaming Stones), Tel Aviv, 1970, 219–37. First published in *Luaḥ Haaretz*, 1943.

15. Yehoshua Porat relates to the warm reception to "*Ha-Drasha*" by local youth, who took it at face value and soon were to identify it with the "Canaanite" movement. Yehoshua Porat, *Shelaḥ Ve-Et Be-Yado* (Dagger and Quill in Hand) (Tel Aviv, 1989), 190. See also the article by Dan Laor, "'*Ha-Drasha' Aḥarei Ḥamishim Shana*" (The Homily, Fifty Years Later), *Ha'aretz*, 29 September 1993.

16. Berl Katznelson, "*Be-Ikvot Siḥa al Ha-Golah*" (Following a Talk on the Diaspora), in *Ktavim* (Tel Aviv, 1950), 12:224.

17. Katznelson, "*Be-Ikvot Siha al Ha-Golah*," 224–25.

18. See Anita Shapira, "Ben-Gurion and the Bible: The Forging of an Historical Narrative?" *Middle Eastern Studies* 33, no. 4 (October 1997): 645–74.

19. See, for example, Yiẕḥak Tabenkin, "*Ha-Mekorot*" (The Sources), in *Sefer Ha-Aliyah Ha-Shniya* (The Second Aliyah Book), ed. Brakha Ḥabas (Tel Aviv, 1947), 23–30.

20. Katznelson, "*Be-Ikvot Siḥa al Ha-Golah*," 22–23.

21. Yehoshua Porat, "'*Massa Ha-Ptiḥa' Ve-Netel Ha-Massa*" (The Opening Essay and Its Load), in *Shelaḥ Ve-Et Be-Yado*, 186–203.

22. Ḥaim Gouri, "*Prakim Mi-Viduyei Ḥaẕot*" (Passages from Midnight Confessions) *Maariv*, 26 December 1975.

23. On the history of "Canaanism," see Yaacov Shavit, *Me-Ivri ad Canaani* (From Hebrew to "Canaanite") (Jerusalem, 1984); Porat, "*Shelaḥ Ve-Et Be-Yado*" (Dagger and Quill in Hand), in *Ve-Ha-Canaani az Ba-Areẕ*" [(And the "Canaanite" Then in the Land), special issue of *Proza* devoted to "Canaanism," August–September 1977; Ziva Shamir, *Le-Hatḥil Me-Alef, Shirat Ratosh: Mekoriut U-Mekoroteha* (Starting at "A," Ratosh's Poetry: Originality and Sources) (Tel Aviv, 1993); Ḥanan Ḥever, "*Kehila Yelidit Medumyenet: 'Sifrut Canaanit' Ba-Tarbut Ha-Yisre'elit*" (An Imagined Native Community: "Canaanite Literature" in Israeli Culture), *Soẕiologgia Yisra'elit* (Israeli Sociology) 2:147–66; Nurit Gaertz et al., *Ha-Kvuẕa Ha-Canaanit—Sifrut Ve-Idiologgia* (The Canaanite Group—Literature and Ideology) (Tel Aviv, Open University, 1987); and Dan Laor, "American Literature and Israeli Culture: The Case of the Canaanites," *Israel Studies* 5, no. 1 (spring 2000): 287–300. On the archaeological roots of "Canaanism," see A. G. Ḥoron, *Kedem Ve-Arav—Toldot Ereẕ Ha-Ivrim* (East and Arabia—History of the Land of the Hebrews) (Tel Aviv, 2000).

24. "*Ha-Derekh Le-Iḥud Ha-Moledet*" (The Way to Unify the Homeland), *Ba-Maavak*, December 1947. See also "*Le-Gius Totali—Le-Mishtar Hagana!*" (Total Enlistment—to a Regime of Defense!), in the same issue, where "Arab masses" are mentioned.

25. "*Teshuvateinu*" (Our Response), *Ba-Maavak*, May 1947.

26. "*Teshuvateinu.*"

27. H̲aim Gouri, "*Ha-Nekhed Ve-Ha-Manggina*" (The Grandchild and the Melody), from "*Ha-Shaa Ha-Canaanit*" (The Canaanite Hour), *Maariv*, 31 October 1980.

28. Baruch Kurz̲weil, "*Al Ha-Ivrim Ha-Z̲e'irim*" (On the Young Hebrews), in *Sifruteinu Ha-H̲adasha—Hemshekh o Mahapekha?* (Our New Literature—Continuity or Revolution?) (Jerusalem and Tel Aviv, 1971), 285, 287.

29. See, for example, Amos Keinan in a special issue of *Proza* called "*Ve-Ha-Canaani az Ba-Arez̲*" (The Canaanite Then in the Land), August–September 1977, 4.

30. H̲aim Gouri, "*Ha-Shaa Ha-Canaanit,*" *Maariv*, 14 September 1980.

31. See "*Ve-Ha-Canaani az Ba-Arez̲.*"

32. Kurz̲weil, "*Al Ha-Ivrim Ha-Ze'irim,*" 274–79.

33. Yonathan Ratosh, "*Mi-Niz̲ah̲on Le-Mapolet*" (From Victory to Downfall), in *Me'asef Aleph* (Tel Aviv, 1976), 56–57.

34. Amos Keinan, "*Ve-Ha-Canaani az Ba-Arez̲,*" *Proza*, 11.

35. Moshe Dayan, *Leh̲iot im Ha-Tanakh* (Jerusalem, 1978) (English ed.: *Living with the Bible* [New York: William Morrow, 1978]).

36. On the background to the building of the Shrine of the Book, see the article by Adolpho Roitmann, "*Me-Ulam Funkz̲ionali Le-Binian Idiologgi: Toldot Ha-Bniya shel Hekhal Ha-Sefer*" (From a Functional to an Ideological Hall: The Construction History of the Shrine of the Book), in *Al Meggilat Sefer* (On a Scroll), ed. Leah Mazor (Jerusalem, 1996), 98–111. My thanks to Meir H̲azan for drawing my attention to this article.

37. This committee was preceded by another, set up by then Education Minister Benzion Dinur in 1954, that apparently did not make any progress on the matter. "Protocol of the Committee for Israeli-Jewish Consciousness in School Curricula," 7 August 1956, doc. 5.25/16, Archive of Jewish Education in Israel and the Diaspora, Tel Aviv University.

38. "*Haamakat Ha-Todaa Ha-Yehudit Be-Veit Ha-Sefer Ha-Mamlakhti, Hanh̲ayot Ve-Tokhniot Limudim*" (Reinforcing Jewish Consciousness in State Nonreligious Schools, Teaching Principles and Curricula) (Jerusalem: Ministry of Education and Culture, 1959), 8.

39. Barukh Ben Yehudah, "Protocol of the Committee for Israeli-Jewish Consciousness in School Curricula."

40. Yehudah, "Protocol of the Committee for Israeli-Jewish Consciousness in School Curricula."

41. Yehudah, "Protocol of the Committee for Israeli-Jewish Consciousness in School Curricula."

42. Elimelekh Rimalt, "Protocol of the Committee for Israeli-Jewish Consciousness (Fourth Session)," 10 September 1956, Archive of Jewish Education in Israel and the Diaspora, Tel Aviv University.

43. Rimalt (as well as Ephraim Urbach), "Protocol of the Committee for Israeli-Jewish Consciousness (Fourth Session)."

44. Israel Yeshayahu, "Protocol of the Committee for Israeli-Jewish Consciousness (Fourth Session)."

45. "Reinforcing Jewish Consciousness in State Non-Religious Schools, Teaching Principles and Curricula," Ministry of Education and Culture, Jerusalem, 1959.

46. "Reinforcing Jewish Consciousness in State Non-Religious Schools," 14.

47. Porat, "'*Massa Ha-Ptiha' Ve-Netel Ha-Massa*," 197–99.

48. Aliza Bukholz, "*Ahdut mul Kera—Bnei Ha-Arez Ve-Ha-Golah*" (Unity versus Rift—Native Sons and the Diaspora), from *Yalkut La-Madrikh* (Counselor's Manual) (Adar, 1944), epilogue: republished in Aviyahu Ronnen, *Dapim Le-Heker Tekufat Ha-Shoah* (Teaching Manual, Studying the Holocaust Period) 16 (1999): 262.

49. Two proposals for the theoretical program of the seniors, *Shnot Ha-Mahanot Ha-Olim* (Years of the Mahanot Ha-Olim) B, were compiled and edited by Yizhak Kafkafi (Yad Tabenkin, 1985), 420–23.

50. See the author's articles "*Bein Shoah Le-Milhama*" (Between Holocaust and War), in *Yehudim Hadashim, Yehudim Yeshanim* (New Jews, Old Jews) (Tel Aviv, 1997), 104–21; Jehuda Reinharz, "Native Sons," in *Essential Papers on Zionism*, ed. Anita Shapira (New York: New York University Press, 1996), 790–822; and "Historiography and Memory: Latrun, 1948," *Jewish Social Studies* 3 no. 1 (fall 1996): 20–61.

51. Uri Avneri, "*Re'akzia shel Ha-Avot*" (Reaction of the Fathers), *Ba-Maavak*, May 1947; "*Tshuvateinu*" (Our Response), *Ba-Maavak*, May 1947.

52. Yehiam Weitz, *Ha-Ish She-Nirzah Paamayim. Mishpato U-Moto shel Yisrael Kastner* (The Man Who Was Murdered Twice. The Trial and Death of Israel Kastner) (Jerusalem, 1993).

53. Amir Gilboa, "Yizhak" (Isaac), *Al Ha-Mishmar*, 12 May 1950, literary section. The poem appeared in the anthology *Shirim Ba-Boker Ba-Boker* (Early Morning Poems) (Tel Aviv, 1953). I would like to thank Galia Sagiv of the Katz Institute, Tel Aviv University, for drawing my attention to it.

54. Hanokh Bartov, *Shesh Knafayim La-Ehad* (Six Wings to One) (Tel Aviv: Merhavia, 1954).

55. Yehudit Hendel, *Anashim Aherim Hem* (Those People Are Different) (Tel Aviv: Merhavia, 1950).

56. Gad Ufaz, "Ma Meizik?" (What Rankles?), *Shdemot* 37 (spring 1970).

57. The prime minister's broadcast on Independence Day, *Davar*, 21 April 1961.

58. See, for example, the contention by Uzi Ornan that Eichmann's capture and prosecution in Jerusalem fit in wonderfully with the program to foster Jewish consciousness and was meant to inoculate youth against exile-negating ideas. Uzi Ornan, "*Ha-Todaa Ha-Yehudit—Hirhurei Kfira*" (Jewish Consciousness—Heretical Reflections), *Ha-Hinukh* (Education) 48 (1976). See also Idith Zertal's claim that the trial was meant to foster Holocaust consciousness and reinforce nationalistic tendencies and existential anxietyin "*Mi-Ulam Beit Ha-Am el Kotel Beit Ha-Mikdash: Zikaron, Pahad U-Milhama (1960–1967)*" (From a Public Hall to a Temple Wall: Memory, Fear and War [1960–1967]), *Teorya u-Vikoret* (Theory and Criticism) 15 (1999): 19–38.

59. Hannah Jablonka, *Medinat Yisrael neged Adolph Eichmann* (The State of Israel versus Adolph Eichmann) (Tel Aviv, 2001).

60. Yizhak Tishler, "*Ha-Hitut Be-Pratim Ve-Ha-Semel She-Enenu*" (Picking at Details and the Symbol That Is Missing), *La-Merhav*, 30 December 1960.

61. Bo'az Evron, "*Eichmann—Ha-Miflezet Ba-Shiviya*" (Eichmann—The Monster in Captivity), *Etgar* 2 (June 1960).

62. Idith Neumann, "*Mishpat Eichmann hu Siluf Ha-Historiya*" (The Eichmann Trial Is a Distortion of History), *Ha-Boker*, 18 July 1961; Yonatan Ratosh, "*Be-Dalet Amot Zarot Meod*" (Within Four Very Narrow Walls), *Davar* 1 September 1961.

63. Uri Avneri, "*Mishpat Eichmann*" (The Eichmann Trial), *Etgar* 5 (May 1961).

64. Uri Avneri, "*Ha-Pogrom shel Etmol*" (Yesterday's Pogrom), *Etgar*, third year, 18 April 1963.

65. H̱aim Gouri, *Mul Ta Ha-Zkhukhit: Mishpat Yerushalayim* (The Glass Cage: The Jerusalem Trial) (Tel Aviv, 1962).

66. Gouri, *Mul Ta Ha-Zkhukhit*, 249.

67. See also Anita Shapira, "*Mishpat Eichman: Dvarim She-Ro'im Mi-Kan lo Ro'im Mi-Sham*" (The Eichmann Trial: Different Perspectives from Here and There), and *Iyun Ve-H̱eker*, *Harz̲aot U-Massot* (Study and Research, Lectures and Essays), vol. 2 (Jerusalem, 2002).

68. H̱aim Gouri, *Iskat Ha-Shokolada* (The Chocolate Deal) (Tel Aviv, 1965).

69. H̱aim Gouri, *Ad Alot Ha-Shaẖar* (By Daybreak) (Tel Aviv, 2000).

70. There is an interesting analogy between Nurit Orẖan's words and Nahum Goldmann's in his debate with Ben-Gurion on a related issue: Ben-Gurion's "historical leap." Goldmann held that "a people can not select those parts of its history it cherishes and jettison what it dislikes" (*Hazut* [Aspect] 4: 154), cited in Shapira, "Ben-Gurion and the Bible," 671.

71. Nurit Orẖan, H̱ulsha Ve-Hi Mekor Koaẖ (Weakness as a Source of Strength), *Ha-Shavua* (This Week), 19 December 1965. It appeared also in *Shdemot* (spring 1966) under the heading "*Ha-Shoa Ve-Ha-Zehut Ha-Yehudit shel Ben Ha-Arez̲*" (The Holocaust and the Jewish Identity of the Native Son).

72. *Shdemot* 20 (winter 1966).

73. I wish to thank Alon Gan, who wrote a doctoral dissertation on the second kibbutz generation in the 1960s and 1970s and made the material available to me.

74. Muki Tsur, "*Khaf Heh Shanim Le-Mered Ha-Ghettaot*" (Twenty-Fifth Anniversary of the Ghetto Uprising), *Ha-Shavua Ba-Kibbutz Ha-Arz̲i* (This Week in the Kibbutz Ha-Arzi—HaShomer Ha'Za'ir) 815, 26 April 1968.

75. See, for instance, the article by Benjamin Tammuz, "*Bein Az̲ma'ut 1948—Le-Az̲ma'ut 1966*" (Independence 1948 versus Independence 1966), *Ha'aretz*, 29 April 1966. "At the most difficult hours, no one imagined failure to be an option."

76. Yehuda Amichai, addressing the Hebrew Writers conference on Israel's twentieth anniversary on 17 April 1968, appeared in the *Bulletin of the Hebrew Writers Association*, no. 31 (May 1968). See, too, the rejoinder by Aharon Megged, "*Misdar 'Dor Ba-Arez̲'*" (The Order of the "Generation in the Land"), *La-Merẖav*, May 10, 1968, and Moshe Dor, "*Dvarim Aẖadim al 'Riv Ha-Dorot'*" (A Few Words on the "Generation Gap"), *Maariv*, 17 May 1968.

77. *Siaẖ Loẖamim*, *Pirkei Hakshava Ve-Hitbonenut* (The Seventh Day, Episodic Listening and Looking) (Tel Aviv, 1968), 162.

78. H̱agor (Gouri's pseudonym), "*Mi-Saviv Le-Z̲iduk Ha-Din*" (About "Divine Justice" [from the Burial Service]), *La-Merhav*, 26 January 1968.

79. *Siaẖ Loẖamim*, 167–68.

80. An example of the country's centrality can be found in the discussion by three generations of the Shelem family in *Siaẖ Loẖamim*, 174–82.

81. Ornan, "*Ha-Todaa Ha-Yehudit.*"

82. For example, the interviews of former MK Ge'ula Cohen with Moshe Shamir, Aaron Z̲eitlin, Leah Goldberg, and Dahlia Ravikovitch, "*Ha-Im Amda Sifruteinu al Dam Ha-Shoah Ve-Ha-Tkuma?*" (Did Our Literature Tell the Story of the Holocaust and Rebirth?), *Maariv*, 2 October 1963. As for the centrality of the Holocaust in Israeli culture today, I would like to mention the works by Aharon Appelfeld, David Gross-

man, David Schitz, Rahel Eitan, Nava Semel, and so on as well as artists such as Ben-Zion Tommer, Motti Lerner, and Orna Ben-Dor. On the centrality of the Holocaust in consciousness and the changing attitudes toward it, see Uri Prago, "*Todaat Ha-Shoah Be-Kerev Noar Lomed Be-Yisrael—5743*" (Holocaust Consciousness among Israeli Pupils—1983), *Dapim Le-Heker Ha-Shoah* (Holocaust Research Bulletin) 3 (1984): 159–78. He makes the interesting diagnosis that among the children of the native sons (i.e., those who had been the "generation reared in the land"), there is less empathy with the Holocaust than among other Jewish population groups in Israel.

83. Nili Keren, "*Massaot Bnei Noar Le-Polin—Hirhur Sheni*" (Youth Trips to Poland—A Second Look), *Skira Hodshit* (Monthly Review), November 1992; "*Todaat Ha-Shoah Ve-Ha-Siurim*" (Holocaust Heritage and the Trips), *Hed Ha-Hinukh* (Education Clarion) 70, no. 1 (1995); Avraham Azili, "*Mass'ot Polin*" (Trips to Poland), *Yalkut Moreshet* (Heritage Notebook) 66 (1998): 105–15.

84. See, for example, the interviews with young artists on the subject of the Holocaust, interviewed by Yael Ben-Yisrael, "*Tiyul bein Zalakot*" (Journey amid Scars), *Al Ha-Mishmar*, 9 May 1986.

85. Dan Ben-Amotz, *Ziyunim zeh lo Ha-Kol* (Tel Aviv: Metzuith Publishers, 1979), 82.

86. Y. Frischman, "Tipuah Ha-Zika Li-Yehudei Ha-Golah Ke-Ikar Hinukheinu," *Ha-Hinukh* (1967): 289–94.

87. Gabriela Avigur-Rotem, Hamsin Ve-Zipporim Meshuggaot (Easterly and Crazy Birds) (Tel Aviv, 2001).

88. See Shapira, "Ben-Gurion and the Bible."

Chapter 4

The Diaspora Factor in Israeli Life

Eli Lederhendler

The Jewish diaspora plays a profound role in Israeli life, first and foremost because immigrants from the diaspora function as subcommunities within Israeli society. Israel—the 77 percent of it that is Jewish—*is* the diaspora, transposed geographically and concentrated in one place. The diaspora, in contrast, is not Israel dispersed, and it therefore lacks multifaceted, direct, participatory capacities in Israeli life. Only secondarily is the diaspora involved in Israeli affairs in the form of activities undertaken by Jewish communities abroad, their leaders, or institutions in concert with Israeli agencies, groups, or communities.[1]

The Jewish diaspora is not like the Indian or Chinese or any of the other diasporic ethnicities in today's mobile world because the Jews who live in dispersion have not themselves emigrated (nor did their parents or direct forebears emigrate) from the ethnic homeland.[2] It would be equally inapt to say that the diasporic Jewries today at all resemble cultural satellite communities of an Israeli center, as had been projected in the thought of Ahad Ha'am and his school of "spiritual Zionists."[3] Therein lies the basic asymmetry in the ostensibly reciprocal relationship between Israel and the diaspora. Simply put, the diaspora is not *Israel*'s diaspora—a truism that bears stating at the outset simply to avoid confusion later on in our discussion. When Jews of today's diaspora refer to themselves as such, it is their ancestors' historic dispersion and their own continued residence in the lands of their birth to which they allude; it is not normally a reference to Israel in its role as nation-state.

The historical term "Jewish diaspora" derives, as is well known, from the exile and dispersion of the people of Israel from its homeland in successive stages during Babylonian, Hellenistic, Roman, and Byzantine times.[4] Between the third and seventh centuries C.E., dispersion and exile were internalized in the Jews' culture and self-awareness as the underlying context of everything "Jewish." Indeed, on both theological and socioethnographic grounds, it is clear that Judaism (as distinct from the biblical religion of ancient Israel) and the variegated cultures of the Jews were shaped primarily in the diaspora.

The symbolic tie to the land of Israel that diaspora Jewish communities perpetuated over the centuries was incorporated into the diasporic mentality as a quality or pedigree of ancient theocratic coherence, ritualized in a few selective ongoing sacred practices and preserved as an eschatological hope. This religious orientation to the land of their ancestors was not, nor could it have been imagined as, a political program with practical ramifications. Within a fundamentally diaspora-constructed Judaism, as one writer recently put it, "the *reference* to Israel rather than Israel itself operates as a dynamic agent, as a catalyst of utopia."[5]

It was only from the late nineteenth century that Jewish political activists grafted the old, spiritualistic Zion myth onto a European nationalist model of nation building and state formation. For purposes of political mobilization and cultural reconstruction in the *yishuv* (Jewish community in prestate Palestine) and in the early years of the state, it proved effective to draw on the imagery of the ancient Israelite heritage and the messianic-utopian hopes for a "return." The truth, however, is far more ambiguous. The latter-day reversal of Jewish dispersion, as represented in *aliyah* (immigration) to Israel, has been partial at best. By 1948, after some 70 years of Zionist settlement activity, the Jewish population of the Yishuv (some 600,000) was still merely a fraction (some 5.5%) of the world aggregate of about 11 million who remained after the decimation of European Jewry. Since 1948, the Jewish population of Israel has indeed burgeoned (totaling just over 5 million and, given current growth rates, will probably represent half the world's Jewish population by the time this book is out of print), and the diaspora is indeed shrinking as a proportion of the world's Jewish population (down from almost 95% to about 62%); yet there is not necessarily a direct causal relationship between these two processes. Rather (with exceptions to be noted presently), the attrition of the diaspora communities is due mainly to assimilation and low birthrates, not emigration, and is thus quite independent of the growth of Israel's Jewish population.[6]

The Jews who have immigrated to Israel are not, by and large, representative of the current centers of Jewish diaspora life, anchored largely in English-speaking countries (predominantly the United States, with its nearly 5.7 million Jews). Only slightly more than 1 percent of American Jews have ever immigrated to Israel, so that the social, cultural, and religious disparities between Israeli and diaspora Jews are most pronounced in the American case.[7] Some western European and Latin American Jewries, as well as South African Jewry, have had somewhat higher *aliyah* rates (ranging from 10% to 25%), but their modest numbers, when added up, do not appreciably alter the discontinuities between Israeli culture and that of the larger diaspora communities of today.[8]

Notably different is the pattern among Jews from the Muslim world (a population that totaled some 850,000 at the end of World War II) and from the former Soviet Union (upwards of 1.3 million of whom have emigrated since 1989). Both groups have contributed very heavily to the post-1948 waves of immigration to Israel, and in both these cases there is a direct correlation between the numerical decline of the diaspora communities and the increase of the Israeli population. The Arab and Muslim world today is virtually empty of Jews, save for a tiny remnant scattered from Morocco to Iran that no longer functions as a viable diaspora community. The half million Jews who remain in the former Soviet Union belong disproportionally to the over-40 age-group, with one-third 65 and above, so that despite the recent invigoration of communal and religious activities, little chance exists that they might retain their present numbers for long, to say nothing of potential regeneration.[9] Even more than the counting of noses, however, it is the remarkable vote of no confidence in a post-Soviet future, cast by so many Jewish émigrés—almost three-quarters of all those who made up Soviet Jewry in the 1980s—that signals the dwindling of this diasporic center, once second only to the United States.

Thus, the major lands of emigration from the diaspora to Israel have been those of eastern Europe and the Middle East, while the bulk of diaspora Jewry today, in contrast, is accounted for by the English-speaking world followed by western Europe and Latin America. The result is a psychosocial and cultural disparity—not to say a gulf—between different parts of Jewish world that tends to obstruct reciprocity. Israel's "ingathered" groups have little or no connection to the noningathered (apart from family connections maintained by Israeli immigrants). By the same token, because the diaspora is not an Israeli diaspora, whether by origin, culture, or direct affiliation, the potential for diaspora involvement in Israel is minimal.[10] Moreover, because the diaspora owes its existence to preexisting historical realities, the new national Jewish "center" has not entirely been able to fulfill the latent potency of an *actual* center vis-à-vis the diaspora communities. Jews of the diaspora have not been renationalized as "overseas Israelis" but continue to live as citizens of the various countries to which they or their parents or grandparents migrated in the course of the past century or two.[11]

Yet there is a point at which radical discontinuity between Israel and the diaspora (historically rather than geographically speaking) becomes an absurd proposition. Israel has grown out of the diaspora experience. Therefore, while diaspora is not in any parallel sense an outgrowth of Israel, both parts of the Jewish world accept that they are linked.

The issue of defining that linkage comes down to an operational question: given the disparities between the diaspora and Israel, what are the linkages that "work," and what sort do not? In the present discussion, we will address two key topics: (1) immigrant groups in Israel and their role in "diasporizing" Israeli society and (2) philanthropy, the "second channel" (after immigration the most effective one) of diaspora influence and mutual Israel–diaspora interaction.

IMMIGRATION TO ISRAEL: DIASPORA, CONTINUED

Immigration is the engine that animates the diaspora–Israel process. If the Israeli political system today is more than a little reminiscent of Polish Jewish politics between the two world wars—indeed, some of the same political parties are still with us—it is because immigration from Poland played a substantial role in the formation of the Israeli polity. If Israelis who occupy the large middle ground between arch-secularists and the ultra-Orthodox appear to be as moderately tradition oriented as Jews of the Sephardic diaspora or central Europe have been in former times, it is because Israelis' attitudes to Judaism quite often are shaped by sensibilities imported from those parts of the world.[12] If the Beta Israel of Ethiopia have succeeded at all in becoming more than a tiny, distant blip on the radar screen of world Jewry, it is by virtue of their dramatic immigration to Israel.

Thus, in its process of nation building through immigration, Israel again and again becomes a palimpsest of Jewish life in other places, preserving as well as discarding elements of the diasporic experience. Past observers have tended to overemphasize the discarding—in one case, perhaps now all but forgotten, going so far as to declare that Israel represented "the end of the Jewish people."[13] It is well, then, in seeking a more realistic view that we take to heart a point recently made by literary historian Ruth Wisse, who noted that secular Israeli writers' discomfort with the "burden of Jewish history" is quite congruous with similar strains that characterized modern Yiddish fiction several generations ago, in what was ostensibly another world.[14]

It is undeniable, of course, that classical Zionist ideology rested on a declared "negation of the diaspora." In the slogan perpetuated by the Zionist pioneering anthem, "*Anu banu artza*," it was proclaimed that Zionist settlers—*'olim*—had come "up" to the Land of Israel in order "to build and to be rebuilt." The human rebuilding alluded to both a physical and a moral reconstruction, and the slogan clearly stigmatized diaspora Jewish life in both senses.

Such attributions of negativity to the diaspora experience might explain the tendency, still widespread in some sectors of Israeli society, to eschew country-of-origin identities in favor of a national-civic, "Israeli" identity. Studies on the subject have found that this point of view is strongest among Israelis who stem from east-central Europe, that is, among those groups that were well established in the country before World War II and then slightly augmented during the 1950s. Populations made up of relatively later immigrants (notably from the Middle East and North Africa) have not exhibited this deliberate atrophy of "diaspora-of-origin" identity.[15]

If we assume that immigrant integration (the favored Israeli term is "absorption") would tend to progressively erase memories of the "old home" and promote the blurring, through marriage, of originally distinct immigrant groups, there may be nothing remarkable here. On both counts—memory effacement and cross-subgroup marriages—more recent arrivals would not "yet" have processed their collective and individual Jewish identities entirely into new, generically Israeli configurations. Such a hypothesis would be more persuasive were it not for the fact that the overt denial of diasporic homeland attachments was in fact undertaken from the start, among the more veteran groups, as an ideological component of their immigration itself ("to build and be rebuilt") and therefore cannot be attributed to the passage of time and long-term integrative processes.

The question to be raised, then, is whether the diaspora-negation ideology was as effective in actual practice as it was strident in its declarative affirmation. As I have already intimated, my thesis is that underlying patterns and modes of self-expression have in fact been retained (though in adaptive formats) from the previous diaspora experience. How, indeed, could it have been otherwise, unless we conceive of an Israeli society created from scratch, with no Jewish experience that preceded it and preconditioned most of the ways in which it might develop?

Some of the same studies that found the previously mentioned tendency among Ashkenazi Israelis to downplay their diaspora backgrounds also found no resonance at all—to the point of its being virtually extinct—of the hardline, antidiasporic position, years ago popularized under the banner of the so-called Canaanite group (intellectuals who demanded a sharp break with diaspora Jewishness in favor of a "purely" local, homegrown, secularized Israeli identity). Rather, the same Ashkenazi Israelis who preferred to dispense with such particular diasporic labels as Polish, Rumanian, Galician, and so on were far indeed from shedding the label "Jewish," an identity tag that alludes to ethnoreligious ties of long standing with other Jews, whether in Israel or not.[16]

Even the more moderate stigmatizing of the diaspora experience that has been part of Israeli discourse has lately undergone a mellowing out. Summarizing the findings on diaspora-origin identities cited previously, sociologist Stephen Sharot notes this change of ideological ambience: "Such negative orientations toward Diaspora Jewishness were less important among later Ashkenazi immigrants and they have lost the prominence they once had, [although] there has been no ethnic revival of Ashkenazi *edot*."[17]

I can attest to this relative decline of diaspora negation, if only anecdotally, from my experiences over the years teaching a B.A. course on "the contemporary Jewish world." (The registration for this course invariably exceeds 100, of whom about a third are retirees and mature, returning students over 40, the remainder being in their early to mid-twenties). As part of the course requirements, I ask students to write a term paper on a diaspora community of their choice, and they almost always pick their own families' community of origin. I receive reports about Poland, Hungary, Rumania, France, or Italy less frequently than reports about Morocco, Tunisia, Yemen, and Iraq, but the Europeans are certainly well represented, as are such "Anglo" communities as South Africa, Australia, and England. This sort of ethnic identification and diaspora pride is not lacking. As Sharot maintains, these subgroup identities coexist with Israeli, national-civic identity.

Moreover, the observed dearth of a public ethnic revival among veteran Ashkenazi populations must be understood in context: some social and cultural patterns that were diasporic in origin have become so generalized within the Israeli milieu and civic culture as to require no overt notice or particular identification, yet they reinforce European Jewish culture just as their counterparts reinforce Sephardi and *mizrachi* (Middle Eastern) diasporic identity. That would be the case with the examples cited earlier (the "Polish" characteristics of Israel's political life, for example) as well as with other instances, from art to cuisine, from habits of dress to an overheated style of journalism. Cynics would no doubt add bureaucratic bungling (the "Chelm" syndrome)[18] to the list. And according to a famous quip, my own university is the "last German university in the world."

Without disputing that diaspora subgroup ethnicity may have a lower profile among European populations, I would submit that closer attention needs to be paid to the ways in which "diasporized" variations of cultural, social, and religious discourse exist as accepted modes of an increasingly pluralistic Israeli identity. To some extent, such disaporic patterns also overflow their subgroup sectors and affect the rest of Israeli society.

Let us consider, in the first instance, the *haredi* (ultra-Orthodox) groups in Israel, among whom a Zionistic diaspora negation never found substantial resonance—very much in line with the diaspora rootedness of classical rabbinic Judaism. Indeed, it may be said that *haredi* Israelis constitute a veritable bastion of diasporic identification as opposed to a neo-Jewish, Israeli one. They express this, first, by pointedly referring to themselves, in their various subgroups, as having originated elsewhere and by affirming the heritage brought from "there" (Gur, Mir, Slobodka, Vizhnitz, Satmar, and so forth). Second, they maintain current diaspora connections (pilgrimage to such sacred sites in the diasporic homeland as the grave of Rabbi Nachman of Bratslav in Uman, the Ukraine, or the courts of various hasidic rebbes in Brooklyn, New York). Third, the politicization of *haredi* groups (as in the case of Shas—the "Sephardi Torah Guardian" party founded in 1983) is unabashedly ethnic.[19]

The case of the *haredim* is interesting as well because their construction of a diaspora-rooted identity has been shaped and indeed motivated by a correspondingly deliberate social distance from mainstream Israeli culture, civic-national norms, and secularism. Their trademark diasporism, therefore, is partly a latter-day construct, and in that sense it does not simply reflect continuity with preimmigration Jewish life in their places of origin—witness the "Lithuanization" of the North African adherents of Shas, apparent in attire as well as the promotion of a yeshiva lifestyle and the adoption of a "Torah sages council" form of leadership. Indeed, the Shas Party itself was created in large part at the urging or behest of Rabbi Eliezer Shach, the late doyen of the "Lithuanian" yeshiva world of Bnei Brak.

While many of the *haredi* groups cultivate marginality as a virtue, not to say an art form, that cannot be said of the Shas group, which aims at broadening its political base and social influence wherever it finds a foothold in Israeli society. The party has garnered votes in recent elections in numbers far surpassing the ranks of its core constituency. Thus, Shas projects a diasporic-based mode of identity beyond the bounds of the classical anti- or non-Zionist *haredi* world into mainstream sectors of society that accept and uphold a national-religious ethos of Israeliness.[20]

In contrast to the *haredi* groups and the Shas constituency, who are veteran Israelis, the immigration from the former Soviet Union has created an entirely new diaspora-identity sector within Israeli society. Now about a million strong, this immigrant cohort represents a fifth of all Israeli Jews and cannot be dismissed as "marginal," although it is well known that feelings of mutual alienation continue to divide many of the "Russians" from veteran Israelis.

The abiding distance between these immigrants and the rest of Israeli society is expressed, among other things, by the avid consumption of Russian-language culture and entertainment (easily accessible in Israel from Russian television) in broad sections of this community and the flourishing of a local, self-contained, Russian linguistic "ghetto." Clashing with other modes of Israeli culture, whether of the Hebraist-humanist variety (emphasizing a modernized Hebrew culture as a natural evolution of national Jewishness) or of the various Orthodox-religious varieties (national-religious or *haredi*), this relatively compartmentalized "Russianness" has nonetheless had few ramifications thus far for "Israeliness" per se.[21]

It is rather the ex-Soviet mode of *Jewish* identity, transplanted to the Israeli setting, that does affect Jewish Israelis at large. Sharot and others note that "a Jewish community in an organizational sense had ceased to exist in the former Soviet Union, and when a Jewish identity was retained it was largely divorced from specifically Jewish cultural content . . . Jewishness [rather] took on the meanings of cosmopolitan intellectualism and a strong achievement drive to overcome the barriers to occupational mobility."[22] These high-culture, cosmopolitan proclivities and the drive for middle-class mobility have already had notable spin-off effects in Israel. The expansion of academic institutions since the early 1990s has been remarkable (especially the many new colleges geared to professional, managerial, or scientific-technological accreditation), as has the flourishing of orchestras, quartets, ballet, and classical music performance generally.[23] These developments have had more than an incidental connection with the arrival of "the Russians," but whereas their consumption of Russian culture tends to isolate the immigrant community linguistically and culturally, the broadened academic and artistic fields in which they are so active are expansive and inclusive. To these we should also add the field of competitive individual athletics, for men and women (from pole vaulting and weightlifting to gymnastics and figure skating), another Soviet-vintage form of achievement and self-advancement. This area of sport was relatively underdeveloped in Israel prior to the recent Russian immigration but has since grown exponentially as part of the Israeli physical culture scene.

The ambiguities of Soviet-style Jewishness have affected Israeli realities and sensibilities in an altogether different, more tragic direction. The ex-Soviet immigrant population of the 1990s included substantial numbers of family members who are not themselves Jewish.[24] A relative handful (several hundred) is converted to Judaism each year, but under the circumstances, this represents but a small fraction of the non-Jewish immigrant population. Were these ordinary times, this might be of little immediate consequence to the general Jewish public because a "presumption of Jewishness" operates in favor of identifying all non-Arabs as belonging to the Jewish majority.

For the past decade, however, Israel has been plagued by tragic and violent deaths due to war and terrorism. Casualties sustained by the Israel Defense Forces, first at the hands of the Hizbollah in Lebanon and subsequently in Palestinian terror attacks, as well as the hundreds of civilian deaths from those terror attacks, inevitably included Israelis from all walks of life. When there have been victims not deemed Jewish under rabbinical law, the issue of burial rites has arisen very suddenly and very publicly. Each and every victim's name is reported in the news, and every funeral is an occasion of public mourning, often televised. When soldiers or civilians who died "as Jews"—that is, as victims of the common enemy—cannot be buried as Jews, this strikes a deep, embarrassed, and sensitive chord.

In the present context, the religious merits of the issue are not pertinent; what is relevant, however, is that once again we have a case of diasporic modes of Jewish life, transplanted to Israeli soil, that have begun to affect the texture of Israeli life as a whole. To Israelis, accustomed to operate according to the "presumption of Jewishness," the need to face up to a more complex variety of identities within the "Jewish" majority is something new and unsettling, and it promises to make itself increasingly felt over the coming decades.

The final case to consider is that of the North Americans who have settled in Israel. Their number is hard to fix because there has always been a degree of return migration to America among this population, but 75,000 to 80,000 is a fair estimate.[25] Of a different order of magnitude than the "Russian" *aliyah*, the much smaller American group nevertheless enjoys several advantages with respect to its integration. First, many if not most of the Americans have, in their diaspora lives, experienced a more positive and certainly more institutionalized form of Jewish identity than did the "Russians," and they therefore possess a stronger initial ethnoreligious link with many Israeli Jews. Second, Americans enjoy the advantage of a native command of English, which is Israel's high-status, second language in fields as varied as information technology, commerce, medicine, popular entertainment and the arts, and the academic world.[26] When coupled with their less insular approach to integration (compared with the "Russians," whose numbers alone allow for a great deal of self-sufficiency in linguistic and cultural terms), these considerations suggest that the American *aliyah*, despite its small size, enjoys a position closer to the Israeli mainstream. Its own sectoral contribution, though modest, could therefore have a disproportionate impact on the Israeli public at large.

Of the various aspects of Israeli life in which the American presence has been noted,[27] the most distinctive involves the infusion of non-Orthodox, American-bred forms of Jewish religious observance and education. It should be noted that the bulk of American immigrants in recent years has been Orthodox (as has been the majority of teenage and college-age students who regularly come from North America for yearlong study programs, thus swelling the Orthodox American presence). By and large, they have sought to integrate religiously into already existing permutations of Orthodox groups, institutions, and ideological camps, though some retain a profile of their own. That profile can be distinctive, as in the case of Orthodox thinker Rabbi David Hartman, who has gathered around him and his Shalom Hartman Institute a liberal-Orthodox and non-Orthodox intellectual following. Other such examples could be cited in this regard as well, but the overall picture is one of more conventional integration by Orthodox Americans into Israeli Orthodox life.[28] The non-Orthodox, in contrast, who predominated in the 1970s, have a distinctly nonconformist profile and have generated a different kind of notice.

With virtually no meaningful development prior to the late 1960s, Conservative (known in Israel as *masorti*, i.e., "traditional") and Reform Judaism (known in Israel as *mitkademet*, i.e., "progressive") appeared only when an American *aliyah* of significant size began to arrive after the Six-Day War.[29] These movements' synagogues and institutions of higher learning were established wherever an appreciable core group of American Jewish immigrants was available. Initially, that meant chiefly in Jerusalem, but by now such congregations have spread to the other large cities (Tel-Aviv, Haifa, and Ashkelon); "yuppie" suburban communities (Modi'in, 'Omer, and the like); older, so-called "development towns" with substantial immigrant populations (such as Carmiel); and a few kibbutzim. Moreover, many of these congregations now include roughly equal proportions of Americans and non-American Israelis—native-born, veteran Israelis as well as immigrants from Argentina and the former Soviet Union. The first Ethiopian *masorti* rabbi was ordained in 2002.

The numbers involved are still very small: the Conservatives, for example, with more synagogues than the Reform, claim some 40 congregations countrywide; they also have a student body of some 300 students at their college in Jerusalem, Machon Schechter. Both figures are miniscule when compared with the number of Orthodox synagogues and Orthodox yeshiva students. The Reform movement, with some two dozen congregations, is perhaps best known in Israel for the activities of its Israel Religious Action Center (IRAC), under the leadership of Rabbi Uri Regev. This group petitions the Israeli Supreme Court on matters related to religious liberty and civil rights and engages in active lobbying for religious pluralism. When both the Jewish Theological Seminary (Conservative) and the Hebrew Union College (Reform) established rabbinical seminaries and Jewish studies colleges in Jerusalem *for Israelis*, granting M.A. degrees and ordination (in addition to the one-year-abroad programs that they run for their American students), they opened a window on the Israeli mainstream that may someday play a role in a public reconsideration of the spiritual dimensions of Israeli Jewish identity.[30]

The same is true of the TALI schools (the acronym in Hebrew translates as "Augmented Jewish Studies"), a network of elementary and high schools that closely approximates in spirit and conception the Solomon Schechter day schools that the Conservative movement established in the United States. In Israel, the concept was applied by a core group of American immigrant families in Jerusalem who established the very first such school in 1976. The TALI network today includes 60 schools, from elementary to high school, and 50 kindergartens and preschools, with a total of some 20,000 students throughout the country. Positioned ideologically midway between the secular and the Orthodox school systems, the TALI schools operate within the secular stream as a separate option.[31]

Despite a certain amount of media attention, however, neither of the non-Orthodox movements can claim to have reshaped Israel's basic religious paradigm, which rests on a normative, public foundation (including governmental support and quasi-constitutional recognition) quite foreign to American concepts of church–state separation and religious pluralism. For the future, non-Orthodox Jewish denominations have the potential to move off the edge of mainstream Israeli consciousness to a point somewhat closer to the center, particularly given the integrative advantages enjoyed by North Americans, but that will depend largely on continued immigration from the diaspora, especially the United States, without which these movements may very well "miss the boat."

Summing up thus far, we may conclude that diaspora-related affinities are not limited to one type of group in the Israeli Jewish population, whether we select for size, religious profile, or timing of immigration. Moreover, the examples described here are by no means an exhaustive list. The Ethiopians constitute yet another good case, as do immigrants from Latin American countries, but the point is already sufficiently established. These place and lifestyle-attachments are at once a confirmation of the Zionist slogan of "ingathering of exiles" and a negation of its "melting pot" version. That is, "Israeliness" is not necessarily constituted by expunging other Jewish experiences but rather, at least in recent decades, constructed in good measure by rearranging immigrants' attachments to their diaspora identity within the context of their new home.[32]

I recently encountered this phenomenon in the case of a young mother of three, dressed in strictly Orthodox garb, who remarked that she communicates with her small children solely in English in order to preserve their native-speaking ability and would rely on the environment to immerse her children within a culture of Hebrew proficiency. This attachment to English runs counter to the normative culture of most Israeli Orthodox Jews and to most Israelis' traditional sense of "correct" integration procedures. The young woman's point of view was perfectly legitimate, however, within the observant, "Anglo" subgroup that constituted her immediate social world and was not at all directed negatively against her Orthodox identity or her adopted Israeli identity.

The idea that the diaspora mind-set is rather different from the stereotypically Israeli one yet that diasporic identities might be viewed as enriching and complicating Israeli culture and *mentalité* rather than as mounting a frontal challenge was eloquently formulated many years ago by political scientist and scholar of contemporary Jewry Charles Liebman when he was himself a relatively recent immigrant. In the preface to his book on Israel–diaspora relations, written just prior to the Yom Kippur War of 1973, he wrote as follows:

> I am a Diaspora Jew. This, I believe, makes me no less proud of Israel or less committed to her survival. But it does make me different from many other Israelis. It permits me a sense of wonder at Israel's very existence, but makes me a little less confident of her future. I think that in general it makes me a little less provincial than most Israelis, and little less self-confident. [. . .] I need hardly add, however, that I find many other Israelis who are basically Diaspora Jews. [. . .] I dedicate this book to my children [who] bear my personal vision—to raise a generation of Diaspora Jews in Israel.[33]

Diasporic patterns of behavior and consciousness persist in Israel among immigrant groups and at least some of their offspring because (1) Jewish identity is, as a rule, rooted in local contexts, as is true of identity in general in any group, and (2) the process of immigration perpetuates diasporic heritage affiliations insofar as "place" is transformed into subcommunities who share the same space. The process by which subcommunities take shape and assert their presence in Israeli civil society is neither abnormal nor erosive of the national identity (despite recent wildly misleading assertions to the contrary).[34] Rather, it can be said of Israel, as of most if not all other modern, complex societies, that none is constructed all-of-a-piece in either cultural or social terms. Over the longer term, diaspora-rooted patterns can and quite often do "overflow" the boundaries from the subcommunity to the larger society, thus enabling a continued evolution of those patterns in a new, Israeli setting.

PHILANTHROPY

Continued immigration from the diaspora to Israel establishes the concrete "presence" of the diaspora for veteran Israelis, in some sense even an attitude of responsibility *toward* the diaspora, and in any event a perception of common fate. The immigrants themselves often retain family and community ties with diaspora Jews and therefore represent a human connection that may last beyond a single generation.

The other overt form of diaspora input into Israeli society, second only to immigration, is the transfer of monetary resources. Financial transfers are less personal, perhaps, but they entail intangible ramifications in the form of mutual regard and responsibility no less than does immigration. Immigrants arrive as individuals or as families and do not actually "represent" an aggregate Jewry from any given diaspora country. In contrast, monetary assistance for institutions and agencies in Israel does derive, in most cases, from organized Jewish bodies abroad and therefore entails the maintenance of a relationship between recipient entities in Israel and the diaspora community that the donor entities represent. Indeed, there are ample grounds to suggest that such donors in the diaspora become representative of their community by virtue of the collective link they establish for their community with Israel. When diaspora Jews delegate to their organizations—through the funds that they donate—the task of forging a link with Israel, they endow those organizations with a collective (one might even use the term "national") legitimacy in the realm of diaspora–Israel relations.

For our purposes here, it is relevant as well that part of the funds raised by Jews of the diaspora for the support of Israel goes toward institutions that have their origin in diaspora initiatives (Jerusalem's Hadassah Hospital, for example, or the ORT vocational school network), make some direct contribution toward the welfare of diaspora Jews settling in Israel (as is the case with the Jewish Agency's immigrant-absorption work), or maintain intensive training programs for senior Jewish educators who then return to work in their diaspora communities.

Moreover, the bulk of monetary assistance comes from precisely those diaspora communities that contribute the smallest number of immigrants. Philanthropic linkages, therefore, compensate for the weakness of more personal linkages, thus becoming indispensable for the maintenance of a significant diaspora–Israel relationship. Although other forms of linkage are theoretically possible, they are largely impracticable (as we will discuss shortly), leaving philanthropy as the chief and most effective mode of interaction. In recent decades, there has been an effort to humanize this interaction and make it both more transparent and more reciprocal: the governance of the Jewish

Agency has been reshaped to give added voice to diaspora representatives ("the funders"), much attention has been paid to "twinning" donor communities with towns and cities in Israel (under the late 1970s "Project Renewal" rubric and the more recent "Partnership 2000"), and individual donors have become far more interested in hands-on participation in the formulation, design, and execution of projects that they fund. But all this is in the nature of getting a "bigger bang for the buck" in terms of personal involvement and reciprocity rather than a qualitative change in the centrality of philanthropy for the Israel–diaspora process.

Such links with Israel provide diaspora philanthropy with an explicitly *Jewish* function that complements its health-and-welfare-related or social functions (which, in many instances, has no specific ethnic content). In a very real sense, the ability to forge philanthropic ties with Israel is crucial to a diaspora community's ability to carry on a more intensive organizational life. This has been misunderstood by a variety of well-meaning critics. There are those who would rebuild the Israel–diaspora relationship on a basis of parity rather than the historical pattern of Israel's client or recipient role, and they therefore propose that diaspora communities invest much more in their own domestic needs.[35] The point, however, is that donating funds to Israel *is* an investment in diaspora Jewish life, even as it represents tangible input into Israeli society.

Understanding the background of this situation requires a brief historical digression. Modern Jewish philanthropy (and the social services that it has funded) emerged in the nineteenth and early twentieth centuries and served primarily integrative functions for Jews living in Western societies.[36] Philanthropy helped to ensure that Jews qua Jews would not be considered a burden on society at large, while it also provided an avenue by which Jews qua citizens could do their part for improving the general well-being of their society. (In American Jewry, for example, it has long been the practice of wealthy Jews to donate funds to nonsectarian as well as to Jewish causes.) Organizing Jewish charities did not require the reconstruction of separate, corporate communities of the traditional *kehillah*[37] type; indeed, it went against the grain of that earlier, insular, religious tradition, and it arose *because* of the demise of the old kehillah. Modern philanthropy was neutral when it came to religious considerations per se, and it avoided the establishment of authoritative or broadly representative Jewish bodies. Instead, it followed the forms of rationalized philanthropy that developed in Western, capitalist countries, taking on the accepted Western form of nonprofit organizations ("funds," "appeals," "campaigns," "boards," and "federations"), established and governed by a voluntary elite. It thus formed a quasi-public and quasi-secular sphere that was based entirely on the voluntaristic premise of private initiative.

Unlike the old, religious injunction to provide charitable relief for the poor (*tsedakah*), this new pattern of institutionalized philanthropy was intended to solve problems that were adversely affecting not just the private welfare of individual Jews but also the quality of Jews' relations with non-Jews in the modern state and economy. In short, it represented a key strategy by which Jewish elites managed their social integration into developed societies, in response to Western notions of poverty, social engineering, and proper economic development and in the context of the modern "Jewish question."[38]

With the expansion of European and American interests and influence in such areas as the Middle East and Latin America and with the concurrent mass emigration of Jews from eastern Europe (1880s–1920s) came a further expansion of Jewish philanthropic activities. An enlightened philanthropic policy that looked beyond the immediate, local situation and was conducted under Western aegis was a positive and farsighted response to problems of poverty, political unrest, and demographic turmoil on a global level. Rendering assistance to Jews in the Middle East or eastern Europe could be legitimated variously as denominational work in underdeveloped parts of the globe (parallel to work done by Western Christians under the auspices of church missions), as the projection abroad of the national interest (as in the activities of the Alliance Israélite Universelle, which promoted French culture in the Levant and North Africa), or as occupational and social rehabilitation that would inevitably make it less necessary for Jews to emigrate to the United States. As for supporting the resettlement of Jews in areas such as Argentina, where European migration and investment was becoming well established, this fit legitimately within the frame of progressive and rational redistribution of "surplus populations" for the sake of colonization and development. None of this departed from the accepted integrationist scheme.[39]

Along with so much that has changed in the Jewish world since then, and in particular since the waning postwar years and the high drama of the 1960s, 1970s, and 1980s, the terms of Jewish integration in the Western diaspora countries have also shifted. In philanthropy, as in such other fields as politics, education, and literature, the older integrationist paradigm of submerging "Jewishness" within a nonsectarian civic identity has given way to a desire to gain for Jewishness, for *difference* itself, an accepted place in a more open and pluralistic civic or national culture.[40] In all these realms, including philanthropy, it has been the function of the Israel connection, above all, to enable Jews to assert a responsible role for themselves in world Jewish affairs, *as Jews*, thus upholding Jewish distinctiveness as an integral part of their other social and civic roles and not as a concession to divided identities.

It is, therefore, a serious error to view the diaspora's philanthropic activity in Israel as somehow representing a minimalistic form of commitment. Invidious comparisons have been made between the sacrifices that Israelis are called on to make for the sake of their country and the money sacrificed by diaspora Jews.[41] Such facile, not to say ridiculous, comparisons miss the rather elementary point, stressed at the very beginning of our discussion, that the diaspora is not *Israel's* diaspora—that is, Jews in the diaspora are not a national periphery of the Israeli state. More substantively, in light of the foregoing discussion, the transfer of funds from the diaspora to Israel represents something of real existential value to those who give and is not to be belittled. The relevant formula for the present diaspora–Israel constellation is *not* "minimal involvement at minimal risk" but rather "maximum *feasible* involvement." At present, short of a significant increase in *aliyah* from the West (which no one predicts), philanthropy represents precisely those maximal, practicable limits because other alternatives have proven unworkable.

One major reason why philanthropic work represents so open and pragmatic a channel between diaspora Jews and Israel is that it is freely given—it is not a tax. It reinforces a mutual recognition of commonality without demanding that either party shed its own specificity or prerogatives. Philanthropic relationships require no *additional* or *prerequisite* cultural or political interaction and therefore can be effectual without the need for substantial face-to-face experience or political hierarchy.[42] Indeed, were such "thicker" connections necessary, philanthropy would be as weak a link as are culture, religious exchange, and political participation. (I stress again that minimal cultural and political involvement should not be confused with minimal existential *commitment*.) In arguing for the superior feasibility of philanthropy as a form of linkage, it is crucial to recall the sociocultural differences, noted at the outset of our discussion, that separate Israeli society from today's diaspora, due to the prevailing immigration patterns: the Jewish communities that have contributed the bulk of Israel's population are no longer representative of diaspora culture, while those most representative of diaspora culture today are not well represented in Israeli society.

First and foremost, the dissimilarity is a linguistic one. Israel's languages (I use the plural here in recognition of the salience of immigrant languages such as Russian) are foreign tongues to the vast majority of diaspora Jews, making it very difficult indeed for meaningful cultural interchange to take place. Two and three generations ago, Yiddish was the lingua franca that permitted that sort of interchange through much of the Jewish world. Today, English has become the most effective channel of Israel–diaspora communication in certain sectors of society (including the academic sector; this book is itself evidence of that), and the high prestige of English in Israel generally, as a world language, has already been noted. Beyond that, the impact of the Internet in terms of communication within the Jewish world may have some important ramifications for the future. For now, however, and for most cultural purposes, from everyday communication to the transmission of experience through various media, the language barrier is very real and shows little sign of being lowered. Kindergarten children in Israel are raised as Hebrew speakers; diaspora children are not. To cite but one example: the Conservative movement, which still represents roughly half the synagogue-affiliated, non-Orthodox Jews in the United States, has been preaching the importance of Hebrew education and Hebrew literacy for a hundred years and has been doggedly putting that doctrine into practice in synagogues, congregational schools, summer camps, and day schools, yet is not appreciably closer today than it was in Solomon Schechter's time to the goal of creating a Hebrew-literate public.[43]

The language problem, however, is only the beginning. Parallel difficulties exist at the political and ethical levels as well. The World Zionist Organization (WZO), founded in 1897, espoused the outlandish idea that the Jews were a political entity (a "nation") and as such had the standing under international law to demand rights of political self-determination. Indeed, Zionist parties formed parliamentary factions as Jewish national delegations in such countries as interwar Poland precisely because they were predicated on the idea that the Jewish people at large, even before achieving independent statehood in Palestine, constituted a political nation with political rights in the diaspora. When the State of Israel was established, it embodied those political rights, but that left the WZO and the dispersed "nation" it ostensibly represented in political limbo. In effect, the nation of Jewry was now to be limited to those who became Israeli citizens, thus availing themselves of their rights to political self-determination; but at the same time, Israel's Law of Return, the basic law concerning Jewish peoplehood, recognizes all diaspora Jews (and their close kin regardless of their religious identity) as eligible for Israeli citizenship at any time should they immigrate.

The WZO remained a representative forum of world Jewry, transcending the boundaries of the State of Israel but unable to confer any civic or political rights or perform any political function within the state or abroad or in the international sphere. Israelis, after all, function politically by virtue of their citizenship, while diaspora Jews may regard the WZO as a conduit for diaspora Jewish opinion but cannot make it politically relevant to either Israel or their own societies. (A friend of mine who attended the 2002 World Zionist Congress in Jerusalem had to cancel a coffee date one evening because the caucus session he was attending was bogged down in a difficult debate. Yet the Congress merited only a brief mention on the evening news, and, needless to say, I never did learn what it was that was so hotly debated there.)

It is for these and related reasons—including a feeling of discomfort with the limitations of the philanthropic mode of interaction—that figures in both Israeli and the diaspora have, over the years, agitated for the replacement of the moribund WZO by some new entity, to re-create a context for a meaningfully shared public life for Israelis and diaspora Jews. These have ranged from proclaiming a new, worldwide Jewish "covenant," a quasi-sacred founding document for an entirely new, nonpolitical, Jewish "world nation"—an idea seriously put forth by American Jewish philosopher Mordecai M. Kaplan in the 1950s; to a new, voluntary, mass-membership world organization to be called "Beit Yisrael—the House of Israel," first floated a decade ago and brought up again, most recently by Israeli politician Yossi Beilin; to a diaspora representation in the upper house of a proposed bicameral Knesset, a notion suggested by Arik Carmon, head of the Israel Democracy Institute; and to an AIPAC-like lobby, in Israel, to represent American Jewish interests at a less formal level in the Knesset.[44] None of these schemes has ever been seriously considered, let alone put into practice, because imagining a common public life that transcends Israel and the diaspora is so inherently difficult.

Along similar lines, philosophers, historians, and political scientists have been marshaled in an innovative effort to mine, classify, and interpret a usable "Jewish political tradition" that ostensibly might serve to guide Jewish political thought and political ethics across diaspora-Israel boundaries.[45] Others have merely speculated that the desire on the part of the human race to "re-establish . . . some kind of moral order above the sovereign states," without actually interfering with "the fulfillment of legitimate national aspirations," would have its Jewish parallel, "some new equilibrium between full national self-determination and international cooperation."[46]

To date, and with one exception, it has not proven possible to square this particular circle. Thus, the diaspora and Israel are pretty much where they were before, with minimal possibility for either party to mesh its political life with the other's. The one exception, which further underscores our point about the practical merits of philanthropy, is in the realm of political funding. In that area, philanthropy has been taken a step further as some (though by no means many) diaspora Jews have, in response to Israeli solicitation, begun to support political parties, election campaigns, extraparliamentary pressure groups, nonprofit organizations, and research centers with defined goals for social or political change in Israel.[47] Money, it turns out, transcends political boundaries easily enough and yet does not entail changes in existing civic or political identities. Although these practices have raised a few eyebrows, no one has mounted a serious challenge to their legal or political propriety.

The desire for something "beyond survival and philanthropy" (the title of one interesting collection of essays on the subject) has brought to light much of the frustration Jewish scholars and community figures experience when seeking an ethical rather than a utilitarian bridge between Israel and the diaspora. This has provided grist for countless "dialogues" and encounters, both at the official level (on numerous, if irregular occasions at the residence of the president of Israel) and at unofficial levels (beginning with the annual "dialogues" first sponsored by the American Jewish Congress and continuing in various "forums" that have sprung up from time to time to acquaint Israelis and diaspora Jews from the business, academic, and civic fields with one another's views). There is now even a Center for Israel-Diaspora Cultural Relations, headed by a theater director formerly of the United Kingdom who hopes to use Jewish theater as a bridge between diaspora communities and Israel.[48]

The spirit of such groping for a common language is not really new. It goes back to the offer of Israel's presidency to Albert Einstein (an offer that he sagaciously declined) and to David Ben-Gurion's famous invitation to prominent diaspora thinkers, scholars, and rabbis to advise him on the matter of the "who is a Jew?" controversy. It is noteworthy, however, that the same issues exist today, a half century later, and that the deference that each party believes is its due, in the name of solidarity, is still a source of tension.

Once again, the obstacles lie in dissimilar mentalities, lifestyles, and underlying prevailing values. Religious pluralism, for example, has been a perennial issue; but given the fact that it is particularly a Western (primarily American) concern, largely undervalued by the bulk of Israelis, it is difficult to see how it can be addressed in Israeli terms, unless and until non-Orthodox immigration from the West takes on larger dimensions. Likewise, the twin bogeys of anti-Semitism and assimilation continue to trouble the Israeli imagination with regard to Jewish life in the diaspora, which some Western Jews may find disturbing but to which they are handicapped in offering an adequate response, given the language barrier and related cultural differences.[49]

It is this situation, more or less predetermined by the prevailing immigration patterns that have left both parties on different cultural wavelengths, that perpetuates the need for philanthropy as a more reliable—some might say irreplaceable—bonding agent between the diaspora and Israel. It is what diaspora Jews are best able to do, from the diaspora, with regard to Israel.

It is true that philanthropy, too, causes some discomfort on both sides. Diaspora intellectual and spiritual figures chafe at the limits of a partnership based on a resource that engages the heart but does not seem to engage the intellect, and they question its ability to offer the wider Jewish public (most of which, after all, does not belong to the class of major donors) a positive and intensive exposure to Israel. Israeli critics, for their part, are irked by the anachronisms of the patron–client relationship that philanthropy inevitably reinforces, and they, too, wonder about the depth of such a relationship. As such critics on both sides correctly sense, it is difficult to uncouple the philanthropy question from all the other variables in the relationship. Their question is, Given the relative weakness of mutual input and sharing in such primal areas as religion, language, culture, or security, what sort of "solidarity" is accomplished through philanthropy?

The answer, clearly, is that funding is an acknowledgment of shared interests that can be expressed in actions, not just in words, with the potential of producing visible results "on the ground." Precisely these down-to-earth qualities are well appreciated watchwords of the Israeli mentality, and they are equally honored by pragmatists such as the Americans and throughout the diaspora among the business class that is chiefly involved in philanthropy. This link possesses content only insofar as it is backed up by program, and therefore it also becomes a conduit for thinking together, not merely a financial transaction. It is perhaps not the best conceivable mode of interaction for either side, but given the constraints, it remains an effective one.

In conclusion, we may say that there are actually two Israel–diaspora processes of some significance. One involves immigration to Israel. Its effects are mainly felt in Israeli society rather than abroad because the diaspora communities that have contributed the most to this migration are either no longer viable or less likely to remain part of the diaspora scene in coming generations. The diasporic experience that is transmitted to Israel via these immigrants is a determining factor in the ongoing evolution of Israeli identity and has, to date, been largely responsible for whatever degree of pluralism that Israeli Jewish culture entails.

Immigration and its subsequent effects has considerably less impact on the relationship that Western diaspora communities have with Israel, with the partial exceptions of a few communities such as South Africa and Argentina. The Israel–diaspora process in the major Western communities, chiefly the United States, is perceived mainly as an internal one; that is, given the limited possibilities of personal participation in Israeli life, it is what Israel represents to Jews *in* the diaspora—more particularly, what Israel represents as a feature of Jewish distinctiveness in the diaspora—that is the crux of the matter.

Establishing that distinctiveness is today, as in the past, accomplished not only through outwardly directed political activity but also through an inner-directed prioritization of Israel on the communal agenda. That prioritization receives its most concrete expression in the inclusion of Israeli causes within the Jewish communal budget.

The philanthropic connection does open up the chance for diaspora groups to seek greater influence within Israeli affairs, but this is a secondary consideration. This may motivate targeted giving among those with particular axes to grind (yeshivas, political groups, non-Orthodox congregations, and the like), but because such giving is divided over a wide range of causes, its overall impact within Israel is by definition diffuse and the resulting influence slight. It is diaspora Jewry that is far more influenced by its philanthropic link to Israel, insofar as it establishes an Israel–diaspora dimension in Jewish life that is otherwise difficult to sustain.

NOTES

1. Stephen Sharot, "Jewish and Other National and Ethnic Identities of Israeli Jews," in *National Variations in Jewish Identity: Implications for Jewish Education*, ed. Steven M. Cohen and Gabriel Horenczyk (Albany: State University of New York Press, 1999), 299–316.

2. On the comparison of modern ethnonational diasporas with the Jewish diasporic model, see Gabriel Sheffer, "Hatefutsah hayehudit vehairgunim hayehudiim habeinleumiim bahistoriah uvapolitikah hakelalit," in *Hatsiyonut vehahazarah lahistoriah: ha'arakha mehadash*, ed. Shmuel Noah Eisenstadt and Moshe Lissak (Jerusalem: Yad Ben-Zvi Press, 1999), 389–413, and "The Loyalties of Ethno-National Diasporas and the Case of the Jewish Diaspora," in *Still Moving: Recent Jewish Migration in Comparative Perspective*, ed. Daniel J. Elazar and Morton Weinfeld (n.p.: Transactions, 1999), 311–36.

3. The Ahad Ha'amist, or "spiritual Zionist," school of thought—once quite popular in Jewish cultural and intellectual circles—floated the notion that the Jewish "national home" in Palestine (statehood in the sovereign sense was not deemed essential)

would never actually reabsorb all the millions of Jews from around the world; rather, such a homeland could be expected to radiate its cultural influence (e.g., via a modern Hebrew literature) throughout the Jewish world, thus providing Jewry with one national-cultural center and reconstituting the essence of "diaspora" life. In America, Ahad Ha'am directly influenced such major Jewish communal and religious leaders as Mordecai M. Kaplan. There is an extensive literature on Ahad Ha'am (Asher Ginzberg, 1856–1927). See, for example, Gideon Shimoni, *The Zionist Ideology* (Hanover, N.H.: Brandeis University Press and University Press of New England, 1995), 104–12, 270–78; Steven. J. Zipperstein, *Elusive Prophet: Ahad Ha'am and the Origins of Zionism* (London: Peter Halban, 1993); and Leon Simon, ed., *Selected Essays of Ahad Ha-'Am* (New York: Atheneum, 1970).

4. The diasporist historian Salo W. Baron wrote a fascinating though little-known essay in 1962 on the provenance and development of diaspora–Jewish relations with the center in Palestine in antiquity that he ended with remarks relevant for contemporary Israel and the Jewish diaspora in the West. See Salo W. Baron, "The Jewish Commonwealths and the Dispersions," in *The Ethic of Power: The Interplay of Religion, Philosophy, and Politics*, ed. Harold D. Lasswell and Harlan Cleveland (New York: Harper and Brothers for the Conference on Science, Philosophy and Religion in their Relation to the Democratic Way of Life, 1962), 1–24.

5. Régine Azria, "The Diaspora-Community-Tradition Paradigms of Jewish Identity: A Reappraisal," in *Jewish Survival*, ed. Ernest Krausz and Gitta Tulea (New Brunswick, N.J.: Transaction Books, 1998), 22.

6. Sergio DellaPergola, "World Jewish Population, 2001," *American Jewish Year Book* 2001: 540–41.

7. Deborah Dash Moore and S. Ilan Troen, eds., *Divergent Jewish Cultures: Israel and America* (New Haven, Conn.: Yale University Press, 2001). Compare Stephen Sharot, "Judaism and Jewish Ethnicity: Changing Interrelationships and Differentiations in the Diaspora and Israel," and Naftali Rosenberg, "Jews in Israel and the United States: Diverging Identities," in Krausz and Tulea, *Jewish Survival*, 87–106 and 163–68, respectively.

8. Immigration rates from various diaspora communities may be estimated by comparing Jewish population figures, cited in the *American Jewish Year Book* (e.g., 1991, 452, 456, 462), with the data in *Immigrants to Israel, 1999*, publication no. 1173 (Jerusalem: Central Bureau of Statistics, 2002), 36–37, 40–41. Argentina, for example, thus had an *aliyah* rate of some 26 percent; Brazil, 12 percent; and Chile, an exceptionally high rate of 40 percent. The United Kingdom had 10 percent; France, 12 percent; Switzerland, 22 percent; Holland, 26 percent; and South Africa, 18 percent. Compare Sergio DellaPergola, "The Global Context of Migration to Israel," in Elazar and Weinfeld, *Still Moving*, 13–59.

9. Norman Stillman, *The Jews of Arab Lands in Modern Times* (Philadelphia: Jewish Publication Society, 1991), 141, 155–77; S. Landshut, *Jewish Communities in the Muslim Countries of the Middle East* (Westport, Conn.: American Jewish Committee and the Anglo-Jewish Association, 1950); George E. Gruen, "The Dwindling Jewish Communities in the Muslim Countries of the Middle East: Their Current Status and Reasons for Mass Emigration," in Elazar and Weinfeld, *Still Moving*, 355–97; DellaPergola, "World Jewish Population, 2001," 554; Mark Tolts, "Jewish Demography of the Former Soviet Union," in *Papers in Jewish Demography, 1997*, ed. Sergio DellaPergola and Judith Even (Jerusalem: Avraham Harman Institute of Contempo-

rary Jewry of the Hebrew University, 2001), 113. Tolts reports that 1.24 million people who were considered Jewish under Israel's law of return emigrated from the former Soviet Union from 1989 to 1998, of which some 770,000 immigrated to Israel (113). DellaPergola cites a total emigration of 1.4 million from 1990 to 2000, of which some 900,000 immigrated to Israel and 300,000 to the United States and 200,000 went to other destinations (554). Current estimates for Jewish population in the former Soviet Union hover between 460,000 and 540,000, in addition to an "extended" population of household members and relations who are not themselves Jewish, perhaps doubling the estimated core Jewish population. The rate of out-marriage for Jews was close to 70 percent of Jewish marriages in Russia in 1988 and close to 80 percent for Jewish marriages in Ukraine in 1996. The median age of Ashkenazic Jews in Russia in 1999 was 58, which meant that a third of all Russian Jews were age 65 and over. There were 2.8 Jewish births in Russia per thousand in 1993–94 but 30 deaths per thousand. In Ukraine, the respective figures were 4.2 and 35.9. The data appear in DellaPergola, "World Jewish Population, 2001," 555, and in Tolts, "Jewish Demography of the Former Soviet Union," 126.

10. See Irving Louis Horowitz, "Minimalism or Maximalism: Jewish Survival at the Millennium," in Krausz and Tulea, *Jewish Survival*, 8–15. Horowitz contends, "Diaspora participation in affairs of state in Israel is limited to rhetorical flourishes and editorial anguishes. It is true that certain key leaders in the American Jewish community have some marginal voice in Israeli life. But this is primarily a consequence of philanthropic and monetary power; not any special policy-making acumen that is essential to Israeli political affairs" (15).

A similar assessment was made some 25 years earlier by political scientist Charles S. Liebman in his book *Pressure without Sanctions: The Influence of World Jewry on Israeli Policy* (Rutherford, N.J.: Fairleigh Dickenson University Press; London: Associated University Presses, 1977): "Diaspora Jewry exercises very little influence over Israeli public policy. It is not true to suggest that it exercises no influence. . . . But it is fair to say that in the sum total of factors that constitute influences on the sum total of Israeli policies, Diaspora influence is slight" (232).

11. See the implications of this issue as summed up in my introductory essay, "The Six-Day War and the Jewish People in the Diaspora," in *The Six-Day War and World Jewry*, ed. Eli Lederhendler (Bethesda: University Press of Maryland, 2001), 1–8. There is to my knowledge only one well-known case in which a Jew still living in the Western diaspora undertook to "renationalize" himself as an Israeli: Jonathan Pollard, still serving a prison term in the United States for transmitting classified intelligence from U.S. sources to Israeli intelligence.

12. For an illuminating discussion of modernization of religious thought in the Middle Eastern Jewish societies of the nineteenth and twentieth centuries, see Zvi Zohar, *Heiru penei hamizrah: halakhah vehagut etsel hakhmei yisrael bamizrah hatikhon* (Tel Aviv: Hakibbutz Hameuhad, 2001).

13. Georges Friedmann, *The End of the Jewish People* (Garden City, N.Y.: Doubleday: 1968), translated from the original French edition, *Fin du peuple juif?* (Paris: Éditions Gallimard, 1965).

14. Ruth R. Wisse, *The Modern Jewish Canon: A Journey through Language and Culture* (New York: Free Press, 2000), 326, 338, 344–46.

15. Sharot, "Jewish and Other National and Ethnic Identities of Israeli Jews," 307, 309–10. In studies that Sharot helped conduct in the 1980s and 1990s, immigrant

populations in Israeli society were compared according to how they selected and ranked their "identities." The great majority among all groups ranked "Jewish" and "Israeli" in either first or second place, before any subethnic, country-of-origin identities; but whereas two-thirds of the immigrants from Poland and Romania ranked their Israeli identity first in importance and Jewish identity second, Moroccan and Iraqi respondents "split evenly in placing Israeli or Jewish identity in first or second place." In addition, "more than twice as many Poles and Rumanians (over 40 percent in these groups) as Moroccans and Iraqis refused to accept [subethnic, *edah*] identities" altogether (309).

16. Sharot, "Jewish and Other National and Ethnic Identities of Israeli Jews," 302, 314.

17. Sharot, "Jewish and Other National and Ethnic Identities of Israeli Jews," 310.

18. Chelm, an actual Polish town with a considerable prewar Jewish population, was folklorized in Yiddish humor as a "town of fools." To this day, wrongheaded mismanagement is dubbed worthy of Chelm.

19. Sharot, "Jewish and Other National and Ethnic Identities of Israeli Jews," 302, 303, 314.

20. As already noted (n. 15), Sharot found that Moroccan and Iraqi immigrants indicated no preference for their "Israeli" over their "Jewish" identity. Thus, "Among North African Israelis, Israeliness is a source of great pride, but it has not yet overtaken Jewishness as the most encompassing identity" (309–10).

21. On former Soviet Jews' link to Russian language and culture and their cultural self-sufficiency in Israel, see Larissa I. Remennick, "Identity Quest among Russian Jews of the 1990s: Before and after Emigration," in Krausz and Tulea, *Jewish Survival*, 251, 253–54; Carmel Zilber, "Russiah haketanah biyisrael," *Yediot aharonot*, June 1, 1997; Eliezer Ben-Rafael, Elite Olshtain, and Idit Geijst, "Identity and Language: The Social Insertion of Soviet Jews in Israel," in *Russian Jews on Three Continents: Migration and Resettlement*, ed. N. Lewin-Epstein, Yaacov Ro'i, and Paul Ritterband (London: Frank Cass, 1997), 364–88; Natalia Damian and Yehudit Rosenbaum-Tamari, "The Current Wave of Former Soviet Union Immigrants: Their Absorption: An Ongoing Survey (1990–1995)," in Elazar and Weinfeld, *Still Moving*, 141–76.

22. Sharot, "Jewish and Other National and Ethnic Identities of Israeli Jews," 312. Compare Fran Markowitz, "Emigration, Immigration and Cultural Change: Towards a Transnational 'Russian' Jewish Community," in *Jews and Jewish Life in Russia and the Soviet Union*, ed. Yaacov Ro'i (London: Frank Cass, 1995), 403–13; N. Lewin-Epstein et al. *Russian Jews on Three Continents;* Remennick, "Identity Quest among Russian Jews of the 1990s," 242, 245; and Robert Brym and Rosalina Ryvkina, "Russian Jewry Today: A Sociological Profile," *Sociological Papers* 5, no. 1 (Ramat Gan: Sociological Institute for Community Studies, Bar-Ilan University, 1996). Ethnographer Betty N. Hoffman made similar observations independently in her study of former Soviet Jews living in Hartford, Connecticut, in *Jewish Hearts: A Study of Dynamic Ethnicity in the United States and the Soviet Union* (Albany: State University of New York Press, 2001): "Without much of the cultural material that traditionally defines Jewish life, Soviet Jews have imagined a new 'Jewishness' . . . that employ[s] the old symbols in new ways as . . . focus on education for substantive economic production and family solidarity as Jewish values, generally without religious expression" (238).

23. For data on the absorption of musicians in Israel, see Yehoash Hirshberg, Bella

Brober, and Michal Ben-Zur, *Hamiktso'a: musikai: Tahalikhei klitah shel hamusikaim ha'olim* (Jerusalem: Jerusalem Institute for Israel Studies, 1997).

24. See note 9 for DellaPergola's figures on emigration from the former Soviet Union in 1990–2000. Some 980,000 (70%) were "core" Jews, while the rest were related to Jews and therefore eligible to enter Israel under the Law of Return. About 900,000 ultimately settled in Israel. Assuming that more "core" Jews than mixed-identity emigrants moved to Israel, the proportion of non-Jewish family members who entered under the Law of Return would still have been considerable, perhaps 20 percent in that decade alone. DellaPergola, "World Jewish Population, 2001," 554. According the Israel's Central Bureau of Statistics, the immigrant population from the former Soviet Union over the period from 1990–98 contained a global average of some 17.3 percent whose religion was Christian or nonclassified. That average percentage varied considerably, however, across age-groups, from a low of 5.1 percent among immigrants age 65 and older to 22.6 percent among children age 5 to 14 and 25.8 percent for adults age 25 to 34. See *Immigrant Population from the Former USSR: Selected Data, 1998* (Jerusalem: Central Bureau of Statistics, 2000), 45 (table 12).

25. Yair Sheleg, citing Nadav Zeevi's estimate for North American Jewish *'olim* published in the *Ha'aretz* supplement on January 1, 1995, puts the number at 80,000, counting Jewish immigration to Israel from 1948. He notes that in fact the number of such immigrants was larger (some 120,000) but that the sizable return-migration results in a net figure closer to 80,000. Yair Sheleg, "The North American Impact on Israeli Orthodoxy" (pamphlet published by the Institute on American Jewish-Israeli Relations of the American Jewish Committee and the Argov Institute for the Study of Israel and the Jewish People of Bar-Ilan University, February 2000), 3.

26. On the "Americanization" of Israel, see Uzi Rebhun and Chaim I. Waxman, "The 'Americanization' of Israel: A Demographic, Cultural and Political Evaluation," *Israel Studies* 5, no. 1 (2000): 65–91. Israeli actress Tamy Ben-Tor recently performed a show exclusively in English in a Tel Aviv theater filled with native Israelis, as the *Ha'aretz* English edition reported in its Friday supplement for 13 September 2002: "America is all over the place," she told the paper. "Nearly everything we watch on TV is American. We all have a relationship with [America]. No one says to me, 'What is this obscure, exotic culture you are dealing with?'" (A9).

27. Interesting reports on the role of Americans in Israeli feminism, religious Orthodoxy, and politics have been published in a pamphlet series by the Institute on American Jewish-Israeli Relations of the American Jewish Committee and the Argov Institute for the Study of Israel and the Jewish People of Bar-Ilan University: Rochelle Furstenberg, "The Women's Movement in Israel" (November 1994); Avi Kay, "Making Themselves Heard: The Impact of North American Olim on Israeli Protest Politics" (January 1996); and Sheleg, "The North American Impact on Israeli Orthodoxy."

28. Sheleg's report on American Orthodoxy in Israel, cited previously (nn. 24, 26), stresses the underrepresentation of American Orthodox rabbis in national-political discourse and their corresponding overrepresentation in academic and spiritual matters. A good case could also be made for the impact made on the lifestyle of Orthodox women in Israel by American Orthodox women. On the feminization of Orthodox life in Israel, see Tamar Ross, "Modern Orthodoxy and the Challenge of Feminism," in *Jews and Gender: The Challenge to Hierarchy. Studies in Contemporary Jewry*, ed. Jonathan Frankel. Vol. 16 (New York: Oxford University Press, 2000), 3–38. Compare Sylvia Barack Fishman, "Women's Transformations of Public Judaism: Religiosity, Egalitar-

ianism, and the Symbolic Power of Changing Gender Roles," in Lederhendler, *Who Owns Judaism?*, 146–48.

29. There were only four Conservative congregations in Israel in 1972.

30. An indication of the small size of the non-Orthodox sector is the fact that non-Orthodox rabbis who live in Israel are significantly underemployed even during the High Holidays. This surplus of non-Orthodox rabbis over congregations has contributed directly to the phenomenon of annual trips by such rabbis to serve in American and European congregations over the holiday season. See *Ha'aretz* English edition, 13 September 2002, A7.

Instructive comments on the problems of the non-Orthodox movements in relation to religious life in Israel are made by Ezra Kopelowitz, "Shifting Boundaries of Religious Authority: A Comparative Historical Study of the Role of Religious Movements in the Conflict between Jews in Israel and the United States" (Ph.D. diss., The Hebrew University, 2000). Compare Allon Gal and Alfred Gottschalk, eds., *Beyond Survival and Philanthropy: American Jewry and Israel* (Cincinnati: Hebrew Union College Press and Wayne State University Press, 2000), and Ofer Schiff, "Hashonut keideologiah shel solidariut yehudit," *'Iyunim bitekumat yisrael*, Vol. 10 (Sde Boker: Ben-Gurion Research Center and Ben-Gurion University of the Negev, 2000), 701–2.

For the history of the Jewish Theological Seminary and the Conservative movement's efforts to develop its ties in Israel since 1948, see Eli Lederhendler, "The Ongoing Dialogue: The Seminary and the Challenge of Israel," in *Tradition Renewed: A History of the Jewish Theological Seminary: Vol. II—Beyond the Academy*, ed. Jack Wertheimer (New York: Jewish Theological Seminary of America, 1997), 179–270. Compare Harvey Meirovich, *The Shaping of Masorti Judaism in Israel*, copublished by the Institute of American Jewish-Israeli Relations of the American Jewish Committee and the Argov Center for the Study of Israel and the Jewish People of Bar-Ilan University.

31. On several levels, it may be said that the Israeli TALI network has done what the Solomon Schechter schools in America cannot hope to accomplish: (1) Because TALI schools are public, not private, schools (as the Schechter schools in America must be), they are part of the state educational establishment, and their potential pool of student registration is far more variegated in terms of social class. (2) The "general" and "Jewish" subjects taught in TALI schools both belong to the same curriculum, both are taught in Hebrew, and both derive from largely overlapping cultural discourses of "Israeliness" and "Jewishness"—thus enabling a level of pedagogic, linguistic, and cultural interpenetration of Jewish and general learning that cannot be fully realized in the American setting.

32. On the coexistence of ethnic and Israeli identities, see Sharot, "Jewish and Other National and Ethnic Identities." On "place attachment" and shifting diaspora identities, see also Rebecca Kobrin, "Conflicting Diasporas, Shifting Centers: Migration and Identity in a Transnational Polish Jewish Community, 1878–1952" (Ph.D. diss., University of Pennsylvania, 2002).

33. Liebman, *Pressure without Sanctions*, 10–11.

34. Baruch Kimmerling's recent book, *The Invention and Decline of Israeliness: State, Society, and the Military* (Berkeley: University of California Press, 2001), takes a monochromatic approach to Israeli national identity, viewing its complex network of subgroups as "Jewish" identities competing or dissolving "Israeliness" in a new pattern of "cultural segmentation" (234) and "the evaporation of the image of a single, unified Israeli society [and] the diminishment of a hegemonic secular Hebrew culture" (1–2).

Some of the new subcultures, he asserts, aim "to replace the previous hegemony with a new one by achieving political and cultural dominance, and either to force their own rules of the game and versions of collective identity on all the other sociocultural segments or to exclude them from the collectivity" (234–35). Driven to hyperbole by his own rhetoric and perhaps by his political leanings, he writes further, "At the present time, cultural wars between the segments oscillate and vary between periods of dormancy and sudden eruptions of open conflict, sometimes approaching civil war" (112). The author of such words has obviously never witnessed civil war.

For a different, more nuanced view, see Israeli author Amos Oz's recent remarks on the extremely variegated nature of "Israeli" lifestyles and values, not as a recent innovation but as originating in the prestate Yishuv itself. "And what came of it?" he asks about the present situation: "Neither the kingdom of David and Solomon, nor the shtetl, nor a Marxist paradise, nor yet a commonwealth of anarcho-religious communities, [but] a Mediterranean country, hot-tempered, sometimes generous, at times terribly involved in its own complexes, a veritable cultural volcano, a religious, social, ethnic volcano—and I must say, that in itself is not so terrible." *Yahadut umedinah: Masot umehkarim*, no. 1: *Yisrael—Halomot umetsiut. Du-siah: Harav Yonatan Sacks—Amos Oz, 24 bemai 2001* (Ramat Gan: Bar-Ilan University, 2002), 17.

35. Yossi Beilin, *Moto shel hadod meamerikah: Yehudim bameah ha-21* (Tel Aviv: Yediot Aharonot "Hemed Books," 1999), makes the combined argument that (1) diaspora Jews who wish donate funds to specific institutions in Israel or Israeli cultural causes, as a means of expressing their involvement and commitment, ought to do so (giving the example of the women of the Women's International Zionist Organization who support a network of day care centers for preschoolers) but that (2) under no circumstances ought diaspora Jewry in organized concert be continuing a blanket subsidy of Israeli social welfare budgets in an effort to aid the poor in Israel, a task properly belonging to the State of Israel through its Ministry of Labor and Welfare and that (3) the "beggarly" image of Israel in the eyes of the diaspora communities is anachronistic, unfortunate, humiliating, and counterproductive to a decent reciprocity between Israel and Jews elsewhere (118–21, 161–65).

From another angle, it has been alleged by an economist at Bar-Ilan University that financial donations to Israel have actually done the Israeli economy more harm than good. This counterintuitive contention is the sort of thing that makes noneconomists cringe. See Warren Young, "The Impact of American Jewry on the Israeli Economy," published by the Institute on American Jewish-Israeli Relations of the American Jewish Committee and the Argov Center for the Study of Israel and the Jewish People of Bar-Ilan University, April 2001.

36. My discussion here is heavily indebted to Derek J. Penslar's masterful study *Shylock's Children: Economics and Jewish Identity in Modern Europe* (Berkeley: University of California Press, 2001), esp. chaps. 3, 5, and 6.

37. *Kehillah* (Hebrew; Yiddish, *kehile*): the term for a local Jewish community.

38. *Kehillah.*

39. On the Alliance Israélite schools, see the documentary study by Aron Rodrigue, *Images of Sephardi and Eastern Jewries in Transition: The Teachers of the Alliance Israélite Universelle, 1860–1939* (Seattle: University of Washington Press, 1993). Compare Aron Rodrigue and Esther Benbassa, *Sephardi Jewry: A History of the Judeo-Spanish Community, 14th–20th Centuries* (Berkeley: University of California Press, 1993), 83–89, and Penslar, *Shylock's Children*, 227–32.

Social historian Daniel Soyer raises another interesting, even subtler point regarding philanthropic work and its effect on Jewish integration. In his study of New York Jewish immigrant hometown societies (*landsmanshaftn*) between the 1880s and the 1930s, he found that by coming to the financial assistance of their hometowns in World War I and the interwar era, these immigrants helped transform their own self-image from that of poor immigrants requiring aid from wealthier Jews to that of "American" Jews capable of using their hard-won economic success on behalf of others. See Daniel Soyer, *Jewish Immigrant Associations and American Identity in New York, 1880–1939* (Cambridge, Mass.: Harvard University Press, 1997). See also Kobrin, "Conflicting Diasporas," chap. 3, on philanthropy and *landsmanshaftn*.

40. Robert Wistrich, ed., *Terms of Survival: The Jewish World since 1945* (London: Routledge, 1995); Marc Dollinger, *Quest for Inclusion: Jews and Liberalism in Modern America* (Princeton, N.J.: Princeton University Press, 2000), 214–27; Ted Solotaroff and Nessa Rapoport, eds., *Writing Our Way Home: Contemporary Stories by American Jewish Writers* (New York: Schocken Books, 1992); Judith Friedlander, "The Six-Day War and the 'Jewish Question' in France," in Lederhendler, *The Six-Day War and World Jewry*, 125–36; Pierre Birnbaum, "French Jews: Between Citizenship and Community," in *Values, Interests and Identity: Jews and Politics in a Changing World. Studies in Contemporary Jewry*, ed. Peter Y. Medding. Vol. 11 (New York: Oxford University Press, 1995), 37–49; L. Sandy Maisel and Ira N. Forman, eds., *Jews in American Politics* (Lanham, Md.: Rowman & Littlefield, 2001); David Biale et al., eds., *Insider/Outsider: American Jews and Multiculturalism* (Berkeley: University of California Press, 1998); and Jonathan Webber, ed., *Jewish Identities in the New Europe* (London: Littman Library of Jewish Civilization and Oxford Centre for Hebrew and Jewish Studies, 1994).

41. Matti Golan, *Kesef temurat dam: Yahadut amerikah neged medinat yisrael* (Tel Aviv: Kinneret, 1992).

42. There are also internal structural reasons why philanthropy is the dominant mode of relating to Israel. Jewish communities in the diaspora, being voluntary societies, are organized but have no true "governing" body; instead, there is a network of interlaced groups whose existence depends directly on the ability to raise funds to support any collective purpose and thus relies on a relatively small number of very wealthy donors. As political historian David Vital comments, "These [wealthy leading donors] are the real makers and breakers in the organized communities of the Diaspora, especially in the United States." David Vital, *The Future of the Jews* (Cambridge, Mass.: Harvard University Press, 1990), 123.

43. Solomon Schechter (1847–1915) moved from Cambridge, England, to New York in 1902 to take charge of the Jewish Theological Seminary. In some ways there has even been a regression: shortly after I completed my undergraduate studies at the Conservative movement's Jewish Theological Seminary (in 1974), the language of instruction at the Seminary College was switched from Hebrew to English.

44. Mordecai M. Kaplan, "Toward the Formulation of Guiding Principles for the Conservative Movement," supplement to *Conservative Judaism*, no. 6 (May 1950): 18, and *A New Zionism* (New York: Herzl Press and the Jewish Reconstructionist Press, 1959): chap. 4. Compare Lederhendler, "The Ongoing Dialogue," 204–5; Beilin, *Moto shel hadod meamerikah*, 170–75; Arik Carmon, *Mamlakhtiut yehudit* (Tel Aviv: Hakibbutz Hameuhad and the Israel Democracy Institute, 1994), 133, 139–42; Samuel Norich, *What Will Bind Us Now? A Report on the Institutional Ties between Israel and American Jewry* (West Palm Beach, Fla.: Center for Middle East Peace and Economic Coop-

eration, 1994), 74–75; and Israeli-American Forum, unpublished memoranda and correspondence, 1998–2001 (in the possession of the author). Of special interest are suggestions raised in papers regarding U.S. Jewry's possible participation in the Israeli political process, including lobbying for changes in the Israeli electoral system and the establishment of an international Jewish "academy" to promote pluralism in Israel: "Report on Study Group, Israel-Diaspora Discussion, June 18, 1998," by Steven L. Spiegel; "Summary and Discussion Points for Study Group—Israel-Diaspora Meeting, August 17, 1998," by Steven L. Spiegel; "Parliamentary and Institutional Reform," committee report, 1–2 May 2000, at a meeting held in Washington, D.C., which "noted the emergence of a proposal to create a kind of AIPAC representing American Jews in Israel, perhaps, as Haim Shaked proposed, a watchdog committee representing and lobbying for American Jewish interests" (2). The now-defunct Forum was cosponsored by the Institute for Jewish and Community Research in San Francisco, California. On the individuals involved and their ideas, see "Group of Senators, Mega-Givers Drafts New Covenant," *Forward*, October 1, 1999, and "Israeli, Yank Bigs Huddling in Secret to Map Future of Diaspora Relations," *Forward*, May 5, 2000. AIPAC, the America-Israel Public Affairs Committee, is the pro-Israel lobby in Washington, D.C.

45. Michael Walzer et al., eds., *The Jewish Political Tradition. Volume 1: Authority* (New Haven, Conn.: Yale University Press, 2000).

46. Baron, "The Jewish Commonwealths and the Dispersions," 24.

47. Examples in this area would include the activities of the New Israel Fund, which has supported progressive nonprofit organizations involved in Arab–Jewish cooperation, gender equality, and the like; the Rabin Center in Tel Aviv and the Shalem Center in Jerusalem, research centers with pronounced political profiles; and the bankrolling by foreign donors of Binyamin Netanyahu's, Ehud Barak's, and Ariel Sharon's campaigns for election as prime minister in the three most recent electoral contests.

48. On the most recent attempt, the previously mentioned Israeli-American Forum (see n. 40), see unpublished memoranda and correspondence. On the Center for Israel-Diaspora Cultural Relations, whose director refers to it as a Jewish version of the British Council, see "If Culture Be the Food of Jews, Play On," *Ha'aretz* English edition, supplement, 20 September 2002, A7.

49. Israel Radio has a weekly talk show that often takes up news items from around the Jewish world. I have invariably been called to give a telephone interview for this program when the host wishes to speak about anti-Semitic attacks against American Jews but not on any other occasion.

CHAPTER 5

Fifty Years of Israeli Discourse on the Holocaust: Characteristics and Dilemmas

Dalia Ofer

> I have nothing to add, everything is so clear. On the other hand, everything is so obscure and incomprehensible.
>
> —Sala Novokovitz, a schoolgirl, during a visit to Maidanek

> When will the Holocaust finally turn into a myth, a parable, a national ceremony one day a year? [And when] will one cease to discuss it, to argue, to quarrel, to pester?
>
> —Aharon Megged, Holocaust Memorial Day 1989
> (*Yediot Aharonot*, May 2)

Public discourse about the Holocaust, which already began in the 1940s in what was to become a painful, lengthy process of trying to define and understand it, has not ceased to this very day. This discourse is comprised of various and diverse themes whose roots lie in the effort to understand the fate of the Jewish people and to comprehend how such an absolute collapse of human values was possible. This dilemma was most succinctly phrased by Rabbi Yitzhak Meir Levin, a representative of the ultrareligious Agudat Yisrael Party in the Knesset, the Israel parliament: "Our human intellect is too limited to understand what happened here, and we also lack a prophet and seer to explain and interpret it for us."[1]

A "true" interpretation of the past was needed in order to understand the present and future tendencies in the area of relations between Jews and non-Jews, between Israel and the Diaspora Jewish communities, and how Jewish identity will be shaped in Israel. As is the case with every historical examination and analysis, the present and contemporary conditions of daily life are weighty factors in shaping our conceptualization of the past and constructing the collective painful memory.

Hesitancy concerning these issues was overt, expressed in various ways and diverse forums already in the second half of the 1940s and during Israel's first decade. There were stormy outbursts in the 1950s over key political events, such as the reparations agreement with West Germany, the Grünwald trial and "Kasztner Affair," and relations with and the sale of arms to Germany. However, the Holocaust was also placed on the public agenda in the wake of debates in the Knesset concerning the "Law for the Punishment of Nazis and Nazi Collaborators," exemption from property taxes of crippled Holocaust survivors, the law establishing Yad Vashem, and the discussions concerning the character of the Holocaust Martyrs' and Heroes' Remembrance Day. In addition, public attention was attracted by publication of Holocaust memoirs and diaries as well as anthologies such as *The Book of the Partisans* and *The Ghetto Fighters Book*, the staging of a dramatized version of Anne Frank's diary by the Habimah Theater, and more.

In this chapter, I examine some substantial issues that are central to an understanding of the discourse on the Holocaust in Israel. These reappear in changing forms and formulations in relation to many other issues that gained the attention of the Israeli public at different periods of time. It is only natural that the foci of the discourse are central events such as trials, wars, political confrontations, and changing cultural and national perceptions. Elsewhere I have argued that the many hues and shades in the Israeli discourse on the Holocaust did not develop in a linear upward projection. Yet, despite the fact that there were ups and downs in its development, I believe that there has been a constant dialogue between the events of World War II and the Holocaust and the Jewish public in Israel.[2]

One of the characteristics of the discourse on the Holocaust is that it is replete with opposites. Rhetoric on the Holocaust was, in the widest sense, of a political, ideological, and personal nature, reflecting a wide consensus on the one hand and continuous criticism of the manner in which that consensus was interpreted on the other. Criticism took the form of arguments between secular and religious Jews or between the Left and the Right and even diverse nuances within each of these camps. These confrontations were marked by their content and language, and in my opinion their roots lie in the substance of the Holocaust itself: it represents the very essence of evil, an evil that undermines the ability to behave in accordance with the accepted norms and values of regular circumstances. At the same time, we are witness to events and the acts of human beings that reflect an impressive ability to contend with the ultimate evil. A painful and troubling past such as the Holocaust is both confusing and challenging. This emotional complexity leads to hesitation between two paths: between the moral duty to remember and not forget as a guarantee of life and the difficulty of choosing what and whom to remember on both the national and the individual level.

REMEMBRANCE: THE INDIVIDUAL AND THE COLLECTIVE

On Remembrance Day in 1956, Abba Kovner said, "He who says: forget nothing—in the end will remember nothing, for remembering everything leads to a state of madness; but to forget everything is in effect a betrayal of life."[3] Kovner pointed to two paths that seemingly contradict one another. On the one hand, he spoke of restricting remembrance, for remembrance may frustrate the ability to face up to life; on the other hand, he saw remembrance as the key to life. To forget is not betrayal of the massacred or their memory but betrayal of life itself. The right degree of remembrance—of commemoration and examination of the past—is the key to the proper shaping of life that continues to unfold in the State of Israel. Works of belles lettres that re-create the inner world of the survivors and their life in the post-Holocaust period most impressively indicate the manner in which various persons chose to seek a balance between remembrance and day-to-day reality and show to what degree memory was fleeting and uncontrollable during certain periods of their lives.[4] The tension between reshaping memory and relinquishing memory is characteristic of the discourse of both the individual and society.

From the point of view of society at large, former Foreign Minister and Prime Minister Moshe Sharett came forward with an excellent formulation of the issue in an address to the Remembrance Day ceremony on April 30, 1954:

> Our nation was saved from total destruction thanks to the memory of its past and its sons' lust for life. . . . We are heading toward a future loaded with memory, and we must shape this future—and that is one of the roles of Yad Vashem. It must turn suffering, disgrace, blood, and bravery into a heritage for all generations to come. Our state and freedom will not survive if for one day it forgets the vale of tears out of which it arose.[5]

Sharett drew a connection between the future of the Israeli state and society and remembrance, claiming that freedom and the existence of the state are dependent on remembrance. Remembrance bears within it opposing components: disgrace, blood, suffering, and bravery. Sharett did not elaborate on these components, and it would seem that all his listeners needed no further explanation. He limited himself to stressing that remembrance could continue to exist only if the narrative of the Holocaust was imparted to the future generations, that is, through intentional study. Therefore, the establishment of Yad Vashem as the institution responsible for shaping and preserving the memory of the Holocaust is both an important and a wise act. What emerges from Sharett's address is that Yad Vashem should shape a hegemonic narrative of the Holocaust, its lessons, and its meaning.

Though there was widespread agreement concerning the importance of Yad Vashem as a national state institution for the commemoration of the Holocaust, at the same time there was also public recognition of the value of other institutions that had preceded Yad Vashem and stressed various aspects of Holocaust history. The experience gained during the short period between the end of World War II and the passing of the Remembrance of the Holocaust and Heroism Law (Yad Vashem) in 1953, indicates that ideological and political differences lead to differing historical interpretations and that it is difficult to arrive at one dominating narrative of the Holocaust.[6]

Collective memory, then, is shaped by active acquisition of knowledge and by the patterns of commemoration; it is these that influence how one relates to the past and one's ability to shape the future. In the Knesset debate after the Yad Vashem Bill was first tabled, Minister of Education and Culture Ben-Zion Dinur pointed out that this was a unique law that deviated from the normal process of legislation, for it dealt with remembrance, even commanding one to remember, whereas normally a law deals with actions. So the minister went on to delineate the areas in which Yad Vashem would act, whose result would be the preservation and shaping of the "collective memory." Dinur presented the proposed law as a direct continuation of efforts that Jews had begun to make under Nazi oppression and in the death camps. The exhortation that was issued (already in occupied Europe) by historians Simon Dubnov and Emmanuel Ringelblum as well as by other leaders calling on Jews to record their experiences and to collect documentation was one of the cornerstones of the Yad Vashem Law. Just as they had encouraged literati and simple folk to keep diaries and to hide them or entrust them for safekeeping into the hands of trustworthy people, so would Yad Vashem assemble these source materials, record testimonies, and collect documentation on all aspects of the Holocaust; these materials would then serve the authors and historians who would labor to reconstruct the historical narrative. Dinur read from a proclamation issued by Jewish inmates in Auschwitz who planned to publish a documentary record of life in the camp:

> And so, comrades, write, jot down short and sharp [notations], as short as the days that are left us to live, as sharp as the knives that are pointed at our hearts. A few pages will survive for YIVO, for the archives of Jewish suffering; they will be read by those of our brethren who will survive and be free, and perhaps they will also learn something from them. And we ask of Fate: May it please You to place our tears in your water bag, so that they come into trustworthy hands and achieve Redemption.[7]

Thus, preservation of memory and shaping it into collective or national memory calls for purposeful, premeditated action and the establishment of one central institution in which the various efforts related to preservation of the memory of the Holocaust and the commemoration of its victims would be organized and concentrated.

What was expressed over and over again in the speeches of Knesset members during the debate on the proposed legislation and in the press was the fear that the younger generation would know nothing about the Holocaust and would not understand its significance because members of that generation lacked personal experience and memories of that horrendous event and because they had no affinity for the culture and knowledge without which it was impossible to understand that period in Jewish history. That is what lent great importance to the didactic objectives that underlay the establishment of Yad Vashem: to teach the younger generation, which is unfamiliar with Jewish life in the Diaspora, so that it comes to know and understand the meaning of its existence.[8] The Yad Vashem Law, together with the formal declaration of 27 Nissan (generally in April) as Holocaust Martyrs' and Heroes' Remembrance Day, created, already during Israel's first decade, a framework in time and space in which the ritual for remembrance and commemoration was forged. These two acts provided legitimization to the efforts to shape remembrance, with the intention of limiting it to public, state-originated rituals. However, the Yad Vashem Law was enacted after many other frameworks had already been established and had set up their own patterns and sites of commemoration. These included Kibbutz Lohamei Hageta'ot and its Ghetto Fighters Museum; Kibbutz Yad Mordechai, which served as a commemoration site for members of Hashomer Hatzair; and the Holocaust Cellar on Mount Zion in Jerusalem.

Fear that the Holocaust would be forgotten was common to individuals, to the public at large, and to the political leadership. Survivors related their experiences time and again to acquaintances and family members and also began to collect and publish them in books commemorating communities that had been annihilated. Public gatherings and commemoration ceremonies were also convened by survivors together with members of their former communities or only with other survivors, at which they repeatedly reminisced about their past life. Lizzie Doron shares with us one such bizarre ritual. Lizzie's mother and four other lady friends met regularly for coffee every two weeks. This was a ritual in which they expressed their anger, sorrow, and pain—a sort of regular self-cleansing. These women used to close the shutters and windows so that light and the outside world would not penetrate and disturb their intimacy. It was only then that they began to sigh, weep, and curse, all accompanied by drinking coffee. This would continue until one of the participants would express a desire to invite an "external element"—God—into the room. At this stage, the ritual came to an abrupt end. No force in the world could join the "club" if it had not been "there," in the camps. God had been absent then, so there was no room for Him now.[9]

Despite all these efforts, some of the survivors began to fear that remembrance of the Holocaust was fading away and that the events of everyday life were taking center stage. The title that Yehuda Ariel gave his article in *Ha'aretz* in 1964, "They Have Begun to Write because Remembrance of the Past Is Fading," was a true depiction of the emotions of individuals. His article concerned the motives of authors who decided to deposit their manuscripts of personal memoirs in the archives of Kibbutz Lohamei Hageta'ot. He quotes one of them as saying,

> I began to write after realizing that the experiences I went through during the Holocaust were beginning to blur in my mind. The first to disappear from my consciousness were family names and dates, the names of friends with whom I shared a terrible fate and whom I was sure that I would remember to my dying day; today I only recall them with difficulty. Out of fear that other details and memories would also become obscured, I set out to write. . . . Time has passed, and everyone has rearranged his life in some manner. What we then believed to be just and correct now causes us to have reservations and feel revulsion. What we once thought to be a right now seems to us to be a crime. Children will grow up who have been educated differently and think differently. I don't know if my writings will interest anyone, but I am not writing for fame. I am sitting down to write because I believe this to be an obligation toward myself, so that I will depict things as they really were. The decision to begin writing has been part of me for a long time. In the past, however, when I set down reminiscences on paper I destroyed them.[10]

Such writings resulted from motivations different from those that prompted the documentation of the Holocaust noted previously that Jews in Europe had begun to collect in the camps and ghettos while the war was still being waged. Those Jews collected documentation and began to record testimonies because the events they experienced seemed to be so incredible that, even during the first stages of Nazi occupation, they feared that no one would believe that they had actually occurred. When the deportations began, the fear that no one would survive to tell the tale increased. It was their wish that future generations should be aware of the historical narrative of the Holocaust and of the terrible experiences they had undergone.

In the 1950s, many survivors began to forget, and their memories of the Holocaust became blurred, so they began to set down their past experiences in writing. This became very widespread as time passed, resulting in an enormous number of volumes of memoirs and documentation committed to writing many years after the event. Publication of memoirs or the deposit of such manuscripts in archives is an expression of the authors' desire that their personal experiences should serve as a source for study and thus contribute to forging the historical narrative of the Holocaust.

Another motive for recording or publishing memoirs and introspective thoughts was that survivors were now looking back at their past from the vantage point of a person who had reached old age. They wanted to share with others "how a person in his late fifties contemplates passages of memory and imagination that remain [with him] from the questioning world of the child in those days."[11] This was no well-ordered narrative, nor did it have literary merit; however, it does reflect a desire to bring past experiences and the reaction to them into the public domain. Thus, the purpose of such memoirs, which historian Dov Kulka has called "scenes from the metropolis of death" or "childhood scenes from Auschwitz," was to add another detail or vantage point to the collective memory.

The tension between memory and forgetfulness, which is a common trait of individuals, is in my opinion one of the causes of the conflicting emotions and verbal contradictions that we encounter in the discourse on the Holocaust. On the one hand, there is a voice that sees in the blurring of memory a positive development that perhaps symbolizes the return to "normal" life. On the other hand, a second, accompanying voice bemoans what is missing or lacking. The individual who survived and continues to live out his life cannot escape the feeling that the dead are also his partners. As survivors have testified, images of the dead turn up at important turning points in their post-Holocaust lives: holidays, wedding festivities, births, and deaths. The visages of family members, friends, and neighbors from hometowns and villages have remained as they were, while the survivors have changed greatly. While the suffering, hunger, and fear they experienced in those dark days are gradually becoming blurred, their traumatic significance continues to accompany their lives.

This is how Lizzie Doron begins her book:

> "On a high hill, somewhere in far-away Europe, stands a castle in which resides a royal dynasty; no one knew about the dynasty, and I am the only witness to the history of the castle." That is what Helena told us and said no more, she did not speak. She may have added a few sentences, closing or opening sentences, sometimes short, sometimes long; the longer ones all referred to the present, the shorter to the past, and there was no [reference to the] future. At every opportunity she thought of the castle once again, for that is where she was born and there she had seen other days.
>
> And in daily life, in the big city, in a dull neighborhood which contains neither a hill nor a castle, at the intersection of Victory Street with Heroism Street, Helena lives a different life in the second story of a two-story house.[12]

It is only fair to ask whether it is possible to part with the past, as was often suggested to survivors after the war, or perhaps such a breaking away is impossible, and the association between past and present, between family members who are no longer and those recently born and added to the family, takes on a new form. Are the relationships between past and present supported by the public commemoration ceremonies, by programs about the Holocaust in the electronic media, and by the profusion of discussion and examination of the Holocaust that is conducted in cultural and artistic frameworks?

This tension, prevalent among individual survivors, can take an opposite form, as we learn from one of the protagonists in Lizzie Doron's book. She has this to say about her sister: "She suffered there, but here too, here too, poor soul, she is still there, and there is no suffering greater than that."[13] This is a perfect example of what Abba Kovner was referring to in the passage quoted earlier.

The difficulty of transferring the experiences undergone by individuals to the public sphere is sometimes formulated positively. Consider the following passage from an article titled "Faithfulness to Historical Memory":

> Every Jew, by his very being a Jew, was a potential victim. And if in the Haggadah[14] we read words of heartfelt identification, "In every generation a man must consider himself as if he participated in the exodus from Egypt," then we may say—without any exaggeration and without fantastic associations—that every Jew in our generation must see himself as if he was physically in the Nazi inferno.[15]

This is a frightening and oppressive demand to make, and it is difficult to say whether it can be realized. It blurs the distinction between here (Israel) and there (the Diaspora) and forcefully claims that the Israeli Jew is a potential victim.

The author of this article criticizes Israeli government policy vis-à-vis Germany (he is referring to the sale of Uzi submachine guns to Germany in 1959) and remonstrates against the erasure from public consciousness of the Holocaust as one of the founding experiences of Israeli reality. This argument brings him from the realm of the individual to that of the collective. He claims that the desire to forge Israeli identity by means of a bridge to the distant past of biblical times whose objective is to make one forget that the recent past—the Holocaust—cannot succeed.

According to this author, then, knowledge of the Holocaust period is necessary not only to safeguard freedom but also for the forging of Israeli identity. Internalizing the past becomes, in effect, an important step in the creation and shaping of Israeli identity. He believes that without an understanding of the recent past—the reality of diverse Jewish life in the Diaspora—one cannot gain a true understanding of the Israeli experience. Historical interpretation that creates an abyss between the Holocaust and the establishment of Israel, claims the author, distorts the ability to understand reality. Despite the tremendous difference between these events, one that is marked primarily by despair and isolation and the other by victory and independence, "both events spring from one root. Each of them—the Holocaust of the People of Israel and the independence of the State of Israel—are a true reflection of the People of Israel in our generation."[16] Once again, we are faced with the internal contradiction between destruction and redemption.

These four examples represent attitudes toward the Holocaust and the shaping of the historical narrative expressed on different occasions. Kovner and Sharett addressed Holocaust Memorial Day ceremonies, occasions intended to preserve and shape historical memory. Their messages, therefore, are phrased in uncompromising and clear language. Individual memoirs expose personal soul-searching and seeking of direction, while the decision to deposit such written memoirs in the archives of Kibbutz Lohamei Hageta'ot represents an act of transferring personal experiences to the public sphere.

Finally, the article "Faithfulness to Historical Memory" presents this connection between the individual and the collective in language that bears a didactic message: faithfulness means remembering the Holocaust and facing up to its meaning and significance, while forgetting, ignoring. or causing one to forget the Holocaust means unfaithfulness. In this case, we are witness to the transfer of remembrance of the Holocaust from the personal to the public and political spheres.

REMEMBRANCE, FORGIVENESS, AND REVENGE

After having discussed the relationship between individual and collective memory, it is fitting to examine a phrase that crops up on different occasions in the Israeli discourse on the Holocaust: "To remember and not to forget, to remember and not to forgive," or, in another formulation, "We shall not forget and shall not forgive."[17] Remembrance is presented as contrasted to forgiveness and forgiveness as contrasted to revenge. In the public discourse, forgiveness and revenge are two opposites that cannot be reconciled: on the one hand, there is no act of revenge that can fit the immensity of the crimes; on the other, forgiveness is impossible, for that would entail betraying remembrance of the Holocaust, which has become a moral duty that is central to the Israeli experience. The renewal of Jewish life in Israel and the strengthening and firm establishment of the State of Israel are generally viewed as a form of revenge. Such "revenge" is also connected to what many understand to be "the lesson of the Holocaust," to which we shall return. For the moment, however, it is necessary to ask, What is the relationship between remembrance, forgiveness, and revenge?

This problematic relationship arose during a public debate over the Israeli government's decision to sell Uzi submachine guns to Germany in 1959. The decision became public knowledge only many weeks after it was taken and led to another round of stormy public debate about Israeli–German relations.[18] An editorial in *Ha'aretz* asked, "Are the efforts to inculcate 'Jewish consciousness' and to establish institutions to further the remembrance of the Holocaust compatible with this agreement?"[19]

In short interviews conducted by *Ha'aretz*, those polled were asked for their opinion on the arms transaction. A minority thought that since the Holocaust is a personal memory for many Israelis and because its history and meaning are being imparted to the general public by means of state institutions in public commemoration ceremonies, there is no danger of it being forgotten. Therefore, it is justified to treat the sale of arms in a matter-of-fact manner. Active public memory will ensure that the Germans are not forgiven, while the transaction serves Israel's economic and political interests. Others thought that the arms deal indicates that there is a tendency to blur the memory of the Holocaust, to forgive the Germans, and to conduct an absolutely normal relationship with them. There were even some who supported this stance by claiming that the past is behind us and that action should be based on rational considerations. Many of those polled believed that the past, in the form of the Holocaust period, should not determine Israel's policy in the present.

In letters to the editor, readers wrote that we must learn the lesson of the Holocaust, and that lesson is an obligation to understand why it happened and to prevent its recurrence. The lesson of the Holocaust also obliges us to take active steps to preserve the memory of the Holocaust through its study and by setting a certain date on which formal memorial and commemorative ceremonies will be conducted. The intention of those who opposed the arms deal was to prevent the rearming of Germany, while its supporters believed that it would strengthen Israel; in other words, the two sides used "lessons of the Holocaust" to support their opposing stands. These two contentions appear as complementary or contradictory arguments in statements by both the supporters and the opponents of the arms deal.[20]

Another question that came to the fore during the public controversy was, What would the Holocaust victims have said about the conduct of Israel's leaders, Ben-Gurion and Dayan, had it been possible for them to express an opinion? Those who raised this question conferred on the issue at hand a mystical aspect out of a desire to lend it an aura of historical authenticity, for had the victims (who seemingly reflect collective memory, in contrast to personal memory, which reflects only the individual) been able to reply, their answers would be free of all contemporary political distortions.[21] Such a claim seems to be affording memory an independent status, as if it could be objective and not constructed by contemporary social, political, and cultural forces.

What is the connection between forgiving and forgetting? He who does not remember cannot forgive. Thus, we see that the terms "remembrance," "forgetting," and "forgiving" are not clearly delineated and defined in Israeli public discourse. Some of the participants in the discourse clearly state that applying rational considerations in relation to Germany does not mean forgiveness.

An additional question raised at this time was whether Holocaust survivors or Israelis who did not experience the Holocaust could forgive in the name of the victims. Among the respondents, there was clear differentiation between those who personally went through the Holocaust and whose family members perished in the camps and those whose only experience of the Holocaust was through the social agents of remembrance and commemoration. Among the respondents were Israelis whose families had been annihilated in Europe and others who had come to the country from outside Europe.[22]

Another scene from Lizzie Doron's book exemplifies, in simple yet forceful language, the gap between persons of different backgrounds. She accompanied her mother's search for family members or acquaintances from her hometown. In one of these efforts, they came to a *moshav* (smallholders' village) near Haifa where a man from Poland bearing their family name lived. Helena introduced herself. "I remember something like that," he answered in fluent

Hebrew, his eyes seemingly closed under twitching eyelids. "How much can I remember?" he asked himself. "I left Poland as a kid and my parents broke off all contact with me." We sat down on a bench, and he asked, "Why is your girl so pale and skinny? What is this Diaspora-style clothing? And tell me, why didn't you come before the war?" Helena didn't answer his questions. Mark went on and related, with great satisfaction, that he had always been a Zionist and admired himself for the fact that he had rebelled against his parents at such an early age and saved his life. Helena recited the names of those who had died and asked, sorrowfully, on the verge of tears, "Maybe you heard [of them]? Perhaps you know [them]?"And he repeated, "I left at a very early age. I don't remember and don't know."[23]

This young Israeli who changed his name to Meir Zabar[24] and whose original given name, Mark, was used only as a nickname cut himself off from the past and finds it difficult to remember. And despite the fact that he cut himself off from the Diaspora before the war and before the annihilation of the communities in which he grew up, he himself and his inability to remember his childhood surroundings embody the difficulty in bridging the gap between the experiences of the individual and the experience that state institutions wish to impart as "the lesson of the Holocaust." At the same time, he does very forthrightly express the "Zionist lesson" of the Holocaust, for his self-separation from the Diaspora was his way of ensuring his life, and he was very proud of it (see discussion later in this chapter).

Yet the blurring of the memory of the Holocaust is rectified to some degree through a somewhat vague way in Israelis who did not personally experience the Holocaust yet who repeat the narrative of that horrendous event to themselves. We can see this, almost allegorically, in another scene included in Lizzie Doron's book. She recalls that at times "visitors" used to join the regular meetings her mother conducted with her survivor lady friends once every two weeks. Since the visitors were from "there," they could participate. As a young girl, Lizzie would inform her mother who the arrivals were, before she was sent off:

> Occasional additional participants would regularly join the regular foursome. I remember them all only as numbers. Their names, Heaven forbid, were teeth breakers and tongue twisters, and the numbers [tattooed] on their arms were for me a simple substitute for pronouncing and remembering [the names]. I would announce from the porch, or sometimes from the window: "546772 is arriving!" or "98426 is on the way!" Helena would pale, her heart skipping a beat. When she took hold of herself she would say: "Elizabeth, you are right, that's the way we will not forget, that's the way we will not forget."[25]

Thus did both those for whom the memory of the Holocaust was a personal one and those for whom Holocaust history was no more than imparted knowledge, experiences, and memory contribute to the shaping of the remembrance and the narrative of the Holocaust.

There are varied, and at times conflicting, answers to the question, How much and to what degree should one remember the Holocaust? However, there is a very wide consensus that one *must* remember and that remembering is of itself an act. This turns the issues of "how to remember the Holocaust" and "what to remember of the Holocaust" into very significant ones for the Israeli discourse.

UNIQUENESS AND MISSION—THE HOLOCAUST AND ITS SIGNIFICANCE

These two issues—the uniqueness and mission of the Holocaust and its significance—have been part of the public discourse on various occasions. I shall begin by quoting from speeches delivered at the Knesset plenary sessions, for what is said in the Knesset is quoted in the press and the electronic media, and Knesset members at times also present their thoughts on the matter outside that forum.

Ben-Zion Dinur, the minister of education at the time and responsible for implementation of the Yad Vashem Law, dealt with the Holocaust historically. He saw it as part of the continuum of Jewish history in the Diaspora, a chronicle replete with persecutions and destruction. He compared the Holocaust not to the destruction of the Second Temple but rather to catastrophes that took place in Europe, such as the Crusades and the expulsion of the Jews from Spain toward the end of the fifteenth century. All this notwithstanding, Dinur did emphasize that the Holocaust was a unique event because of the following features: the Nazi objective of total annihilation of the Jews, mass murders executed by state agencies and under state law, and precise and pedantic planning coupled with the employment of scientific and technological techniques. All these were done with the acquiescence and active cooperation of the majority of Germans.[26] In the wake of the Holocaust, the historical pattern of Jewish life in the past, marked by the rise and decline of Jewish centers in the Diaspora, was irrevocably destroyed. Dinur's analysis pointed at one and the same time to continuity and uniqueness, even though the two were diametrically opposed one to the other.[27]

Dinur concluded that the three vows declared by the Talmudic sage Rabbi Yossai ben Hanina—which included the prohibition of large-scale Jewish immigration to Israel ("They shall not ascend the wall")—should be nullified. Today the only answer to the destruction was to immigrate to the Land of Israel (i.e., to "ascend the wall"), upbuild it, and carry out there the "ingathering of the exiles."[28] In this article, Dinur provided a very generalized interpretation of the role of the Holocaust in Jewish history. He pointed to only one contradiction that lies at the root of Jewish existence in the modern age: the reality of Jewish life in the Diaspora and Jewish expectations for full integration into nations and states despite the fact that the Jews are a nation unto themselves. In his opinion, there is no basis for such expectations. Wide sectors of the Israeli public agreed with this conclusion, which may be termed "the Zionist lesson of the Holocaust."[29]

The Israeli public discourse of the 1950s is replete with efforts to find some explanation for the Holocaust, even to discover some comforting interpretation of it. This was an indication of yet another essential contradiction in the Israeli experience: on the one hand, the depressing sense of loss, mourning, and death that was common to many, both in the wake of the Holocaust and because of the death of thousands in the War of Independence, and, on the other, a sense of satisfaction and joy at the new reality of Israel.[30]

Yet side by side with the Jewish and national lesson or explanation of the Holocaust, some found that it imparted a universal significance to Jewish existence. During the debate on the Yad Vashem Law in the Knesset, Knesset member Yona Kesse (Mapai) stressed the value and importance for Israelis of Yad Vashem as a memorial, a memorial that makes it very clear to what a state we must not descend. We must prevent our becoming soulless lest we, as victims, become insensible to the suffering of others.[31]

In 1963, Naomi Zorea, a member of Kibbutz Ma'agan Michael, emphatically wrote that she would like her children to gain two lessons from this horrendous episode in Jewish history: "A. That they grow up to be proud people who would retaliate against any violence perpetrated against them; B. That they remain free of Nazi-type defilement."[32] Arieh Kubovy, chairman of Yad Vashem, developed this theme to an even higher level, adopting a term coined by Aharon David Gordon: "*am adam*" (literally, "a nation of human beings"). He was referring to the duty of the Israeli Jew, in the wake of the Holocaust, to be morally obligated to the humanistic code. "The nation, too, must be created in the image of God. The nation or any other collective entity is not permitted 'to commit any form of ugliness and abomination' that is forbidden to man." He stressed that self-accusation and self-justification are alien to the tradition of Judaism and ended his address by quoting from the prophet Zephaniah: "The remnant of Israel shall do no wrong and speak no falsehood; a deceitful tongue shall not be in their mouths." That is the most important message for the continuation of Jewish life after the Holocaust.[33]

The tendency to link national and universal components continued to be part of the public discourse in the 1980s and 1990s. By way of example, I shall once again turn to the political arena, that is, to debates in the Knesset conducted during the summer and fall of 1992 concerning visits by organized groups of Israeli pupils to Poland and about the character of the Auschwitz death camp as a tourist site. Knesset member Ovadiah Eli (Likud) said, "Auschwitz is a memorial to the most terrible of tragedies that has befallen our people, and a symbol of man's baseness and cruelty." Eli Dayan (Labor Party), who together with Ovadiah Eli raised the issue on the Knesset floor, said, "There is no better way to bring home [to the youth] the Holocaust period and perhaps even to educate [them] to love their fellow men, than a visit there."[34] Knesset member Shevah Weiss (Labor Party), himself a Holocaust survivor, added his insight: [The death camp is] like a permanent monument of everlasting ignominy to the greatest crime ever committed against humanity, and especially against the Jewish nation. Therefore millions of persons come and will continue to come there to shed a tear, to light a candle in memory of the millions of victims, and to express their anger against those who brought the sense of death to the world.[35]

And Knesset member Dedi Zucker of the Meretz socialist party adopted a more universal view in a session of the Knesset commemorating the "*Kristalnacht*": "The Holocaust is not only the story of the Jews, but also of the Germans and Western civilization as a whole. It is, as I said, not our story alone but that of an entire civilization that failed, that collapsed."[36]

Yet it was precisely in connection with this issue that the question was raised whether the visits of Israeli youths to the death camps in Poland did perhaps encourage the adoption of a nationalistic outlook and perhaps added to intolerance of the different, the stranger. That, for example, is what Minister of Education Shulamit Aloni argued: "The youth return from such journeys with more Right-wing and nationalistic inclinations," for which she was sharply criticized at a session of the Knesset, particularly by Knesset member Abraham Hirchson (Likud).[37] (This issue was given more prominent attention in the late 1990s following the inappropriate behavior of groups of pupils who visited Poland.)

During the 1990s, expressions adopted from the terminology connected with Nazi Germany and the Holocaust were used in discussions of ethnic conflicts and even in political controversies. Expressions such as "the other Germany," "Nazi barbarity," "the world's silence," "a *Judenrat* government," and "the borders of Auschwitz" served as codes that needed no further elaboration or explanation. In August 1992, in the midst of the war in Bosnia, Knesset member Rafi Elul (Labor Party) asked, "Why does Israel not issue a statement condemning death camps and the transfer of the Muslim population in Bosnia? [These are] acts that remind us of the horrors of the Holocaust. . . . They [the Serbs] tightly pack hundreds of people, exactly as the Nazis did to the Jews, and the world is silent."[38] He went on to question the actions of Israeli diplomats and the Jewish lobby in the United States who, he claimed, were thwarting efforts to have the mass murder of Armenians by the Turks in World War I from being placed on the American calendar of public events. The connection of the Holocaust to acts of genocide in the past and the present is indicative of the extent to which the terminology of the Holocaust has been internalized and the use to which it is put in connection with other political and social milieus.

Another, much different sphere in which the national, personal, and universal outlooks meet and in which those involved sought some significance and meaning in the Holocaust is the writings of young boys and girls after their visits to Poland and the extermination camps. Studies that have analyzed the reactions of youngsters to visits at commemoration sites and death camps abroad as they faced commemorative monuments or the remains of Jewish life in Poland have indicated that a distinction can be made on the basis of schools from various sectors: there is a difference in the reaction of children from urban or kibbutz schools, from different social classes, and from secular or religious schools. I shall not go into this point here. I should, however, like to give examples of how the national and universal aspects are expressed when facing the death camps, this in poems written by two schoolgirls. I chose these two poems not for their literary merit but because I believe that they are representative of the most direct emotions that the encounter with the camps aroused in the young writers. These poems reflect highly significant elements in the public discourse. The first is taken from an anthology of personal impressions, in drawings and writings, collected by the pupils of the Emek Hefer School; the second first appeared in the organ of the Ma'agan Michael regional school. The national and universal significance of the Holocaust are clearly expressed in both these poems.[39]

Treblinka

Dalia Savir

That which the eyes
of a small stone have seen
cannot be comprehended
by a person:
all the atrocities
that passed before it
the pain, the fire, and the blood.
That which its eyes have seen
it has borne within itself,
all these years.
it wants to cry out
to those who observe it:
"I saw it all happen!"
But no one listens to a stone.
And so, through the years,
all that is revealed
are the cracks that lie
within.
If only the forests
that flank the tracks
might tell what happened
on that road . . .

If only those villages could speak . . .
But stones have no power of speech,
only man does.
But when it all happened,
Man was struck dumb.

The direct subject of Dalia Savir's poem are the scenes that passed before the eyes of a small stone at Treblinka, sights that human eyes cannot describe. We understand them because for us Treblinka is not a place but a code, and we know what Treblinka means. The poetess describes the scenes as atrocities, pain, fire, and blood, in general and symbolic terms. The stone bears knowledge of what happened and the sights it saw, and for many long years it had wanted to cry out, "I saw it all happen!" But, of course, one quality of a stone is that it is unable to utter a scream. Moreover, no one is attentive to its desire to cry out. Does the stone—which knows and wants to cry out—symbolize man? Or perhaps it is precisely its silence that is symbolic of man. For Savir's stone has internal cracks, the result of the suffering and silence from which it cannot detach itself. Man is like a stone in the field. But man, who is endowed with the power of speech and who can (and must) cry out, tell, and talk, did exactly the opposite of what his nature and very essence dictated. "But when it all happened, man was struck dumb." The underlying theme of the poem is the contrast between silence and the cry, between the ability and the inability to speak, between the human heart and a heart of stone. Nowhere in the poem does it refer to Jews or use the term "my people." It does not mention Nazis or Germans, only human beings and nature, the two elements most universal in character. If nature could replace man, it would cry out.

This Is My Mother

Tsofit Singer, Poland, 1987[40]

You are the ones who murdered her
my mother
you are the ones
who humiliated her,
reduced her to dust
yes, yes, my mother.
You starved her, beat her,
put her in a bunk
with three other girls,
caused her to sit for two days
in a latrine
yes, yes, my mother.
You killed her father,

her mother,
and two brothers,
but she did not give in.
she ran, starving, stumbling,
but did not give in.
yes, that was my mother.
And today
she is a proud Jew
living in the Land of Israel,
and I am her daughter
also a proud Jew,
living in the Land of Israel,
thanks to my mother.
my mother
she was the victor this time
yes, yes, my mother.

Tsofit Singer's poem is a personal, biographical, and national message that takes the form of a scream, one of pain and perhaps also a victory cry, while giving vent to a sense of revenge.

The poem is written in the second-person plural, the word "you" appearing over and over again. The specific "you" is not identified by name or appellation, but their deeds clearly identify them: you murdered, you humiliated, you starved, you beat, you put, you caused her to sit, you killed, and so on. Toward the end of the poem, the use of the third person refers to her mother: "she did not give in." And in the last stanza, the first-person singular is the author herself, who contends with the might of "you" and the heroism and victory of "she"—her mother. The challenge and the cries of victory are expressed in the switch to the first-person singular: "I am her daughter—also a proud Jew, living in the Land of Israel, thanks to my mother."

I shall conclude this topic by turning once again to the address delivered by Dov Kulka when he was awarded the Buchman Prize at Yad Vashem in December 1998. He shared with the audience his memories of the children's choir at Birkenau, in which he participated at the age of 11. The conductor, a huge prisoner whose name was Imre, taught them Schiller's "Ode to Life" from Beethoven's Ninth Symphony. The young Kulka did not understand the words but remembered the music. Some time later, while still in Auschwitz and after the children's camp had already been destroyed, he learned the meaning of the text from another inmate who heard him playing the melody on a mouth organ. Kulka related,

I think that he also tried to make me realize this horrible absurdity, this terrible wonder, that an ode to joy and the fraternity of nations, Schiller's "Ode to Life" from Beethoven's Ninth Symphony, should be performed in front of the crematoriums of Auschwitz, only several hundred meters from the biggest site of execution and cremation known to that humanity which is the subject of the ode, and this at the very moment while we were talking and during all the months that we were there. . . . Of course, the question I ask myself to this very day is, what motivated this Imre [the conductor], not the fact that he organized a children's choir, for one may say that . . . it was necessary to somehow preserve sanity, some form of keeping busy, but what did he believe in, if he did believe.[41]

In sum, it may be said that the Israeli discourse on the Holocaust adopted a conceptual framework that tried to confront the narrative of the Holocaust by imparting to it a meaningful national character. This discourse rejected nihilism.[42] And yet it is a multivocal narrative. The national and universal values that characterized the discourse from its very beginning continue to play a central role, even though there has been a sort of competition between them ever since the 1970s. Only a very detailed historical, political, and social analysis will be able to pinpoint when, by whom, and under what circumstances does the clash between the two take the upper hand over the tendency for them to join in dialogue. No doubt, confrontations between the national and universal values are engendered particularly when the Holocaust is discussed in relation to controversial issues touching on Israel's foreign relations and the Arab–Israeli conflict.

THE JEWISH RESPONSE TO THE HOLOCAUST

Throughout the entire period since the Holocaust, the Israeli discourse on how Jews responded to Nazi persecutions is replete with contrasting images: hero versus coward, honor versus humiliation, those who put up a fight versus collaborators, and active versus passive. Controversies over this issue were particularly sharp, in effect reflecting differences of opinion both among elements already active among the Jews under Nazi rule and among political parties in Israel whenever this issue appeared on the public agenda.

During the debate in the Knesset on the proposed Yad Vashem Law, Dinur praised Jews who rebelled in the ghettos or joined the partisans. To him, they epitomized the height of human heroism in this period: "This uprising, in which a few and tattered remnants were besieged in the ghetto, cut off from the world, alone and isolated, without equipment, without arms, without any hope of victory or rescue, without any prospect of help, symbolized the heroism of Israel in the Holocaust." For Dinur, heroism does not end in glorious victory: this is not the heroism of the fighter who awaits rescue or victory but the heroism of the fighter who knows that victory will never be his. This is the heroism of David whose battle with Goliath ends in tragedy, a Samson in David's clothing who calls out, "Let me die with the Philistines," for what is important is that the Germans will die.

But the beginnings of heroism in the Holocaust, from Dinur's viewpoint, lie in the day-to-day struggle for survival in which the public gave expression to Jewish solidarity as well as to its belief in victory over the Nazis. This was remarkable heroism, considering the humiliating conditions under which it was enacted, heroism that he termed "bravery of the spirit" and "heroism of the spirit":

> The Jewish struggle for life . . . in the early years the people carried on a struggle for life, a struggle for the possibility to remain alive, to keep going until the enemy should fall, not to give him an opening. This struggle of the nation to maintain the image of human beings under conditions of humiliation, abuse, and torture, is a unique heroic episode, for every effort of the enemy . . . was aimed and planned to break the spirit of the nation.[43]

Dinur proposed a discourse of reconciliation, one that would bridge the gap between the heroism of those Jews who fought to maintain the honor of their nation, seeking to take revenge on the Nazis, and ordinary people who engaged in the daily struggle for survival. He also drew a connection between the Israeli soldiers who fought in Israel's War of Independence and the ghetto fighters, seeing the two as one link in the chain of Jewish heroism, one continuous episode of Jewish bravery. In this manner, he drew a connection between the Holocaust and the establishment of Israel and the shaping of Israeli society during the state's first years. Dinur created an all-encompassing yet not clearly defined discourse that showed understanding for the difficult situation of the Jews under Nazi occupation and at the same time propounded an ideological interpretation concerning the continuity of Jewish history.

Dinur's outlook, however, did not represent the discourse that was dominant in the Israeli Left. Ya'akov Hazan, a Knesset member representing Mapam, and Avraham Berman, a left-wing activist and a member of the leftist Po'alei Zion Party in the Warsaw ghetto, embraced a much more specific definition of the heroism of the ghetto fighters and the partisans. Theirs was not a definition of reconciliation but one of opposites. They rejected the distinction made in the press, noted previously, between active and passive heroism. In its stead, they saw a threefold division: the fighters, as opposed to the Jewish public at large; the public (which was helpless and led by a corrupt leadership of collaborators); and the heads of councils, members of the *Judenrat*, and the Jewish police. Berman and Hazan sharply criticized the heads of the *Judenrat* who, they claimed, misled the public, bringing it to resign itself to Nazi policy and thus lose its will to survive even before the deportations began. Their treachery went beyond collaboration with the enemy to safeguard themselves and the interests of those who were personally close to them; they also betrayed the interests of the entire community by cutting the ground out from under the will of ordinary folk to live, by adding to the desperation of many Jews and leading them to moral corruption. They saw no importance in preserving human dignity or the honor of the nation.[44]

In contrast to the corrupt leadership, Hazan and Berman portrayed the armed resistance of the ghetto fighters as a choice between the possibility of saving themselves and of honorable death—and they chose to die honorably. Unlike Dinur, who presented the ghetto revolts as a war of despair and as a situation that held no hope of survival, Berman interpreted them as the outcome of a conscious decision to fight Nazism or fascism and linked the struggle in the ghettos to the war that had been waged by the Soviet Union. Though Hazan did not make the connection between the fighting in the ghettos and the war effort of the Soviet Union, he did agree with Berman that the choice to resist was on the whole a conscious decision to defend Jewish honor, this in view of the fact that the masses went meekly to their deaths.

Religious circles reacted differently to the Nazi occupation and anti-Jewish policy. They too expressed much admiration for the heroic acts of the ghetto fighters, even pointing to the great number of religious Jews in their ranks. However, they believed that heroism was not the lot of the fighters alone. One could find heroism of the highest degree among all Jews, even those who were slaughtered just because they were Jews; therefore, all should be considered martyrs. The religious discourse on the Holocaust was replete with references to persons who continued to study religious law and fulfill religious commandments despite the harsh conditions under which they existed and to those who sought sacredness even in the midst of Nazi defilement. Acts of heroism were attributed to such persons, who were considered martyrs. Knesset member Zerah Warhaftig, one of the central figures in the efforts to establish Yad Vashem and commemoration patterns, sharply criticized the distinction made by the Left between one Jew and another:

> When people speak of our victims and their commemoration, I sometimes feel that it is a form of blasphemy when they begin to differentiate between the victims, as if some are more saintly and others—less. And also when they begin to point to those singular occurrences—if only there had been more such occurrences—such as the ghetto uprisings and the like: these included only very small numbers [of participants].[45]

Knesset member Mordechai Nurock, a member of the Mizrahi religious Zionist Party, expressed the same concept: "It is the duty of the People of Israel to commemorate our martyrs whose souls left their bodies as they recited 'Hear, O Israel.'" And Rabbi Yitzhak Meir Levin of Agudat Yisrael forcefully declared, "The parents who sacrificed themselves for the sanctification of Heaven, perishing in the Holocaust with 'Hear, O Israel' on their lips, their dying instruction to their children was: emigrate to the Holy Land and live as Jews."[46]

These spokesmen interpreted Jewish behavior in the Holocaust as the will to continue to live as Jews according to traditional concepts: to carry on the Jewish culture and heritage that had developed in the Diaspora. Not only did these not contradict life in Israel, but it would be impossible—so they believed—to ensure a continued Jewish existence, even in Israel, without them. It was absolutely necessary, therefore, to establish *yeshivot*[47] and to continue the study of Jewish Law and a religious lifestyle.

A careful reading of the Yad Vashem Law as tabled in the Knesset indicates that the text of the law did not tend toward polarization; it did not point to heroes and victims "like sheep to the slaughter," as opposites.[48] And yet, from the title given to Yad Vashem as "The Holocaust Martyrs' and Heroes' Remembrance Authority" and that of the "Holocaust Martyrs' and Heroes' Remembrance Day Law" passed in 1959, the general public received the impression that they emphasized the distinction and separation between the two. (It is noteworthy that Knesset member Emma Talmi, of Mapam, proposed calling the law "The Holocaust and Ghetto Uprising Remembrance Day Law," thus returning to the formulation adopted by the Knesset when it had originally determined that 27 Nissan was to be the day of commemoration of the Holocaust and the ghetto uprisings.) Despite this, representatives of the ghetto fighters and the partisans claimed at meetings of the Yad Vashem Council and in other frameworks that Yad Vashem purposely tended to play down the importance of the rebellions and the fighting in partisan units when shaping national remembrance of the Holocaust.[49]

I should like to sum up the issue of Jewish response to the Holocaust with another powerful excerpt from a work of literature. Lizzie Doron describes an Independence Day celebration in her home neighborhood. This was already after the Six-Day War of 1967. Helena invited herself to an Independence Day party at the home of a family whose son was a friend of her daughter Elizabeth. She came to the party elegantly dressed in festive clothes and with makeup on her face. Her outward appearance differed from the others at the party. This is how her daughter described the moment when Helena met her host, who came forward to greet her:

> The host, muscular, cheerful, and tanned approached her and introduced himself: "My name is Komem[50] Shealtiel," he said, shifting his head so that his forelock would change position, and extended his right hand. "And I," said Helena in a metallic voice that momentarily broke and trembled, "my name is Helena Like Sheep to the Slaughter" and extended her hand Komem Shealtiel wrinkled his forehead and brow and asked: "What?" Helena repeated, saying as she shook his hand: "Helena Like Sheep to the Slaughter. You certainly know." And she repeated the name once again, only slower: "H-e-l-e-n-a L-i-k-e S-h-e-e-p t-o t-h-e S-l-a-u-g-h-t-e-r." I returned home alone with Helena on the eve of the holiday. And I never saw Ariel Komem again.[51]

The character of Jewish behavior in the Holocaust was stricken from the public agenda in Israel after the Six-Day War, particularly from the 1970s on. There are no vestiges of the fierce arguments, dressed in ideological wrappings, that raged between the Left and the Right. Research and teaching contributed to a more balanced appraisal of the Jewish fighters and leadership during the Holocaust. The outlook that widened "heroism" to include the attempt to contend with the difficulties of daily life gave birth to a new term in the historical discourse, which also became part of the public discourse: *amidah yehudit* (literally, "the Jewish stand"). All this notwithstanding, in the political discourse one still comes across various terms and expressions that include remnants of ideological censure or apologetics, such as "borders of Auschwitz" or "*Judenrat* government"; such phenomena are indicative of the durability of imagery and concepts even in changing circumstances.

CONCLUSION

By way of conclusion, I will quote a poem published in a newsletter of a delegation to Poland of pupils from the Emek Hefer School, a poem marked by personal soul-searching:

Maidanek

Noga Berger

Maidanek,
In this G-d forsaken place
one begins to ponder
the meaning of life,
the nature of human beings,
of what is man capable?
the heart cries out from within,
the soul wants to scream,
you feel helpless
in the presence of so much evil,
recognizing its dominion here.
you can't believe
that the world knew but remained silent,
that the world knew but did not cry out,
that the Shoah happened
right here
and here the cries went up
but were not heard at all.
In this God forsaken spot
I began to believe
in the sacredness of life

At a Remembrance Day assembly in 1959, Arieh Kubovy, then chairman of Yad Vashem, rhetorically asked why the element of revenge does not form part of such ceremonies. This was the answer he provided:

I believe that the true explanation lies in the fact that at our commemoration ceremonies we first of all turn inwards to ourselves. We congregate at assemblies that are devoted to moral stocktaking and to all the seventeen millions of Jews who lived before the catastrophe. We want to gain an understanding of those who are no longer with us, and we want to understand ourselves, whose fate was unlike theirs. We try to find an answer to why they reacted as they did, and to give a reckoning of our response—we who live in the lands of freedom.[52]

Kubovy portrayed the remembrance of the Holocaust as soul-searching, internal stock taking—as taking stock of the past, the present, and the future. In his view, the establishment of Israel and the "ingathering of the exiles" were more than attributes of redemption; they were also expressions of expiation for helplessness or for the fact that Jews who were outside the area of Nazi rule were far away from the tragic events when they occurred.

Collective soul-searching and stock taking took on a more central role in the public discourse on the Holocaust during the 1970s and 1980s. The 1990s, in contrast, were marked by a growing tendency for individual soul-searching and the search for a link between the individual and the events of the past.

NOTES

1. *Divrei Haknesset* (Knesset Debates), session of 18 May 1953, 1337 (in Hebrew).

2. Dalia Ofer, "Israel Reacts to the Holocaust," in *The World Reacts to the Holocaust*, ed. David Wyman (Baltimore: Johns Hopkins University Press, 1996), 836–923.

3. "This People's Heart Is Not Made of Stone," *Al Hamishmar*, 13 April 1956 (in Hebrew). For the literary example par excellence of this saying, see Yoram Kaniuk, *Adam Resurrected* (New York, 1971).

4. I could point to many and diverse examples. I shall mention only the following: Savyon Liebrecht's short story "Cut" (*Kritah*) in her *Horses on the Highway* (Tel Aviv, 1988; in Hebrew), and *A Man, a Woman, and a Man* (New York: Pesea Books, 2001); Saul Friedländer deals with these issues differently in his *When Memory Comes* (New York: Farrar Straus, 1980); see also Lizzie Doron, *Why Didn't You Come before the War* (Tel Aviv, 1998; in Hebrew), to which I shall return.

5. *Ha'aretz*, 30 April 1954 (in Hebrew).

6. See, for example, the address of Ya'akov Hazan, a Knesset member representing Mapam, in the parliamentary debate on the Yad Vashem Law, *Divrei Haknesset*, session of 18 May 1953, 1332.

7. *Divrei Haknesset*, session of 12 May 1953, 1311. The Institute for Jewish Research (Yidisher Visenshaftlikher Institut [YIVO]) was established in Vilna in 1925 following a decision taken by a conference of Jewish scholars in Berlin in August 1925. In 1940, following the occupation of Poland, the American branch took over, and a large part of the collection was transferred to New York. A number of YIVO scholars managed to immigrate to the United States before the Nazi occupation in June 1941. YIVO is still an important library and archive of Jewish research on East European Jewry.

8. Elimelech Rimalt, *Divrei Haknesset*, session of 18 May 1953, 1333; Baruch Azania, *Divrei Haknesset*, session of 18 May 1953, 1334.

9. Doron, *Why Didn't You Come before the War* (n. 10), 19–23.

10. *Ha'aretz*, 9 April 1964, 4 (in Hebrew).

11. Dov Kulka, from an address at the Buchman Prize ceremony, Yad Vashem, Jerusalem, 9 December 1998.

12. Doron, *Why Didn't You Come before the War*, 9. See also her breathtaking and stunning description (36–37) of her mother's memories on the Passover Eve. The mother expressed her astonishment at the fact that the features of members of her family, whom she saw seated around the Seder table just like "then and there," had not changed or grown older, even though many long years had passed.

13. Doron, *Why Didn't You Come before the War*, 19.

14. The text read every Passover Eve that relates the story of the Exodus from Egypt and admonishes the Jews to pass this lesson on from generation to generation.

15. *Hashavu'a Bakibbutz Ha'artzi*, 22 April 1960, 1 (in Hebrew).

16. *Hashavu'a Bakibbutz Ha'artzi*, 22 April 1960, 1 (in Hebrew).

17. Dov Shilansky, *Divrei Haknesset*, session of 30 November 1992, 767; Yigal Allon, *Ha'aretz*, 21 April 1963 (in Hebrew).

18. For Israeli–German relations, see Neima Barzel, "Israel and Germany 1945–1956: Development of the Attitude of Israeli Society and State to Germany Following the Holocaust" (Ph.D. diss., University of Haifa, 1990; in Hebrew). For the sale of Uzi submachine guns and the public uproar it caused, see Shlomo Shapiro, "Communicating Interests across History: German–Israeli Security Cooperation," in *Germany and the Middle East: Past, Present, and Future*, ed. Haim Goren (Jerusalem, 2003), 320.

19. *Ha'aretz*, 26 June 1959, 2 (in Hebrew).

20. B. Ben-Zion, "The Lessons of the Holocaust," *Ha'aretz*, 6 July 1959, 4 (in Hebrew), and "Sale of Israeli Arms to Germany," *Ha'aretz*, 28 June 1959 (in Hebrew), with Abraham Schweitzer in favor and Eliezer Livne against.

21. Mark Geffen, "A Deal in Return for a Deal, *Al Hamishmar*, 30 June 1959, 2 (in Hebrew); see readers' reactions by Reuven Leib of Beit Hakerem, Jerusalem, and Shalom Ben Yehuda of Givatayim, who signed his opinion, "Auschwitz inmate A 19341," in "Ha'aretz's Readers Express Their Opinions on the Arms Deal," *Ha'aretz*, 6 July 1959, 4 (in Hebrew).

22. *Ha'aretz*, 20 June 1959, 2 (in Hebrew).

23. Doron, *Why Didn't You Come before the War*, 13–14.

24. The choice of surname is significant. *Zabar* (cactus) is the term popularly used to denote native-born Israelis who, like the fruit of the cactus, are said to be prickly without and sweet within.

25. Doron, *Why Didn't You Come before the War*, 21.

26. *Divrei Haknesset*, session of 12 May 1953, 1310–14.

27. Ben-Zion Dinur, "Diaspora Communities and Their Destruction," in *Knesset: Contributions by Authors in Memory of H. N. Bialik*, ed. Y. Cahan and F. Lachover. Vol. 8 (Tel Aviv, 1943–44), 60 (in Hebrew).

28. Dinur, "Diaspora Communities and Their Destruction," 60. The Talmudic tractate Ketubot 111a concerns three "vows" of God: (1) God made the Jews promise not to rebel against the Gentile nations who rule over them, (2) the Jews as a nation should not immigrate to Israel ("ascend the wall"), and (3) God made the Gentile nations promise not to brutally confine the Jews.

29. Dinur, "Diaspora Communities and Their Destruction," 60. See also the *Divrei Haknesset* speeches of 18 May 1953 by the following members: Y. Hazan, 1331; Baruch Azania, 1334; Idov Cohen, 1331; and Yitzhak Meir Levin, 1338. The latter's unease is discernable, for he mentions time and again that we lack a prophet or a seer who can interpret contemporary events: "Again, we lack an Isaiah, a Jeremiah, prophets and seers who could explain the words of the Lord to the House of Israel in these stormy days." See "To Redeem the Heritage of the Destruction," *Ha'aretz*, 9 April 1964, 2 (in Hebrew); Reuven Hammer, "The Holocaust: No Simple Answers," *Ha'aretz*, 4 May 1978 (in Hebrew); "Destruction and Renewal," *Ha'aretz*, 13 April 1980 (in Hebrew); and Aharon Megged, "An Ancient Fear Whispers to Us: It May Happen Again," *Yediot Aharonot*, 2 May 1989, 10 (in Hebrew).

30. See the speech by Elimelech Rimalt, *Divrei Haknesset*, session of 18 May 1953, 1333.

31. Rimalt, *Divrei Haknesset*, session of 18 May 1953, 1350–51. See also Moshe Prager, "The Jewish People Has Not Been Defeated: From Holocaust to Redemption—The Twenty-Year Balance Sheet," *Tarbut* 14, no. 1 (October–November 1959): 14–18 (in Hebrew);, and Asher Barash, "The Change within Redemption," *Iggeret* 18, no. 47, 20 April 1952, 3–4 (in Hebrew).

32. Naomi Zorea, "About the Ideology of Hatred," *Bulletin of Kibbutz Ma'agan Michael* 292 (15 March 1963) (in Hebrew), copy in Ma'agan Michael Archives, quoted in Micha Balf, "Between Mt. Carmel and the Sea: Development of Public Utterances on the Holocaust in Kibbutz Ma'agan Michael and Kibbutz Ma'ayan Zvi" (M.A. thesis, The Hebrew University of Jerusalem, 1998), 58 (in Hebrew).

33. Address at the closing ceremony of Holocaust Memorial Day, 1 May 1962. See Yad Vashem Archives, Jerusalem.

34. *Divrei Haknesset*, session of 9 September 1992, 521–22.

35. *Divrei Haknesset*, session of 9 September 1992, 522.

36. *Divrei Haknesset*, session of 11 November 1992, 372.

37. *Divrei Haknesset*, session of 28 October 1992, 119; see also the reply of Shulamit Aloni to the statement by Rabbi Yosef Azran, session of 30 November 1992, 771.

38. *Divrei Haknesset*, session of 5 August 1992, 376.

39. *Written There*, by the delegation to Poland in March 1994, Emek Hefer School. An unpaged booklet for internal distribution.

40. *Written There*, by a delegation to Poland in March 1987, Emek Hefer School. An unpaged booklet for internal distribution.

41. See note 13.

42. It is noteworthy that there has recently been no little criticism of this discourse. Some forms of commemoration in schools even exhibit some cynicism and black humor. Some of these elements are visible in Eyal Sivan's film *Remember, Slaves of Memory* (1987) and surfaced in part of the Holocaust Memorial Day ceremony conducted at the Kedma School in 1988.

43. *Divrei Haknesset*, session of 12 May 1953, 1310.

44. *Divrei Haknesset*, session of 18 May 1953, 1339, 1351.

45. *Divrei Haknesset*, session of 8 May 1953, 1345.

46. *Divrei Haknesset*, session of 8 May 1953, 1336, and 1338, respectively.

47. Academies for talmudic studies.

48. For a more extensive discussion of this issue, see Ofer, "Israel Reacts to the Holocaust," 861–62; Roni Stauber, "Jewish Behavior in the Holocaust as Conceived

by Public Opinion in Israel in the 1950s" (Ph.D. diss., Tel Aviv University), 128–46, 201–32 (in Hebrew).

49. *Divrei Haknesset*, session of 18 June 1958, 2118; "The Fourth World Council of Yad Vashem," *Yad Vashem Bulletin* 17 (18 December 1958): 30–31 (in Hebrew).

50. Doron, *Why Didn't You Come before the War*, 56–57.

51. The meaning of the first word Komem means independence or being upright.

52. Arieh Kubovy, "Jewish Tradition Sees in Suffering the Path to Redemption," address to Holocaust Memorial Day assembly in the Mann Auditorium, Tel Aviv, 1959, in Arieh Kubovy, *If I Forget Thee, O Holocaust* (Jerusalem, 1967), 19 (in Hebrew).

CHAPTER 6

Israeli Identity: The Jewish Component

Charles Liebman and Yaacov Yadgar

INTRODUCTION

This chapter addresses a troublesome question first alluded to in the book *Choosing Survival*, coauthored by one of us.[1] Every survey of Israeli Jews suggests that the overwhelming majority, even among those who do not define themselves as "religious," observe many Jewish rituals. In addition, Israeli Jews report that Judaism and the Jewish people are important to them. Yet Judaism and Jewishness, as we shall see, play a decidedly secondary role in mainstream Israeli culture. At a speech before members of the Jewish Agency Board of Governors, one participant, a representative of Reform Judaism in the United States, asked why there was so little Jewishness in Israel. A colleague reports that a Swedish Jew (nonreligious, i.e., non-Orthodox) who immigrated to Israel with his wife and daughters was asked by his now grown daughters if they could return to Sweden for the Jewish holidays so that they could once more feel their Jewishness. This chapter is devoted, first of all, to describing what we know about the extent of religious observance and the strength of Jewish identity among the "nonreligious." We then go on to describe the absence of a significant Jewish dimension in mainstream Israeli culture, and finally we try to explain this apparent contradiction. But before we turn our attention to the nonreligious, we want to make a brief observations about the Israeliness/Jewishess of the roughly 20 percent of Israeli Jews who define themselves as *dati* (religious). We will deal with three segments of that population: the *haredim* (ultra-Orthodox), the West Bank settlers, and the modern Orthodox.

Yair Sheleg has written a comprehensive study of virtually all segments of the Israeli religious population, and it is this study, in addition to our own impressions, on which we rely.[2] The major point that Sheleg amply illustrates is the Israelification of the religious, especially its youth. Paradoxically, the agencies for change in many instances are parallel cultural institutions established by the religious community because the nonreligious agencies neither serve their needs nor engage their interests. But the books, magazines, radio and television programs, theaters, comedy acts, and even bars that cater to the religious segment of the population are often the carriers of these new ideas. Some of these new ideas, conceptions, practices, and values can be traced directly to an Israeli influence, and in some (and perhaps most) cases, Israeli culture is simply the medium through which developments in the Western world penetrate religious circles. An example of the former case is the sense of comfort and even the loyalty that the new generation of *haredim* now exhibit toward Israel and their strong identification with Israel's condition. An example of the latter is the penetration into religious circles of many modern notions and most especially the value of "an open mind," of "nonjudgmentalism" (avoiding judging the behavior, especially the religious behavior of others), of the search for "self-fulfillment" and the relative disinterest in collective concerns. That these tendencies extend to the children of the original West Bank settlers is perhaps the most remarkable phenomenon of all. The Israelification of the religious is indicated in lifestyle as well as ideological change. Trips to the Far East by young religious Jews, including unmarried couples traveling together, is increasingly common. One now sees young religious men and women at rock concerts, waving their arms, moving their bodies, and screaming as uninhibitedly as the nonreligious. These tendencies are found most forcefully among the modern Orthodox, where, as one of us noted in a recent article, the level of criticism directed against the Orthodox establishment, against traditional Orthodox practice, and against the traditional manner of interpreting Jewish law bears seeds that threaten to undermine Orthodoxy itself.[3] But it has penetrated *haredi* circles as well, albeit in a more moderate manner and more attuned to traditional *haredi* sensibilities. A good example is the increased sensitivity to Judaism's patriarchal biases. Among the modern Orthodox, voices are increasingly heard that demand a reinterpretation of the tradition's attitude toward women. Religious practice has also undergone change in an effort to accommodate women's demand for greater participation in ritual activities that were heretofore exclusively male. The pace of change in this regard in the past ten years has been dramatic. But even among the *haredim*, one finds frequent meetings of women (sometimes hundreds and even thousands) where speakers no longer exhort their listeners to obey their husbands or their rabbis but rather speak to them of the basic equality (though not the interchangeability) of the sexes.[4] The appearance of *haredi* couples sitting together in coffeehouses is a sure sign of changing attitudes toward the role of women in that community.[5]

ATTITUDES TOWARD JEWISHNESS AND OBSERVANCE OF JEWISH PRACTICES AMONG THE NONRELIGIOUS

Positive attitudes toward Jewishness and the observance of Jewish (religious) practices are not the same thing. Among the pioneer settlers who came to Palestine in the first decades of the twentieth century, there was generally a positive attitude toward Jewish ethnicity, that is, membership in the Jewish people and concern for Jews throughout the world, a nostalgia for many traditional Jewish practices, but a principled objection to "religion" and hence to the observance of Jewish rituals.

The creation of the State of Israel, along with the influx of new immigrants still closely tied to traditional practice, breathed new life into the Jewish tradition. Jewish symbols were now adapted to build and to strengthen national identity and loyalty. Israel's civil religion was built on traditional Jewish symbols. It still is.[6] The problem is that the civil religion itself no longer evokes the allegiance and the emotion that it once did.

In addition to the presence of Jewish symbols and transformed rituals in the national celebrations that strengthened the ethnonational or Jewish side, there was probably more observance of religious ritual at the familial level than scholars have credited. This was certainly true of *mizrahim* (new immigrants from Arab-speaking countries) but also of many *ashkenazim*, especially the displaced persons from eastern Europe who arrived in Israel following the establishment of the State. Just as recent studies, described in this chapter, surprised many Israeli observers by the ubiquity of traditional Jewish practices and the strength expressed concerning Jewish affiliation, so it is possible that in the pre-1967 period, for which there are hardly any survey studies, observers may have been misled about the level of religious observance because of the ignorance, indifference, and even hostility of the cultural and intellectual elite to religious traditions.[7]

The Six-Day War of 1967 and the Yom Kippur War of 1973 and the events that succeeded them strengthened Israeli Jewish identity. A discussion of the purported impact of these events takes us beyond the limitations of this chapter.[8] We confine ourselves, therefore, to more recent surveys of the Jewish identity of Israelis and the analyses of these surveys.[9] Many of the studies rely heavily on Simon Herman, but all were conducted subsequent to his own summary study of Jewish identity.[10] Almost all were conducted in the late 1980s and 1990s, all before the outbreak of the second intifada in September 2000.

All the studies yield, more or less, the same conclusions. We divide them into four major findings. First, although there are significant differences between groups of Israeli Jews in terms of both their Israeli identity and their Jewish identity, the two identities, Israeli and Jewish, are positively related except in the case of the *haredim*. Jewish identity was measured by questions such as ties to the Jewish people, how proud one was to be Jewish, or wishing that if one were to be born again, one would be born Jewish. Israeli identity was defined by measures such as the wish that if one were to be born again, one would be born an Israeli and how certain one was that one would continue living in Israel. Yair Auron found that the attitudes of the nonreligious toward the Jewish people and the self-image of the nonreligious as part of the Jewish people is much less meaningful to them than other identity components, such as their attitudes toward the State of Israel or to the land of Israel. Stephen Sharot, on the other hand, in his review of identity studies conducted through the mid-1990s, concluded that the extent to which Israelis distinguish their Israeliness from their Jewishness is not always clear. This may well be true for the majority of Israelis. We shall have more to say on this subject in the section that follows.

The correlation between the strength of the Israeli and Jewish identities suggests the second major finding. Respondents who define themselves as religious have stronger Jewish and Israeli identities than respondents who define themselves as traditional, and these in turn have stronger Jewish and Israeli identities than those who define themselves as secular. But it seems to us that the category of "religious" or Orthodox is far clearer both objectively and to the respondent him- or herself than are the terms "traditional" or "secular." In many respects, the term "secular" is the least clear. In the as-yet-unpublished study by Kopelowitz and Franco that surveyed a group of secular college students at a small Israeli college, many not only reported some observance of Jewish ritual (a quarter are careful to eat only kosher outside their homes) but also testified to the depths of their own religious beliefs.

The third and perhaps most important finding is that whereas secular Jews have the weakest identity both as Israelis and as Jews, the vast majority of them do observe at least some traditional Jewish practices, do see themselves as part of the Jewish people, and do feel loyalty to the State of Israel. Ninety percent of the secular college students in the Kopelowitz and Franco study reported that they were proud to be Jewish. Seventy-nine percent of the nonreligious respondents in the Auron study reported that being Jewish played a very important or a very, very important role in their lives. In the broadest set of studies of Israeli Jewish attitudes toward religious practice and religious beliefs (studies conducted by the Guttman Institute), a majority of nonreligious reported that they would like their children to be more observant than they themselves. The overwhelming majority felt some attachment to the Jewish tradition and celebrated at least some Jewish holidays and some customs and rituals. Even among the Russian immigrants who arrived in the past decade from the former Soviet Union—immigrants who continue to define their Jewishness in ethnic rather than religious terms—there is evidence of adaptation to the Israeli pattern of Jewishness. Twenty-two percent report that they are more religious today than in the past, only 9 percent report that they are less religious, and 76 percent want their children to observe the tradition in one form or another. There are exceptions. Among young Israeli Jews who identify themselves as secular, a minority express negative attitudes toward religion and the Jewish tradition and alienation from Diaspora Jews. But such feelings have declined since the Six-Day War. Auron points out that the war marks the beginning of a crisis of Israeli identity.[11]

The fourth major finding is that there are few differences by age or gender but marked differences by ethnicity, that is, country of origin. *Mizrahim*, those born in Arab-speaking or predominantly Muslim countries or those whose fathers came from such countries, have stronger Jewish and Israeli identities than *ashkenazim*, those born in European or North American countries or those whose fathers were born in these countries. According to the latest (2000) Guttman Report (the most comprehensive survey of Israeli attitudes toward Judaism and Jewishness), 50 percent of the *mizrahim* define themselves as traditional and 9 percent as nonreligious or antireligious. Comparable figures for *ashkenazim* are 19 percent traditional and 34 percent nonreligious or antireligious.[12]

When we try to get behind these identities and ask what they really mean to the respondents themselves, the survey data are less helpful and the authors of these studies less confident. Yair Auron, whose studies of students in teachers' seminaries is most instructive, feels that for his secular respondents, the Holocaust is the central element in their Jewish identity. Attitudes toward the Jewish people, he says, are mediated by way of the Holocaust, and the tie to the Jewish people is a tie to a dead people. His analysis recalls that of Amos Elon, who, in the 1970s, stressed the importance of suffering and victimhood in the Jewish identity of Israelis.[13] Laura Zarembski describes this crisis in terms of a lost sense of defining characteristics—what it means to be an Israeli. She contrasts the insecurity of the secular community to the self-confidence of the religious community.[14] What this suggests to us is that the root of the problem lies not in the dissociation from religion or from tradition but in a loss of belief, by significant numbers of secular Israelis, in secular Zionism—an ideology that until now had nourished their sense of identity with Judaism and the Jewish people. Yet this crisis to the contrary notwithstanding, the majority of Israelis continue to report high levels of traditional behavior and strong ties to the Jewish people.

JUDAISM AND JEWISHNESS IN ISRAELI CULTURE

In this section, we are interested in tracing the attitudes of those who produce and transmit the dominant symbols of Israeli society through the major agencies of middlebrow culture (television, radio, daily newspapers, and popular fiction). We suspect that a study of popular advertising, which we did not undertake, would yield similar results. In other words, we are looking at popular culture in Israel, which, as one scholar notes, "is the product of mass culture especially as it is mediated by, in, and through printed and electronic sources."[15]

The critical change that has taken place in Israel in the past few decades is the weakening and gradual replacement of Zionist conceptions, myths, and symbols—what might also be called the Zionist metanarrative—with what we term the universalistic-humanist narrative.[16] Three methodological caveats are in order. First, what we describe are mainstream agencies of Israeli culture and cultural transmission. In the past 20 years, cultural agencies appealing to particular segments of Israeli society (the national religious, the ultra-Orthodox *ashkenazim* and the ultra-Orthodox *mizrahim*, and the Russians) have proliferated. Their presence means that other cultural agencies, many of them intensely Jewish, are now available to the Israeli audience. They are excluded from our analysis because they cannot be said to shape Israeli culture (although this may become less true in the future). They generally reach a rather specific audience, and their audience excludes most of the "nonreligious"[17] whose behavior and attitudes are of interest to us. Second, the current intifada, in past year or two, has produced some change in Israeli culture in the direction of greater Jewishness. How permanent this change will be remains to be seen. Finally, we are describing what we call the public or civic culture of Israel, not the State or political culture, that is, the culture generated by the government itself.[18]

Indeed, the separation of the two cultures is the key to our story. Until the Yom Kippur War, Zionist ideology, conceptions, and perceptions of history, what we call the Zionist metanarrative, dominated both the public culture of Israel—the system of symbols generated and transmitted by independent cultural agencies—and the statist or political culture—the system of symbols generated and transmitted by the government. But following the Yom Kippur War, basic beliefs on which the Zionist narrative was built began to be questioned.[19] Historical, social, and cultural "truths" that were heretofore unquestioned were now challenged. The "shattering of myths" that became a national pastime in the late 1980s and early 1990s were but a symptom of the broader collapse of the Zionist metanarrative[20] in the public culture (though never in the political or statist culture). But, as we already suggested, the political or statist culture has lost its influence as the population increasingly loses confidence in government and the political leaders of the state and loses interest in issues of collective rather than private concern. Without the Zionist metanarrative in the public culture, Israeli Jews, nonreligious in particular, remain without a mediated tie to Judaism and Jewishness and without a narrative that would help formulate their Israeli identity. The dominant narratives that have replaced Zionism—at least insofar as one can identify them at this stage of the development of a collective Israeli identity—have abandoned the effort to construct a Jewish Israeli identity. At the cultural level with which we are dealing, the dissociation of Judaism and Israeliness leaves Judaism as the property of the Orthodox and the rabbinical establishment, to whom, it should be noted, this condition is quite satisfactory. They now have a monopoly on the definition of Jewishness, and since the realm of secular culture is void of Jewish content, it is a less threatening one. Indeed, the changes in Israeli popular culture may be attributed, in part, to the rise in political importance of the Orthodox sector.

The manner in which Israel's major newspapers treat the Jewish component in the Israeli national identity illustrates our contention regarding the decline of the Zionist metanarrative.[21] With the Six-Day War and Yom Kippur War, we reach the apogee of a process in which, under the influence of the Zionist narrative, the press portrayed Judaism and Jewishness as an integral component of Israel's ethnonational identity. The soldiers of the Israel Defense Forces were pictured as the ultimate heroes of the Israeli collective and as the model of authentic Jews. It is not too far-fetched to say that they were portrayed as the ultimate *religious* Jews. The soldiers, dressed in "the prayer shawls [*tallitot*] of khaki,"[22] hardly represented the classical notions of Judaism, but they were, at least in the minds of those who produced Israeli culture, representatives and guardians of authentic Judaism.

As we suggested, this metanarrative gradually lost is hold in the 1970s and 1980s. It was replaced, certainly in the press, by a postnational narrative, built around the values of universalism and humanism. In the framework of this narrative, both the Jewish religious identity and the Israeli Zionist ethnonational identity (with its accompanying Jewish component) were perceived as anachronistic identities that served only to isolate Israelis from the rest of the world. The Zionist metanarrative was viewed as a threat to both individual and collective self-realization and as an obstacle to peace. The new narrative, which emphasized the motif of peace and the consequences of peace, contained messianic and eschatological elements, and some interpreted this too as a version of Jewish messianism. There were even those who, under the cry for a "return to the Jewish bookshelf," sought a new interpretation of Judaism in which universalism and humanism became the major values of the Jewish tradition. But these voices were a minority among the cacophony of opposing voices that emphasized the tie between Judaism/Jewishness, religion, and the Orthodox establishment. Judaism/Jewishness was now portrayed as the obstacles to truth and peace and the symbol of extremism, violence, and ultranationalism. In their private lives, Jews continued to observe some Jewish ritual (folk practice might be a better term) and in their minds and hearts continued to harbor feelings of association with Jewishness and the Jewish people, but the public culture provided neither a language nor a symbol system for its expression.

The consequence of all this was that in the realm of public culture, a bifurcation of Judaism/Jewishness on the one hand and Israeliness on the other emerged. Israel is a Jewish state, and Judaism/Jewishness continues to play a role in its public culture—in the media, in art, and in music in literature. But at the risk of oversimplification, we think it fair to generalize and say that in the eyes of the producers of middlebrow Israeli culture (the agents of cultural transmission), Judaism/Jewishness was distinguished from Israeli culture. It has an assigned place in the cultural agenda, but it is not to be confused with "real" culture. For example, in both Israeli cinema and television, the Jewish tradition does not appear as a natural, daily, "normal" element in the life of the Israeli protagonist. Compare this with the manner in which daily life is portrayed in the American media. The Simpson family is a good example. Church attendance on Sunday is a regular part of the family schedule. The Simpsons are not a religious family. Homer can't stand church attendance. He presents a constant challenge to the pastor whenever the pastor extends his sermon. The pastor in turn represents corruption and religious close-mindedness. The religious character in the show, Ned Flanders, is grotesque and negative. In other words, the show hardly caters to organized religion. But this is our point. Religion is part of the American scene whether one likes it or not. Homer, the average American, does go to church. There is no counterpart in Israeli television serials. We would not expect Israeli television serials to show the average Israeli attending synagogue. Only a quarter do so, according to the Guttman survey referred to previously. But according to that same report, 85 percent indicate that they participate in a Passover Seder, 71 percent light candles on the Sabbath, 67 percent fast on Yom Kippur, 55 percent have a special Sabbath meal, 48 percent recite (or hear) *Kiddush* before the Friday night meal, and 41 percent build a *succah*. Forty-one percent also report that they refrain from working in public on Shabbat. In other words, Jewish ritualistic elements plays a role in the lives of the vast majority or a strong minority of Israeli Jews, but this finds little place in the behavior of those portrayed on Israeli television screens or in the Israeli cinema. The notable exception is the portrayal of the older generation of *mizrahi* Jews. Scenes that depict *mizrahim* are likely to express some form of religious traditionalism. Some will wear skullcaps (*kippot*), the family might sit around the Sabbath table and hear the patriarch invoke traditional blessings, and one even finds scenes depicting a visit to the synagogue. But these practices are played out by the older parental generation. The media make clear that the protagonists are uncomfortable in such settings and find them inappropriate and unsuitable.

We are not arguing that Jews, Judaism, and even religion are ignored (although, as discussed later in this chapter, this too happens). They have their place in both television and the cinema, indeed in literature as well, but they are representative of the "religious other"—of "them" and not "us." In the 1990s, when the dichotomy between religious and secular became so critical in the construction of the Israeli identity, one finds a greater maturity in the handling of the Jewish/Judaic element. But Judaism/Jewishness continues to be identified as "religious" and generally represented by a stereotypical character. Religious Jews might cavil at such treatment. But it is the nonreligious Jews who affirm their Judaism and participate on a selective basis in Jewish ritual and ceremony that are simply ignored. It is the nonreligious Israeli whose Jewish lifestyle is ignored by the agents of Israeli culture.

There is no more dramatic evidence of how secondary Judaism/Jewishness is to the producers of Israeli middlebrow culture than a recent incident. Israel has three television channels. Channel One is governed by the Israel Broadcasting Authority and is noncommercial. Channels Two and Ten are commercial channels. However, their programming must be approved by a government-appointed public committee. In August 2002, the committee rejected channel Ten's programming for September. September is the month filled with Jewish holidays. In 2002, it included the Jewish New Year, Yom Kippur (the holiest day of the Jewish calendar), and the seven-day festival of Succoth. However, the Channel Ten programs for the month of September "made no reference to these days. . . . Members of the committee asked the directors of the channel to add programs which carry associations to the Hebrew calendar."[23]

The manner in which the movie *Avanti Popolo* treats the tension between Israeliness and Jewishness provides another example of the Jewish–Israeli dichotomy. The movie takes place in the last moments of the Six-Day War, and the heroes are Israeli and Egyptian soldiers. But the widespread interpretation of the movie's theme, an interpretation expressed by movie critic Uri Klein, was the conflict between Israelis and Jews. He observes that

> the Israelis in the film are represented by the Israeli soldiers . . . and the Jews are represented by the two Egyptian soldiers. At the climax of the film, one of the Egyptian soldiers, who is a theater actor by profession, recites Shylock's well known monologue from Shakespeare's *Merchant of Venice*.[24]

In other words, here is an example of an Israeli production that does contain a Jewish element, but it is expressed by Arabs, the ultimate "other" in Israeli Jewish identity.

The attitude of Israeli culture to the notion of penitence or becoming a born-again Jew (*hazara b'tshuvah)* also illustrates our point. Dan Urian, for example, found that during the 1980s, Israeli television portrayed *hazara b'tshuvah* in a positive light. The description of the penitent was that of a secular, antireligious, leftist, drug-addicted suicidal criminal who embraces religious observance as a solution to the meaningless of his life. Such persons turn into righteous, family-oriented, quiet, positive people. However, during the 1990s, television adopted the stance of the Israeli theater. *Hazara b'tshuvah* was now depicted as a questionable and grotesque act based on a culture of lying whose outcome, for example, undermines the family and destroys the world of the individual as well as the world of the Israeli collective.[25]

We see in the treatment of *hazara b'tshuvah* by the disseminators of Israeli culture a representative case, exemplifying the attitude toward the Jewish components in Israeli identity. The notion that lies at the heart of this treatment is the binary distinction, as we have argued, between Israeli culture and Jewish culture, and *hazara b'tshuvah* becomes a ritual act of crossing lines and abandoning one camp—the camp of "us," the Israelis—for another camp—the camp of the "other," the camp of the "religious," which is identical with the camp of Jews and Judaism. Israeliness and Jewishness become mutually exclusive categories, and their integration becomes impossible, undesirable, and unnatural. Any in-between category, such as traditional rather than religious Judaism, is presented, in the best case, as an anomalous identity that will inevitably dissolve in a process of identifying with one side or another. In the worst case, it is hypocritical and disloyal.

Uri Zohar (the prominent actor who became a *hozer b'tshuvah*) is a kind of role model for this sort of interpretation. A great deal of attention is paid to the manner in which Zohar's *hazara b'tshuvah* serves the ultra-Orthodox *haredi* community as a myth and symbol to attract more penitents. Zohar himself plays an active role in the confirmation and continual reconstruction of this myth and has placed himself at the service of those who would mobilize him for political purposes. We are not arguing that the manner in which Zohar, the individual, is perceived by the cultural elite does any injustice to the truth of his particular case. What we are saying is that there is no reason for Zohar to be viewed as the paradigm for *hazara b'tshuvah*. One could point to contrary examples where an artist has successfully melded the two identities. This is especially true of artists from a *mizrahi* background. The case of the musician Ehud Banai is instructive. Banai has gradually turned to greater religious observance and has reached the point where he openly adopted a traditional lifestyle. Nevertheless, he did not cross any red lines but continued to conduct one of the most successful musical careers in Israel in tandem with his growing affirmation of tradition. But it is the Zohar case that remains paradigmatic for the generators of Israeli culture. In their eyes, Zohar's *hazara b'tshuvah* means that he is "lost" to the world of Israeli culture and further demonstrates the notion that one must choose between "us" and "them"—Israeliness or Judaism/Jewishness. Zohar's *hazara b'tshuvah* provides the ostensibly perfect model of the choices that an Israeli faces. You are either an Israeli or a religious Jew. There is no melding of the two identities.

The treatment of the Jewish holidays is an example of the changing manner in which the media treat the Jewish component in Israeli identity. We already mentioned how one television channel simply chose to ignore them. The situation in the press is not that extreme, but the changes in the past few decades have been dramatic. A glance at the newspapers of the 1950s through the 1970s reveals that the holiday issues of the papers are indeed "holiday issues." In addition to their coverage of the news, they concerned themselves with the traditional aspects of the holiday as these aspects were transmitted via the Zionist prism. This was also true of the Friday (i.e., the Friday-Shabbat) issues. This accent on the traditional nature of the holidays has declined in the past few decades. It has almost entirely disappeared from the two most widely read Israeli dailies,[26] *Yediot Aharonot* and *Ma'ariv* (although not at all from *Ha'aretz*, a less read but more prestigious daily). The popular dailies will carry columns by a rabbi or religious personality commenting on the Jewish holiday or on the biblical portion of the week appropriate to a particular Sabbath, but the columns are written from an Orthodox perspective and serve as a gesture to the religious reader. The orientations of most Israelis (nonreligious yet interested, involved, and sympathetic to the tradition) receive little expression.

A similar treatment of the Jewish holidays is found on television. Israeli television made its appearance after the Six-Day War, and Channel Two began airing only in 1994, when the undermining of the Zionist metanarrative reached its peak. Except for those programs specifically intended for the religious public, it is difficult to identify the place of Jewish holidays on Israeli televisions channels. The most prominent expression of the holiday spirit, with the previously noted exception, is the filming of a Hollywood movie on the festival eve. The most prominent characteristic of the holidays, as reflected in the listings of Israeli public television, is that of family. Programs are those that the whole family can enjoy together. In some cases, the program decision makers air historical docudramas on biblical personalities who might bear some connection to the holiday. These are often programs produced in the United States with a Christian perspective. Only rarely does one find television programs relevant to the holiday from a Jewish perspective—then it will usually be a learned roundtable discussion of the holiday by scholars rather than some original production. The ninth of Av (*Tisha B'Av*) lends itself to this kind of treatment. This is not true of the national holidays, specifically Holocaust Memorial Day and Independence Day. On those occasions, the television channels devote themselves entirely to the significance of the holidays.

The way in which Channel One airs the reading of the *megillah* on Purim is an example of the nature of the concession that Israeli culture offers to Judaism.[27] The public channel feels obligated (or is obligated by its charter) to provide some coverage of the most traditional holidays. Coverage of Purim should be easy because its carnival-like nature offers the least tension between secular and religious values. But Purim does have its strictly religious moments, and the reading of the *megillah* is the most important of them. Channel One positions television cameras in some Orthodox synagogue and covers the event in the most formal manner possible, as if it were saying "We are obliged to handle this topic, we have no idea how to do it, so we turn the production over to those to whom it belongs, that is, the religious." As one television critic remarked, it has no place for the nonreligious Jew who might know little of the ritual aspects of the holiday but wants to learn more.[28]

A segregation between what is thought of as Jewish or religious and what is considered real culture is also reflected in the guides to leisure-time activity in the Israeli press. *Ahbar Hair*, which advertises itself as "the Bible of leisure," omits describing events of a Jewishly traditional nature.

What we are witnessing in the relationship between Judaism and Israeli culture has an ethnic component as well. As we have seen, there are differences between the attitudes of *ashkenazi* Israelis and *mizrahi* Israelis to the Jewish component of their Israeliness, and this too is reflected in Israeli culture. *Ashkenazi* Jews are far more likely to adopt an understanding of Judaism that imposes sharp distinctions between secularism and religiousness and leaves little space for what is best termed religious traditionalism—religious behavior that is based on custom and family tradition tied to a sense of ethnic or national identity rather than religious behavior that is dictated by authoritative interpretations of sacred text. Jews from Islamic countries have retained a strong measure of traditionalism that is dictated by family custom rather than rabbinic fiat, but *mizrahim* are minor voices within the ranks of those who dominate the agencies of Israeli culture, and many of them have adopted the regnant attitudes of *ashkenazim.*

Attitudes toward Judaism/Jewishness are more complex in modern Hebrew literature.[29] We confine ourselves to the observation that the retreat from the collective to the personal in the past few decades characterizes Hebrew as well as other Western literature. However, it is more surprising in Israel given the challenges that Israeli society faces. There are those who see signs of a crisis of meaning in the retreat of the younger generation of Hebrew writers to the personal and the private (to the point where there is avoidance of narrative writing in the customary sense):

> One gets the impression that in this artistic revolution of young writers there is nothing new . . . not so much a withdrawal of an embattled artistic vanguard from some dominant cultural community but a colony of forced exiles trying to create a minimum space for itself in what appears to be a cultural vacuum.[30]

This vacuum, we believe, stems at least in part from the decline of meaningful frameworks of collective identity that had previously existed. There is little place in this "cultural vacuum" for Judaism/Jewishness, whether in its traditional or in its Zionist, ethnonational formulation.

CONCLUSIONS

The question with which we introduced this chapter has an easy answer. There is no real contradiction between the absence of Judaism/Jewishness in the public culture and the observance of Jewish ritual and practice at the private, familial level. Israel's public culture has never been especially sympathetic to ritual observance (and is even less so today than in the past), but the majority of the public continues to observe whatever traditions it does observe without regard to the public culture. Perhaps the most remarkable finding of this study is how little the public culture impinges on private observance. This may be especially true within the Jewish tradition. As long as

Jews had no state of their own, religious life necessarily carried on in the home and family circle rather than in public festivals and rites. Hence, Jewish ritual was able to sustain itself despite the public culture.

This answer, while correct, is a bit too facile. After all, times have changed, there is a Jewish state, and it did develop a panoply of rituals and rites built around the Jewish symbols. These rituals and rites have become increasingly bereft of meaning and content. Why, then, has ritual observance at the private or familial level sustained itself despite its minor importance in the public culture? On the other hand, there is some evidence for the gradual decline of ritual observance. How is this to be explained? Finally, how are we to explain the differences between *ashkenazim* and *mizrahim*? We note seven points with regard to these three questions. They are not mutually exclusive. In fact, some of them say the same thing from a slightly different perspective.

The first point is methodological in nature. Perhaps the absence of Judaism and Jewishness in Israeli culture does affect private observance, but people don't change their behavior overnight. Precisely because ritual behavior and a sense of Jewishness are deeply embedded in the behavior of the Israeli Jew, he or she carries on with this behavior and the same attitudes even though the underlying basis is atrophying.

Second, it is possible that whereas attitudes toward Judaism and the practice of Jewish religious observance have declined dramatically, respondents are reluctant to admit that changes have taken place in their own lives, that they no longer observe as much or care as much as they once did. It might take a few decades or another generation before the changes that our analysis of Israeli culture suggests find expression in survey data. We cannot dismiss the opposite possibility. In light of the absence of Jewishness and Judaism and even the negative attitudes toward Judaism and Jewishness by the cultural elite, respondents may report less Jewish practice than is truly the case.

A third point to note is that Jewish identity—that is, calling oneself a Jew and acting out basic Jewish ritual—is a consequence of an absence of real alternatives. The alternative to being Jewish may be unacceptable to our respondents. Despite the secondary and segmented place of Judaism and Jewishness, Israel remains a Jewish state. This is reflected in a number of ways. The symbols of the state are Jewish, it is the Jewish holidays that are celebrated as national holidays, it is Jewish history and not the history of Palestine that youngsters learn as their history, and it is the Holocaust that continues to serve as the central myth of Israeli society and that forms the prism through which the present is understood. Israel is also, as Smooha calls it, an ethnonational state[31] in the sense that public policy favors the Jewish sector of the population. The stark reality of one's Jewishness and the importance of one's Jewishness are reinforced by growing demands by Israeli Arabs for greater benefits and demonstrations of empathy with the Palestinians in the occupied territories. The alternative to being Jewish in Israel is not the same as it is in the United States or many parts of western Europe. Israeli society, even middle-class, high-tech, globalized Israeli society, hardly recognizes a neutral or a cosmopolitan or global identity—the real alternative that strikes everyone except a small coterie of intellectuals as the alternative to being an Israeli Jew is to be an Israeli Arab. This is a powerful force in maintaining the Jewish population's sense of Jewishness in the face of other tendencies that act to trivialize it. And if Jews cannot act out their Jewishness in public rites and ceremonies, all the more reason to do so at the private level.

A fourth point is that the observer of Israeli society is mislead about the absence of Jewishness because Israeli culture is described and defined by a small group of Israeli Jews who are indeed distanced from and dissociated from Judaism and Jewishness but who represent only the cultural and academic elite. According to one study, the most secular are least aware of how small a percentage they constitute the Israeli Jewish population.[32] This would not be the first time that the patrons of Israeli culture, out of enmity to the Jewish tradition, have distorted the reality around them. Dalia Manor argues that Israeli artists in the 1920s who portrayed Jewish themes were criticized for doing so by the art critics and that the work embodying these scenes was ignored.[33] In an observation of immediate relevance to our topic, Peter Berger says the following:

> There is a thin but very influential stratum of intellectuals—broadly defined as people with Western-style higher education, especially in the humanities and social sciences. They constitute a secular internationale, whose members can be encountered in every country. . . . When they travel to, say, Istanbul, Jerusalem, New Delhi, they almost exclusively meet with other intellectuals—that is, people much like themselves—and they can jump to the conclusion that this faculty club faithfully reflects the cultural situation outside—a fatal mistake indeed.[34]

A mistake, we would add, that leads them to believe that their own cultural representations are rooted in reality.

Fifth, the fact that the majority of Israeli Jews report an unanticipated level of traditional practice may be understood, by way of analogy, to other forms of personal practices. Respondents, after all, are being asked a question about their behavior and beliefs. Whereas they may be responding truthfully, the fact that they are responding to a question posed by an outsider may mislead us about the significance to them of what they report.

Related to the previous explanation is our sixth point: the dissociation of religion and culture that also helps account for the slow decline of religious observance. At the risk of oversimplifying a complex historical picture, it is fair to say that until the nineteenth century, most Jews in eastern Europe and Islamic countries lived within the confines of a religiously traditional culture. That is, the norms and the values and beliefs—the very rhythms of the society with which they identified themselves and with which they were identified by others—was imbued with a Jewish religious aura in the same way that the society in which the vast majority of Muslims lived was imbued with a Muslim aura. Some (many) Jews, especially in eastern Europe, strove to enter into the broader culture, a condition made possible by the release of the Jews from many legal constraints and the fact (or at least the appearance of the fact) that that culture was becoming religiously neutral.

The breakout from the confines of a strictly Jewish culture meant the necessity to think through what being Jewish meant. Here we find the seeds for the representation of Judaism or Jewishness as a religion with a precise set of demands in one area of life but with little or no relevance to another area of life. This is what fundamentalists of all religions (in the case of the Jews, we mean the Orthodox, the religious party that emerged out of the dissociation of religion and culture) mightily resisted. That association of religion, culture, Judaism, and Jewishness (i.e., religious obligation and ethnic tie) that had been so natural in the premodern society now became an artificial construct. As far as the Orthodox were concerned, this required the reconstruction of a religious Jewish society that was self-consciously insulated from the larger society. The vast majority of Jews, however, rejected this effort, and the Orthodox were left as a distinctly minority party. Some groups of Jews developed alternate ideologies to that of the Orthodox. Many members of these ideological groups, and certainly the mass of Jews who belonged to none of the ideological camps, persisted in living and in some cases even advocating a pattern of life that recalled though did not replicate the older Jewish tradition. This is what we mean by religious traditionalism. Holidays were observed more or less, synagogues were visited at least on the holiest of days, and home rituals were recalled but without the punctiliousness or the sense of obligation or even the sense of the divine, which the Orthodox demanded. It is impossible to say whether this stemmed from a desire to preserve custom, from nostalgia for the manner in which one was raised, from family obligation as a mode to teach the young about their Jewish roots, or simply because many looked to ritual and holy days to impart a sense of order into their own lives. This was the pattern of life that the first modern settlers brought with them to the land of Israel, and this was the pattern of life that we suspect the masses of eastern European immigrants brought with them when they arrived in Israel between the end of the war and the first years of statehood. Zionist ideology, once it shed it socialist overtones, strengthened this pattern of behavior. Although Zionism was a secular movement, it incorporated Jewish symbols in its public celebrations and in most cases left room for observance of private ritual. Nevertheless, in the decades following the establishment of the State, it would appear that the pattern of traditional living slowly declined at the private level, at least among the *ashkenazim*, because it bore little relationship to the new Israeli culture, which was increasingly patterned on Western consumerist culture. It was not so much challenged by that culture as it was rendered irrelevant. The more recent disappearance of Zionism as the culture of Israel further contributed to that process. Only Orthodoxy, what in Israel is called "religion," offered an alternative. In the case of the *haredim*, it offered an alternative culture. In the case of the religious Zionists, it offered a partial culture but provided an ideology that made participation in Israeli culture religiously legitimate. In other words, religious Zionism defined Israeli culture in its own terms, thereby rendering it compatible with religious observance. But Orthodoxy, whether of the *haredi* variety or even of the religious Zionist variety, challenged the traditionalists and their behavior. To the Orthodox, the behavior of the traditionalists was religiously incoherent. The Orthodox made clear to the traditionalists that their pattern of Jewish living was illegitimate. That traditional behavior constituted a watered-down version of "authentic Judaism" and no substitute for what Judaism required. Pressed between the temptations of the consumerist culture and the admonitions of the rabbinic elite, some traditionalists joined Orthodoxy. But the greater number, with no ideology to buttress their traditional mode of behavior and no rational justification for continuing the practices of the past, appear to be abandoning them (albeit slowly) when they appear onerous or bothersome or inappropriate to other cultural patterns.

The pattern among the *mizrahim*, those who come from Islamic countries, is slightly different, perhaps no more than a slower process compared to what took place among *ashkenazim*. But *mizrahim* are different because they acquired not only an Israeli identity but also, after arriving in Israel, a *mizrahi* identity, a result of their unique experiences in the Israeli context. Behaving in a religiously traditional, albeit non-Orthodox manner was built into *mizrahi* identity, thereby attenuating the process of decline. Iraqi, Tunisian, or Moroccan Jews did not identify themselves, nor were they identified by others as Iraqi, Tunisian, or Moroccan Jews in their countries of origin. They were just Jews. So they retain the notion that their Iraqi, Tunisian, or Moroccan Jewish identity is simply Judaism. Indeed, when they speak of their Jewish identity, they may mean their ethnic identity. This, in turn, makes their Jewishness more encompassing than their Israeli identity, and it is therefore no surprise that they feel themselves more Jewish than Israeli. Hence, the strengthening of *mizrahi* identity was accompanied by attenuation in the process of decline in traditionalist religious behavior. This may change for two reasons. First, the consumerist culture presents pressures or temptations. Children of *mizrahim*, according to the latest Guttman Report, are even less traditional than their parents than are children of *ashkenazim*. Second, traditional *mizrahim* find themselves under increased pressure from ultra-Orthodox *mizrahim* (Shas) and Rav Mordecai Eliyahu of the religious Zionist camp, who delegitimates traditionalist behavior.

It is instructive to compare what has happened and is happening in Israel with what happened in the other great center of Jewish population, the United States. The masses of Jews who arrived from eastern Europe at the turn of the twentieth century until World War I were also traditionalists in their behavior. A minority was aligned with some ideological camp—Bundists, Anarchists, and so on—but the majority had no particular ideological affiliation. But among all of them, traditional Jewish behavior, transplanted from eastern Europe and adapted to the exigencies of life in the urban ghettos of the United States, dictated the rhythms and patterns by which they lived. The ideological parties disintegrated under the impact of American life. But those who continued in their traditionalist patterns of behavior and certainly those who had no previous ideological home could find one in the newly established movement of Conservative Judaism. This took time. The Conservative movement grew slowly, and it was not until the end of World War II that one can speak of its rapid expansion. But as Marshall Sklare has demonstrated,[35] the movement was home to the ethnically sensitive traditional Jew of eastern European origins almost from it very beginning. Jewish leaders, the rabbis, and the elite of the Conservative movement developed an ideology that need not concern us here. What is important is that the Conservative movement deliberately sought to lessen the tensions between the religious demands that it raised and the behavior of its adherents. In other words, it welcomed into its synagogues the traditionalist Jew and offered a kind of legitimacy to traditionalist behavior. Actually, the process described here was more often reversed. The traditionalist Jews established synagogues and then sought to employ Conservative rabbis who would conduct their own lives in the manner expected of elite religious figures but who would minimize the demands made on the traditionalists themselves and would focus their major attention on ethnic issues, combating antisemitism and, later in support for Israel, issues with which traditionalists were in full sympathy. The point is that the Conservative movement provided a home that offered an alternative to Orthodoxy. In many cases, this was a de facto "ethnic" or "cultural" alternative, though it called itself "religious." They were able to reestablish a tie between Jewish culture and religion, albeit a partial culture in the context of the larger American culture. This may have slowed the process of declining traditionalist observance. Perhaps it did not, but it did offer the sense in which being Jewish—carrying the label and identity of a Jew—fit into acceptable patterns of American culture. It was impossible for the vast majority of the immigrants and their children to be Orthodox. Indeed, Orthodoxy is a pattern of Jewish life that was foreign not only to them but even to their parents and grandparents. What Conservative and later Reform Judaism did was to legitimize the Jewish religion in American terms and offer a framework into which the immigrant and his or her descendants could fit their own pattern of Jewish behavior. Effectively speaking, there is no such home, no such alternative in Israel. The reasons for this is are beyond the purview of this chapter.

Finally, our seventh point is that paradox of paradoxes: that Israeli culture dissociates the Jew from the Israeli has less of an impact today than it might have had in the past because the very retreat to the private and the familial that we noted as characteristic of contemporary Western culture and, in its wake, Israeli culture means that what one does and how one behaves at the private and familial level is less affected than ever by the nature of the public culture. The retreat into oneself means that it no longer matters if public meaning systems are inconsistent with how one conducts one's life.

NOTES

1. Bernard Susser and Charles S. Liebman, *Choosing Survival: Strategies for a Jewish Future* (New York: Oxford University Press, 1999).

2. Yair Sheleg, *The New Religious Jews: Recent Developments among Observant Jews in Israel* (Jerusalem: Keter, 2000; in Hebrew).

3. Charles Liebman, "Modern Orthodoxy in Israel," *Judaism* 47 (fall 1998): 405–10.

4. Kimmy Caplan, "The Internal Popular Discourse of Israeli Haredi Women," *Archives de Sciences Sociales des Religions* (2004).

5. Tamar Elor and Eren Neria, "The Wandering Haredi: The Use of Time and Space among the Haredi Population of Jerusalem," in *Text, Rhetoric and Behavior: Collected Articles on Haredi Society in Israel*, ed. Emanuel Sivan and Kimmy Caplan (Jerusalem: Van Leer Institute and the Kibbutz Hameuchad, 2004, in Hebrew).

6. On the role of religion and the use of traditional symbols in the *yishuv* (the Jewish settlement in Palestine prior to the creation of the state) and on the role of religious symbols in the strengthening of national identity, see, for example, Charles S. Liebman and Eliezer Don-Yehiya, *The Civil Religion of Israel: Traditional Judaism and Political Culture in the Jewish State* (Berkeley: University of California Press, 1983); Anita Shapira, "Religious Notions of the Labor Movement," in *Zionism and Religion*, ed. Shmuel Almog, Jehuda Reinharz, and Anita Shapira (Jerusalem: Mercaz Zalman Shazar, 1994; in Hebrew), 301–27, and, in that same volume, Shmuel Almog, "Religious Values in the Second Aliyah," 285–300; Moti Zeira, *Rural Collective Settlement and Jewish Culture in Eretz Israel during the 1920's* (Jerusalem: Yard Yitzhak Ben Zvi, 2000); and Nili Aryeh-Sapir, "Shaping an Urban Culture: Rituals and Celebrations in Tel-Aviv in Its Early Years" (Ph.D. diss., Tel Aviv University, 2000; in Hebrew).

7. Even in the prestate period, there was probably more observance of "religious" rituals than many scholars acknowledge. In an interesting letter from Chaim Weizmann to the American Jewish leader Louis Marshall in 1924, Weizmann, as an afterthought, perhaps to reassure Marshall that the *yishuv* was not totally atheistic, writes that "the picture of Jaffe on Rosh Hashana and Yom Kippur was divine. I was told that 17,000 of the 27,000 Tel Aviv residents went to synagogue. The large synagogue of Tel Aviv (there are three such synagogues) was filled all day and every day. I saw this myself. Halutzim from all over Eretz Israel came to the cities to pray, just as in the past, and at the end of Yom Kippur, after the fast, the joy, the Hebrew songs were like a hymn rising to the God of Israel as a thanks for the great privilege." This is surely an exaggerated picture. It is unlikely that 17,000 people could have found a place to worship in Tel Aviv even if private places of worship were established for the holidays. We must also recall that a good portion of the *yishuv* were not pioneer settlers but petit bourgeois. But the letter also points to an atmosphere that may be as close to the truth as the opposite image—the settlers as atheists in rebellion against established religion. (We are indebted to Zvi Zameret, director of Yad Yizhak Ben Zvi. for providing us with this document.)

8. For an extended discussion, see Liebman and Don-Yehiya, *The Civil Religion of Israel.*

9. Shlomit Levy, Hanna Levinsohn, and Elihu Katz, *Jewish Israelis: A Portrait* (Jerusalem: Avi Chai and the Israel Democracy Institute, 2002; in Hebrew) (the highlights of the study appeared as a separate booklet under the same name as the report; we cite the highlights unless otherwise noted); Shlomit Levy, Hanna Levinsohn, and Elihu Katz, *Beliefs, Observances and Social Interaction among Israeli Jews* (Jerusalem: Louis Guttman Institute of Applied Social Research, 1993) (the highlights of that report are reprinted in *The Jewishness of Israelis,* ed. Charles Liebman and Elihu Katz [Albany: State University of New York Press, 1997], which also includes an analysis of the 1993 report); Yair Auron, *Jewish-Israeli Identity* (Tel Aviv: Sifriat Poalim Publishing House, 1993); Michal Shamir and Asher Arian, "Collective Identity and Electoral Competition in Israel," *American Political Science Review* 93 (June 1999): 265–77; Uri Farago, "The Jewish Identity of Israeli Youth, 1965–1985," *Yahadut Zmanenu* 5 (1989): 259–85 (in Hebrew); Uri Farago, National Identity and Regional Identity in Israel," in *Between I and We,* ed. Azmi Bashara (Tel Aviv: Van Leer Institute and the Kibbutz Hameuchad, 1999; in Hebrew), 153–68; Eliezer Ben-Rafael and Stephen Sharot, *Ethnicity, Religion, and Class in Israeli Society* (Cambridge: Cambridge University Press, 1991); Yochanan Peres and Ephraim Yuchtman-Yaar, *Between Consent and Dissent: Democracy and Peace in the Israeli* Mind (Jerusalem: Israel Democracy Institute, 1998; in Hebrew); an unpublished study by Ezra Kopelowitz and Hadar Franco of 160 students in Rupin College in 2001 (for a report of the study with a summary of the findings, see *Ha'aretz,* 12 September 2002, 3B); Jacob Shamir and Michal Shamir, *The Anatomy of Public Opinion* (Ann Arbor: University of Michigan Press, 2000); Stephen Sharot, "Jewish and Other National and Ethnic Identities of Israeli Jews," in *National Variations in Jewish Identity,* ed. Steven M. Cohen and Gabriel Horenczyk (Albany: State University of New York Press, 1999), 299–316; Eliezer Leshem, "The Aliyah from the Former Soviet Union and the Religious-Secular Cleavage in Israeli Society," in *From Russia to Israel: Identity and Culture in Transition,* ed. Moshe Lisak and Eliezer Leshem (Tel Aviv: Hakkibutz Hameuchad, 2001; in Hebrew), 125–48; Alek Epstein, "The 'Russian' Road to Being Jewish: Thoughts Following the Research Report *Jewish Israelis: A Portrait* (lecture delivered at a conference to discuss the 2002 Guttman Report, Jerusalem, 27 May 2002).

10. Simon Herman, *Jewish Identity: A Social Psychological Perspective* (Beverly Hills, Calif.: Sage Library of Social Research, 1977).

11. Auron, *Jewish-Israeli Identity,* 30–31.

12. Levy, Levinsohn, and Katz, *Jewish Israelis,* 14.

13. Amos Elon, *The Israelis* (London: Penguin, 1971).

14. Laura Zarembski, *The Religious-Secular Divide in the Eyes of Israel's Leaders and Opinion Makers* (Jerusalem: Floersheimer Institute for Policy Studies, 2002).

15. Catherine Albanese, "Religion and American Popular Culture: An Introductory Essay," *Journal of the American Academy of Religion* 64 (fall 1996): 737.

16. The term is from Yaacov Yadgar, "From the Particularistic to the Universalistic: National Narratives in Israel's Mainstream Press, 1967–1997," *Nations and Nationalism* 8 (2002): 55–72.

17. The Russian media is a special case.

18. As Habermas notes, this distinction between the civic-public realm and the state realm is necessary for the maintenance of a democratic society. Jürgen Habermas, *The*

Structural Transformation of the Public Sphere: An Inquiry into a Category of Bourgeois Society (Cambridge, Mass.: MIT Press, 1992); Craig Calhoun, ed., *Habermas and the Public Sphere* (Cambridge, Mass.: MIT Press, 1992).

19. Stephen Sharot, "Traditional, Modern, or Postmodern? Recent Religious Developments among Jews in Israel," in *Postmodernity, Sociology and Religion*, ed. Kieran Flanagan and Peter C. Jupp (London: Macmillan, 1996), 119. It is important to note that the weakening of Zionism is paralleled by the strengthening of Jewish identity, as we indicated in the previous section. This suggests to us, as we note in the concluding section, that the public culture is less important than we might have otherwise thought.

20. Uriel Dan, "Zionism in the Israeli Theater," *Israel Affairs* 8 (autumn/winter 2002): 43–55.

21. For a comprehensive review of Israeli newspaper treatment of the national tradition, see Yaacov Yadgar, "Intellectuals and Tradition: The Attitude of the Israeli Press to the Israeli National Narrative, 1967–1997" (doctoral diss., Ramat Gan, 1999; in Hebrew).

22. *Ma'ariv*, 7 October 1973, 1.

23. *Ha'aretz*, 23 August 2002, 23.

24. Uri Klein, "National and Personal Cinema," *Kesher* 31 (May 2002): 47e–55e.

25. Dan Urian, "Touch the Sky: Jewish Identity in Modern Israeli Culture," *Kesher* 30 (November 2001): 31–41 (in Hebrew).

26. For example, in 1971, the front page of the Rosh Hashanah edition of *Ma'ariv* included the headline "Masses Will Gather Tonight in Five Thousand Synagogues for the Rosh Hashanah Services" (*Ma'ariv*, 19 September 1971). The same edition, in separate stories, reports on religious services in Jewish communities around the world and (in keeping with the Zionist metanarrative) their difficulties. Ten years later, a similar headline on the front page read "Preparations Were Completed for Handling Thousands of Worshipers at the Western Wall." The report was accompanied by a column discussing the holiday rituals (*Ma'ariv*, 28 September 1981, 1). The literary supplement included several references to the holiday. Ten years later, the front-page reference to the holiday was headlined "Security Forces Are Preparing for the Holiday" (*Ma'ariv*, 8 September 1991, 1). The holiday supplement included a special guide for hikes and tours headlined "Special for the Holidays." The literary supplement made no mention of the holiday. The September 2001 Rosh Hashanah edition did not contain any front-page reference to the holiday. The back-page headline read "For the First Time: Armed Guards at Synagogues." Three secondary headlines of the same report read "Vacation: Tens of Thousands Are Flying Abroad but Not to the U.S.A.," a second read "Money: The ATM Machines Will Be Filled with Cash," and the third read "Missing You: Rosh Hashanah Cards to the Soldiers Kidnapped in Lebanon." The literary supplement made no reference to the holiday (*Ma'ariv*, 17 September 2001).

27. Sagi Green, "Television: Redundant," *Ha'aretz*, 26 February 2002, 16.

28. In a judgment that we think is too extreme, Benjamin Harshav writes with empathy that "the essence of Israeli literature today is not 'Jewish' other than in its language and its readers—just as the essence of any other literature is not necessarily national. . . . The framework is 'Jewish' but the content is human, or better put, it is 'literary.' And to the extent that one can speak of literature as representing, in the

wider sense of the word, the consciousness of its authors and readers, this cosmopolitan viewpoint also represents them."

29. Benjamin Harshav, "The Modern Jewish Revolution: Notes toward Its Understanding," *Alpayim* 23 (2000): 44 (in Hebrew).

30. Gadi Taub, *The Dispirited Rebellion* (Tel Aviv: Hakibutz Hameuchad, 1997; in Hebrew), 47.

31. Sammy Smooha and Theodor Hanf, "The Diverse Modes of Conflict: Regulation in Deeply Divided Societies," *International Journal of Comparative Sociology* 33 (1992): 26–47.

32. The material is found in the 1993 Guttman Study and is described in Liebman and Katz, *The Jewishness of Israelis*, 95–96.

33. Dalia Manor, "The Dancing Jews and Other Characters: Art in the Jewish Settlement in Palestine in the 1920's," *Journal of Modern Jewish Studies* 1 (April 2002): 84.

34. Peter Berger, "The 2000 Paul Hanly Furfrey Lecture: Reflections on the Sociology of Religion Today," *Sociology of Religion* 62 (winter 2001): 445.

35. Marshall Sklare, *Conservative Judaism: An American Religious Movement* (New York: Schocken Books; new augm. ed. with new preface, 1972).

CHAPTER 7

Immigrants from the Former Soviet Union: Their Influence and Identity

Theodore H. Friedgut

As several of the authors in this volume have pointed out, Israel's national identity is as yet uncrystallized, resembling more a montage in the making than any fixed and stable whole. Changes are introduced constantly by the influence of developments both domestic and global and not least by the successive waves of immigration. The result has been that in place of the compact, homogeneous, relatively ideologized prestate *yishuv*, Israel's society today is a "cosmopolitan, pluralistic, and heterogeneous society with an increasingly sectarian orientation of an ethnic and religious nature that weakens collective values of various subgroups."[1]

In this chapter, we will analyze the influence of the million-plus immigrants from the former Soviet Union (FSU), themselves a highly heterogeneous public subject to a rapid transition in identity, on this process. Some of the changes that have taken place over the years act to maintain the suspicion and patronizing condescension with which new immigrants have always been regarded and, despite the official abandonment of the "melting pot" model a decade or more ago, pressure the immigrants to conform to the absorbing society, abandoning their own distinctive identities. Other changes ease the way for the newest and most intensive wave of immigrants to assert its own identity within the national montage. The hundreds of thousands who arrived with and immediately after the State's establishment have, on the whole, made a secure place for themselves in Israel. Perhaps most important of all is that 62 percent of the Jewish population of Israel are today native born and grew up in the public environment of the Israeli Zionist ethos and the Hebrew language, whatever their home culture might be.[2] No more is there an ideological minority attempting to socialize a mass immigration to Israel's norms and values. Earlier, in Israel's prestate and early state history, the monopoly of the Hebrew language, the creation of a Hebrew children's literature, and a Zionist historical narrative had been important developments in laying a foundation for a national identity.[3] Though these have been challenged and changed over the years, they remain a part of Israel's founding myths.

The new tolerance of communal traditions gave the FSU immigrants opportunity to insert some of their own holidays into Israel's calendar. While some of these innovations have been accepted easily, others engendered conflict. For a generation or more, religious and ultra-Orthodox commemorations of various festivals and life cycle ceremonies have challenged the secular, national, and agriculture-related ceremonies that once dominated Israel.[4] Beyond this, the differences in understanding of cultural symbols has been ground for conflict.

In the Soviet Union under Communist rule, Christmas was not celebrated publicly. In its place, New Year celebrations were popular, and the symbols of Christmas, stripped of religion, were transferred to the New Year, with Santa Claus becoming Grandfather Frost and the Christmas tree simply a New Year tree. As the one nonpolitical holiday in the Soviet calendar, New Year became a favorite for family and friends to get together. But for veteran Israelis from Catholic countries of Europe, New Year's Eve remained St. Sylvester's night—a traditional night for Jew baiting and pogroms.[5] For those less familiar with this central and eastern European tradition, even among nonreligious Israelis, the Santa Claus figure and the fir tree were redolent of Christian culture and therefore foreign and even hostile, a feeling that the FSU immigrants simply could not comprehend or accept. Today, under the pressure of the immigrants and despite fierce opposition of ultra-Orthodox religious circles, this celebration has become firmly ensconced in Israel's calendar, though the Gregorian New Year is not (as yet) recognized as a nonworking day.

This was not the only change that the immigrants helped introduce to Israel's calendar. The veterans' organization of the FSU immigrants also succeeded in getting the Knesset to pass a law in May 2000 (in the context of a political wooing of the immigrant vote) publicly marking May 9 as a day of solemnities marking the World War II victory over the Nazis in Europe. This involved a reordering of Israel's historical narrative, raising the consciousness of World War II and not only the Holocaust. Last but not least, March 8, marked in the Soviet Union as the International Day of Working Women, has been adopted widely in Israel today as a day of recognition for women at their places of work, marked by the distribution of flowers and sweets. The adoption came when merchants saw the economic potential and began advertising the date and the event, drawing in the general public, as tens of thousands of FSU immigrants sought bouquets for their wives, mothers, and girlfriends. Here, no conflict—cultural, religious, or historical—was encountered.

As a different aspect of such misunderstanding, Israeli teachers have encountered active hostility on the part of immigrant students in the teaching of the Bible in secular secondary schools. The students, overwhelmingly secular in their outlook, regarded this as an attempt to proselytize them, totally unaware that in these schools biblical studies are an introduction to the national history and literature rather than theological.[6] This secular–religious antagonism was perhaps compounded by the particular disorientation suffered by immigrant youth of the 1990s. They came from the massive identity crisis that accompanied the collapse of the Soviet Union, in which all institutions of authority—state and governmental as well as parental and societal—lost status and immediately entered the disorientation of immigration to Israel that further exacerbated all these instabilities. As a result, youthful immigrants were frequently suspicious of any attempts to exercise authority over them and attempted to determine their own values and courses of action.[7] But such misunderstandings were not limited to teacher–student relations. Even in discussions between immigrant teachers and their veteran Israeli colleagues, great misunderstandings arose, with the veterans' feelings ruffled by what they regarded as the immigrants' lack of commitment to Jewishness and the immigrants offended by the veterans' unwillingness to relate positively to aspects of religions other than Judaism.[8] Neither side can easily comprehend the cultural background that the other brings to these symbols.

The reaction of any given group to another introducing new and different values may well depend on the receiving group's understanding of what constitutes culture. One research study found that the residents of Israel's development towns, largely Oriental Jews for whom a traditional religious culture held high priority, had a much more negative evaluation of the cultural contribution to Israel of immigrants from the FSU, a largely secular and modernist group, than did the population of the larger cities, who were much closer oriented to the literary, musical, and scientific heritage of the immigrants and found their secularism much less offensive.[9]

Though immigrants from the Soviet Union were a familiar phenomenon over a long period of Israel's existence, the great wave of the 1990s proved quite different from what had previously been known, "an entirely different sociological generation."[10] Who and what are these new immigrants?

VARIETIES OF RUSSIANS

As we noted, the FSU immigrants are a complex and heterogeneous group who have come to Israel from widely differing backgrounds. We may divide them into two main groups, "moderns" and "traditionals," with each group subdividing further.

The "moderns" divide into "westerners" (*Zapadniki*), coming from the Soviet Union's western borderlands, annexed to the Soviet Union between 1939 and 1945, thus still carrying some live memories of Jewish and Zionist life, and "heartlanders," from the interior of Russia and the Ukraine, under Soviet control since 1917 and cut off more and more from any living Jewish memories, particularly since World War II.[11]

The "traditionals" are Jews from Georgia, the Mountain Jews of the Caucasus, and the Bukharan Jews. Their common feature is that each maintained, even throughout the Soviet period, a Jewish religious life and a traditional family and community structure, and each was an ethnic minority within a similarly traditional ethnic society. All three groups, on arrival in Israel, tend to settle in compact communities, preserving the family connections and community relations familiar to them from their former places of residence. In this, they are not unlike the Moroccan, Kurdish, or other traditional Jewish communities that had been absorbed earlier into Israel. Their traditionalism is, quite naturally, under constant pressure from Israel's predominantly modern culture, and there is a constant tension between the conservative and the modernizing elements of the society, compounding the difficulties of transition. At times, this develops into an intracommunal tension as with the founding, within Israel's religious educational system, of a school for girls of Bukharan origin, financed by a wealthy member of the Bukharan immigrant community, teaching the young women self-esteem, aspirations for education and for a career, and the value of equality with their spouses in place of the traditional subservience of wife to husband.[12] It was noted that within the Bukharan immigrant community, support for this change of tradition was far from unanimous.

Just as Israel's identity is in a state of constant flux, so is that of the immigrants from the FSU. We will therefore have to examine them within a broad and dynamic framework, uncovering tendencies and incipient trends rather than static states of being. On arrival in Israel or on taking the decision to leave the FSU and beginning preparations for *aliyah*, the immigrant is first faced with the question of adopting as his own the basic Israeli narrative or, alternatively, selecting some portions of that narrative while rejecting others, thus essentially exerting an influence for change in the foundations of a national identity. In broadest terms, the fundamental narrative of Israel is based on the history of the Jewish people in the land of Israel in ancient times, a narrative of the rise, fall, and eventual renaissance of a nation and its state. This narrative minimizes the period of life in the Diaspora as one of dependence and submission.[13] While the immigrants could accept the first element of this narrative, having maintained through Soviet times some awareness of Jewish heroes of antiquity, the second element was more difficult for them, for, as we shall see, the Russian culture in which most of them lived was regarded as something of value, not to be surrendered.

THREE WAVES OF IMMIGRATION

There have also been differences in the circumstances accompanying the exodus of Jews from the Soviet Union in different periods as well as differences in the circumstances of their reception in Israel. There have been essentially three distinct waves of post–World War II immigration to Israel from the Soviet Union.

The first wave, beginning from 1955 and lasting until 1967, brought 12,132 Jewish immigrants.[14] This was an immigration mainly though not exclusively of older people, separated during the war from relatives who were living in Israel. Of small dimensions and given little or no publicity, this wave of emigration was easily absorbed by Israel, consisting as it did of persons for whom Israel held a specific attraction. The vicissitudes of this wave also demonstrated the political nature of the emigration in the Soviet period. It was almost completely cut off after the 1956 Sinai campaign, recovering only slowly as Soviet–Israeli relations became normal, reaching 1,892 *olim* in 1966, only to be cut off again in the wake of the 1967 Six-Day War.

The second wave began in mid-1968 and lasted until the early autumn of 1989. In that period, an additional 178,180 Soviet Jews came to Israel, while additional tens of thousands went to the United States, Germany, and numerous other countries.[15] This emigration differed from its predecessor in that it was marked by an open, public struggle, initiated from within the Soviet Union by Jews there. The emigration wave was thus accompanied by a heightened consciousness of national solidarity and attempts to acquire knowledge of all aspects of Jewish life. In addition, particularly in the first years of this wave, a large percentage of the immigrants were "westerners" from the Baltic republics and the western Ukraine or "traditionals," particularly from Georgia. All these factors eased the integration of the new immigrants into Israel and its institutions without creating great pressures for change of existing cultural or political patterns.

The third wave of immigrants began in October 1989 and continues to the present. To the end of 2002, this wave has brought 1,132,768 FSU immigrants to Israel.[16] The rate of arrival in 2002 was an average of 1,500 immigrants per month. To understand the behavior patterns of this wave in Israel and their creation of an influential pressure on the country's identity, we must examine three factors: numbers, quality, and intensity of immigration. In addition, the political environment of the period played a part in the initial developments.

The tidal wave of immigration transformed the FSU immigrants from simply the most recent of a series of immigrations to be absorbed into Israel into by far the largest single ethnic community in the country, with the exception of the native born. At the beginning of 2003, immigrants from the FSU are 21 percent of the Jewish population of Israel. Here was a significant proportion of the population, appearing in circumstances that were bound to change the equilibrium of society. There were simply too many of them to ignore or to absorb as their predecessors had been absorbed. Their numbers were also sufficient for maintaining a distinct and influential community, affecting politics, culture, and the economy.

The quality of the immigrants was also a factor. This was a feature of the

Soviet immigration noted in the earlier waves, making them a welcome addition to the society. In the third wave, there was no great diminution of the high educational level and the prominence of writers, musicians, artists, technical intelligentsia, and scientists. Fifty-five percent of the immigrants of this wave have more than 13 years of education, compared to 28 percent in the Jewish population of Israel in 1990 at the onset of the third wave.[17] The immigrants were thus an important force in raising Israel's level of education. In this wave, an entire intelligentsia arrived. Between 1989 and 1998, 116,900 immigrants arrived from Moscow, St. Petersburg, and Kiev, the three intellectual metropolitan centers of the FSU.[18] This intelligentsia provided the articulate leadership needed to formulate a dialogue with the veteran Israeli intelligentsia and stimulate change in the direction of developing Israel's identity.

The third important factor determining the influence of the third wave is its intensity, a factor rarely discussed in analysis of the immigrants. If the second wave averaged 715 immigrants per month over a period of 20 years, the third wave was nearly 10 times that, averaging 6,742 immigrants per month. Almost 400,000 arrived between October 1989 and the end of 1992. The intensity of the immigration meant that there was a huge mass of people caught up in the early stages of immigration, when the immigrants' difficulties and dislocations are greatest. This sharpened the sense of community and urgency—a community of suffering and an urgency to take action as a community to find relief.

At this point, Israel's government was controlled by a party espousing a doctrine of minimizing state intervention in many fields of life, among them immigrant absorption. In place of detailed government control and tutelage in the framework of state-run absorption centers, a policy of "direct absorption" was adopted. The immigrant was given a lump sum of money to cover initial expenses and was expected to find housing and employment much as did any other citizen.[19] In addition, the Ministry of Immigrant Absorption at the start of the wave was controlled by a minister from one of the ultra-Orthodox parties in the coalition who gave spiritual absorption preference over the material aspects of the immigrants' lives. The emphasis at this time on circumcision for all male immigrants, including adults, and the arbitrary assignment of Hebrew names to the "newborn Jews" as part of this procedure aroused widespread resentment and even ridicule in the immigrant community.

Two other aspects of this wave should be noted. First of all is that this wave had a very different social composition than had the previous two waves.[20] It was composed mainly of "heartlanders," many of them from the peripheral cities of Russia and the Ukraine, along with the previously mentioned metropolitan intelligentsia. As was only natural, the percentage of mixed marriages was higher among these immigrants, rising steadily over time, and their Jewish identity and knowledge were weaker. Most of them were born after World War II, and many were born after the death of Stalin, "a generation that knew not Joseph" since the average age of the immigrants was in the late twenties. In addition, this wave was precipitated more by the deteriorating conditions and the economic and political instability of the Soviet Union in 1989–1991, "push" factors driving them out of the Soviet Union rather than the "pull" factors of their historical, religious, or ethnic connection to Israel. To the extent that "pull" factors operated, they were based mainly on the attraction of family members, friends, and former colleagues or neighbors who had succeeded in establishing themselves in Israel. This tidal wave of immigrants was washed up on Israel's shores rather than elsewhere in the world in no small measure because as of October 1, 1989, the United States no longer granted refugee status to Jews emigrating from the Soviet Union. Instead, it admitted them in limited numbers under the general immigrant quota for that part of the world.

An added influence on the identity development of this wave was the presence of prominent cultural and political personalities who had arrived in the latter stages of the second wave and who gained an understanding of Israeli society. Furthermore, they were willing to devote themselves to making the FSU immigrants into an independent institutionalized community within Israeli society. These included Anatolii Sharansky, whose international standing gave the immigrants' situation a high profile and whose organizing ability in putting together and financing the Zionist Forum laid a solid institutional basis for the cultural and political development of the community. Another prominent influential among the immigrants was former prisoner of Zion Edward Kuznetsov, who probed the possibility of an immigrant political party as early as 1980 and became the editor of *Vesti*, to this day the most prominent and influential of the Russian-language newspapers in Israel, providing a persuasive basis for internal communication of the community's sorrows and aspirations. Other immigrant intelligentsia leaders and opinion makers found abundant outlets for their opinions in the many Russian-language journals and periodicals that appeared in Israel. The immigrant community's views on Israel and the incipient dialogue with Israel's veteran society was often initiated and formed by the writings of Maya Kaganskaya, Raphael Nudelman, Larissa Gerstein, Dina Rubina, Grigorii Kanovich, and a large number of others.

Where observers had noted that the second wave had formed relatively few institutions and that its members, though politically sensitive and active, had been slow to rise to leadership positions on the Israeli political scene, the massive arrival of the third wave changed this. Very rapidly there appeared an intricate network of institutions, at first informal and based on personal connections but later structured through the Zionist Forum and its multitude of constituent organizations. The formalization of this community structure was eventually crowned by the appearance of an immigrant-based political party that had a marked influence on Israel's politics and that, after only seven years of activity, has merged, as have most of its former voters, with a veteran Israeli party.[21]

Though the arrival of the third wave reawakened fears of the economically and educationally weaker portion of Israel's population that they would be crowded out of the economy by the newcomers, this never happened, and the fear has since passed.[22] In fact, the arrival of a host of new consumers in need of housing, furnishings, and automobiles and hungry for all kinds of consumer goods was the basis of Israel's rapid economic growth throughout the 1990s. The size of the immigrant consumer market and the competition for its purchasing power caused a change in advertising patterns. Though English words and phrases had long been used in advertising for their snob appeal, now Russian began to appear and is today almost ubiquitous on packaging. The wave was so intense that Russian-language advertising on the shelves made economic sense in any case, and thus non-Hebrew communication as part of daily life was given a strong legitimation, something not looked on with favor in earlier generations.[23] The immigrants thus had an influence toward widening Israelis' international perspective and cultural horizons.

The immigrants' contribution to the economy was not, however, solely as consumers. They also brought with them a massive injection of professional manpower into the workforce. Among the immigrants arriving from the beginning of 1989 to the end of August 2001 were 98,928 engineers; 20,875 physicians and dentists; 19,965 musicians, artists, and writers; 23,598 nurses and paramedicals; and 45,380 teachers.[24] Much of this vast human capital was not put to use, whether because of age, language difficulties, or the limited size and particular structure of Israel's economy. However, the immigrants made a significant contribution both to the quality and to the variety of enterprises in the economic, social, and cultural sectors. International medals in kayaking, pole vaulting, swimming, and even ice skating caught the attention of veteran Israelis and were a source of pride to the immigrants. The expansion of Israel's musical establishment, already well known, became almost legendary. But on the economic side, there were equally significant if less well-known achievements. Numerous research "hothouses" were set up in which immigrant scientists were given seed money by the government and enabled to bring research ideas to the point that foreign investors might be attracted to bring them into production. Work on fuel cells, hydromagnetic dynamics, computer software and hardware, biotechnology, and electronics as well as a host of other subjects often initiated by immigrants and staffed by immigrant scientists and technicians boosted Israel's technological level. On a wide variety of subjects and on many levels of daily life, the immigrants could feel themselves as valuable contributors to Israel, people who improved and advanced the country rather than as unfortunate immigrants to be treated as objects of charity and transformed from "diaspora luftmenshche," into productive citizens.

The integration of the third-wave immigrants into the labor force was, however, less rapid than in the 1970s. While immigrants of the 1970s were earning a higher-than-average income after three years in the country because of their high qualifications and their high rate of participation in the labor force, the third-wave immigrants took close to five years to achieve that level. They had largely to content themselves with a lower level of employment than their formal training and employment before immigration would have led them to expect.

Only after the immigrants had organized themselves as an autonomous community, more precisely after their achievement in the 1996 elections, did the consciousness of this immigration's uniqueness penetrate and a serious dialogue begin, defining relations between the immigrant community and veteran Israel. The high educational level of the immigrants brought with it an articulate consciousness of what "ought to be" and a high level of activism in attempting to create a reality in consonance with that consciousness. Where Israel's realities diverged from the immigrants' vision, the immigrants were both willing and able to exert pressure for change and, where this was slow in forthcoming through existing Israeli institutions, to create their own cultural, social, and political institutions. At this point, we can see the beginnings of an influence on Israel's overall identity.

RELIGIOUS AND ETHNONATIONAL IDENTITY

But we may ask what identity the immigrant institutions promote. An examination of the dynamics of self-identification of the immigrants reveals a truly complex and constantly changing picture. Fortunately, we have a large number of sociological research projects on the subject that follow immigrants from the former Soviet Union through the decade of the 1990s in Israel and that are today probing the changing ethnic, national, and religious consciousness of those who may well be the immigrants of the current and coming decades.

One of the young generation of Moscow activists of the 1980s who attempted to revive some measure of Jewish culture in the Soviet Union described the identity of Soviet Jews as Jews only by passport, cut off from all national roots but nevertheless knowing that they were Jews because those around them would not let them forget their ethnic origins. All overt and subtle reminders of Jewishness in the Soviet media of this period were negative in nature, but the State of Israel and its brilliant victory in the Six-Day War served as a positive focus of pride. Jewish identity in this period was based not on knowledge or practice but on the need for some pride—some personal and group dignity in an environment that was perceived as ranging from humiliating to openly hostile. A sociological study of Jews in Russia in the mid-1990s found that only 5 percent felt strongly attached to Jewish culture, 31 percent felt a marginal attachment, and 58 percent had no attachment whatsoever. Only 1 percent attended synagogue regularly, and 75 percent never visited a synagogue. When asked to which culture they felt closest, 62 percent named Russian, only 5 percent named Jewish, while 28 percent claimed equal closeness to both cultures. These same persons were asked two further questions: what they considered as their nationality and what the national registration was in their passports. On the first question, 74 percent declared their nationality as Jewish, 6 percent said Russian, and 19 percent declared a mixed nationality (Jewish Russian or Russian Jewish). The nationality registration in their passports was quite different. Eighty percent were registered as Jews, 17 percent as Russians, and 3 percent as some other nationality. The researcher found a tendency of reidentification with the Jewish community on a basis of utility, an attempt to be identified with the social and commercial prominence of successful Jews in post-Soviet Russian society.[25] This reidentification was seen as a first step to acquiring a cognitive and affective link to Jewish life. While 70 percent of the Jewish families surveyed had one or more non-Jewish members in them, these "non-Jews" were often descendants of Jewish antecedents who after years of estrangement from Jewish life are now reidentifying with the Jewish components in their identity.[26]

As noted previously, the religious element of Jewish identity in Russia has been particularly weak. As far back as 1976, a sociological survey of 1,191 Jews carried out by Moscow Jewish scientists found that only 7 percent (mainly the elderly and less educated) classified themselves as religious, 53 percent "respected all religions equally," and 32 percent had no interest at all in the Jewish religion.[27] A similarly low level of religious knowledge, observance, and belief was found in two other surveys conducted in the mid-1990s. Significantly, both of these indicate a continuity in the trend of many Jews' viewing other religions as equal or preferable to Judaism.[28] These characteristics brought one of the leaders of today's Jewish community of Russia to define it as a postassimilatory entity in which religion plays only a marginal role: "The Jewish community of Russia is ethno-national more than religious and is assimilating into its ranks the descendants of mixed marriages. This community represents a new identity whose educational values demand new teachers of tradition, university professors rather than rabbis."[29]

However, the Jewish life of the potential immigrants in Russia is no less dynamic than is that of the immigrant community in Israel. We have already mentioned the phenomenon of reidentification of persons formerly considered by themselves and others as non-Jews but who are descendants of Jewish grandparents or perhaps even great-grandparents. Meanwhile, a recent comparative survey of Russian and Jewish students in institutions of higher education in Russia, including some students in courses of Jewish studies, found that although only 2 percent of the Jews surveyed claimed that they observed all the Jewish religious commandments, 30 percent stated that they observed the Jewish religion to some degree, and only 12 percent said that they led totally irreligious lives.[30] This indicates a sharp difference from the previous generation and, coming as it does in the future intelligentsia of the Jewish community of Russia, should be regarded as significant. The same study found similarly interesting identity changes regarding national identity. Of the 408 students surveyed who defined themselves as Jews, almost half were from families with two Jewish parents, 43.9 percent were from families with one Jewish and one non-Jewish parent, and 5.6 percent of the Jewish respondents said that both their parents were non-Jews. Among the children of mixed Jewish and non-Jewish parentage, three-quarters declared themselves Jewish.[31] This also fits Ryvkina's findings that youth expressed closeness to Jewish culture at a rate 2.5 times greater than that of their parents' generation.[32]

A similar, perhaps even stronger dynamic may be observed among the immigrants in Israel. The question of "who is a Jew" has vexed the Israeli public for decades and has never been definitively decided, even after being tested in courts of law. The coincidence of religious and ethnonational identity is the main complicating factor. While persons of other ethnic backgrounds can become recognized as Jews by adopting the Jewish religion, persons of Jewish ethnic background and national identity who adopt other religions are seen as ceasing to be Jewish (though they may remain Israeli citizens).[33] Varying conceptions of Jewishness in different communities, such as Satanovsky's, to which we referred earlier, have been noted by scholars.[34] Clearly, an understanding by veteran Israelis of the self-definition of the FSU immigrants and an understanding by the immigrants of the society they are entering must of necessity influence the degree of success in creating relations between the two communities. Moreover, the resolution of the immigrant community's national identity around the ethnic or the religious pole influences greatly both the intracommunal relations and relations with the social and political institutions in its new environment.[35]

Not surprisingly, the findings among the Jews of Russia regarding religious and ethnonational self-identification were sustained in surveys of the immigrants of the 1990s. A survey of 500 new immigrants in 1991 found three-quarters defining themselves as ethnic Jews, some of these as Russian Jews, some as Soviet Jews, and about half simply as Jews. As to nationality, 20 percent responded "new immigrant," and only 2 percent defined themselves as Israelis. Many saw themselves defined as non-Israeli by their veteran Israeli neighbors. Given the immigrants' past, these findings are in no way unexpected. It should also be noted that on arrival in Israel, the immigrant is confronted by an ethnonational definition with an inseparable religious component, a new and unfamiliar ethnic-related language, and even unfamiliar holidays and a new workweek, all defined by ethnic and religious custom.[36] These aspects, together with the very personal civic disabilities that many of them suffer, account for the "distance" or degree of alienation from religious individuals and institutions found particularly among the third-wave immigrants.[37]

In another survey, conducted in the summer of 1999 among 400 immigrants selected to represent proportionally the immigration of the third wave, 8 percent identified themselves as Israeli, while 47 percent called themselves Russians and 45 percent Jews. A control group of veteran Israelis declared themselves 48 percent Israelis and 33.5 percent Jews, the rest identifying as Ashkenazim or Sephardim.[38] When the immigrants were allowed a compound choice of identity, Israeli as the more prominent element was still only at the 8 percent level, but an Israeli component (Russian Israeli and Jewish Israeli) as the secondary factor raised the percentage to 42.[39]

Moreover, time has proved to be an important element, though for both schoolchildren and for the elderly it is an insufficient remedy for their adjustment difficulties. The longer immigrants are in the country, the larger the percentage defining themselves as Israelis. In the previously mentioned sample, 11 percent of those who arrived in the years 1989–1992 defined themselves as Israeli, as compared with only 4 percent of those who arrived in 1997–1999.[40] It has been suggested that in the contemporary world, identity is becoming more and more a matter of multiple factors that the individual arranges hierarchically or compartmentally, preferring one element in one situation and another elsewhere. These different elements of identity may at times even be contradictory to one another.[41] This is particularly true of an immigrant population undergoing a transition in all the elements of its life. The immigrant functions in at least two languages and has two different identities that vary in influence in different sectors of his life. He is simultaneously immersed in two cultures and forms from them his own personal synthesis that becomes a new part of the evolving pluralistic society in which he makes his way.[42]

With regard to religion, Gitelman found only 5 percent of his 1991 interviewees who would include a religious component in their definition of Judaism, while the other 95 percent defined it either as a nationality (as Jewishness had been officially defined in the Soviet Union) or as a historical and cultural phenomenon. Indeed, Gitelman concluded that the religious component of Jewishness as officially defined in Israel inhibited a wholehearted Jewish identification in many of the immigrants. As part of their affective distance from religion, the FSU immigrants are overwhelmingly in favor of civil marriage and of the opening of places of business and entertainment and operation of public transport on the Sabbath.[43] While the cognitive and affective dimensions of the immigrants' attitude to religion appear to remain largely stable, a significant difference is found in a study at the end of the 1990s, when the behavioral aspect is examined. In a sample in which only 1.4 percent defined themselves as religious and another 24.7 percent called themselves "traditional," 33.6 percent stated that they always fasted on the Day of Atonement, and 13.2 percent always ate kosher food.

While on the face of it the immigrants' secular outlook is similar to the secularism that was so prominent in the Israeli culture of the prestate and early state periods, there is a completely different basis for the two. The antireligious outlook of the early Israeli settlers was an ideological revolt against a culture regarded as passive and backward, looking to the next world to make up for the ills of the earthly existence. The "Revolt of the Son" was a deliberate, conscious negation by young people closely acquainted with Jewish law and tradition, many of them graduates of religious seminaries. The secularism of the FSU immigrants comes largely from a void of Jewish knowledge, stemming from the cultural, historical, and religious deprivation of the generations that grew up under Soviet rule. Finding themselves in a society in which there are widely accepted social norms, a segment of the immigrants, having no ideological opposition to religion, finds it useful to adopt the prevailing modes of behavior. The "traditionals" largely observed these norms in their communities even in the Soviet Union, while some of the "westerners" still had the living memory of a community that included such behavior patterns in its pre-Soviet identity. What has been left uninvestigated so far is the extent to which "traditionals," while actively identifying with Orthodox Judaism, show sympathy and understanding for their fellow immigrants' demands for nonreligious ways of life. Certainly similar patterns of behavior are to be found in many North American or European Jewish communities today. Thus, an element of religious behavior may be found in the identity of the immigrants even when the cognitive and affective aspects of religion are largely rejected. Their overall influence, however, is to revive the secularist influence in Israel's national identity, and in this the immigrants of the third wave have thus far had a considerable impact, strengthening the secular social, economic, and political institutions active in Israel. Particularly striking has been the immigrant support for the Shinui Party in politics, a new list based primarily on a platform opposing religious coercion and the influence of the ultra-Orthodox parties. First running in the 1999 elections, this party garnered six seats in the Knesset, one of them held by an immigrant from the FSU, Professor Victor Brailovsky. In the elections of 2003, Shinui became the third-largest party in the Knesset with 15 seats, two or three of them from the votes of FSU immigrants who suffer particularly from civic disabilities due to the religious monopoly on personal status and the draconian policies toward non-Jews adopted by the Ministry of the Interior under a series of ultra-Orthodox ministers.[44]

THE POLITICS OF THE FSU IMMIGRANTS

Surveying second-wave immigrants at the beginning of the 1980s, Gitelman noted that as they entered the cultural, social, and economic life of Israel, the immigrants also entered actively into its political life but were slow in achieving leadership positions.[45] This was the period in which the first abortive attempt was made, led by Edward Kuznetsov, to found a party based on Soviet immigrants. The situation changed under the intense pressure of the hundreds of thousands of immigrants in the first two years of the third wave of immigration. By 1992, when elections were on the horizon in Israel, a poll showed 68 percent of the new immigrants favoring a party of "their own" to voice their needs.[46] While this party, led by Yulii Kosherovsky, a former Moscow refusenik leader (and two lesser groupings), failed to gain representation in the Knesset, it mobilized sectors of the immigrant society, paving the way for the 1996 campaign of Yisrael Ba'Aliyah, headed by Sharansky. This party's success in winning seven Knesset seats was based in large part on the rich institutional foundation that had grown up in the first half of the 1990s. Around the Zionist Forum, founded by Sharansky as an umbrella group, there were already 35 organizations by 1993 and 55 by 1996.[47] These social, educational, and cultural groups, reaching into all parts of the immigrant community, provided one of the channels of mobilization for the new party. Alongside Sharansky, there was a leadership of second-wave immigrants who had been active in various parties but found no understanding or acceptance of the particular needs of the immigrants and so brought their skills and dedication to the new party. In addition, its activists succeeded in bringing together large numbers of pensioners and unemployed, turning them into canvasers and propagandists and giving them the pride of being wanted and useful. Thus, the most alienated of the new immigrants were drawn into the political system and given the sense that they as citizens counted for something. This feeling of civic efficacy, the idea that things can be changed for the better through politics, became one of the keys to the integration of formerly estranged sectors of the FSU immigrant community into Israel's society. Political socialization was a stepping-stone to a broader Israeli socialization.[48]

Even in 1996, when 175,000 immigrant voters put "their own" party into the Knesset, it could be seen that the longer one was in Israel, the greater the likelihood of voting for one of the older, nonsectoral parties. In 1996 and again in 1999, Yisrael Ba'Aliyah was regarded as the "party of pensioners" and of the newest and least integrated immigrants.[49] Like other ethnic lists before it, Yisrael Ba'Aliyah had two relatively successful terms in the Knesset but has now followed its voters, with the party organization formally joining the Likud, while its left- and right-wing fringes joined general Israeli parties identifying with their views.

While the general public impression is that the FSU immigrants are a right-wing group, an analysis of their voting history shows that this is an oversimplification. The stereotype is perhaps based on the impression left by such high-profile figures as Avigdor Liberman, leader of the "National Union," by Anatolii Sharansky's steady movement from centrist liberalism to the right or the journalist Edward Kuznetsov, under whose editorship *Vesti*, the flagship of the Israeli Russian-language press, strongly urged the immigrants toward the right wing of political activism, a position that eventually led to his being dismissed from the newspaper. However, in 1992, some 47 percent of the FSU immigrants voted for Labor as against 18 percent for the Likud and even fewer for Kosherovsky's DA (Democracy and Aliyah) and two lesser immigrant-based lists. Again in 1999, 56 percent of the immigrants supported Labor and

Ehud Barak, the same percentage as supported him in the general public. In 1996, 2001, and 2003, the majority of the immigrants supported the Likud candidates.[50] The FSU immigrants, having come to a fully developed political system, have less commitment to any single party than do veteran Israelis, most of whom grew up in a highly politicized system in which everything from medical care to sport was associated with a particular party and loyalty to that party was an inherited tradition. The immigrants are more reserved in their loyalties and look for responses to their own particular concerns.[51] In addition, they are willing to change their attitudes toward specific political problems in keeping with changing circumstances, though they are less changeable regarding abstract political concepts, such as freedom versus anarchy, or fundamental orientations toward politics.[52]

To understand the basis of political participation of the immigrants, it is necessary to look at the circumstances of their arrival in Israel and the first years of their life in the country. The claim that the immigrants have no tradition of civil culture should perhaps be reexamined. Though the Soviet political system left no room for individual civic judgments or initiative, one of its paradoxes was that it made great propaganda as to the rights and freedoms of Soviet citizens. This sharpened the citizen's awareness of the limitations on him and the internal contradictions of the system. Each person was sharply aware of the areas of life in which he could complain and made full use of such opportunities.[53] On arrival in Israel, the immigrant found that politics were different, that there were real fundamental choices to be made, that the individual's sense of having been wronged by the authorities had a remedy at election time, and that the community's numerical and organizational strength could bring political benefits. The primary benefit sought was to defend the security and the growing possessions earned by each one. For the third-wave immigrants in particular, leaving the Soviet Union or its successor republics was motivated primarily by the economic and political insecurity there. In Israel, the immigrant supports that candidate or party that appears best able to defend personal security and hard-won economic status. As we have already noted, the longer an immigrant is in Israel, the more likely he is to give his vote to one of the established parties rather than to an immigrant list.[54] In 1999 some 56 percent of immigrant votes went to Sharansky's Yisrael Ba'Aliyah and 15.6 percent to Liberman's Yisrael Betenu (15.6%).[55] A survey two years later found that only 15 percent of the immigrants voiced support for the immigrant lists, a decline that, judging from the results of the 2003 elections, appears to have continued steadily.[56] Yesterday's immigrants vote today as all Israelis vote.

The situation may well be different on the local level. While the immigrant lists have declined in the arena of national politics, the high concentration of immigrants in a large number of the development towns of Israel has maintained the identity of the immigrant community. In the 1999 municipal elections, FSU immigrants elected 100 municipal councillors and in a number of municipalities became part of the ruling coalition and elected deputy mayors and, in one town, a mayor.[57] These local notables come in addition to the 30 immigrant Knesset members, senior civil servants, and leading party activists counted by Khanin. All together, a group numbering 200 immigrants may be counted as part of the political elite of Israel.[58] Thus, Gitelman's 1982 observation that the immigrants are slow in achieving leadership positions, while accurate for its time, was changed by the size and intensity of the third wave of immigration. No less important than these political activists, Khanin identifies a group of nonparty intelligentsia with broad connections in all political camps and easy access to the Russian-language Israeli press. These are opinion makers who often form ad hoc public committees to investigate and press for solutions to numerous problems affecting the immigrant community.[59] Their energy and success in mobilizing public support attests to the active civic consciousness of the community.

Many of the local councillors ran on locally organized lists that reflected the immigrants' interest in having a say in local community centers, schools, municipal bylaws on Sabbath observance, and such.

The glaring social and economic inequalities developed by Israel in the latter half of the 1990s and particularly since the autumn of 2000 have struck hard at some sectors of the immigrant community and in addition have increased the overall social tensions within Israel's society. This, together with the religious–secular rift, may work to maintain the distinct political identity of the FSU immigrants in municipal affairs. Thus, much of the test of the immigrants' influence on Israel's national identity in the spheres of religious–secular lifestyles and social equality may lie in the near future.

ISLANDS OF SEPARATENESS

As we have noted, the immigrants of the 1990s created a multitude of institutions—social, cultural, and political. Many of these were "islands of separateness" in which purely Russian cultural forms and language persisted. Such, for instance, was the St. Petersburg Club in Jerusalem, a group boasting 500 members whose activities revolved around the celebrations, news, and events of their former home city (the inaugural meeting was a New Year's Eve celebration) and were conducted solely in the Russian language.[60] This was perhaps an extreme case, for the members were mainly women aged 45 and up, with a third of the members over 65 years of age. Yet it serves to emphasize the value placed by a large proportion of the immigrants on Russian language and culture as long-term components of their identity.[61] In the extreme case, this can find expression in the attitude held by Alexander Goldstein, a journalist and writer who glories in the Russian literary culture and is repelled by anything that smacks of the Orient—an attitude that he developed in his childhood, growing up in Baku, Azerbaijan. He professes only disdain for Israel's material and spiritual culture. Yet his identity contains contradictions.

"Russian is my language, but Russia is not my country. Israel is my country." He claims to write Israeli literature in the Russian language.[62] While there is an entire spectrum of immigrant organizations, varying from isolationist to integrationist, the "islands of separateness" do not disappear.[63] Among the prominent successes is the system of *Mofet* schools, initiated by a small group of immigrant teachers in cooperation with the principal of a Tel Aviv high school and later with the active support of the Union of Immigrant Teachers as an expression of their professional reservations regarding Israeli schools in addition to its being a way of helping find employment for the union's constituents.[64] Originating as after-hours schooling in mathematics, science, and Russian language and literature—staffed by former teachers from the immigrant community and offered to the immigrant parents who found the ways of the Israeli schools inadequate and the intellectual level lower than what they were used to for their children—the *Mofet* system has spread across Israel and has spawned kindergartens and a full secondary school, recognized by Israel's Ministry of Education. Where there was a demand, Russian language and Russian literature were added to the regular curriculum in the secondary schools. In addition, retired teachers—such as a teacher of physics in Acre and one of mathematics in Jerusalem's Kiryat Menachem district—began by offering private lessons in Russian to immigrant children but attracted attention by their excellence and were integrated into the general educational system. Throughout the *Mofet* system, veteran Israeli parents who have recognized the academic excellence achieved in these schools have started registering their children there. While maintaining its own identity, *Mofet* has gained recognition as part of the educational system, bringing the community's resources to bear on the content and forms of Israeli education.

"Russian" restaurants, dancing classes for children, discos patronized exclusively by FSU immigrant youth and featuring Russian rock artists, visiting artists and theater groups from Russia, and, perhaps most of all, family events—birthdays, weddings, bar mitzvahs, and so on—persist and flourish as a cultural phenomenon. The relatively large concentrations of immigrants in a number of development towns provide the economic as well as the social framework for such institutions. Over 80 percent of the immigrants live in localities in which they make up one-third or more of the population.[65] There is a combination of a significant percentage of the population, lending legitimacy to the tendency to maintain that community's identity, together with the "critical mass" to support such claims, forming an audience, a market, and an interested public capable of sustaining institutions. For example, the city of Bat Yam has 43,730 FSU immigrants (30% of the total population), Ashdod 59,759 (34.9%), and Beer Sheva 51,955 (30%).[66] The key to understanding the psychology of this phenomenon of maintaining the community's separate culture alongside its integration into an Israeli identity lies, perhaps, in applying within the framework of Israeli life a saying that became popular among non-Jews in Russia after the fall of the Soviet Union. Asked as to their attitude toward Jews, the Russian might answer, "Lunch, but not dinner" (*obed no nye uzhin*). To work with a person and share the lunch break is normal, but it does not mean that this person will necessarily be invited for dinner or to family or other social events. So it is (not surprisingly) with the immigrant. He is integrated into Israeli society in work, study, or army service but, for moments of relaxation and celebration, chooses the forms and companions familiar to him from early life. The circulation of *Vesti* as a daily newspaper has fallen steadily in recent years, but the weekend edition, to be read in the leisure of the Sabbath, holds its own, selling eight times the regular weekday number.[67] Particularly in the early years of their life in Israel and in an inverse correlation to age, relatively few of the immigrants, 20 percent in a survey done in the mid-1990s, were found to read the Hebrew-language press.[68] A later survey found 9.3 percent reading the Hebrew press regularly and another 25.7 percent who read it sometimes.[69] Radio, television news, and the Russian-language press supplied the bulk of their communicational needs. But the picture becomes more complex as the years pass. Rejecting the dichotomy of ghettoization or integration that appeared to fit earlier, Adoni and Cohen posit four distinct groups of immigrants in accordance with differing patterns of communications consumption: (1) dualists, who are consumers of both Hebrew- and Russian-language media (these they found to be 26.1% of their sample); (2) adapters, who are oriented primarily to the Hebrew-language media (18.1%); (3) isolationists, who consume mainly Russian-language communications (44.9%); and (4) isolated, who have no exposure to mass communications (10%).[70] While this is as yet far from complete integration, it shows progress in that direction, with close to half the immigrants using Hebrew-language media to some extent, as compared with the survey cited earlier, and in addition indicates a tendency to retain a "Russian" component of identity even while moving toward integration. The significant percentage (44.9%) who consume primarily Russian-language media formed the basis of justification for Israeli television to open a Russian-language channel, felicitously named Israel Plus. Previously, three or four Russian channels, available on cables, had dominated the immigrants' television time. Today, just as they have an Israeli press in the Russian language, they have Israeli television, in which the news and discussion programs present in large measure Israeli questions, discussed by Israelis, including Hebrew speakers who are given simultaneous translation into Russian, while much of the Russian spoken text is given Hebrew subtitling. Once more we see the compound of Israeli and Russian identities in action.

BECOMING ISRAELIS

While a generation or more will be needed before the "islands of separateness" of the FSU immigrants become part of the Israeli cultural and social mainland, such a process is clearly under way. The *Gesher* (Bridge) Theater, founded in 1991, began as a group of professional immigrant actors who from the outset wanted to give plays in both Russian and Hebrew and employed a language coach to assist them in learning their lines in Hebrew, a language in which none of them was proficient. Their professionalism and the dramatic originality of their director's stagings soon brought them an award as the finest theater group in Israel.[71] Today a number of their actors are Israeli raised and trained, mostly from Russian-speaking families, and while they still present many plays in Russian, the dominant language of spectators in the lobby in some of their Hebrew-language performances of such Russian classics as Bulgakov's *Master and Margarita* may well be Russian. Both the theater and its audience begin to feel at home with the Hebrew language. The success of *Gesher* pushed the "Top Hat Theater" (*Teatr' Tsilinder*), a Jerusalem-based group that has struggled to maintain itself for five years, to attempt something similar, taking a talented and experienced immigrant director and young, Israeli trained, Russian-speaking actors to present a broad spectrum of audience-pleasing plays in Hebrew. Another such success is *Musica Aeterna*, initiated by its conductor, Il'ya Plotkin. This is a chamber choir of professional choral performers who began with a repertoire of Slavic liturgical compositions and have since broadened their appeal to include Jewish liturgy and classical choral pieces that have brought them participation in all of Israel's choral festivals as well as performance dates throughout the country. The publication of an anthology of Hebrew literature in Russian translation, alongside a periodical, *Zerkalo* (the Mirror), that publishes Hebrew translations of Russian-language poetry, prose, and essays by new immigrants strengthens this tendency of broadening audience horizons in both directions, creating a dialogue of equals.[72] This dialogue has accelerated and broadened with the appearance of a new generation of immigrant writers. In the early 1990s, the immigrant writers focused their view primarily on life in Russia and the leaving of Russia. The epos of the mass immigration was a central event in their lives. The new generation begins to take up daily problems of life in Israel: the culture shock facing the immigrant, a society of greedy landlords and unfair employers (not infrequently the immigrant's first acquaintances in Israel), and the trauma of what appears to the immigrant intellectual as an intolerant, sometimes hostile society and a provincial culture.[73] Thus, while the language of this literature remains Russian, its focus is now the nature of Israel's society and the place of the immigrant within this society. Coming to grips with these problems is a first step in the immigrants' establishing their own new Israeli identity and determining the relations of this identity to the other components of the national identity.

CONCLUSIONS

To be an immigrant is, in almost all cases, to condemn oneself to some degree of individual marginalization. Adopting a new national identity and culture means rearranging much of the individual's historical memory, focusing on new heroes, new narratives, and new forms of commemoration while pushing previous memories into the background.[74] A dissonance is set up here, for the immigrant's history remains constant, even though memory is changed, and as a result a conflict is created between the newly adopted memory and the historically based countermemory. In many cases, particularly with mature adult immigrants, this conflict remains throughout life, whatever the wish of the person to be part of his new society and nation. In effect, this is the mirror image of the conflict that motivated the decision to emigrate from the FSU to Israel. Until a new identity has been synthesized and taken root, most individuals can only minimally affect their society. For the third-wave immigrants, a group with a lower general level of Jewish and Zionist motivation than their earlier compatriots, this conflict may be particularly sharp.[75] However, the existence of a large and cohesive community, with a strong self-consciousness, does much to attenuate this marginalization, providing, as we have seen, numerous institutional shelters that serve to preserve and reinforce the individual's self-image and give the community's culture and norms a fulcrum from which to exert influence on the dominant identity. In addition, it provides a familiar and supportive environment for the immigrant, helping him through the alienation and confusion that almost inevitably accompanies immigration.

As we have demonstrated in this chapter, such a community is the hallmark of the third wave, created by the sheer numbers and intensity of their arrival in Israel and the quality of intellectual leadership that spearheads the community. The FSU immigrant community has, from the beginnings of the third wave, been imbued with a strong awareness of the value of its institutions and tends to act as a community through them.[76] Thus, the St. Petersburg Club, mentioned earlier, adopted as its slogan a line from a song by a popular Russian bard of the 1960s and 1970s: "Let us join hands, brothers so that we are not lost each one by himself." An early community activist, himself a second-wave immigrant, Vladimir Glozman, wrote, "The community is not a ghetto in which the lives of the Soviet immigrants are posited in contradiction to the life in Israel. Rather it is the way in which we can prove ourselves in Israel both as individuals and as a collective, bringing the greatest possible benefit to Israeli society. As individuals we get lost, but as a community we can give—and receive—much more."[77]

In specific terms, we can point to a number of sectors in which the FSU immigrant community has affected the national identity of Israel, reinforcing existing characteristics, some of which had been weakened over the years by Israel's changing economics and demographics, and introducing others that broaden that identity into new areas. The first that we will mention is a heightened sense of the ethic of excellence in all fields of endeavor. At the time of the founding of the State of Israel, there was a sharp awareness that the country was poor in natural resources and that its main wealth was the quality of its population. There was an explicit molding of identity toward a modern "Western" culture and an openly expressed rejection of "Levantinization" of any and all aspects of Israel's life. With the growth and change of Israel's population, the routinization of life, and the general deideologization, this aspect was dulled somewhat. The FSU immigration has revived it in many ways. The renewed emphasis on high levels of professionalization in theater, sports, education, and in work ethics in general has been a result of the high educational level and the need-induced ambition of the immigrants.

In many of the previously mentioned fields, the Soviet society had world-leading levels of professionalism. In addition, the immigrants combine the ethos of their past—that they had to be better than those around them just to gain acceptance and to hold a position—with the motivation so commonly seen in new immigrants all over the world. They work harder and more than veteran Israelis in order to establish themselves and to earn the material wealth that they see their veteran neighbors enjoying. The long-term importance of these characteristics lies with the trainers and teachers in various fields, such as *Mofet*'s mathematics and physics teachers or the athletic coaches and theater directors whose dedication to high professional standards and methodologies will spread to younger generations and become part of Israel's collective personality. In its overall influence, this trend will return Israel, for better or for worse, to a predominantly "Western" orientation in its broad culture.

A second area of influence, acting particularly through the political system, is the FSU immigrant community's secularizing influence. This is a complex process, for, as we have seen, there has been a trend toward behavioral integration into Israel's religious practices, while the cognitive and affective resistance to religion is maintained. This is less a reaction against religion itself than a resentment of religion's prominent place in state life. The disabilities and indignities that are the lot of all too many of the immigrants drive the community to side with the separation of religion from the state. With the continuing immigration, the percentage of immigrants who are not regarded as Jews by the Orthodox establishment continues to grow. But these enter Israel under the provisions of the Law of the Return and either consider themselves ethnic Jews rather than religious or bind their future lives and those of their children with the State of Israel and its nation and in return expect full citizen rights. As they continue to enter the FSU immigrant community, the question of state–religion relations will become even sharper. Having shown their civic awareness and found the key to political efficacy, the immigrant community is most likely to persevere in pursuing a solution that will solve their problems of personal status. Their success in this quest, however long it may take, will mean a basic redefinition of Israel's identity, carrying the society beyond the ideological secularism that was a prominent feature of the prestate community.

In what is perhaps a less tangible change, the FSU immigration has given impetus to the broadening and opening of Israel's society to influences from the world. The pressure of a million immigrants seeking to establish a new identity but unwilling to take a ready-made prescription from Israel as the receiving society has created a resultant in which both sides are changing. Yet the incipient changes that we have noted are as yet only tendencies. The exact nature of the new integrative identity that will result is still in the future, for the bulk of the immigration, the third wave, is not yet a full generation old, and identity changes may come to full realization only in the third generation. Meanwhile, the dialogue between veteran Israel and the immigrant community forces a reexamination of founding myths and dated truths, a procedure that is natural to any society and that had already started in Israel but was given greater impetus by the size, quality, and intensity of the third wave.

Looking back over a decade in Israel, 79.5 percent of the third-wave immigrants declare themselves "satisfied" or "very satisfied" with their absorption in Israel and declare that coming to Israel was a good decision.[78] They have a feeling of having contributed to the development of the country's economy and culture. At the same time, they maintain a critical attitude toward much in the government, the educational system, and the society of Israel. Perhaps in this combination of being happy *in* Israel while at the same time being dissatisfied *with* Israel, they prove themselves to be well on the way to being true Israelis.

NOTES

1. Majid Al-Haj and Elazar Leshem, *Immigrants from the Former Soviet Union in Israel: Ten Years Later* (Haifa: University of Haifa Press, 2000), 1–2. For additional discussion of the changes in Israel's society and culture in the decades before the mass immigration from the FSU, see Eliezer Ben Rafael, Elite Olshtein, and Idith Geijst, "Identity and Language: The Integration of Jews from the FSU in Israel," in *MeRussia L'Israel: Zhut Utarbut Bamaavar*, ed. Moshe Lissak and Elazar Leshem (Tel Aviv: Hakibbutz Hameuchad, 2001), 82–83 (in Hebrew).

2. *Israel Statistical Annual*, no. 53 (Jerusalem: Central Bureau of Statistics, 2002), table 2.21.

3. Yael Zerubavel, *Recovered Roots: Collective Memory and the Making of Israel's National Tradition* (Chicago: University of Chicago Press, 1995), esp. 79–83.

4. See Zerubavel, *Recovered Roots*, 236, for a discussion of this development.

5. Those who have seen Roman Polanski's film *The Pianist* will doubtless remember the scene in which a drunken Nazi officer, beating Jewish workers indiscriminately, tells them that the reason for the beating is the marking of St. Sylvester's night.

6. Inna Shapiro, "Joys of Christmas, Horrors of the Crusades," *Ha'aretz*, 20 August 2002, B5 (in Hebrew).

7. Tamar Horowitz, "Immigrant Children and Youth in the Educational System: Assimilation, Mono-Lingualism, Mono-Directionalism and Stereotyping," in *Diukana shel Aliyah: Tahalikhei klita shel yehudei Brit Hamoatzot L'sheavar, 1990–1995*, ed. Moshe Sicron and Elazar Leshem (Jerusalem: Magnes Press, 1998; in Hebrew), 403. For a broad, comparative discussion of the identity of Jewish youth both in Israel and in

Russia, with a copious bibliography, see Kirill Demidov and Alek D. Epstein, "The Formation of Jewish Identity in the Secular Schools of Israel and the Diaspora," *Evreiskoe obrazovanie*, no. 2 (2001): 28–29, and footnotes 10–18.

8. Shapiro, "Joys of Christmas, Horrors of the Crusades." Zvi Y. Gitelman, Vladimir Cherviakov, and Vladimir Shapiro, "Judaism in the National-Self Consciousness of Russian Jews," *Vestnik Evreiskogo universiteta v Moskve* 3, no. 7 (1999) 136 (in Russian), found that 13 percent of their sample regarded various Christian denominations as more attractive than Judaism.

9. Sabina Lisitsa, Yohanan Peres, and Eliezer Ben Rafael, "The Attitude of Veteran Israelis toward Immigrants from the CIS: A Multi-Cultural Perspective," *Diaspora* 20–21 (2002): 198.

10. Moshe Lissak and Elazar Leshem, "The Russian Intelligentsia in Israel: Between Ghettoization and Integration," *Israel Affairs* 2, no. 2 (1995): 31.

11. See Zvi Y. Gitelmen, "Jewish Soviet Identity in a Period of Transition," *Yehudei Brit Hamoatzot Bamaavar* 1, no. 16 (1994) 149 (in Hebrew). Professor Gitelman coined the terms "Westerners" and "Heartlanders."

12. Israel Television, Channel Two News, 11 February 2003.

13. Zerubavel, *Recovered Roots*, 15–17, 214.

14. Sidney Heitman, "The Third Soviet Emigration: Jewish, German and Armenian Emigration from the USSR since World War II" (mimeograph, 1986), 21. From 1945 to 1954, only 18 Jews were allowed to leave the Soviet Union for Israel. In 1955, 105 emigrated, and in 1956, 753. The total given above excludes approximately 30,000 Jews who left the Soviet Union for Poland in 1956–57 under a Polish–Soviet repatriation agreement and after a six-month interval continued on to Israel with the full knowledge and tacit concurrence of the Soviet authorities.

15. The figure for Israel is from "Statistical Data," *Jews of the Soviet Union in Transition* 4, no. 19 (2000): 136. The number of Jews who left the Soviet Union and went to countries other than Israel during this period is given here as 178,885.

16. Spokesman of the Ministry of Immigrant Absorption, *Ha'aretz*, 30 December 2002, 10A.

17. Moshe Sicron, "The Human Capital of the Immigrants and Their Integration into Employment," in Sicron and Leshem, *Diukana shel Aliyah*, 132–34, gives a detailed analysis of the educational level of the immigrants, differentials by republic of origin, and variations during the decade of the 1990s.

18. Elazar Leshem and Moshe Lissak, "The Social and Cultural Consolidation of the Russian Community in Israel," in Lissak and Leshem, *MeRussia L'Yisrael*, 34. See also the discussion in Elazar Leshem and Moshe Lissak, "The Development and Consolidation of the Russian Community of Israel," in *Roots and Routes: Ethnicity and Migration in Global Perspective*, ed. Shalva Weil (Jerusalem: Magnes Press, 1999), 143.

19. For detailed discussion and analysis, see Elazar Leshem, "Immigrant Absorption Policies and the System of Services to Immigrants: The Initial Absorption Stage," in Sicron and Leshem, *Diukana shel Aliyah*, 41–126.

20. For development of this theme, see Lissak and Leshem, *MeRussia L'Israel*, 31.

21. On the alacrity with which the immigrants of the second wave engaged in politics and the slowness of achieving leadership positions, see Zvi Y. Gitelman, *Becoming Israelis* (New York: Praeger, 1982), 344. On the rich informal subculture of the third wave, see Zvi Y. Gitelman, "Jewish Soviet Identity in a Period of Transition," *Yehudei Brit Hamoatzot Bamaavar* 1, no. 12 (1994): 153 (in Hebrew). For a discussion of the

process of community formation, see Leshem and Lissak, "The Development and Consolidation of the Russian Community of Israel," 135, 157–161.

22. For confirmation that there was no growth of unemployment among veteran Israelis and no lowering of wages as a result of the entry of the immigrants into the workforce in the first half of the 1990s, see Moshe Sicron, "Hahon Haenoshi," in Sicron and Leshem, *Diukana shel Aliyah*, 177.

23. The author has in his possession a letter written in 1919 by his father, then a soldier in the Jewish Battalions of the British army, commenting that it was difficult trying to communicate with the settlers of Rishon L'Tzion because the latter insisted on speaking "Hebrew and only Hebrew."

24. Ministry of Immigrant Absorption (http://www.moia.gov.il).

25. Rosalina Ryvkina, "Changes in the National Self-Identification of Jews in the 1990s," in *Problemy sushchestvovaniia v diaspore*, comp. F. Dektor and V. Mochalova (Minsk: MET, 2001), 145, 155–56.

26. Ryvkina, "Changes in the National Self-Identification of Jews in the 1990s," 156.

27. Mikhail Chlenow, "The Interrelation of Religious and Ethnic Identification in Jewish Self-Consciousness," in *Problemy sushchestvovaniia v diaspore*, comp. F. Dektor and V. Mochalova (Minsk: MET, 2001), 60.

28. See Zvi Y. Gitelman, Vladimir Cherviakov, and V. Shapiro, "Judaism in the National Self-Consciousness of Russian Jews," *Vestnik Evreiskogo universiteta v Moskve* 3, no. 7 (1994; in Russian); Rosalina Ryvkina, *Evrei post-Sovetskogo Rossii: kto oni?* (Moscow: URSS, 1996; in Russian).

29. Eugene Satanovsky, "Organized National Life of Russian Jews in the Late Soviet and Post-Soviet Era: A View from Moscow," *Jewish Political Studies Review* 11, no. 1–2 (spring 2002): 41.

30. Vladimir Sobkin and Aleksandr Vladimirov, "The Particularities of the National Self-Identification of Jewish Students in Russia," *Evreiskoe obrazovanie*, no. 2 (2001): 43, 52.

31. Ryvkina, "Changes in the National Self-Identification of Jews in the 1990s," 155–56.

32. For a broad discussion of this theme, see Abram Torpusman, *Spory ob opredeleniiu Evreistva* (Jerusalem: Te'enah, 2001; in Russian).

33. Chlenow, "The Interrelation of Religious and Ethnic Identification in Jewish Self-Consciousness," 29.

34. Chlenow, "The Interrelation of Religious and Ethnic Identification in Jewish Self-Consciousness," 63–64.

35. Gitelman, "Jewish Soviet Identity in a Period of Transition," 150–51. In a survey conducted by Gitelman in Chicago, only one out of 150 immigrants who had been in the city for 20 years declared his identity as American.

36. Sabina Lisitsa and Yochanan Peres, "Problems of Self-Identification of Immigrants to Israel from the FSU, and Their Interrelation with Native-Born Israelis," in *Migratsionnye protsessy i ikh vlianie na Izrail'skoe obshchestvo*, ed. Alek Epstein and A. V. Fedorchenko (Moscow: Institute for the Study of Israel and the Middle East, 2000; in Russian), 261.

37. Lisitsa and Peres, "Problems of Self-Identification," 254–55.

38. Lisitsa and Peres, "Problems of Self-Identification," 257.

39. Lisitsa and Peres, "Problems of Self-Identification," 256.

40. Lisitsa and Peres, "Problems of Self-Identification," 251.

41. See the discussion in Hanna Adoni and Akiva Cohen, "Communications Consumption and Social Structuring of Identity in the 'Russian' Community in Israel," *Yehudei Brit Hamoatzot L'sheavar BaYisrael Uvatfutzot* 20–21 (2002): 208 (in Hebrew).

42. Gitelman, "Jewish Soviet Identity in a Period of Transition," 151–52; Lisitsa and Peres, "Problems of Self-Identification," 261, show a similar alienation from religion and religious people. Al Haj and Leshem, *Immigrants from the Former Soviet Union in Israel*, 46, present similar findings regarding civil marriage and Sabbath transport and so on.

43. Al Haj and Leshem, *Immigrants from the Former Soviet Union in Israel*, 41–42.

44. For a particularly poignant exposition of such disabilities, only one among hundreds or even thousands, see Vered Levi-Barzilai, "Our Mischael? Well Actually Not," *Ha'aretz*, Supplement, 24 January 2003, 45–48. It may be proposed that one of the reasons for the decline of the FSU immigrant party, Yisrael Ba'Aliyah, was the failure of its leader, Anatolii Sharansky, to ease the personal status of the immigrants during his term as minister of the interior from 1999 to 2000.

45. Gitelman, *Becoming Israelis*, 144.

46. Theodore H. Friedgut, "Generations and Politics: Changes in Status, Outlook and Identity in Israel," in Epstein and Fedorchenko, *Migratsionnye protsessy i ikh vlianie na Izrail'skoe obshchestvo*, 61.

47. Narspy Zilberg, "Russian-Jewish Intelligentsia in Israel and the Search for New Models of Integration," in Epstein and Fedorchenko, *Migratsionnye protsessy i ikh vlianie na Izrail'skoe obshchestvo*, 198–227.Gitelman, "Jewish Soviet Identity in a Period of Transition," 153, notes the highly developed subculture of the 1990s immigrants as compared with the second-wave immigrants.

48. For a comprehensive discussion of the concept of civic efficacy and its importance in the socialization of new immigrants, see Gitelman, *Becoming Israelis*, 310–14, 337, 345–46.

49. For reference to the 1996 elections, see Theodore H. Friedgut, "Generations and Politics," 64. For the same phenomenon in 1999, see Vladimir Khanin, "Political Elites, Social Structures, and Socio-Political Conflicts in the Community of Immigrants from the USSR/CIS in Contemporary Israel," in Epstein and Fedorchenko, *Migratsionnye protsessy i ikh vlianie na Izrail'skoe obshchestvo*, 237–38.

50. For detailed analysis of the electoral behavior of the immigrants, see Friedgut, "Generations and Politics," 60–67. and Etta Bick, "Sectarian Party Politics in Israel: The Case of Yisrael Ba'Aliya, the Russian Immigrant Party," in *Israel at the Polls, 1996* ed. Daniel J. Elazar and Shmuel Sandler (London: Frank Cass, 1998), 119–45.

51. See the discussion in Lisitsa and Peres, "Problems of Self-Identification," 264–65.

52. Gitelman, *Becoming Israelis*, 338, 344.

53. See Theodore H. Friedgut, *Political Participation in the USSR* (Princeton, N.J.: Princeton University Press, 1979), 224–34. For the statement that the immigrants lack a civic culture tradition, see Elazar Leshem and Moshe Lissak "Formation of the Russian Community in Israel," *Yehudei Brit Hamoatzot Bamaavar* 4, no. 19 (2000): 58.

54. Khanin, "Political Elites," 237–38.

55. Al Haj and Leshem, *Immigrants from the Former Soviet Union in Israel*, 56. The definition of "Yisrael Betenu" as an immigrant party has always been somewhat problematic. Although Liberman himself is an immigrant of the second wave and attained

prominence as director general of the Likud and as an aide to Prime Minister Benyamin Natanyahu and the party's name was clearly associated with one of the political parties of post-Soviet Russia, Liberman claimed to represent all those who suffered under the establishment and named a prominent nonimmigrant senior military figure as his second in command. Later, in forming the "National Union," with parties that had no particular connection to the immigrants, he further diluted any claim to represent the FSU community and indeed in the 2003 elections received far less support from the immigrants than in the previous elections.

56. *Ha'aretz*, 30 July 2001. In the 2003 elections, Yisrael Ba'Aliyah polled 105,000 votes fewer than in 1999, and the "National Union," of which Yisrael Betenu was a part, lost 21,000 votes. See *Ha'aretz*, 30 January 2003, 9A.

57. For a full discussion of the immigrants' participation in the municipal election campaign and its results, see Zev Katz, "Immigrants from the Former Soviet Union in Israel's Political Life in the 1990s," *Yehudei Brit Hamoatzot Bamaavar* 4, no. 19 (2000): 145–57.

58. Khanin, "Political Elites," 234.

59. Khanin, "Political Elites," 231.

60. Zilberg, "Russian-Jewish Intelligentsia in Israel and the Search for New Models of Integration," 212.

61. On this phenomenon, see Al Haj and Leshem, *Immigrants from the Former Soviet Union in Israel*, 69.

62. Uriah Shavit, "Is This a Culture?" *Ha'aretz*, Supplement, 1 March 2002, 42–46. For research showing that immigrant youth hold the Russian language in high esteem but do not have nearly as positive feelings about Russia as a country, see Elite Olshtain and Bella Kotik, "The Development of Bilingualism in an Immigrant Community," in *Language, Identity and Immigration*, ed. Elite Olshtain and Gabriel Horenczyk (Jerusalem: Magnes Press, 2000), 213–15.

63. For a detailed analysis of the varieties of immigrant organizations, see Moshe Lissak and Elazar Leshem, "The Russian Intelligentsia in Israel: Between Ghettoization and Integration," *Israel Affairs* 2, no. 2 (1995): 26–28.

64. For a detailed description of *Mofet*'s origins and development, see Alek D. Epstein, "The Challenge of Excellence as a Response to the Difficulties of Absorption in the Israeli Educational System," *Yehudei Brit Hamoatzot Bamaavar* 4, no. 19 (2000): 189–91.

65. Al Haj and Leshem, *Immigrants from the Former Soviet Union in Israel*, 66.

66. Ministry of Immigrant Absorption, "Dispersion of Immigrants Arriving between 1.1.1989 and 31.12.2002," report of 6 January 2003 (http://www.moia.gov.il).

67. *Ha'aretz*, 12 January 2003, 2A.

68. Lissak and Leshem, "The Russian Intelligentsia in Israel," 29.

69. Al Haj and Leshem, *Immigrants from the Former Soviet Union in Israel*, 23.

70. Adoni and Cohen, "Communications Consumption and Social Structuring of Identity in the 'Russian' Community in Israel," 208.

71. For the story of Gesher's origins and achievements as an allegory for the FSU immigrant community's impact, see Jason Keyser, "Russian Jews, Israel Change Each Other," Associated Press, 16 December 2001, as published by the *Miami Herald*.

72. See the discussion around one issue of *Zerkalo*, in *Ha'aretz*, Book Review section, 29 May 2002, 8.

73. See the discussions in Shiri Lev Ari, "No New Dostoevsky Has Grown Up

Here," *Ha'aretz*, 21 September 2002, D7. As the reader may have noted, *Ha'aretz*, Israel's most intellectual Hebrew-language newspaper, has opened its pages broadly to discussions of the immigrants' plight and problems, explaining them to the veteran Israeli intelligentsia. At one point, the newspaper was considering the idea of publishing a Russian-language edition.

74. For a discussion of this point, see Zerubavel, *Recovered Roots* 10, 257.

75. Lisitsa and Peres, "Problems of Self-Identification," 257.

76. Lissak and Leshem, "The Russian Intelligentsia in Israel," 28.

77. Vladimir Glozman, "Building a Community," *The Soviet Jewry Zionist Forum* 20 (1991)" 6–7, cited in Zilberg, "The Russian-Jewish Intelligentsia in Israel and the Search for New Models of Integration," 198.

78. Al Haj and Leshem, *Immigrants from the Former Soviet Union in Israel*, 13.

BIBLIOGRAPHY

Adoni Hanna, and Akiva Cohen. "Communications Consumption and Social Construction of Identities in the "Russian" Community in Israel." *Y'hudei Brit Hamoatsot L'sheavar Bayisrael Uvatfutzot* 20–21 (2002): 205–16. (in Hebrew)

Al Haj, Majid, and Elazar Leshem. *Immigrants from the Former Soviet Union in Israel: Ten Years Later.* Haifa: Haifa University Press, 2000.

Ben Raphael, Eliezer, Elite Olshtein, and Idith Geijst. "Identity, Language and Social Integration of Jews from the Former Soviet Union in Israel." In *MeRussia L'Yisrael: Zhut Utarbut Bamaavar*, ed. Moshe Lissak and Elazar Leshem. Tel Aviv: Hakibbutz Hameuhad Publishing House, 2001, 77–99. (in Hebrew)

Bick, Etta. "Sectarian Party Politics in Israel: The Case of Yisrael Ba'Aliya, the Russian Immigrant Party." In *Israel at the Polls, 1996*, ed. Daniel J. Elazar and Shmuel Sandler. London: Frank Cass, 1998, 119–45.

Chlenow, Mikhail, "The Interrelation of Religious and Ethnic Identification in Jewish Self-Consciousness." In *Problemy sushchestvovaniia v diaspore*, comp. F. Dektor and V. Mochalova. Minsk: MET, 2001, 28–65. (in Russian)

Demidov, Kirill, and Alek D. Epstein. "The Formation of Jewish Identity in the Secondary Schools of Israel and the Countries of the Diaspora." *Evreiskoe obrazovanie*, no. 2 (2001): 19–36. (in Russian)

Epstein, Alek D. "The Challenge of Excellence as a Response to the Difficulties of Absorption in the Israeli Educational System." *Yehudei Brit Hamoatzot Bamaavar* 4 no. 19 (2000): 181–95.

Epstein, Alek, and A. V. Fedorchenko, eds. *Migratsionnye protsessy i ikh vlianie na Izrail'skoe obshchestvo.* Moscow: Institute for the Study of Israel and the Middle East, 2000.

Epstein, Alek, and Nina Kheimets. "Cultural Clash and Educational Diversity: Immigrant Teachers' Efforts to Rescue the Education of Immigrant Children of Israel." *International Studies in Sociology of Education* 10, no. 2 (2000): 190–210.

Friedgut, Theodore H. "Generations and Politics: Changes in Status, Outlook and Identity in Israel." In *Migratsionnye protsessy i ix vliianie na Izrail'skoe obshchestvo*," ed. Alek D. Epstein and A. V. Fedorchenko. Moscow: Institute for the Study of Israel and the Middle East, 2000, 36–71.

Gitelman, Zvi Y. *Becoming Israelis.* New York: Praeger, 1982.

———. "Jewish Soviet Identity in a Period of Transition." *Yehudei Brit Hamoatzot Bamaavar* 1, no. 12 (1994): 148–57. (in Hebrew)

Gitelman, Zvi Y., Vladimir Cherviakov, and V. Shapiro. "Judaism in the National Self-Consciousness of Russian Jews." *Vestnik Evreiskogo universiteta v Moskve* 3, no. 7 (1994): 121–44. (in Russian)

Heitman, Sidney. "The Third Soviet Emigration: Jewish, German and Armenian Emigration from the USSR since World War II." Mimeograph, 1986.

Horowitz, Tamar. "Immigrant Children and Youth in the Educational System: Assimilation, Monolingualism, Mono-Directionalism and Stereotyping." In *Diukana shel Aliyah: Tahalikhei klitatam shel olei Brit Hamoatzot L'sheavar, 1990–1995*, ed. Moshe Sicron and Elazar Leshem. Jerusalem: Magnes Press, 1998, 368–408. (in Hebrew)

Horowitz, Tamar, and Elazar Leshem. "Immigrants from the Former Soviet Union in the Cultural Sphere of Israel." In *Diukana shel Aliyah: Tahalikhei klitatam shel olei Brit Hamoatzot L'sheavar, 1990–1995*, ed. Moshe Sicron and Elazar Leshem. Jerusalem: Magnes Press, 1998, 291–333. (in Hebrew)

Israel Statistical Annual, no. 53. Jerusalem: Central Bureau of Statistics, 2002.

Katz, Zev. "Immigrants from the Former Soviet Union in Israel's Political Life in the 1990s." *Yehudei Brit Hamoatzot Bamaavar* 4, no. 19 (2000): 145–57. (in Hebrew)

Khanin, Vladimir. "Political Elites, Social Structures, and Socio-Political Conflicts in the Community of Immigrants from the USSR/CIS in Contemporary Israel." In *Migratsionnye protsessy i ikh vlianie na Izrail'skoe obshchestvo*, ed. Alek Epstein and A. V. Fedorchenko. Moscow: Institute for the Study of Israel and the Middle East, 2000, 228–47. (in Russian)

Leshem, Elazar. "Policy of Immigrant Absorption and the System of Services to Immigrants in the Initial Stage of Absorption." In *Diukana shel Aliyah: Tahalikhei klitatam shel olei Brit Hamoatzot L'sheavar, 1990–1995*, ed. Moshe Sicron and Elazar Leshem. Jerusalem: Magnes Press, 1998, 41–126. (in Hebrew)

Leshem, Elazar, and Moshe Lissak. "Development and Consolidation of the Russian Community in Israel." In *Roots and Routes: Ethnicity and Migration in Global Perspective*, ed. Shalva Weil. Jerusalem: Magnes Press, 1999, 135–71.

———. "Formation of the "Russian" Community in Israel." *Yehudei Brit Hamoatzot Bamaavar* 4, no. 19 (2000): 47–66. (in Hebrew)

———. "The Social and Cultural Consolidation of the Russian Community in Israel." In *MeRussia L'Yisrael: Zhut Utarbut Bamaavar*, ed. Moshe Lissak and Elazar Leshem. Tel Aviv: Hakibbutz Hameuhad, 2001, 27–76. (in Hebrew)

Lev Ari, Shiri. "No New Dostoevsky Has Grown Up Here." *Ha'aretz*, 26 September 2002, D-7. (in Hebrew)

Levi-Barzilai, Vered. "Our Michael? Actually, No!" *Ha'aretz*, Supplement, 24 January 2003, 45–48. (in Hebrew)

Lisitsa, Sabena, and Yohanan Peres. "Problems of Self-Identification of Immigrants to Israel from the FSU, and Their Interrelation with Native-Born Israelis." In *Migratsionnye protsessy i ikh vlianie na Izrail'skoe obshchestvo*, ed. Alek Epstein and A. V. Fedorchenko. Moscow: Institute for the Study of Israel and the Middle East, 2000, 244–75. (in Russian)

Lisitsa, Sabena, Yohanan Peres, and Eliezer Ben Raphael. "The Attitude of Veteran Israelis toward Immigrants from the CIS: A Multi-Cultural Perspective." *Ye-*

hudei Brit Hamoatzot L'sheavar BaYisrael Ubat'futsot 20–21 (2002): 193–204. (in Hebrew)

Lissak, Moshe, and Elazar Leshem. "The Russian Intelligentsia in Israel: Between Ghettoization and Integration." *Israel Affairs* 2, no. 2 (1995): 20–36.

———. *MeRussia L'Yisrael: Zhut Utarbut Bamaavar.* Tel Aviv: Hakibbutz Hameuhad, 2001. (in Hebrew)

Olshtain, Elite, and Bella Kotik. "The Development of Bilingualism in an Immigrant Community." In *Language, Identity and Immigration*, ed. Elite Olshtain and Gabriel Horenczyk. Jerusalem: Magnes Press, 2000, 201–17.

Ryvkina, Rosalina. *Evrei v post-Sovetskoi Rossii: kto Oni?* Moscow: URSS, 1996. (in Russian)

———. "Changes in the National Self-Identification of Jews in the 1990s." In *Problemy sushchestvovaniia v diaspore*, comp. F. Dektor and V. Mochalova. Minsk: MET, 2001, 143–58. (in Russian)

Satanovsky, Eugene. "Organized National Life of Russian Jews in the Late Soviet and Post-Soviet Era: A View from Moscow." *Jewish Journal of Political Studies* 11, nos. 1–2 (2002): 29–43.

Segev, Amira. "Larissa Gerstein." *Ha'aretz*, Supplement, 19 October 2001, 34–39. (in Hebrew)

Shapiro, Inna. "Joys of Christmas, Horrors of the Crusades." *Ha'aretz*, 20 August 2002, B5. (in Hebrew)

Shavit, Uriah. "Is This a Culture?" *Ha'aretz*, Supplement, 1 March 2002, 42–46. (in Hebrew)

Sicron, Moshe. "The Human Capital of the Immigrants and Their Integration in Work." In *Diukana shel Aliyah: Tahalikhei klita shel yehudei Brit Hamoatzot L'sheavar, 1990–1995*, ed. Moshe Sicron and Elazar Leshem. Jerusalem: Magnes Press, 1998, 127–81. (in Hebrew)

Sicron, Moshe, and Elazar Leshem, eds. *Diukana shel Aliyah: Tahalikhei klita shel yehudei Brit Hamoatzot L'sheavar, 1990–1995.* Jerusalem: Magnes Press, 1998. (in Hebrew)

Sobkin, Vladimir, and Aleksandr Vladimirov. "The Particularities of the National Self-Identification of Jewish Students in Russia." *Evreiskoe obrazovanie* 2 (2000): 39–62. (in Russian)

"Statistical Data." *Yehudei Brit Hamoatzot Bamaavar* 4, no. 19 (2000): 136. (in Hebrew)

Torpusman, Abram. *Spory ob opredeleniiu Evreistva.* Jerusalem: T'enah, 2001. (in Russian)

Zerubavel, Yael. *Recovered Roots: Collective Memory and the Making of Israeli National Tradition.* Chicago: University of Chicago Press, 1995.

Zilberg, Narspy. "Russian-Jewish Intelligentsia in Israel and the Search for New Models of Integration." In *Migratsionnye protsessy i ikh vlianie na Izrail'skoe obshchestvo*, ed. Alek Epstein and A.V. Fedorchenko. Moscow: Institute for the Study of Israel and the Middle East, 2000, 198–227. (in Russian) (A Hebrew version may be found in *Yehudei Brit Hamoatzot Bamaavar* 4, no. 19 [2000]: 196–212.)

CHAPTER 8

From Melting Pot to Multiculturalism; or, The Privatization of Israeli Identity

Daniel Gutwein

In 1997, Israeli public opinion was stunned by the appeal made by Ehud Barak, the Labor candidate to the premiership, for the forgiveness of Israel Oriental Jews (the *Mizrachim*) for the suffering caused them over the years by the Labor movement.[1] Barak's apology was an explicit recognition of the major transition undergone by Israeli society since the 1970s, leading to the decline of the veteran Labor hegemony and the political empowerment of the *Mizrachim*.[2] Barak's appeal for forgiveness originated, no doubt, in the electoral exigencies of his party, and he might have had in mind the cultural grievances not only of the *Mizrachim* but of the new immigrants of the former Soviet Union as well. Nevertheless, manipulative as his apology might have been, it marked a turning point, albeit a fallacious one, in Israel's identity discourse. Barak, the ultimate Israeli, a kibbutz-born commander of the most prestigious elite unit of the Israel Defense Forces (IDF), and leader of the party of the veteran European middle class (the *Ashkenazim*), actually accepted the *Mizrachi* lower-class narrative of oppression and exclusion and publicly recognized the responsibility of his movement.[3]

In addition to its sociological implications, Barak's apology had important intellectual ramifications as well. He had, in fact, appropriated the multicultural critique of the Israeli "melting pot" ideology and the way it had been implemented by Labor-controlled state agencies in the 1950s and 1960s.[4] Barak's apology actually reflected a growing recognition of the fundamental transformation that Israeli collective identity has undergone over the past three decades.[5] One of the outstanding features of this transformation has been the almost universal condemnation and renunciation of the melting pot ideology and the gradual endorsement of its multicultural-inspired critique. The ideology of the melting pot—or, in the equivalent Hebrew, Israeli term,

Mizug Galuyot—it has been argued, was used to legitimize forcing new immigrants to adopt modern Hebrew culture instead of their original, non-Zionist exilic cultures and molding them into the Zionist ideal of the "new Jew" (the *Zabar*), thus ensuring the continuance of veteran Labor *Ashkenzi* hegemony while perpetuating it.

Different versions, Zionist or Post-Zionist, of this multicultural critique have informed scholarly discussions of the Israeli cultural, social, and political history of the 1950s and the 1960s. Most prominently, it has appeared in Post-Zionist "critical" writings, where the melting pot ideology and policy has served as a proof of the modernistic (i.e., oppressive) nature of Zionism. On the other hand, multiculturalism is portrayed by Post-Zionist ideology as an alternative to the melting pot, born of postmodern and postcolonial theories and critical analyses of Zionist and Israeli history that emerged with the decline of the Labor *Ashkenazi* hegemony and advocated the emancipation of its "others." The scholarly interest in multicultural critique was also the result of nonacademic factors: the contrast between the melting pot and multiculturalism has become the focus of bitter controversy and conflicts, reshaping Israeli society, politics, culture, and identity. Consequently, scholarly discussion has gradually become intertwined in the arguments dividing Israeli society, and ideological positions were very often uncritically accepted as scholarly interpretations.[6]

Barak's apology attests to the importance of the melting pot and its multicultural critique in Israeli identity discourse. The ease with which he appropriated this critique is an ample proof to the confusion between scholarship and ideology, research, and politics that informs it. Moreover, this appropriation by the representative of the allegedly oppressive elite—against whom it was originally made—actually casts doubts on its pretension of emancipating Labor's "others" and seemed to show that it might equally serve the interests of the veteran middle-class hegemony itself.

In order to relocate the discussion of the melting pot and multiculturalism in the setting of critical scholarly analysis, these concepts should be removed from the area of ideological and political controversy in which it has been conducted over the past two decades and should be historically contextualized. The contextual approach, which will be employed here, probes the way in which ideologies acquire historical impact by separating their formal content from the political goals they serve and examines the contemporary specific social and cultural circumstances that impart the relevant ideologies their changing meaning. And, indeed, this approach suggests alternative interpretations to the prevalent ideological reading of the melting pot and multiculturalism.

Contrary to the accepted version, the target audience of the melting pot ideology was not the new immigrants of the 1950s but the absorbers; further, it did not aim at imposing Hebrew culture on the new immigrants since the acquisition of the language and culture of the "new country" is an integral and normal part of almost any immigration process. Rather, the melting pot ideology intended to uphold the ethos of Israeli etatism (*mamlachtiyut*) as a collective alternative to socialism, as the basis for Israeli social engineering and the welfare state, and to overcome the ideological and political opposition it faced in particular within the Labor movement. From this perspective, the multicultural critique appears to be a means of undermining Israeli collective ethos and of providing an ideological basis to the privatization revolution, which has been changing Israeli society since the 1980s, breaking up the welfare state and commercializing its services while widening social and economic gaps.

THE MELTING POT

Chronological facts provide a pertinent starting point for the historical contextualization of the ideology and policy of the melting pot. The multicultural criticism of the melting pot began to play a central role in Israeli scholarly discussion and identity discourse precisely when the *Ashkenazi* veteran elite—the chief beneficiary of the melting pot who, according to this critique, used it to establish and retain its hegemony—explicitly rejected its major, allegedly oppressive premises. The melting pot continues, then, to affect Israeli society long after it lost its weight as a policy or ideology. Hence, the multicultural critique is motivated not by the formal content of the melting pot ideology, which it criticizes, but by its social implications, which will be probed here.

The melting pot ideology was formulated most clearly by David Ben-Gurion, the "founding father" of the State of Israel and its first prime minister.[7] Ben-Gurion frequently spoke of the urgent necessity of merging the hundreds of thousands of immigrants who arrived at Israel in the early 1950s with their varied languages and cultures and molding them into one Hebrew culture as a basis for building the nation. Comparing the Israeli melting pot to that of the United States, he maintained that the sound foundations of the United States enabled the melting pot process there to work slowly, and, in fact, it had still not come to an end after 300 years. In Israel, on the other hand, the distinct structure of society and the special needs and tasks of the state required the adoption of a deliberate state-controlled policy that would speed up the acculturation of the immigrants. Ben-Gurion thus distinguished between the melting pot as a process, like in the United States, and the melting pot as a policy and ideology, as it should be in Israel. His words further imply that the need to conduct a melting pot policy emanated from the special circumstances and conditions arising from the establishment of the Israeli state and the mass immigration. The majority that absorbed the immigrants in the United States constituted a solid, stable group that also defined the hegemonic language and culture. These were not challenged by the constant flow of immigrants, who formed minority groups and, as such, had no choice but to adapt themselves to the common hegemonic culture through the melting pot process. In Israel, by contrast, the relationship between the absorbed and the absorbing population following the great immigration introduced an element of constant instability and created the need for an ideology and policy that would make the melting pot work.[8] On the whole, Ben-Gurion's distinction between melting pot as an ideology and as a process and his view of the exceptional character of the Israeli melting pot as ideology rather than process was accepted in public and academic discourse, and it informs the multicultural critique as well.[9]

In the United States and in other immigration countries, the melting pot is, indeed, a process by which new immigrants acquire the language and culture of the new country as a precondition of their integration into the labor market and society. This process has marked generational characteristics.[10] The first generation suffers the most agonizing experience: deprived of its original culture and seeing its intellectual world abruptly becoming irrelevant, it faces difficulties in acquiring the new language, is forced to accept underpaid manual labor, and consequently suffers economic exploitation, poverty, social control, and exclusion. The acquisition of the new language and culture becomes an interest of the immigrants since it increases their chances of improving their position in the labor market and in society as a whole. This advancement, however, is usually accomplished only in the second and third generations, when the new language and culture are part of the normal upbringing of the immigrants' children, mainly through the school system and other social agencies. Gradually, the second and third generations become integrated into the new society, but it is a dialectic process whereby they demand recognition of their different identity and their heritage, which gradually becomes part of the host culture. The melting pot, then, is not an ideology but rather the cultural facet of the process of the immigrants' integration into the labor market and society in the new country. Changing economic and social policies in the absorbing countries naturally influence the melting pot process. These policies, however, do not initiate the process and cannot forestall it; they can only regulate it.

In contrast to Ben-Gurion's interpretation, however, in Israel, too, the melting pot was a process rather than an ideology. The hegemony of Hebrew as the official national language and culture was not challenged by the mass immigration, and it was uncontested despite fears of Hebrew loyalists. These fears, however, were later used to imbue the process of the melting pot with the appearance of ideology. Moreover, Hebrew culture was not monolithic: from its very beginnings, it was an arena for ongoing struggles between competing viewpoints and trends—such as that between the religious and the secular, which has accompanied modern Hebrew culture from its very beginnings and which frequently reflected political power struggles.[11] The needs of the immigrants' absorption spurred formation of the state school system, which was a source of economic and political power that further exacerbated cultural conflicts.[12] Thus, the change in the demographic composition of Israel in the wake of the great immigration led to an intensification of existing cultural struggles and to the rise of new ones. Nevertheless, these struggles did not challenge the hegemony of the Hebrew culture because they were conducted within it, not against it. The cultural and educational disputes engendered by the immigrants themselves were quickly translated into terms of already existing conflicts between rival forces in the Israeli establishment.[13] These conflicts were then extended to the immigrant population, which thus became absorbed into the framework of the existing Israeli power structure. Thus, more than protest against the melting pot, these cultural conflicts became a part of it.

The distinctive political character of cultural struggles sometimes prompted Ben-Gurion to execute a tactical retreat from the ideology of the melting pot. Thus, referring to the education of immigrant children from Yemen, he sided with those who opposed the speeding up of the melting pot process. He disapproved of any injury to the religious traditions, customs, or beliefs of the Yemenite new immigrants on the grounds that the process of their absorption should be accomplished gradually—that is, in the American fashion, according to his definition. The Labor movement, he argued, should educate these immigrants to its values patiently and with empathy. Ben-Gurion even warned, at a Mapai Party forum, that any attempt at cultural coercion would drive the Yemenites into the arms of rival religious and right-wing parties, such as the Mizrachi and Herut, or even the Communists, whereas a patient, tolerant approach would bring about a gradual cultural transformation, thus bringing this community closer to the Labor movement.[14] He displayed a similar approach in regard to the question of Yiddish culture: in consideration of immigrants who possessed no other culture and in spite of his declared hostility to Yiddish, he was against imposing restrictions on Yiddish theater.[15] It seems, then, that Ben-Gurion himself, while advocating the ideology of the melting pot, acknowledged that it could be realized only gradually, as a process.

As in other lands of immigration, the process of the melting pot took place simultaneously with the process of class structuring in Israeli society. Class stratification involved the inclusion of groups of immigrants, particularly the *Ashkenazim*, in the hegemonic class and the exclusion of others, particularly the *Mizrachim*, who were relegated to the lower classes.[16] This process led to the growth of class cultures marked by the congruence between social class and ethnic affiliation.[17] The *Mizrachim*, who were concentrated in the geographic and social periphery, where they constituted a significant segment of the Israeli working class, created their own "Oriental" culture, which in addition to its ethnic features has the marked characteristics of a working-class culture. Similarly, the *Ashkenazim* became identified with the emerging Israeli middle class, who was closely connected with the ruling establishment, and its culture became the hegemonic culture.

Moreover, the terms "*Mizrachim*" and "*Ashkenazim*" in the accepted Israeli meaning result from the interrelation of the processes of the melting pot and class structuring.[18] Israeli "*mizrachiut*" is an imagined identity, born out of the impact of the melting pot on different groups of new immigrants, mainly from Islamic countries, who were merged in working-class slum areas and peripheral regions of Israel. There they developed a distinct culture, which, as in the case of the "Oriental music," integrated elements from their different, original cultures with the Israeli hegemonic, Mediterranean and rock music. The *Mizrachim* thus became the product of the dissolution of the different identities and cultures of Jewish communities that originated in Islamic countries by the melting pot and their merging into the culture of the Israeli working class. The rise of *Mizrachi* culture was, in fact, not a protest against the melting pot but evidence of its success. What the *Mizrachi* culture really protested against was not the melting pot but the middle-class *Ashkenazi* hegemony and its economic and social privileges. Like *Mizrachiut*, Israeli *Askenaziut* is also an imagined identity, born of the melting together of various groups of immigrants from different European countries whose culture, which became hegemonic, was also the product of the Israeli melting pot and which was structured as the middle class. The melting pot involved, then, two different yet overlapping processes: cultural unification and class stratification, which produced different class cultures.

The disregard of class aspects of the melting pot is closely related to the confusion between political controversy and historical analysis that characterizes the public and scholarly discussion of the melting pot. This confusion is manifested in the prevalent view that posits the rise of *Mizrachi* culture from the 1970s on as an indication of the disintegration of the melting pot ideology. When historically contextualized, however, the rise of *Mizrachi* culture is clearly seen to be the result of the melting pot process: it permeated the hegemonic Israeli culture as part of cultural integration and upward social mobility typical of the second and third generation of the melting pot. Likewise, the apparent Kulturkampf between *Mizrachim* and *Ashkenazim* does not indicate the failure of the melting pot as it is popularly claimed but, on the contrary, seems to be part of the inner workings of the melting pot process and of its inherent class conflicts. These class conflicts, even more than ethnic identity, may well explain the patronizing attitude of the hegemonic, *Ashkenazi* Hebrew culture, as middle-class culture, toward the *Mizrachi* culture, as the lower, working-class culture. This patronizing attitude is, in fact, a practice of social control, well known in other immigrant countries, not least in Jewish immigrant communities.

Israeli melting pot was, then, not an ideology, as suggested by Ben-Gurion, but, like in other immigrant countries, a simultaneous process of economic, social, and cultural integration and class stratification. Hence, it seems that while the multicultural critique attacks Ben-Gurion's ideology of the melting pot, it accepts his unhistorical distinction, the artificiality of which he himself was aware. This raises the question of what were Ben-Gurion's goals in spreading the ideology of the melting pot in the 1950s and why the multicultural critique has made this ideology the target of its assault in the 1980s—thus distorting the scholarly discussion of the melting pot—and reviving it as a factor in Israeli society long after it had lost its relevance.

The melting pot ideology was one of the keystones of the ethos of statehood—*mamlachtiyut*—which served Ben-Gurion to shape the nascent Israeli state and society.[19] As the ethos of Israeli polity, *mamlachtiyut* strove to adapt the institutional structure of Jewish society to the conditions of sovereignty. One of his primary objectives was to dismantle the voluntary organizations that had developed during the *Yishuv* and "state on the way" era, many of which were associated with the Labor movement, and to absorb them into the bureaucracies of the emerging state. *Mamlachtiyut* contained a double message: it committed itself to mold Israeli society in keeping with the values of the Labor movement yet called for replacing the organizational structures that had conveyed these values, claiming that they were no longer able to inculcate these values in the changing reality of the state and the great immigration.

Mamlachtiyut provoked strong hostility within various opposition factions in the Labor movement that put forward an alternative perception of the desirable form of society and polity.[20] They embarked on a fierce struggle against *Mamlachtiyut* out of fear that it did not really intend to inculcate the values of the Labor movement, as it proclaimed, but would renounce them, out of a desire to protect organizational and partisan interests. Among the Labor-oriented organizations that were to be amalgamated into the state bureaucracies in accordance with *mamlachtiyut* were the *Palmach* unit, which was absorbed into the IDF;[21] the *Histadrut* school network, which was dismantled and incorporated into the state educational system;[22] and the youth movements associated with political streams, which were to be replaced by a national, quasi-military youth movement.[23] Since these Labor-oriented organizations had gained high public prestige as some of the most important manifestations of the native Hebrew culture and of the "New Jew," their dismantling became the focus of a prolonged, bitter ideological and political dispute. Ben-Gurion ascribed great importance to neutralizing opposition to *mamlachtiyut* within the Labor movement as a precondition for winning broad public legitimacy for it. The melting pot ideology, as a central component of the ethos of *mamlachtiyut*, played an important role in this attempt. Indeed, there was great similarity between both: *mamlachtiyut* called for the absorption of the Labor movement's voluntary organizations into state bureaucracies, and the melting pot sought to abolish the distinctiveness of various immigrant groups and to assimilate them into the national Hebrew culture.

In contrast to the ambivalence surrounding *mamlachtiyut*, the ideology of the melting pot gained extensive support in the Labor movement.[24] Its members, including those who opposed *mamlachtiyut*, were actively involved in various establishments, whether education, social services, rural settlement, or the army, through and in which the melting pot process was practiced but which at the same time were the targets and agents of *mamlachtiyut*. This overlapping may explain the power and effectiveness of the ideology of the melting pot: the consensus on the ideology of the melting pot was transformed into a means of creating the necessary psychological state of mind for inculcating the disputed ethos and practices of *mamlachtiyut* within the Labor movement and mainly to play down, if not altogether neutralize, the opposition to it. What enabled the use of the melting pot to advance the cause of *mamlachtiyut* was the marked difference between them from the point of view of the Labor movement: in the case of the melting pot, the movements' members were, at least metaphorically, its active agents; in the case of *mamlachtiyut*, they were its passive objects or even victims. Thus, the melting pot ideology paved the way, politically and psychologically, for the acceptance of the ethos of *mamlachtiyut* in the Labor movement and legitimized the incorporation of their own voluntary organizations into the state establishments; at the very least, the ideology of melting pot created a cognitive dissonance to the opponents of *mamlachtiyut*. The goal of the ideology of the melting pot was, therefore, not to acculturate the new immigrants, as it is usually claimed, but to advance and implement the ethos of *mamlachtiyut* among the veteran Labor members.

The ideology of the melting pot should therefore be analyzed not as part of the process of the melting pot but as a means to propagate the ethos of *mamlachtiyut*. *Mamlachtiyut* came to the fore concurrently with the decline of the socialist ethos within the Labor movement, and thus it had two opposite but complementary consequences: it called for state regulation of the economy and social services, and it served the stratification of Israeli society with its in-built class inequality. These developments were reflected in the struggle between contradictory values, such as economic efficiency and social justice, within state institutions. In this context, the melting pot ideology served to reinforce the foundations of state regulation and social responsibility, for it viewed the integration of the immigrants as the state's primary objective, thus paving the way for the concept of a welfare state and justifying its mechanisms. While inculcating these values, the melting pot ideology also served to suppress and replace the socialist, pioneering (*chaluzi*) foundations of the Labor movement and to affirm class relations that had been constructed in Israel as part of the melting pot process, thus reaffirming it.

Contrary to the appearances that dominate contemporary controversies and that prevail in current public and scholarly discourse, the melting pot ideology was directed at the absorbers, mainly the Labor movement, whose socialist ethos of *chaluziyut* it replaced with the ethos of *mamlachtiyut*. Thus, the melting pot ideology helped define the consciousness and boundaries of the emerging middle class, which through its hold on the economy and on the state and public establishments became the core of Israeli hegemonic class. In this context, it would appear that the significance of the melting pot ideology as a historical force was not in the cultural sphere. Rather, by surpassing socialism and nurturing an alternative social solidarity, it granted legitimacy to the social engineering and central regulation of the economy and to the Israeli welfare state functioning within the framework of existing class relations and social order.

MULTICULTURALISM

Since the late 1980s, the multicultural critique of the melting pot has been at the center of public and scholarly discourse in Israel.[25] It provoked a lively controversy, generating both support and opposition from various groups spread across the entire political, ideological, cultural, and social spectrum. The most comprehensive and pointed version of the multicultural critique has been put forward by the Post-Zionists.[26] The radicalism of their criticism, especially of the melting pot, helps contextualize multiculturalism by underscoring the elements in this critique that made it the focus of public interest long after the melting pot has lost its relevance as ideology or policy.

Confusing historical analysis with ideological arguments, the Post-Zionists present the multicultural critique as a means of liberating Israeli society from the yoke of Zionist, *Ashkenazi* Labor oppression. The rise of multiculturalism is portrayed as the adaptation of Israeli society to the conditions of late capitalism and globalization and as part of its transformation from a Zionist-mobilized into a pluralistic, civil society in which the erosion of its Zionist ingredients makes room for hitherto excluded groups, such as the *Mizrachim*, the ultra-Orthodox Jews (*Chardim*), and Israeli Palestinians as well as new groups that emerged as the multicultural discourse developed, such as Jewish and non-Jewish immigrants from the former Soviet Union and foreign workers or labor immigrants. The Post-Zionist critique specifically highlights the affinity between multiculturalism and the sectorialization and privatization processes that Israeli society is currently undergoing, thus presenting multiculturalism both as an outcome of these processes and as a solution to the problems they create.

The emphasis on the interrelationship between multiculturalism, Israel emerging civil society, and late capitalism raises doubts about the Post-Zionist claim that multiculturalism acts as a liberating force on behalf of the excluded, disempowered groups.[27] This claim is rooted in the popular notion of civil society as a free space of voluntary and spontaneous relations that countervails the institutionalized oppression leveled by the state.[28] From a more critical, historical, perspective, however, civil society is just another facet of the market society, whose inherent oppressive power is no weaker than that of the state.[29] Moreover, the oppression of the various groups that the multicultural project claims to liberate is no less practiced in the domain of civil (i.e., market) society—by means of economic exploitation, social control, ethnic and gender discrimination, and cultural and ethnic exclusion—and perhaps even more so.

From this perspective, multiculturalism as the "cultural logic of late capitalism," with its politically correct rhetoric, seems more a means of blurring the oppression inherent in the civil society while adapting to it the excluded groups than a means of liberating them.[30]

The interrelationship and overlapping of multiculturalism and the privatization process reveals a further contradiction in the Post-Zionists' emacipatory discourse. It is indisputable that at the same time that multiculturalism was emerging and celebrating its first victories in the 1980s and 1990s—the most prominent manifestation of which was the gradual incorporation of *Mizrachi* culture into the Israeli canon—economic and social inequality also increased, affecting mostly those excluded and disempowered groups on the Israeli fringe, such as the *Mizrachim*.[31] One of the major reasons for the growing inequality is the privatization and the commercialization of the social services and the replacement of the state as their provider by business ventures and the civil society and its privately financed organizations.[32] It appears, then, that the same factors that encouraged the widening of the socioeconomic gap in Israel were those that informed the rise of multiculturalism.

Advocates of Post-Zionist multiculturalism recognize its affinity to the privatization process, that is, to the social prices it carries.[33] They point to the role of market forces in promoting the multicultural project—to the success of *Mizrachi* "music cassettes," for example—although they concede that the rule of the market forces contradicts distributive justice, fosters economic inequality, and sows the seeds of social destruction. The Post-Zionists believe, however, that the price of social injustice inherent in the market mechanism that informs multiculturalism is worth paying. They base this preference on the Israeli historical lesson and on the political and cultural structuring of Israeli society: the state, they claim, has been acting against the excluded groups by promoting the social hegemony of the veteran elite and the big money; market forces, on the other hand, have enabled the disempowered groups to penetrate the vicious circle of discrimination created by the state. The guiding logic of Post-Zionist multiculturalism is, therefore, one of "market democracy": past experience has taught marginal groups that market forces have a relative advantage over the state because the market mechanisms of oppression are less violent and absolute than those of the state, and they provide more escape routes, which in turn create better, albeit partial, prospects for liberation from the oppression of the elite. The Post-Zionist lesson, however, stands in total contradiction to Israel social history over the past three decades. The privatization process undermines the foundations of the welfare state and concentrates control of the economy in the hands of an increasingly narrow group of capitalists, eroding social security among the middle classes and driving the lower classes below the poverty line. Thus, it steadily increases economic inequality to the detriment of the disempowered groups that the multicultural project purports to represent and emancipate.[34]

The Post-Zionist multicultural critique is therefore characterized by an essential contradiction: while purporting to emancipate the excluded groups, it actually supports privatization, which further excludes them, economically, socially, and even culturally. This contradiction indicates that the significance that has been acquired by multiculturalism since the 1980s should be analyzed apart from its formal contents, namely, the melting pot; it should be historically contextualized. And indeed, while the melting pot ideology promoted the Zionist nation-building project and the ethos of *Mamlachtiyut* that replaced socialism as the foundation of the Israeli social engineering and welfare state, multiculturalism has advanced the ethos of privatization, abolition of the welfare state, and commercialization of its services. An examination of the affinity between multiculturalism, particularly in its Post-Zionist version, and privatization sheds light on the processes that have transformed multiculturalism into an active force in Israeli society and politics during the 1980s and 1990s.

The privatization revolution encountered a powerful ideological obstacle that interfered with its implementation: the Zionist ethos. Despite its decline, Zionism, founded as it is on values of national and social solidarity, is still the hegemonic ethos in Israel, providing legitimacy to its social structure and values. Zionism, especially the version formulated by the Labor movement, charged Israeli consciousness with a profound sense of solidarity that contradicts the values of privatization, presenting it as foreign to Israeli identity and experience and stamping it with a seal of nonlegitimacy. Hence, challenging the hegemony of Zionism on the one hand and privatizing Israeli consciousness and identity on the other became a precondition for abolishing the welfare state, commercializing its services, and transferring control of the economy from government- and public-controlled agencies to the market forces and the private sector.

Post-Zionism is the most comprehensive manifestation of the ideology of privatization in Israel.[35] It began as a negation of the various national and social manifestations of the Zionist collective ethos that accorded legitimacy to the Israeli welfare state and its economic and social structures. The Post-Zionists bases their negation of the Zionist national and social solidarity on a moral denunciation of Zionist ideology and its implementation by the Israeli state apparatus. This Post-Zionist renunciation has gradually become a kind of catechism of guilt: it condemns Zionism as a movement whose past, as well as its present, is contaminated with political, social, and cultural injustices toward Jews and Arabs alike. According to this catechism of guilt, the oppressive nature of Zionism toward the Jews was manifested in the negation of the Diaspora, the abandonment of the Nazi victims during the Holocaust and condemnation of their passive behavior while politically exploiting and making propagandistic use of the survivors' suffering, the ideological and ethnic selection of immigrants, the cultural coercion by the melting pot, the exclusion of the *Mizrachim*, and so on. The goal of this Post-Zionist guilt discourse was to privatize the Israeli collective memory. Its forgone conclusion is that Zionist and Israeli collective is fundamentally immoral and debases any individual who relates to it. The only way for the conscientious Israeli individual to break free of the partnership in Zionist oppression is to negate its ideological foundations and dismantle Zionism's social structures. In this way, the Post-Zionist guilt discourse and privatized collective memory emerged as effective weapons in the struggle of the privatization revolution against the Zionist collective ethos—and values that derived from it—for it attacked its claims, especially those of the Labor movement, to reflect the values of personal, social, and universal justice and ethics on which it based its legitimacy both internally and externally.

The advocates of privatization were aware of the prominence of the Zionist national and social solidarity in Israeli collective identity, so they did no attack it directly, but they usurped its inherent emotional appeal to serve privatization. Moreover, they blurred the inner contrast between the privatized ethos and the Zionist ethos by merging both of them into a paradoxical, oxymoronic pattern of "privatized solidarity."[36] Multiculturalism is a prime example of privatized solidarity: it claims to intensify the sentiment of social solidarity by removing it from the arena of Israeli oppressive universal collective to that of different particular, liberating identity groups. In practice, however, the solidarity guaranteed in multiculturalism is false, for it is realized as a part of the privatization project, which is a prime cause of the increase in economic and social inequality, thus specifically damaging those excluded groups. As economic and social gaps widened with the dismantling of the universal welfare state and the privatization of its services, Israeli society gradually fractured into rival identity sectors, which consolidated themselves politically as they struggled for their share in the diminishing public resources.[37] Multiculturalism is, therefore, the logic of sectorialization, which as privatized solidarity imparts to the privatization revolution the appearance of social solidarity, thereby camouflaging its detrimental effects on disempowered groups.

Sectoralization and multiculturalism were generally presented as the "natural condition" of Israeli society and were disrupted by the melting pot policy. In this perspective, sectorialization is a manifestation of the collapse of the Zionist Labor hegemony and accords room for political and cultural expression by groups and voices that had been oppressed and silenced. However, as an immigrant society, the split of Israeli society into rival sectors in the third generation, when cultural differences in immigration countries normally fade, is not a "natural condition." Quite the reverse; it is the result of a deliberate policy that has been practiced since the Right's rise to power in 1977. By means of sectorialization, the Right sought to abolish the universal welfare state, which had been one of the Labor's power bases, and to replace it with a division of welfare services provided by different rival identity sectors that would constitute the basis of a durable right-wing government. Like multiculturalism, sectoralization, too, is a model of privatized solidarity: the sectors replace the state in providing social services, thereby forming the illusion of continued social responsibility. Sectorialization of social services, however, heralded the beginning of their privatization since the delegitimization of the state bureaucracy as a service provider paved the way for the market to provide them. Indeed, under the aegis of sectorialization, the market has become increasingly dominant in the provision of social services, such as education and health, that have transformed into commodities; accordingly, human entitlement to services has been replaced by purchasing power, a policy that has affected particularly the weaker, disempowered classes.[38]

Since the mid-1980s, sectoralization and privatization policies have also gained the support of the Israeli Left, which now represents largely the middle classes. Acknowledging that the loss of their power after 1977 and its transference to the right-wing *Mizrachim* and *Chardim* was not an "accident" but the result of long-term demographic trends, the mostly *Ashkenazi*, secular middle classes have regarded privatization—namely, reducing state control in the economic and social spheres and transferring it to market forces and professional establishments, where they still maintain power—as an useful strategy for preserving their hegemony. However, the mutual affinity between sectoralization and privatization generated a vicious cycle that affected both lower and middle classes: commercialization of the social services gradually eroded the social security of substantial parts of the middle class, who, endorsing the multicultural logic, began to view favorably the option of a sectorial organization as a means to struggle for their share in public resources. Yet by doing so, they simply reaffirmed privatization policies that continue to injure their social security. Similarly, the more affluent middle classes used multiculturalism to legitimize the creation of segregated, quasi-private service systems, especially in education, whose budgetary base was public but whose high standards were ensured by private payments, thus excluding those without means. It appears, therefore, that multiculturalism proposes the institutionalization of the dynamics of inequality on which the existing economic and social order is based rather than changing it. Thus, the more multiculturalism establishes itself, the greater the legitimacy it accords to sectorialization and privatization of Israeli society to the detriment of the ever-disempowered middle and lower classes.[39]

The affinity with privatization and the inherent increase in inequality challenges, therefore, the claims that the multicultural project promotes the emancipation of the excluded groups. Quite the reverse; multiculturalism is being used as a disguise to transform privatization policies from the cause of the hardships experienced by lower classes to the illusion of a solution. It perpetuates this economic discrimination through privatization policies, in contradiction of its formal content and claims of emancipation. Employing rhetorical indignation that complies with the dictates of political correctness, the multicultural critique forms an illusion of transformation and a fallacious consciousness of liberation and serves to control and domesticate the oppressed strata within the framework of the existing order. Thus, it actually blocks criticism, neutralizes opposition to the process of economic dispossession and the increasing social inequality that dominate Israeli society, and halts public discourse on alternatives to the privatized order. Multiculturalism is, therefore, a type of neoliberal ideology that leaves the regulation of social and economic relations to market forces and civil society, undermining the basic assumptions of the welfare state and serving the privatization revolution. While appearing as the champion of excluded groups, multiculturalism in practice prepared the necessary psychological background for the abolition and privatization of the universal welfare state, thus serving the interests of the affluent strata while helping preserve the existing power structure with its inherent economic, political, and cultural oppression of the lower classes.

Contextualization of the scholarly discussion and public controversies regarding the melting pot and multiculturalism proves them to be ideological agents of the privatization revolution in Israel. This ideological bias explains why the multicultural critique reintroduced the ideology of the melting pot to the center of the public and scholarly debate, presenting it as state intervention in cultural relations, serving the hegemony of the veteran Israeli *Ashkenazi* Labor establishment. Against this background, the multicultural critique could portray sectorialization as emancipation from this intervention, facilitating the emergence of a multicultural condition. Thus, the melting pot becomes a symbol of political coercion, and multiculturalism a symbol of liberation. However, the ideology of the melting pot had a central role in creating and legitimizing the collective ethos that advanced *mamlachtiyut* to become an alternative to socialism as a basis of economic regulation and social solidarity in Israel. Given the fact that the melting pot ideology was intended to consolidate the regulatory powers of the state, its criticism undermined this formulation, which served as the basis for the Israeli universal welfare state, and promoted the privatization and the commercialization of its services. Multiculturalism chose, therefore, to challenge the foundations of Israeli solidarity, presenting them as oppressive and proposing to replace them with its illusory privatized solidarity, which actually promotes the abolishment of the welfare state, a process that harms most severely the lower classes whose interests multiculturalism pretends to represent.

NOTES

1. *Ha'aretz*, 26 and 28 September 1997; Daniel Ben-Simon, "Gilgula shel Slicha" (The Development of the Appeal for Forgiveness), *Ha'aretz*, 29 September 1997. Compare Shlomo Ben-Ami, *Makom Le-Kulam* (A Place for All) (Tel Aviv, 1998), 332–96 ("The State, Politics of Identity and the Minorities Revolution").

2. Dan Horowitz and Moshe Lissak, *Metzukot Ba-Utopia: Israel—Chevera Be-Omes Yeter* (Trouble in Utopia: The Overburdened Polity in Israel) (Tel Aviv, 1990), 198–239; Moshe Lissak, *Ha-Aliya Ha-Gdolah Bi-Snot Ha-Chamishim: Kishlono Shel Kur Ha-Hituch* (The Great Immigration of the Fifties: The Failure of the Melting Pot)

(Jerusalem, 1999); Gershon Shaffir and Yoav Peled, *Being Israeli: The Dynamics of Multiple Citizenship* (Cambridge: Cambridge University Press, 2002), 74–109.

3. Shlomo Swirski, *Lo Nechshalim ela Menuchshalim* (Orientals and Ashkenazim in Israel) (Haifa, 1981).

4. See, for example, Menachem Mautner, Avi Sagi, and Ronen Shamir, eds., *Rav-Tarbutiut Be-Medinnah Demokratit Ve-Yehudit* (Multiculturalism in a Democratic and Jewish State) (Tel Aviv, 1998); Nissim Calderon, *Pluralistim Beal Korcham: Al Ribui Ha-Tarbuiot Be-Israel* (Multiculturalism versus Pluralism in Israel) (Haifa, 2000); Shlomo Ben-Ami, "Israel Ke-Chevra Rav-Tarbutit" (Israel as a Multicultural Society); Yoav Peled and Adi Ophir, *Israel Me-Chevra Meguieset Le-Chevra Ezrachit?* (Israel: From Mobilized to Civil Society?) (Tel Aviv, 2001), 18–23; David Ochana, *Ha-Israelim Ha-Achoronim* (The Last Israelis) (Tel Aviv, 1998); Baruch Kimmerling, "Ha-Yisraelim Ha-Chadashim: Ribuy Tarbuiot Llo Rav-Tarbutiut" (The New Israelis: Multitude of Cultures without Multiculturalism), *Alpayim* 16 (1998): 264–308; Yossi Yonah, "Medinat Kol Ezrachea, Medinat-Leom O Demokratia Rav Tarbutit? Israel Ve-Gvulot Ha-Demokratia Ha-Liberalit" (A State of All Its Citizens, Nation-State or a Multicultural Democracy: Israel and the Boundaries of Liberal Democracy), *Alpayim* 16 (1998): 238–63; Yosi Yonah and Yehudah Shenhav, "Ha-Matzav Ha-Rav-Tarbuti" (The Multicultural Condition), *Teoria Ve-Bikoret* 17 (2000): 163–88; Yehudah Shenhav, "Ha-elita Ha-Shaletet Mefachedet Mi-Pnei Ha-Rav-Tarbutiut Be-Shem Ha-Tov Ha-Klali" (The Ruling Elite Is Afraid of Multiculturalism on Behalf of the "General Good"), *Mussaf Ha'aretz*, 7 June 2000; Ella Shohat, *Zichronot Asurim: Likrat Machshava Rav-Tarbutit* (Forbidden Reminiscences: Toward Multicultural Thought) (Tel Aviv, 2001); Sami Shalom Shitrit, "Milkud 17: Bein Charediyut Le-Mizrachiyut" (Catch 17: Between Ultra-Orthodox and Oriental), in *Shas: Etgar Ha-Israeliyut* (Shas: The Challenge of Israeliness), ed. Yoav Peled (Tel Aviv, 2001), 21–51; Chanan Chever, Yehudah Shenhav, and Pnina Muzaffi-Haller, *Mizrachim Be-Israel* (Orientals in Israel) (Tel Aviv, 2002); and Yhudah Shenhav, *Ha-Yehudim Ha-Aravim: Leumiut, Dat Ve-Etnyiut* (The Arab-Jews: Nationalism, Religion and Ethnicity) (Tel Aviv, 2003).

5. Ephraim Ya'ar and Ze'ev Shavit, "Tahalichim U-Megamot Ba-Zehut Ha-Kolectivit" (Processes and Trends in the Collective Identity), in *Megamot Ba-Chevra Ha-Israelit* (Trends in Israeli Society), ed. Ephraim Ya'ar and Ze'ev Shavit. Vol. 2 (Tel Aviv, 2003), 1129–262.

6. See, for example, Baruch Kimmerling, *Ketz Shilton Ha-Achusalim* (The End of Ashkenazi Hegemony) (Tel Aviv, 2001).

7. On Ben-Gurion and the melting pot, see Zvi Zameret, *Yemei Kur Ha-Hituch* (The Melting Pot: The Frumkin Commission on the Education of Immigrant Children [1950]) (Beer-Sheva: Ben-Gurion University, 1993), 56–70.

8. David Ben-Gurion, *Medinat Israel Ha-Mechudeshet* (Israel, the Renewed State) (Tel Aviv, 1969), 349, and "Kur Mzref Am" (A National Melting Pot), in *Khazon Va-Derech* (Tel Aviv, 1952), 256–57.

9. Devora HaCohen, "Aliya Ve-Klita" (Immigration and Absorption), in Ya'ar and Shavit, *Megamot Ba-Chevra Ha-Israelit*, Vol. 1, 365–74, 380–87; Chever et al., *Mizrachim Be-Israel.*

10. See, for example, Marcus Hansen, "The Third Generation in America: A Classic Essay in Immigrant History," *Commentary* 14, no. 5 (1952): 494–500; Irving Howe, *World of Our Fathers* (New York: Random House, 1976); and Chaim I. Waxman, *Jewish Baby Boomers: A Communal Perspective* (New York: State University of New York, 2001).

11. See, for example, Ehud Luz, *Makbilim Nifgashim* (Parallels Meet: Religion and Nationalism in Early Zionist Movement [1882–1904]) (Tel Aviv, 1985); Smuel Almog, Jehuda Reinharz, and Anita Shapira, eds., *Zionut Ve-Dat* (Zionism and Religion) (Jerusalem, 1994), 21–80, 285–405; and Zameret, *Yemei Kur Ha-Hituch*.

12. Zvi Zameret, *Alei Gesher Tzar* (Across a Narrow Bridge: Shaping the Educational System during the Great Aliya) (Beer-Sheva, 1997).

13. Zameret, *Yemei Kur Ha-Hituch*, 23–48.

14. Zameret, *Yemei Kur Ha-Hituch*, 63–66. For a possible explanation of this contradiction, see Anita Shapira, "Ben Gurion Ve-Ha-Tanach: Yezirato shel Siper History?" (Ben-Gurion and the Bible: Creation of a Historical Narrative?), in *Yehudim Chadashim Yehudim Yeshanim* (New Jews Old Jews) (Tel Aviv, 1997), 217–47.

15. Rachel Roganski, "Attitudes towards Yiddish in Israel, 1948–1958," in *Yiddish after the Holocaust*, ed. Joseph Sherman (in press).

16. Moshe Lissak, "'Eretz Israel Ha-Rishonah' Ve-'Eretz Israel Ha-Shnia': Thalichim Muatzamim shel Kituv Chevrati-Tarbuti Bi-Shnot Ha-Chamishim" (Intensified Processes of Social Polarization in the Fifties], *Bein Olim Le-Vatikin: Israel Ba-Aliay Ha-Gdolah, 1948–1953* (Between Immigrants and Veterans: Israel and the Great Immigration 1948–1953), ed. Dalia Ofer (Jerusalem, 1997); Anir Ben Porat, "Iy-Shivion Chevrati Be-Israel" (Social Inequality in Israel), in Ya'ar and Shavit, *Megamot Ba-Chevra Ha-Israelit*, Vol. 1, 553–78; Shlomo Svirski and Dvorah Bernstein, "Mi Avad Bame, Avur Mi U-Tmurat Ma? Ha-Pituach Ha-kalkali shel Israel Ve-Hitavut Chalukat Ha-Avoda Ha-Adatit" (The Development of Ethnic Division of Labor in Israel), in *Ha-Chevra Ha-Israelit: Hebetim Bikortiyim* (Israeli Society: Critical Perspectives), ed. Uri Ram (Tel Aviv, 1993), 120–47; Yoav Peled, "Chida U-Shma Shas" (A Riddle Named Shas), in *Shas: Etgar Ha-Israeliyut* (Shas: The Challenge of Israeliness), ed. Yoav Peled (Tel Aviv, 2001), 52–74.

17. Motti Regev, "Mavo Le-Tarbut Ha-Israelit" (Introduction to Israeli Culture), in Ya'ar and Shavit, *Megamot Ba-Chevra Ha-Israelit*, Vol. 2, 852–93.

18. Ephraim Ya'ar and Ze'ev Shavit, "Tahalichim U-Megamot Ba-Zehut Ha-Kolectivit" (Processes and Trends in the Collective Identity), in Ya'ar and Shavit, *Megamot Ba-Chevra Ha-Israelit*, Vol. 2, 1225–45; Chever et al., *Mizrachim Be-Israel*.

19. For opposing interpretation of *Mamlachtiut*, see Avi Bareli, "Ha-Mamlachtiut U-Tnuat Ha-Avoda Be-Rershit Shnot Ha-Chamishim: Hanachot Miviniot" (Statism and the Labor Movement in the Early Fifties], in *Etgar Ha-Ribonut: Yetzira Ve-Hagut Ba-Asor Ha-Rishom La-Medinah* (The Challenge of Independence: Ideological and Cultural Aspects of Israel's First Decade), ed. Mordechai Bar-On (Jerusalem, 1999), 23–44; Zvi Zameret, "Ben Zion Dinur Bein 'Mamlachtiut Le-Tnuatiut" (Ben Zion Dinur: Between Statism and Voluntarism in Education), in Bar-On, *Etgar Ha-Ribonut*, 45–61; Israel Kolat, "Me-Miflaga Sotzialistit Le-Miflaga Mamlachtit" (From Socialist Party to Statist Party), *Iyunim Bi-Tkumat Israel* 3 (1993): 292–943; Eyal Kafkafi, *Medinah Mechapeset Am* (State Looking for a People) (Tel Aviv, 1991); Henri Nir, "Chaluzim Ve-Chaluziut Bi-Mdinat Israel: Hebetim Semantyim Ve-Historiyim" (Pioneers and Pioneering in the State of Israel: Semantical and Historical Aspects), *Iyunim Bi-Tkumat Israel* 2 (1992): 116–40; and Eliezer Don-Yehiya, "Political Religion in a New State: Ben-Gurion's *Mamlachtiyut*," in *Israel: The First Decade of Independence*, ed. S. I. Troen and N. Lucas (Albany: State University of New York, 1995), 171–92.

20. See Kafkafi, *Medinah Mechapeset Am*, and Bareli, "Ha-Mamlachtiut U-Tnuat Ha-Avoda."

21. Anita Shapira, *Mi-Piturei Ha-Rma ad Le-Peruk Ha-Palmach* (From the Dismissal of the Chief of Staff to the Dismantling of the *Palmach*) (Tel Aviv, 1985).

22. Zameret, *Alei Gesehr Tzar*, 109–40, 190–219.

23. Zameret, *Alei Gesehr Tzar*, 93–101.

24. Zameret, *Yemei Kur Ha-Hituch*, 71–75; Bareli, "Ha-Mamlachtiut U-Tnuat Ha-Avoda," 23–39.

25. See note 4.

26. See Kimmerling, Shenhav, Yonah, and Shohat in note 4.

27. Yosi Yonah and Yehudah Shenhav, "Ha-Matzav Ha-Rav-Tarbuti" (The Multicultural Condition), *Teoria Ve-Bikoret* 17 (2000): 163–88.

28. Leah Rozen, "Musag Ha-Chevra Ha-Ezrachit" (The Concept of Civil Society), in Peled and Ophir, *Israel Me-Chevra Meguieset Le-Chevra Ezrachit?*, 27–34.

29. Dov Chanin, "Be-Ikvot Granshi al Ha-Chevra Ha-Ezrachit" (Following Gransci on the Civil Society), in Peled and Ophir, *Israel Me-Chevra Meguieset Le-Chevra Ezrachit?*, 73–93; Adi Ophir, "Chevra Ezrachit Be-Ir Lelo Hafsaka" (Civil Society in Modern Cities), in Peled and Ophir, *Israel Me-Chevra Meguieset Le-Chevra Ezrachit?*, 113–80.

30. Danny Gutwein, "Zehut Neged Ma'amad: Rav-Tarbutiyut Ke-Ideologia Neo-Liberalit" (Identity versus Class: Multiculturalism as a Neo-Liberal Ideology), *Teoria U-bikoret* 19 (2001): 241–59.

31. Vaadat H-Chakira Ha-Parlamentarit Le-Noseh Ha-Pearim Ha-Chevratiyim Be-Israel Be-Rashut Chaver Ha-Kneset Ran Cohen (Parliamentary Inquiry Committee on Social Gaps in Israel Headed by M. K. Ran Cohen), *Doch U-Skiraah al Hitpatchut Ha-Pearim Ha-Chevratiyim Be-Israel Be-Esrim Ha-Shanim Ha-Achoronot* (Report and Survey on the Development of Social Gaps in Israel in the Last Two Decades) (Jerusalem, December 2002).

32. Danny Gutwein, "Ha-Dialektika shel Keshel Ha-Shivion: Ha-Smol Ha-Israeli bein Neo-Liberalism Ve-Sozial-Demokratia" (The Dialectics of the Inequality Deficiency: The Israeli Left between Neo-Liberalism and Social Democracy), *Mikarov* 3 (2000): 30–57; Danny Gutwein, "Likroa at Masve Ha-Hafrata" (To Unveil the Costs of Privatization), *Eretz Acheret* 11 (2002): 30–33; Danny Gutwein, "The Privatization Revolution and Social Inequality Policy in Israel," *Sh'ma* 33 (May 2003): 9–10.

33. Yonah and Shenhav, "Ha-Matzav Ha-Rav-Tarbuti," 169–71.

34. See note 31. Menachem Mautner, ed., *Tsedek Chalukati Be-Israel* (Distributive Justice in Israel) (Tel Aviv, 2000).

35. Daniel Gutwein, "Left and Right, Post-Zionism and the Privatization of Israeli Collective Memory," *Journal of Israeli History* 20 (2001): 9–42.

36. Danny Gutwein, "Hafratat Ha-Todaah Ha-Israelit" (The Privatization of the Israeli Mind), *Eretz Acheret* 12 (2002): 72–76.

37. Ephraim Ya'ar and Ze'ev Shavit, "Chevra Merubat Shesaim" (Multi-Split Society), in Ya'ar and Shavit, *Megamot Ba-Chevra Ha-Israelit*, Vol. 2, 1105–96.

38. Daniel Gutwein, "Tmurot Ba-Mediniyut Ha-Kalkalit shel Ha-Yamin, 1977–2003: Me-Hafrata Malima Le-Hafrata Oligarchit" (Changes in the Economic Policy of the Right: From Nationalized Privatization to Oligarchic Privatization), *Avoda, Chevra U-Mishpat*, (2004).

39. Gutwein, "Zehut Neged Ma'amad," 253–55.

CHAPTER 9

The Globalization of Israel: Transformations

Oz Almog

AFTER ALL IS SAID AND DONE, IT'S A SMALL WORLD

The development of a global economy, based both on modern media technology and on the massive power of computers, constitutes an important factor in the formation of the global village. Economic interest binds together groups that are isolated and distant. It transcends national boundaries, sweeping aside individual practices and restrictions as well as particularistic state economic objectives in most areas. There are three outstanding indications of the development of a global economy. They are (1) a united Europe, of importance both symbolically and practically; (2) the development of "world cities"—gigantic metropolises, such as London, New York, Paris, Rome, Toronto, Frankfurt, Tokyo, Singapore, and Hong Kong, which attract thousands of migrants from all over the world and which are foci of tourism, trade, development, and international banking;[1] and (3) The appearance of large multinational corporations, which are global agents in their control of centers of production in large numbers of countries and by means of the marketing and distribution of fashion goods and similar products throughout the world, thus promoting a common culture for people of different nationalities.[2]

Whether the global village is a blessing or a curse is a matter of opinion. In any case, it is still far from being fully realized. For now, at least, differences between states remain sharp and persistent. Nationalism has recently re-erupted from subterranean depths (in Quebec in Canada, the Basque lands in Spain, several states in the previous Soviet Union, and elsewhere), and we have seen the reemergence of undemocratic ethnocentric regimes, often based on religious fundamentalism. When half the world's population has still never conducted a telephone conversation, it is difficult to speak about globalization in the foreseeable future. In a world in which 900 million people suffer from hunger and more than a billion dwell in 61 countries that produce only 6 percent of the world's income and where their per capita incomes are about two dollars per day, it is too early to declare that we have a universal economy. Given that the world's 60 richest countries have doubled their income per head since 1970 and that 60 of the poorest have only made scanty progress, if any, the concept of a "world revolution" should be kept in proper perspective.[3]

Local climates, the territorial instinct, local tradition built and preserved over generations, racial and religious endogamy, and the persistence of national languages are all significant sources of differences among ethnic groups and countries that have persisted over many years.

Despite all the previously stated reservations, a broad historical perspective, combined with an examination of modern trends, indicates that globalization is a sweeping force that, it seems, cannot be held back in the long term. The Israeli experience, to which this chapter is devoted, demonstrates technology's awesome power as an agent of social change. My purpose is to demonstrate how external forces have rendered Israel similar to and more connected to other countries and how it is gradually losing its cultural distinctiveness. It is important to stress that, culturally, the State of Israel is still very different from other countries. It continues to retain quite a number of national features that make the Israelis unique. In the case of Israel, a state detached from Europe and located in a hostile tempestuous Arab region devoid of democracy, the vision of a global village still seems like a fantasy. Nevertheless, the Middle East is becoming an integral part of the world, and it is reasonable to assume that Israel's neighbors will be overwhelmed by the global economic and cultural onslaught (some Orientalists think that there are signs that it is already occurring). In the meantime, even as the winds of war gather momentum and as Islam once again draws its sword, Israel has not ceased to be influenced by the trend toward globalization. Its national colors are fading, and the style of life in Israel is gradually converging with that of Western countries.

FROM A LOCALIZED TO AN INTERNATIONAL ECONOMY

Israel's globalization did not begin on a particular day or in a particular year. In fact, it began as soon as the state came into existence. As its economy developed, so did its relations with other countries. Yet the globalization process certainly accelerated in the 1980s and even more so in the 1990s in the wake of the Israeli economy's transition into a market-based one and as a result of technological and cultural changes that occurred around the world.

Toward the end of the 1980s, especially on the establishment of the second national unity government in 1988, a new economic era was ushered into Israel, the ultracapitalist era. In the course of a decade, the average Israeli's standard of living increased immensely, allowing Israel to approach the "Super League" of developed countries.

In April 1997, the International Monetary Fund added Israel to its list of industrial countries on the basis of the rapid development of its economy and its growth in per capita income. That gratifying decision not only gave the country an economic boost but also symbolized the conclusion of a revolutionary economic decade. The decade's features included a transformation of the structure of capital ownership and a radical change in production and marketing. Israel became an open-market economy in which money and profit were highly prized and where yesterday's luxuries rapidly became items of mass consumption.

THE TELEVISION TRANSFORMATION

In July 1986, the Knesset, Israel's parliament, passed legislation enabling the establishment of cable television in the country. The following October saw the tabling of a bill with the title Second Authority for Television and Radio Law, which mandated the establishment of a second television channel. The second channel began broadcasting that same day under the guise of "trial broadcasts." Another year passed before the cabinet approved the appointment of the new channel's board of directors. Channel Two's broadcasts were then viewed by about 50 percent of the country's television owners. To reach a broader public, the new authority had to add transmitters and even make use of satellite transmission.

By 1990, when the Knesset passed the second broadcast authority law, 94 percent of Israeli homes had a television set.[4] Many people had begun purchasing superior models, and many homes added a second set to allow family members to watch different shows simultaneously. Even local architecture began to show the influence of this new culture of television watching, especially among the middle and upper classes. The living room became a "minicinema" centered around the mesmerizing screen. Those who could afford it added, in their new apartments, a small television room specifically for to small-screen viewing. During the Gulf War of 1991, some 82,000 sets were purchased (a jump of 48%).[5] The huge demand was not just a result of the Israeli addiction to television watching—the Gulf War was the first war that Israelis experienced by television set, mostly via CNN broadcasts.

In November 1993, after a period of trial broadcasts, Channel Two opened commercially. Three companies were chosen by government tender to share time on the channel. Cable television broadcasts began the same year, creating a quantum leap in the number of channels available. Israelis, so research has shown, were quick to hook up to cable television. They adopted the innovation at a rate higher than in any other Western society—some 1,000 subscribers a day during the first year. By 1999, the cable companies had networked some 1.5 million Israeli households, and of these about 1 million decided to establish connections. At the beginning of 2001, a satellite television company, Yes, began operating, increasing competition in the cable market and multiplying the supply and variety of programs to quantities that had seemed incredible just a few years earlier. This company offered, when it first began operating, a plethora of 62 channels, including most of the channels that the cable companies had offered, along with new music, movie, entertainment, sport, juvenile, cultural, and information programs. (In time, the number of channels balanced out, and now the cable companies and Yes offer about 40 channels each.)

As one might expect, the channel revolution led to a huge change in Israeli television-watching culture. By 1995, two years after the cable companies and Channel Two began operating, 41 percent of Israeli's inhabitants had two television sets at home, and 16 percent had three or more sets. The time spent watching television also increased—in a survey conducted that same year, 51 percent said that they watched television two hours a day, while 28 percent said that they generally watched two to three hours a day.[6]

One of the ways religions preserve themselves is by erecting physical or moral walls that block the inflow of "heretical" information and ideas that might flout the religious or ideological dogma or create a focus of interest outside the religion. The Zionist national religion had succeeded in preserving a high level of consensus. Israeli society was something like a snail closed up in its spiral shell, a level of seclusion made possible by the country's geographical, political, and cultural isolation in the Middle East as well as by the limitations of its media. For 25 years, Israelis watched a single state-run television channel that was forbidden to broadcast commercials. Other types of media were also limited. There were two radio stations (Israel Army Radio, better known as Galei Tzahal, and the Voice of Israel) and four daily newspapers with a significant national circulation (*Ha'aretz*, *Davar*, *Ma'ariv*, and *Yediot Aharonot*). The messages characteristic of the Israeli media were national (rather than international): local news stories, interviews with Israeli politicians, and op-ed pieces on political and defense issues. The average Israeli knew very little about what was going on outside his country and had little interest in world news. The media revolution changed and continues to change this reality. The Israeli is now becoming more attentive to events in the world at large and more versed in foreign news.

This statement must be qualified. Israel is certainly still quite ethnocentric in its media approach, especially in its news coverage, but this tendency is becoming less pronounced. The media are reporting more and more foreign news and enlarging the space they devote to foreign cultures. Israelis can now see the world not only through their own Channel One's Saturday night "Viewing the World" show, which was created at the beginning of the 1990s, but also and especially on the English-language international news stations CNN, BBC, and Sky and on the various European channels.

Studies prove that as media exposure to events outside the country increases, interest in events in Israel decreases among Israel's citizenry, especially the educated, nonreligious younger generation. Interest in events outside Israel increases, and the influence of foreign cultures, especially American culture, increases.[7]

THE TOURISM TRANSFORMATION

Until the beginning of the 1980s, most Israelis never left their country and certainly not for travel and vacation. Only a few families—mostly from the upper class—were able to take an overseas vacation once every few years, generally organized tours without children. The reason was the high price of air travel and the small quantity of dollars that travelers were allowed to take with them overseas. At the end of the 1970s, when Israel began its process of adopting a capitalist economy, the overseas tourism industry began to undergo a revolution. One of the first signs of this came in 1978, when Israel opened its airspace to charter flights unrestricted in their point of origin and destination. Up until then, there had been only charter flights from Scandinavia to Eilat and to Ofira at the southern tip of the Sinai peninsula. In 1980, Arkia, an Israeli airline that had been owned jointly by the state and the Histadrut labor federation and had accumulated huge debts, was sold to private investors. The company was rehabilitated and reorganized and began to operate low-cost charter and regular flights to a variety of overseas destinations. The charter flight changed the overseas flight from a one-time event to a routine one. This was not only because of the low cost but also because of other innovations, such as the option of canceling a flight up to 20 days prior to traveling.

Another player in the revolution in overseas travel was Ma'of, another airline. Ma'of was founded in the 1970s and began to offer internal Israeli flights in Cessna planes to construction companies. Toward the end of the 1970s, a special commission headed by Dr. Meir Het recommended that Israel's skies be opened to charter flights. Things moved quickly from there. Ma'of Charter, as it called itself in the press, pressured the authorities to grant it an international license to operate charter flights. In the end (after repeated attempts by El Al to torpedo the agreement), Ma'of was granted the license it craved. It purchased two Boeing 720s and became an international airline.

Ma'of "sold seats," but their planes flew only when all seats were sold. The company also launched a massive advertising campaign that included large newspaper pages looking much like supermarket ads, emphasizing the economy of the trips (the "deal").

By 1983, Ma'of had already flown 92,000 people to and from Israel on 600 flights.[8] But success was short lived. Ma'of did not survive for a number of reasons. These included the economic crisis caused by the Lebanon War, hostile competitors, and bad management. It went bankrupt at the end of 1984. Yet, despite its short life, it managed to contribute to a change in attitudes regarding overseas air travel. Instead of a rare and expensive item to be enjoyed only by the well-off, it became a mass commodity available to many hundreds of thousands of Israeli families.

According to estimates made by Israeli's Central Bureau of Statistics, 3,671,000 people flew to and from Israel in 1989 as compared to 117,000 in 1950, 223,000 in 1960, and 1,050,000 in 1970.[9] In 1990, there were 792,000 exits of Israelis to other countries, 6.2 times as many as in 1970. Also in 1990, according to the Central Bureau of Statistics, Israelis took $1.48 million out of the country, more than the income from overseas tourists in Israel. In 1992, a full 26.9 percent of Israel's Jewish population left the country by air, spending more than $200 million to pay for their trips.[10]

The growing competition in the market—among airlines and among travel agencies—along with further technological developments in aviation (larger and faster airplanes, navigation computers, and so on) led to a steady decline in ticket prices.[11] The concept of the "deal"—a travel package including a flight and hotel accommodations—came more into the awareness of the consumer through the daily press and became one of the symbols of the new era, one in which Israel became materialistic, hedonistic, and wealthy, opening up toward the outside.

An especially significant contribution to the increase in the volume of international flights was made by Israel's increasingly warm relations with Turkey beginning at the end of the 1980s. Turkey offered the Israeli tourist room-and-half-board vacations for ridiculous prices, and a growing stream of "regular Israelis" began flowing to the hotels of Antalya, a pastoral Turkish town on the Mediterranean coast. In an instant, an overseas trip with a stay in a luxury hotel was available at prices close to a family vacation in Eilat or Tiberias. Entire populations for whom such a vacation had once been but a dream could now make a family and personal fantasy come true (another reason a Turkish vacation was cheap for the average Israeli tourist was the difference in local prices between Israel and Turkey). The peace treaty with Jordan opened another new market for an inexpensive trip to another country and increased the flow of Israeli external tourism.

A study of leisure culture conducted by The Hebrew University of Jerusalem in 1990 found that more than half (58%) of the population had taken a vacation outside Israel during the course of the year. About a quarter of the population (27%) had done so at least twice. The study also found that as income and education increased, so did the proportion of those taking such a vacation during the year (from 32% among those with up to eight years of education to 66% among those with an undergraduate education or higher and from 33% among those with the lowest income to 79% among those with the highest income).[12]

By the end of the 1990s, overseas trips had become a national mania, especially at holiday time. Each year broke a new record for travelers; the press was fascinated, even astonished. So, for example, in August 1996, *Yediot Aharonot* reported that in the first three weeks of that month, "more than 635,000 travelers went through Ben-Gurion Airport, 30,000 more than in the first three weeks of August 1995."[13] In August 1998, *Yediot Aharonot* informed its readers that "close to 200,000 Israelis are spending the holidays overseas. Their destinations are varied, as always, as are the prices of the flights, the vacation packages including hotels and car rentals, and other attractive offers that will come at the very last minute."[14]

The wave of flights to overseas affected Israel's globalization in four important ways. First, it opened up the geographic cordon that Israel had lived behind for many years and created a natural flow of population from Israel to elsewhere and back. Second, it placed a large mass of Israelis in contact with foreign cultures and as a result increased the influence (whether conscious or unconscious) of practices and patterns of behavior from other countries on Israeli life and behavior. Third, it made the import of goods from overseas easier, and these imports increased the similarity between Israel and other countries (especially in the West). Fourth, the opening to overseas made such trips routine, even trivial, as both the destinations and the style of such trips changed. In the past, Israelis had tended to go overseas with guides on trips with names such as "All Europe in a Week" or "Classical Europe in Three Days." Now, however, Israelis go to exotic lands all over the globe with a wide variety of purposes. It might be a family vacation, a periodic shopping spree, or a study tour about art, anthropology, or even gourmet food. Overseas has become so close and so accessible that the word itself has almost disappeared from the lexicon. Israelis once announced, "I'm going overseas"—the specific destination was of secondary importance to the fact that they were leaving the country. Now they simply say, "I'm flying to Amsterdam."

The local press has in recent years devoted myriad articles and weekly and special supplements to tourism and trips. There has also been a flowering of globetrotting magazines (devoted to travel, geography, natural history, and world culture). In the past, only adventurers, scientists, and lunatics had any interest in whale hunting in Alaska or funerary practices in the Philippines, but today there is an audience of thousands curious about these subjects.

On television, also, there were a growing number of films offering the viewer eye-catching observations of plants, animals, landscapes, and societies from around the world. A few professional travelers (such a Tzur Shizaf, Doron Harel, and Eyal Peled) became Israeli culture heroes as a result of books and articles they published or films and television programs they participated in and in so doing shared their thrilling adventures.

THE TELECOMMUNICATIONS TRANSFORMATION

During the 1950s, only 7,000 telephones were installed in Israel each year. Most of them went to politicians, their associates, and high officials in the government, the Histadrut labor federation, the Jewish Agency and municipal governments. In the 1960s, the rate reached 30,000 telephones a year, but that was still far from enough to meet the demand. In the decade that followed, an average of 50,000 telephones were installed each year, and, at the end of that decade, when demand grew, 70,000 new telephones were installed each year. By 1974, about 750,000 telephones had been installed in Israel, among them 94,000 in Jerusalem, 335,000 in greater Tel Aviv, and 120,000 in Haifa, with the remainder to the rest of the country. The country's telephone density (the number of instruments per 100 inhabitants) reached 23 in 1974, in comparison with 65 in the United States, 55 in Switzerland, 22 in France and Italy, 6 in the Soviet Union, and 1.3 in Egypt.[15] But despite this progress, the supply was still far from able to meet demand, and there seemed to be no solution.[16]

Malfunctions (disconnections, interference, static, and so on) were a matter of course—to the point that the "Telephone Song," performed by one of the country's favorite comedy teams, won the top spot in IDF Radio's hit parade for 1966. Israelis were nothing if not cynical about their tottering phone system.

By 1980, a good 100,000 telephones were being installed a year, but the waiting list only grew longer and now included 200,000 households. Of these, about 5,000 had been waiting for more than 10 years. A waiting period of two years was routine, unless one had connections in the appropriate places.[17]

In 1981, the country's first digital exchange was installed. On the face of it, it heralded a change in the communications map. But while it was certainly another step toward improving and streamlining the country's communications technology, it was nevertheless what the behavioral sciences term a "first-degree change" rather than the total change of system ("second-degree change") needed to set the system going in a new direction. Thus, four years later, in 1984, Israel still had only a million telephone lines for a population of close to 4 million, operating on an outmoded communications network with overloaded arteries. Many waited hopelessly for a telephone to be installed in their homes, a wait that for some of them had begun more than 20 years previously. Even the happy recipients of phone lines suffered repeatedly from disorders, difficulties making long-distance calls, and obstacles to making overseas calls. There seemed to be no solution on the horizon, and the criticism of the dysfunctional system leveled by the press and public figures had long since become a tired mantra.

The turning point was the establishment of Bezek. The idea of setting up a telecommunications services company outside the Ministry of Communications was conceived in 1978 under the stewardship of Minister of Communications Meir Amit. Amit established a commission to study the issue, and its recommendation for the establishment of Bezek was carried out in 1980 by Minister of Communications Yitzhak Moda'i (the first meeting of the company's board of directors was held that same year). At the end of 1982, the Knesset passed the Telecommunications Law by a 90 percent majority. An agreement was signed between Bezek's management, representatives of the Histadrut, and the joint workers' delegation of the telecommunications workers in the ministry for the transfer of the workers from the ministry to the new company.

Bezek[18] was in practice established in 1984 as a government corporation responsible for communications services in Israel. The idea was to create a commercial company (the plan was for staged privatization) that would gradually gain freedom from the encumbrances of a government corporation. The success was immediate, much swifter than with similar telephone companies set up in other countries. During Bezek's first year of activity, it laid the country's first fiber-optic cable and began the process of digitalization, which for the customer meant the switch to touch-tone phones (a process that was completed in the space of 12 years, seven less than the goal set by the company's founders). Within its first three years, Bezek shortened the telephone waiting list from 257,000 to 41,000. In 1991, there were only 18,000 people waiting. Within 10 years (1984–94), a million telephone lines had been installed, two times more than the number of lines installed up to 1984—that is, over a space of 64 years. In 1984, only 72 percent of the families in Israel had a telephone line; 10 years later, the level was up to 95 percent.[19] In 1980, there were 208 people waiting for a line for every thousand inhabitants, but by 1997 there were only nine waiting (i.e., people whose requests for lines had been processed but who were still waiting for installation) per 1,000 inhabitants. In 1998, the column in the Central Bureau of Statistics' table on the waiting list was blank—no requests for lines had not been filled within a reasonable time.[20] The number of malfunctions also fell dramatically.[21] In 1985, the Government Publications Office still had to broadcast public service commercials urging the public to spread its long-distance calls over the course of the day and night so as to move the excess of calls from peak to trough hours. But less than a decade later, as a result of Bezek's technological innovations, the pendulum swung the other way, and the public was invited "to talk as much as you like." By the end of the 1990s, most of Israel's inhabitants had telephones, and lines were installed within a few days of being ordered. Many thousands ordered further lines for their homes.[22] Calls became much cheaper, including long-distance and overseas calls, as a result of fiber-optic lines that could transmit thousands of calls simultaneously. In 1977–78, incoming and outgoing international calls totaled 36.3 million minutes (with only 13 million of those outgoing calls). In 1983–84, the year Bezek was founded, the total was 108.5 million minutes (35.7 million of them outgoing calls).[23]

Once Israelis had telephones and the system functioned adequately, it was possible to proceed to the next stage in the Israeli telecommunications revolution—the global stage. It arrived in 1997, the year that the international communications market was opened to competition, in the form of two new international call service providers: Kavei Zahav and Barak. The results came immediately—the price of calls plunged by 50 percent, and within two months Bezek's international service had lost about 45 percent of the market. According to a survey conducted in September 2002 among a representative sample of the adult Jewish population (commissioned by the newspaper *Yediot Aharonot*), 56 percent of Israelis call other countries regularly. The majority—21.8 percent—calls via Bezek International. The survey also shows that the residents of Tel Aviv and two of its close suburbs, Ramat Gan and Givataim, made the most overseas phone calls—70 percent of the total number made in the entire country. This demonstrates the gap between the country's center and its periphery. College-educated, nonreligious people also made the most calls (65% of the total).[24]

Cheaper international call rates and the improvement in reception and transmission quality enable Israelis to communicate with family members, friends, colleagues, businesses, and others overseas as a matter of course. This brings the world closer to home. The ease, speed, and low price of international calls today (even from cell phones) has also made overseas trips easier; no longer does a visit to another country mean being out of touch and worried about what is happening at home. Many Israelis now travel overseas equipped with a magnetic card, calling code, or mobile phone that allows them to call Israel from wherever and whenever they wish. In July 2002, *Mamon*, the consumer magazine section of the daily newspaper *Yediot Aharonot*, quoted the deputy chief executive officer for marketing, sales, and business development of the international call company Barak: "Israelis are considered world record-holders in the quantity of telephone calls they made to Israel during their overseas stays. Israelis call home from overseas 30–40 percent more than tourists from other countries."[25] Commercial relations between Israeli and overseas firms have also been eased and simplified by this inexpensive and rapid form of communication, and it has made it easier for international firms to operate in Israel.

THE INTERNET TRANSFORMATION

Israelis, like the rest of inhabitants of the West, began linking up with the Internet during first half of the 1990s. An important turning point in the Internet revolution in Israel came, however, with the establishment of the first major Hebrew-language portal in 1996, called Walla (another, more modest site, Israel On Line—IOL—had preceded it). Five more portals were quickly established: Ahla, Nana, Tapuz, Netking, and Internet Zahav. In 1998, Israel was ranked (according to a survey conducted by the research firm Network Wizards) 15th among 25 countries in its Internet servers. The Scandinavian countries were in first place and South Africa in last place. In Finland, there were 87 Internet servers per 1,000 inhabitants, while in Israel there were 18. In other words, Finland had a server for every 11 inhabitants and Israel one for every 55 inhabitants.[26]

The development of Hebrew portals gave an impetus to the growth of private Hebrew Web sites. A study made in 1996 by the consulting firm Meta Group Israel found 750 Israeli Internet sites. About 20 percent of these belonged to the computer, communications, and high-tech sector.[27]

Toward the end of the decade, the first professional surveys began appearing about Internet access and the number of Web surfers in Israel. The data are not uniform and are sometimes contradictory, perhaps because of the difficulty in quantifying "surfing" and the rapid pace of change in the field. But they provide a certain measure of the growth of the network in Israel. For example, a Gallup poll published in 1998 in *Yediot Aharonot* showed that 11 percent of the 1.4 million households in Israel were connected to the Internet (a total of 155,000 households). The estimate was that, on the average, two family members "occasionally" surf the Web, so that the number of surfers was then about 300,000.[28]

In July 1998, *Ha'aretz* reported on its front page that up-to-date surveys indicated that Israel was in twelfth place worldwide in the percentage of inhabitants connected to the Internet—10 percent of the country's inhabitants.[29]

Even though various surveys showed that the Internet is used largely by a single sector of the Israeli population (well-off, college-educated young men who were born in Israel or have lived here for many years), the network's penetration has rapidly challenged this technological hegemony, and the use of the Internet has made large strides toward becoming as standard as the telephone. In fact, a survey conducted at the beginning of 2001 by TIM (a subsidiary of the research company TNS/Telstar) produced the following statistics:

About 20 percent of the population, about 1.27 million Israeli adults and teenagers, surf the Internet, and 26 percent of them began to surf during the past year (of the survey). The survey ranks Israel in twelfth place in the level of Internet surfing, after Italy and before France. The survey also shows that the number of Internet surfers among the Jewish population (age 13 and up) is 1.17 million. Some 947,000 adults (age 18 and above)—that is, about 28 percent of the adult Jewish population—surf the Internet, along with some 224,000 teenagers—that is, 52 percent of young people of the ages of 13 to 17. According to other Telstar surveys, the number of surfers among the Arab population and the non-Hebrew-speaking population is about 100,000.[30]

The number of Hebrew Internet sites also grew at a dizzy pace. There were several reasons: user-friendly software for setting up sites soon became available, institutions of higher education began to use the network intensively, and the commercial sector internalized the message that "if you're not there you're not anywhere."[31] The TIM survey conducted by TNS/Telstar, conducted at the beginning of 2001, shows that 64 percent of the computerized businesses in Israel used the Internet in the year preceding the survey. Of the businesses connected to the network, 22 percent conduct sales or purchases online.[32]

Reams of articles and books have been written on the Internet and the process of globalization, and Israel is no different than other countries in this respect. But the large distribution of computers in Israel and the relative fluency of the average Israeli in English may well have made the Internet's adoption swifter here than in many other parts of the West.

THE MALL TRANSFORMATION

The opening shot of Israel's personal consumption race was fired with the launch of Atarim Square on HaYarkon Street in Tel Aviv in 1975. The square, whose construction was considered a notable economic event, included a commercial area of 13,000 square meters (140,000 square feet), with 128 stores and an impressive number of cafés. The center of the square was occupied by an innovative round structure that contained the Drugstore, the country's first store of its type, built by the owners of one of the country's department stores, Kol Bo Shalom. The next revolutionary innovation was the construction of the Dizengoff Center Mall in 1983. Located on Tel Aviv's central Dizengoff Street, it was built by businessman Aryeh Piltz.[33] Before the mall opened, the only roofed shopping center in Israel was London Ministore, containing stores, cafés, and a cinema on Ibn Gvirol Street, established in 1968. But this passage made up of two alleys was much smaller and much more modest in what it offered than Western shopping malls. Dizengoff Center was the first Israeli shopping center built on the model of the fashionable malls in the United States. (Israel's mall architects chose American rather than European models—in Europe commerce takes place largely within the cities on pedestrian commercial roads.) The very name, including an English word, *center*, heralded the new consumerist trend that the mall brought with it.

Dizengoff Center was also the first shopping center in Israel to boast full air conditioning. In addition to stores that were elegant by Israeli standards (some of them sold goods then considered scarce, such as computers, posters, special furniture, and original fashion), there were also two cinemas, three cafés, seven restaurants, four banks, the large HaMashbir LeTzarchan department store, and an underground parking garage for 1,000 automobiles.[34]

The next stage in the consumer revolution opened on September 26, 1982, when the cornerstone was laid for the Ayalon Mall in Ramat Gan, adjacent to Tel Aviv, on land that had previously held garages. The project was initiated by David Azrieli, a Canadian businessman who invested some $20 million in the project. Three years later, on July 2, 1985, the mall was opened to the public. The mall's marketing staff called it "a city in a home," and the Ayalon Mall, like other malls around the world, was a roofed shopping city, containing a large variety of commercial activities along with entertainment and leisure services. The complex originally contained 60 stores selling food, clothing, shoes, utensils, furniture, electrical equipment, musical instruments, jewelry, and gifts. There were also a large number of eating places of various levels—snack bars and ice cream parlors as well as cafés and restaurants. Another element, which became a model for other Israeli malls, was businesses of the category of "personal services"—a bank, a travel agency, an optometrist, a pharmacy, a hair salon, and so on. The mall also had four cinemas, which also became a model for other Israeli malls.

As it happened, a general strike broke out on the same day the mall opened in protest against a package deal reached between the Finance Ministry and the country's large employers. But it made no difference to the Israel consumer. Crowds charged the mall's gates just before they were opened, and the result was widely covered in the press. There were headlines such as "Mall Madness," "Tens of Thousands Charged the Ayalon Mall Last Night," and "The Stores in the New Mall Made More Than Three Million Dollars in Ten Days."

Two years after the opening of the Ayalon Mall, mall fever began sweeping the country. There were almost simultaneous openings of other malls: Karyon in Kiryat Bialik north of Haifa, Lev HaMifratz on Haifa Bay, the Horev Center on Mt. Carmel in Haifa, the Lev Mall in Hadera, the Sharon Mall in Netanya, Gan HaIr in Tel Aviv, and Lev Mall in Ashdod. Afterward, in quick succession, came the Jerusalem Mall in the capital city's Malha neighborhood, the Negev Mall in Be'erseheva, and Bat Yam Mall in the Tel Aviv suburb of that name. Soon after its establishment in the winter of 1993, the Mall Association stated that 60 percent of mall managers reported 10,000 to 20,000 visitors a day.[35] By the end of the decade (1999), some 150 malls had been built in Israel, from Kiryat Shmonah in the north to Eilat in the south. Some of them were in small and peripheral locations, such as Upper Nazareth, Migdal HaEmek, Kfar Yona, and Tel Mond. This statistic made Israel one of the world's leading countries in the number of malls relative to the population.[36] The record was set by Rishon LeTzion, which won the nickname "Mall City" thanks to the six malls it boasted as of 1999. In gaining this title, Rishon LeTzion toppled Toronto, Canada, from first place (several of the city's malls have since closed or been rezoned).[37]

The adoption of the American mall method of commerce was accompanied by a large increase in American imports. The entry of American chain stores into Israel surged in 1993, most of them setting up shop in the malls. The Israeli marketing world began to be characterized by the massive penetration of foreign brands in all areas of consumption and in competition with local brands. Central sectors in which this process progressed at a rapid pace were textiles and clothing, shoes, food, cosmetics and toiletries, and toys. It was not only products that penetrated the Israeli market. So did concepts from the American buying culture, such as the "deal" and the "sale," terms that entered the Israeli buying vocabulary.

In October 1993, *Yediot Aharonot*'s leisure and consumer affairs correspondent, Shoshana Hen, published an article in the newspaper's Saturday supplement on the Americanization of Israel. The article included a list—hardly exhaustive—of 43 American brand names that had already "immigrated" to Israel. Among them were Levis, Fruit of the Loom, Canon, Pepsi, Ben and Jerry's Ice Cream, Hershey, Helena Rubinstein, Barbie, and Nike. Not every imported brand name succeeded (for marketing, cultural, or other reasons), but even these left another imprint of America on Israeli society.

As in the United States, the name of the game in Israeli malls became size. Every year, the press wrote of a new mall that broke records for size and luxury, and the sense was that a faucet of plenty had been opened. The list of stores appearing in the brochure (another word imported from American mall English into Hebrew) put out by the company that manages the Grand Mall, Israel's largest (as of 2002), underscores the huge wealth of products on offer today to the Israeli public and the transformation of the mall into a huge capitalist sanctuary of leisure and consumption "just like overseas." This mall boasts 3 stories and 2 department stores, 63 clothing and fashion stores, 2 lingerie stores, 14 shoe stores, 5 purse and fashion accessory stores, 11 watch and jewelry stores, 5 electric appliance stores, 6 cosmetic stores, 4 entertainment and leisure stores and centers (cinema, books, and recordings), 2 photo shops, 4 optometrist establishments, 1 supermarket, 23 restaurants, cafés and fast-food stands, and 7 "miscellaneous" businesses (including lottery ticket stands and a dry cleaners).

More than any other economic phenomenon, the development of the mall succeeded in bringing Israeli consumer culture (and Israeli culture as a whole) close to American and European consumer culture. In the past, one of the main activities Israelis sought out or dreamed of when making overseas trips was visiting large stores such as Marks and Spencer, Gallery Lafayette, and Bloomingdale's. Today, however, the malls of the West are no longer such great attractions for the average Israeli tourist (some say that the variety of products available in Israel is even greater than that normally found in malls overseas). Israeli malls have also significantly increased the similarity between the Israeli culture of consumption and that in the most developed Western countries—and similarity, as noted previously, is an important part of the globalization process.

THE FAST-FOOD TRANSFORMATION

The first American-style fast-food joints (if not yet a franchise of an American chain), selling largely milkshakes, pizza, hamburgers, and pancakes, appeared on Israel's large city streets (King George Street in Jerusalem, Dizengoff Street in Tel Aviv, and HaNevi'im Street in Haifa) as early as the first half of the 1960s. But the real turning point in Israel's fast-food culture was made by the Burger Ranch chain at the beginning of the 1970s. The first Burger Ranch was opened by Barry Skop and Ron Lapid in 1972 on Ben-Yehuda Street in Tel Aviv. The investment paid off, and in 1978 the second branch opened. At the end of that year, Skop and Lapid went to the United States to see up close how to make money from hamburgers, and a year later they sold their first franchise to a branch in Ramat HaSharon. This was the first Burger Ranch to be equipped with a microwave oven, a computerized french fry machine, and backlit pictures of the menu, and it worked. Investors began taking an interest in the potential, and Skop and Lapid sold their franchises according to strict conditions. Identical restaurants began sprouting up in every self-respecting town. First it was the Tel Aviv metropolitan area, then the well-off more distant suburbs of Tel Aviv in the Sharon area, then north and south and even to Jerusalem. Like large American chains, Burger Ranch insisted on a unitary look and menu for every restaurant and compromised only on the subject of kosher certification, without which, as is known, there are several central Israeli markets that cannot be penetrated.[38]

In the 1980s, the chain continued to grow rapidly through the sale of franchises. In 1991, its sales reached NIS 5 million ($2.2 million). It sold 7 million portions of meat that year in 47 branches employing 1,200 people. About 30 people worked in the company's central offices in Rishon LeTzion.

Burger Ranch's success brought on attempted imitations with names such as Chief Burger, Gulliver, King Donald, and Jeffrey's as well as the American Wendy's chain and others. Generally, these collapsed after building up lots of debt. The only competing chain that succeeded in Israel was the native MacDavid's, but this is a small chain with just a handful of branches.

The first significant competition for Burger Ranch did not appear until 1983. October 14 of that year saw the opening of the first branch of McDonald's in Israel in the Ayalon Mall. Israel was the sixty-eighth country in the international spread of McDonald's as the world's largest fast-food company at that time, announcing the opening of a new branch every eight hours.

In 1994, the major international hamburger-flipping competitor of McDonald's entered the Israeli market—Burger King. Competition in the Israeli fast-food market moved up a class. In 1999, McDonald's had 72 restaurants in Israel (including a few MacDrives, serving the food directly to car windows). Burger King had, at this time, 50 branches and Burger Ranch 73.

Fast-food hamburgers quickly turned from a distant American dream into an inseparable part of Israel's culture of eating. Newspaper surveys show that 69 percent of Israel's population of the age of 12 and up visit these restaurants at least two or three times a year. A full 48 percent do so once a month or more. Attendance at hamburger joints is especially common for teenagers—92 percent of 12- to 17-year-olds visit one at least two or three times a year and 75 percent once a month or more.[39] A market survey, conducted of the entire fast-food industry by the Burger King management in 1995, measured a 50 percent increase in Israelis' consumption of hamburgers and a 50 percent drop in consumption of the "national food"—the falafel.[40]

Alongside the multiplication of hamburger joints, there has been a proliferation of pizza parlors. The leading chains are Pizza Hut and Domino's, huge international chains that opened their first outlets in Israel in 1990. In 1995, there were already 17 branches of Domino's in Israel, and its sales had already reached $10 million. In 1994, Israelis eating off the cardboard boxes of Domino's delivery pizzas consumed, according to press reports, 200 tons of cheese sprinkled over the more than million pizzas sold annually by the chain. In 1995, Pizza Hut had 18 branches in Israel, and these consumed 260 tons of Mozzarella, 500 tons of flour, and 30 tons of mushrooms.[41] In 1999, the management magazine *Status* reported that the Domino's Pizza chain, marketed in Israel by the Omani Motzrei Mazon company, had 27 branches and between 750 and 1,000 employees, depending on seasonal trends.[42]

By the end of the decade, other international fast-food chains had entered the Israeli market. These included Kentucky Fried Chicken,[43] Nando's, and Dunkin' Donuts. It is difficult to measure Israelis' average expenditure on eating outside the home, but estimates are that this constitutes about 10 percent of food expenses (Americans, by comparison, spend 40% of their food budgets on eating out), and the number rises each year.

The revolution in fast-food consumption, together with the world communications and transportation revolution, is one of the capitalist warheads that is gradually destroying national particularity and in doing so building a homogeneous international culture characterized by similar visual stimuli, tastes, and organizational models. This process is called "cultural isomorphism." The American fast-food chains that have become international labels thus do more than export new types of food to the four corners of the world. They also export a package of American cultural eating habits and its corollaries. Furthermore, since fast food (street food) is an element that creates popular culture, the import of alternative foods creates competition with local national foods and sometimes shunts them aside. When a country's typical foods, such as falafel, are pushed out of the market, local identity and the local sense of uniqueness also weaken.

"McDonaldization," which nips at the heels of national culture, found an especially picturesque and symbolic expression in Israel when, in 1995, a branch of that restaurant opened at the Golani Junction, next to the memorial for the fallen soldiers of the legendary Golani infantry brigade. The families of the fallen soldiers bitterly protested the sacrilege committed to this sacred national site by the "church of gluttony" and the Big Mac, but their protests were of no use. At the order of the Israeli roads authority, the McDonald's signs were removed, and an aesthetically pleasing Golani sign was put in their place, but the restaurant's drive-in lane, which runs adjacent to the memorial site's fence, remained in place. The hedge that was planted there to block the view of the restaurant, as part of an agreement with the families of the fallen, was a joke. McDonald's remained and in fact changed something of the meaning of this national site. The site is no longer visited just by quiet, respectful people coming for emotional and altruistic reasons to commune with soldiers who fell in the line of duty. Visitors now also include thousands who stop by just because of their material need for something good to eat.

THE HIGH-TECH TRANSFORMATION

The infrastructure for Israel's high-tech industry was put into place in the 1950s with the establishment of the country's military industry in the form of Rafael Armament Development Authority, Israel Aircraft Industries, and MAMRAM, the computerization unit of the Israel Defense Force (IDF) and with the development of engineering research at the Technion–Israel Institute of Technology and the Weizmann Institute of Science. Elron Electronic Industry, established in 1962 by Uzia Galil in an apartment in Haifa, is considered Israel's first high-tech company.[44] Elron was the first factory established as a joint venture between investors and entrepreneurs—a model that is a building block of high-tech industry.

The 1970s saw a second wave in the Israeli high-tech revolution, when new and successful electronics and computer companies were founded, such as Yiskar, SciTech, Elisra, Alta (a subsidiary of Israel Aircraft Industries), Telrad, Leshem, and Vichy-Israel. The expansion of this sector was the result of the following factors: scientific breakthroughs made throughout the world, but especially in the United States, that led to new developments in computers, lasers, communications, and biotechnology; the penetration of Israel by large high-tech companies with the help of Israelis who reached senior positions in very large enterprises in the United States and persuaded the owners to establish subsidiaries in Israel; the halt of computer production at the Weizmann Institute in 1972, which caused a transfer of brains in the computer field from the institute to industry; the establishment of the nuclear reactor in Dimona and the nuclear research facility at Nahal Sorek; the French and British embargoes imposed on Israel after the Six-Day War, which forced Israel to establish its own sophisticated weapons industry, including an electronic weapons industry; and the heavy losses that the Israeli army suffered in the "war of attrition" and the Yom Kippur War, caused by electronic arms technologies developed by the Soviet Union (missiles, radar, and so on). These required the IDF to develop a fitting Israeli technological response. Other impetuses were the establishment of the position of chief scientist of the Ministry of Industry and Commerce and the research-and-development unit of the Defense Ministry, which began supporting and guiding projects in industry, and the quantitative and qualitative development of the computer science faculties at the universities and the establishment of the industrial management faculty (including a division of information systems) at the Technion.

Israel began harvesting the benefits of these high-tech seeds toward the end of the 1980s. Within a few years, high-tech had become Israel's most successful industry and an important impetus for economic growth. In addition, it was a much-talked-about and heavily covered phenomenon, a new subject of local pride and a source of justified new hopes. Concepts such as "start-up," "risk fund," "purchasing control," "financial investors," "strategic partners," "mergers," and "headhunters" appeared daily in the economic press, and the Israeli media began producing scores of articles and special supplements about the subject. The very frequency of the use of the term "high-tech"—carried over as a loanword into Hebrew—expressed the change. The growth of Israeli high-tech is illustrated by the following statistics.

The average growth of the gross domestic product (GDP) between 1992 and 1998 was close to 5 percent, while the rate of growth of exports in the "advanced sectors" (what is popularly called high-tech) was 14 percent during that same period.[45]

In 1990, Israel had less than 10 public technology companies developing products for the civilian market and just a few dozen start-ups. By the end of the decade, there were already 100 public technology companies and 4,000 start-ups.[46] In fact, no one really knows precisely how many such companies there were or are in Israel since many are set up and fail in a short amount of time. The estimate is that at the end of the 1990s, between 1,000 and 1,500 new start-up companies were established each year.[47] (Each start-up begins with one entrepreneur or a small group of partners and generally requires five programmers and an initial injection of development funds.) In July 2000, the monthly magazine *Wired* ranked Israel fourth among the world's high-tech centers. That same year, the monthly *Red Herring* stated that Israel was in third place, after the United States and Canada, in the number of technological firms listed on New York stock exchanges.

At the end of the 1980s, only a very small number of international high-tech companies maintained close ties with Israeli companies. By the end of the 1990s, nearly all the world's largest high-tech companies had already set up shop in Israel—among them Motorola, Intel, IBM, Hewlett-Packard, Digital, Microsoft, and Vichy-Dell—and developed some of their new products there.[48]

In 1991, there were only two venture-capital funds in Israel. At the end of 1998, there were 88 as well as 213 private investment companies.[49] According to the measure of the quantity of venture-capital fund investments in 1998, there was more venture-capital investment in Israel than in 47 of the 50 U.S. states and in all but two European countries.[50]

The dramatic nature of the rise in Israeli venture-capital funds and in the extent of their investments is illustrated by the following example: in the first quarter of 2000, private companies in Israel raised some $686.8 million in 94 deals, an increase of 79 percent compared with the quarter that preceded it.[51]

At the beginning of the 1990, just a handful of Israeli companies were traded on American stock exchanges. At the end of 1990s, there were 70 (at that time, only Canada had a larger number of companies listed).

The rapid development of Israel's high-tech sector amazed the world. Many experts considered Israel to be one of the three countries with the highest level of entrepreneurship, alongside the United States and Canada. At the beginning of May 1996, the British economic daily *Financial Times* published a comprehensive article on Israel's technological industries with the headline "High-Tech Chutzpah." The article described Israel as the most exciting and attractive place for high-tech companies outside California and Boston. The respected newsweeklies *BusinessWeek* and *Newsweek* also published articles describing with wonder the dizzying growth of Israeli high-tech. A comparative international report published by the United Nations each year that ranks the position, status, and activities of the world's countries in various fields showed that in 1998 Israel was ranked seventh in the field of technology. Among that category's subcategories, the rank was even higher. For example, in "turning research into industry," Israel was ranked second in the world and in scientific research and technological sophistication third. In the adoption of new technology, it was ranked fifth and in the number of engineers sixth.

One important caveat must be stated. Israeli high-tech is no longer in its infancy, and despite its huge successes, there have also been no few difficulties and failures. *Red Herring*, the most important monthly in the international venture-capital field, devoted some 100 pages in its September 2000 issue to the various problems being faced by Israeli high-tech. Among the problems Israel had to cope with were the flight of Israeli high-tech companies to the United States, the severe shortage of engineers and other necessary professionals, high local taxation, distance from target markets, and chronic failures of marketing and distribution.

The crisis in which Israeli high-tech finds itself at the time of this chapter's writing—with both global[52] and local causes (in particular, the war with the Palestinians)—is a serious one and threatens some of the achievements made thus far. On the New York stock exchanges' Black Sunday—March 12, 2001—NASDAQ, the index of technological and Internet stocks, plunged, for the first time in two years, under the 2,000-point mark. This completed a one-year decline of 61 percent. The Dow Jones index was also caught up by the avalanche. Israeli stocks suffered a painful blow: for example, the stock of Gilat Satellites dropped by 56 percent. The fall came after a long list of leading companies published profit warnings the previous month, declaring an anticipated slowdown in their growth. High-tech was in major crisis.

The heavy blow has frightened many people because it seems to be one more domino in a toppling row. Investors are fleeing, factories are laying off workers, companies are closing, buyers are beginning to hesitate, and the ebullient atmosphere is being replaced by a melancholy and anxious one.[53] The fall of the dot-coms, an industry that was worth tens of billions of dollars a year, was critical because this industry's "food chain" is particularly large and includes large communications providers; producers of electronic equipment, chips, and optical fibers; satellite companies; and even furniture and food companies. Still, despite the common popular wisdom, this is not a bubble that burst. It is more reasonable to say that this was a correction required by the original euphoria—the kind of euphoria that has also characterized other industrial, commercial, financial, and technological revolutions (the establishment of the railroad, radio, bonds, cable television, and so on). The initial investments in high-tech all over the world were rushed and made without profound judgment. Everything was new, fast, tempting, and unknown. Yet after the storm, the excitement, the unrealistic expectations, and the inflated forecasts generally comes a period of calibration and stabilization. The talk of the death of high-tech, including Israeli high-tech—is thus early and exaggerated.[54]

In honor of Israel's fiftieth anniversary of independence, *Ma'ariv* published a Gallup poll that tried to measure the average Israeli's aspirations and preferences in the "New Israel." One question asked, "If you had no financial or other limitations, which of the following professions would you most like your child to choose?" The answers were first place, high-tech (33%); second place, doctor (15%); third place, lawyer (13%); and fourth place, Torah scholar (12%); officer in the standing army came in only at fifth place, with 5 percent.[55] These numbers express a most profound change in the country.

High-tech sparks the imagination of many educated young people in Israel not just because of its promise of a chance at wealth but also because it has all the romantic elements necessary for the birth of a constitutive myth. There is something electrifying in a start-up company that recalls the atmosphere of the elite military unit. There are crazy work hours; a sense of challenge; total devotion for the sake of success; the desire to excel; the knowledge that you are the small, crafty "David" who can defeat the giant, clumsy "Goliaths" with initiative and determination; the great reward that awaits at the end of the road; work with a team that is young, energetic, ambitious, creative, and competitive; the survival under difficult conditions that hardens and enriches you with inner nostalgia; the responsibility demanded of each member and the sense of partnership (which is almost absent in other industries); chutzpa and belief in oneself; and the informality and organizational flexibility characteristic of the sector.

However, unlike the culture of the elite military unit, which is centered on national service and Zionist culture, high-tech is "postnationalist" and "Post-Zionist" at almost all levels. It is global rather than local, it expresses loyalty to oneself and not to an organization or the state, it centers on money and career and not on social ideals and altruistic motivation, it is brain work rather than manual labor, and its dream is to conquer the world rather than to conquer the homeland.

Israeli culture has begun, in recent years, fostering the myth of the global high-tech entrepreneur just as, in the past, it fostered the myth of the combat soldier. Moreover, it is also establishing socialization frameworks for training a new cadre of high-tech entrepreneurs, just as in the past it invested in the establishment of socialization networks for the creation of "Zionist Spartans" (youth movements, agricultural schools, and so on).

WHAT OF THE FUTURE?

The process of globalization, which seemed, until just a short while ago, to be surging forward as it trampled down national traditions and cultures, has suddenly received new meaning, especially after the catastrophe of September 11. For a moment, it seemed as if the rumors of nationalism's death had been exaggerated. The deadly fireballs that destroyed the World Trade Center in New York and one of the wings of the Pentagon in Washington may not have burned the flag of globalization, but they certainly bent the flagpole and cast light on the cultural abyss yawning between the First and Third Worlds, between suffocating fundamentalism and alienating progress. On second thought, however, it may well be that the new global war now raging about us is an immanent, almost deterministic part of the postmodern cultural revolution—an unavoidable price that humanity pays at the end of every era and the beginning of a new one. In any case, Israel, which was on the front lines of the Cold War, has again found itself, and not to its own benefit, on the front line of a new global campaign. The globalization it has been and is undergoing will thus, in many ways, be the victory of Western globalization as a whole over its enemies.

This is not a simple campaign, and victory is hardly assured because Israeli globalization has many dangerous enemies, both outside and inside. These enemies view globalization as an existential and cultural threat to their existence. Most of them come from among religious Jews, ultra-Orthodox Jews, nationalist Jews, and Muslims. In fact, Jews and secular Zionists with rational worldviews and openness to change fear globalization because it threatens the Jewish and Zionist character of the State of Israel.

Is the global yuppie the new model that will replace the Zionist Sabra? To judge by what has taken place in Israel over the past two decades, the answer is in the affirmative. Can the Israeli yuppie survive? No one can answer that question.

NOTES

1. On this phenomenon and the approximation of Tel Aviv to this model, see Aryeh Shahar, "Global Village? Global City?," *Panim* 12 (winter 2000): 59–68; Baruch A. Kipnis, "Tel Aviv, Israel—A World City in Evolution: Urban Development at a Dead-end of Global Economy," Reseaech Buletine No. 57, http://www.lboro.ac.uk/gawc, 2001.

2. The turnover of some large global corporations is much larger than many state budgets.

3. See World Bank, "World Development Report, 1999/2000, The World Bank World Development Indices, 2000."

4. Elihu Katz and Hadassah Haz, "Twenty Years of Television in Israel: Do They Have a Long-Term Effect?," *Zemanim* 52 (1995): 80–91.

5. Michal Palti, "Big Sister," *Ha'aretz*, 15 April 1999, D1, *Galeria* section.

6. Yoav Birnberg, "Sitting in Your Underwear and Watching the World," *Yediot Aharonot, Sheva Leilot*, 13 October 1995, 2.

7. Quoted in Yehuda Koren and Eilat Negev, "The National Sweetener," *Yediot Aharonot, Sheva Leilot*, 18 September 1998, 26.

8. See Arieh Avneri, "Air Deals," in *The Gamblers* (Bar Publishers, 1987; in Hebrew), 46.

9. Central Bureau of Statistics, "Travelers, Cargoes, and International Air Traffic in Selected Years," *Statistical Yearbook* (Jerusalem: Central Bureau of Statistics, 1992), tables 18.1 and 18.11.

10. The statistics have been gathered from the following sources: "Tourism," *The State of Israel—Supplementary Volume, The Hebrew Encyclopedia*, 774; survey by the Pori Institute, based on a representative sample of the Jewish population from age 18 throughout the country, *Otot* 164 (February 1994): 53.

11. In 1961, there were 10 foreign airlines, in addition to El Al, operating out of Israel's major international airport. In 1989, there were 60 such countries, 23 of them with regular flights. During this period, the number of passengers going through Ben-Gurion International Airport grew from 223,000 in 1960 to 3.5 million in 1989. In this later year, there were some 450 travel agencies operating in Israel. The data come from "Transportation and Tourism," *Within the State of Israel—Supplementary Volume, The Hebrew Encyclopedia*, 774.

12. Eliahu Katz et al., *Leisure Culture in Israel: Changes in Patterns of Cultural Activity 1970–1990* (Jerusalem: Gutman Institute for Applied Social Research, Center for Information and Study of the Public Council for Culture and Art, Ministry of Education, November 1992), 2.

13. Aryeh Egozi, "Nightmare at the Airport," *Yediot Aharonot, 24 Sha'ot*, 26 August 1996, 10.

14. Dani Sadeh, "Celebrating Overseas," *Yediot Aharonot, Tayarut*, 31 August 1998, 4–5.

15. See "Ministry of Communications," *Government Yearbook*, 1975–76 (Jerusalem: Government of Israel), 284.

16. See the report in "Ministry of Communications—General Survey," *Government Yearbook* 1977, 333.

17. In 1970, the telephone waiting list's proportion to the population was 70 homes per 1,000 inhabitants. In 1980, it was 208 per 1,000 inhabitants. Central Bureau of Statistics, National Mail and Communications Services, table 18.12, *Statistical Yearbook*, 1999.

18. "Bezek" is the official Hebrew translation of the term "telecommunications."

19. The data are taken from David Levy Paor, "More Competition, More Regulation, the "Communications Revolution' in Israel and the State's Role," *Politika* 4 (December 1999): 41.

20. Central Bureau of Statistics, National Mail and Communications Services, table 18.12, *Statistical Yearbook*, 1999.

21. The annual growth in the number of phone lines in the 1984–94 period reached 6.6 percent, as compared to 1.8 percent in Sweden, 5.6 percent in Spain, and 4.6 percent in Belgium. The statistics come from Roni Aloni, "Forward March into the Digital Era," *Telekomunikatzia*, special supplement to *Ha'aretz*, December 1994, 29.

22. In 1988, Bezek's telephone network comprised some 2.87 million direct lines. The company's workers installed and moved 450,000 lines in that year, including ISDN lines. *Hadashot Bezek* 139 (June 1999).

23. "International Telephone Traffic," *Government Yearbook*, 1983–84, 348.

24. "The Majority Rules," *Yediot Aharonot*, *Mamon*, 13 September 2002, 5.

25. Shoshana Hen, "They Don't Leave Israel," *Yediot Aharonot*, *Mamon*, 26 July 2002, 8.

26. From "Yedion Otot—Puri—Internet," *Otot* 98, no. 213 (May 1998): 57.

27. "750 Israel Internet Sites," *Reshet Machshevim*, 28 April 1996, 4.

28. David Goldman, "The Israeli Surfer: Ashkenazi, Male, Non-Religious," *Yediot Aharonot*, *Mamon*, 15 March 1998, 7–8.

29. Quoted in Avi Belivosky, "The Government Will Act to Increase the Number of People Connecting to the Internet," *Ha'aretz*, 6 July 1998, A1.

30. Hani Barabash, "1.3 Million Israelis Surf the Internet," *Ha'aretz*, 31 January 2001, C7, *Kalkala* section.

31. See "Business Use of the Internet Expected to Expand in Israel in 2000," *Omanut Digitalit* 58 (January 2000): 27.

32. Hani Barabash, "1.3 Million Israelis Surf the Internet," *Ha'aretz*, 31 January 2001, C7, *Kalkala* section.

33. On the interesting historical background to Dizengoff Center, see Tamar Berger, *Dionysus at the Center*, Sifrei Simat Kirya (HaKivsa HaShehora Series) (Bnei Braks: Ha-Kibbutz Ha-Me'uchad, 1998). In the 1990s, the mall was expanded and reached 100,000 square meters (1.076 million square feet). The data appear in *Dionysus at the Center*, 193.

34. A total of 250 businesses operated there in 1983. Berger, *Dionysus at the Center*, 206.

35. Shoshana Hen, "The Mall Managers," *Yediot Aharonot*, *Mamon*, 8 June 1993, 46–48.

36. Israel is the densest country in the world when it comes to commercial centers, according to the results of a survey conducted in 1997 for *Yediot Aharonot*'s *Mamon* supplement by the research division of the Anglo-Saxon real estate network. The statistic comes from Ofer Petersburg, "Jurassic Park," *Yediot Aharonot*, *Mamon*, 17 October 1997, 5. In 1998, Israel had one mall for every 75,000 people. This statistic appears in "Coming Soon: The Next Malls," *Yediot Aharonot*, *Zemanim Modernim*, 18 February 1998, 9.

37. Anat Shinkman, "Grand Mall," *Iton Tel Aviv*, 4 August 1995, 46–48.

38. See Yuval Natan, "20 Years between Two Halves of a Warm Bun," *BaMahaneh*, 17 June 1992, 22–25.

39. Shoshana Hen, "Computerization Survey," *Yediot Aharonot*, *Mamon*, 3 February 1998, 2.

40. Hadas Manor, "The King of Burger King," *Ma'ariv*, 25 April 1995.

41. Ravit Naor, "And My Grandmother Used to Say: That's Not Food," *Ma'ariv*, 15 February 1995, 5.

42. "$3.22 Million in 65 Countries," *Status* 101 (November 1999): 44.

43. Kentucky Fried Chicken opened its first Israeli outlet in the 1980s in Herzliyya's Neve Amirim neighborhood. It was a failure; only in the 1990s did the chain manage to penetrate the Israeli market, this time with greater success.

44. Dan Tolkovsky, who had then left the post of commander of the air force and was appointed director of Discount Investments, began to channel financing and administrative support to high-technology industry. See Ben-Tzion Naveh, *The Management of High-Tech Industries in Israel* (Ramot: Tel Aviv University, 1995), 53.

45. Orna Berry (chief scientist of the Ministry of Industry and Commerce), "Great Potential for Israeli High-Tech in the Next Millennium," *Hi-Tek HaMilenium* (advertising supplement), *Ha'aretz*, December 1999, 7.

46. According to data published in 2000 by the periodical *Red Herring*. The Israeli *Guide for High-Tech Workers 2001* lists 600 well-established high-tech companies.

47. In October 1999, *Ha'aretz*'s economics section published a poll conducted among Israel's six largest accounting firms about the establishment of start-ups. According to these firms, 1,500 start-ups were established in 1999. For comparison, 600 companies were traded on the Tel Aviv stock exchange that same year. Guy Rolnik, "Another Country," *Ha'aretz*, *Mea BeKalkala*, 15 December 1999, 58–60.

48. On the products developed in Israel by foreign high-tech companies, see Nisan Cohen, "50 Years of Excellence," *Ha'aretz*, *Mussaf Hitek 98*, December 1998, 12–16.

49. Berry, "Great Potential for Israeli High-Tech in the Next Millennium."

50. Yigal Erlich (chairman of the Israel Association of Venture Capital Funds), "Deep Pockets," *High-Tek HaMilenium*, December 1999, 39.

51. *Ha'aretz*, *Kalkala*, 1 May 2000, C9.

52. See Baruch Kipnis, "The Global Crisis and Israel's High-Tech Industry," Reseaech Buletine No. 72, http://www.lboro.ac.uk/gawc, 2002.

53. See "The Week Reality Returned" (special supplement), *Ma'ariv*, *Asakim*, 16 March 2001.

54. Sever Plotzker, "The NASDAQ Is Dead, Long Live High-Tech," *Yediot Aharonot*, *HaMusaf LeShabat*, 16 March 2001, 4.

55. *Ma'ariv*, *Atzma'ut*, special supplement (*Mi Anahnu, Ma Anahnu*), 20 April 1999, 9.

Index

Abdulla, King, 3, 16, 22
Adalah, 40
Adoni, Hanna, 202
Agnon, Shmuel Yosef, 96
Agudat Yisrael, 137
Ahad Ha-am. *See* Asher Ginsburg
Ahbar Hair, 173
Ahdut Ha-Avoda, 88
Ahla, 242
AIPAC, 124
al-Aqsa intifada, ix, 17, 31, 48, 53
Alaska, 239
Aleph, 83
aliyah, 100, 110, 117, 123, 188
Alliance Israelite Universelle, 122
Allport, Gordon, 5
Almog, Oz, xii
Aloni, Shulamit, 150
Alterman, Nathan, 90
am adam, 149
American culture, 237
American Jews, x, 116–18, 197
American Mall, 245
Amichai, Yehuda, 97–98
Amidah yehudit, 158
Amir, Aharon, 80, 82, 85
Amir, Eli, 10
Amit, Meir, 241
Amotz, Dan, 99
anarchists, 179
Anderson, Benedict, 19, 25
Antalya, 238
anti-Semitism, 72, 74, 86, 126
Anti-Zionist, 35, 87
Arabic, 81
Arab-Israeli conflict, 8, 11–12, 16, 22, 25, 154
Arab-Jewish relations, 31–67
Arabs, viii, ix, x, 2–4, 7, 10, 13–14, 16–18, 20, 22, 26–27, 31–67, 81, 171, 176, 225
Arafat, Yasser, 26
Aran, Zalman, 86
archaeology, 85
Arendt, Hannah, 19
Argentina, 117, 122, 127
Ariel Yehuda, 141
Arkia, 237
Armenians, 150
Ashkelon, 117
Ashkenazi Jews, vii, viii, xi, 7, 102, 113–14, 165, 167–68, 174–75, 177–78, 196, 215, 216–17, 219–20, 223, 227, 228

Ashkenaziut, 220
Atar, Moshe, 80
Atarim Square, 244
Auron, Yair, 166–67
Auschwitz, 143, 149–50, 153
Australia, 114
Autonomists, 70–71
Avigur-Rotem, Gabriela, 102
Avneri, Uri, 81–82, 84–85, 88, 102
Ayalon Mall, 244, 247
Azrieli, David, 244

Baba, Homi, 24
Baer, Israel, 1
Baku, 200
Balad Party, 53–54
Balfour Declaration, 39
Ba-Maavak, 81
Banai, Ehud, 172
Barak, 242
Barak, Ehud, 199, 215
Bar-Kochba, 15–16, 77–78, 85, 91
Bar-On, Mordechai, x
Bartov, Hanoh, 90
Baruch, Baba, 9
Basque lands, 233
Bat Yam, 201
Bat Yam Mall, 245
Baudrillard, Jean, 24
BBC, 236
Bedouin, 45, 48, 50
Beersheva, 201
Beit Yisrael, 124
Belgium, 32
Ben-Aharon, Yariv, 98
Ben-Ami, Issachar, 9
Ben-Eliezer, Uri, 18
Ben-Gurion, David, 1, 7, 14, 18, 22, 69, 78, 85, 89, 90–91, 97, 103, 125, 146, 217–20
Ben-Gurion Airport, 239
Ben-Hanina, Yossai, 148
Ben Yehuda, Baruch, 86
Berdyczewski, Micha, 72
Berger, Noga, 158
Berger, Peter, 176
Berman, Avraham, 155–56
Bezek, 240–42
Bialik, Haim, 73–74, 79
Bilu, Yoram, 9
Bin Nun, 78
binational state, 14, 34, 51, 58
Birkenau, 153
Bosnia, 150
Boston, 251
Brailovsky, Victor, 197
Brenner, Josef, 72, 74
Britain, 13, 16, 114
British Mandate, 37
Bundists, 178
BusinessWeek, 251

California, 251
Camp David Talks, 38
Canaanism, 79, 80–85, 89, 96, 98–99, 101–3
Canada, 32, 250–51
Carmiel, 117
Carmon, Aric, 124
Center for Israel-Diaspora Cultural Relations, 125
Chelm syndrome, 114
Choosing Survival, 163
Christians, 31, 43, 173
CNN, 235
Cohen, Akiva, 202
Cohen, Eric, 20
Committee of Israeli-Jewish Consciousness, 85–87
Committee to Consolidate Hebrew Youth, 79
communists, 219
conservative, 117, 123, 179
consociational democracy, 32, 34

Davar, 236
Dayan, Eli, 149
Dayan, Moshe, 15, 85, 146
Dead Sea Scrolls, 85
Democracy and Aliyah Party, 198
Democratic Front for Peace and Equality, 52
Derrida, Jacques, 24
Diaspora, viii, x, 11, 47, 50, 59, 69–103, 109–27, 137, 141, 188, 225
Dimono, 249

Dinur, Zion, 140, 148, 154, 155
Dizengof Center, 244
Doron, Lizzie, 141–42, 146, 157
Dow Jones, 251
Druze, 31, 43
Dubnow, Simon, 70, 140

education, 44
Egypt, 240
Egyptian Army, 97
Eichmann, Adolf, x, 90–96
Eilat, 237–38, 245
Ein-Ha'Horesh, 96
Einstein, Albert, 125
Eisenstadt, Baruch, 76
El Al, 237
Eli, Ovadiah, 149
Eliyahu, Mordechai, 178
Elon, Amos, 167
Elul, Rafi, 150
Emek Hefer School, 151
English, 119, 192, 246
En Harid, 75
Eretz Israel Ha-Ze'ra, 81
Erikson, Erik, 4–6, 9, 14, 23, 27
Ethiopian Jews, 100, 112, 117
ethnic democracy, 33
Europe, 234
European Jewry, x, 110
Evron, Bo'az, 85

Fast Food Stores, 246–49
Feniger, Ofer, 98
Financial Times, 251
Finland, 243
Flanders, Ned, 170
Flapan, Simha, 1, 13–14
forgiveness, 145–48
Foucault, Michel, 24
France, 32, 114, 240, 243
Frank, Ann, 138
Frankfurt, 233
Friedgut, Theodore, xi
Frischmann, David, 72
Furnival, J. S., 32

Gahal, 88
Galilee, 31
Galilee Judaization Program, 47
Gaza Strip, 36, 43, 46, 51, 56
Gelber, Yoav, 16
Georgia, 188, 189
German, 77, 152
German Jews, xi
Germans, 145, 148, 150, 154
Germany, 189
Gerstein, Larissa, 191
Gesher Theatre, 202–3
Ghanem, As'ad, 35
Gilboa, Amir, 89–90
Ginsberg, Asher, 70, 83, 109
Gitelman, Zvi, 196, 197, 200
Givataim, 242
globalization of Israel, 233–53
Glozman, Vladimir, 204
Golan Heights, 46
Golani Brigade, 247
Golani, Motti, 17–19
Goldstein, Alexander, 200
Gordon, Aharon David, 149
Gordon, J. L., 73
Gordon, Judah Leib, 72
Gouri, Haim, 80, 82, 96, 98
Gramsci, Antonio, 24
Greater Israel, 21
Great Revolt of 1936–1939, 14
Greek music, 10
Greenberg, Uri, 71, 78–79
Grodzinsky, Yosef, 69
Group identity, 5
Gulf war, 235
Gur-Horon, Adiya, 83
Guttman Institute, 166
Guttman Report, 167, 170
Gutwein, Daniel, xi, 3

Ha'aretz, 145, 173, 236, 243
Habermas, Jurgen, 24
Hadari, Yona, 18–19
Hadassah Hospital, 120
Hafat, 16
Haifa, 117, 240
Hamshbir Letzarchan, 244
Haredi Jews, 114–15, 163–65, 168, 172, 178, 223, 227, 253
Harel, Doron, 239

Hartman, Rabbi David, 117
Ha-Savua, 96
Hashomer Hatzair, 89, 141
Hasidic, 114
Hazan, Ya'akov, 155–56
hazara b'tshuvah, 171–72
Hazaz, Haim, 77, 80, 85
Hazoni, Yoram, 12
Hebrew, 8, 23, 41, 45–50, 73, 78–83, 86, 115, 119, 123, 174, 185, 190, 202–3, 216–19, 221, 242–43, 246, 250
Hebrew Union College, 118
Hebrew University, 238
Hen, Shoshana, 246
Hendel, Yehudit, 90
Herman, Simon, 8, 165
Herut, 219
Herzl, Theodor, 70–71
Het, Meir, 237
high-tech industries, 249–53
Hirchson, Abraham, 150
Histadrut, 42, 52, 221, 240
Hizbollah, 116
Hobsbawm, Erik, 25
Holocaust, viii, x, 2, 14, 19, 39, 50, 69–71, 76–77, 79, 82, 86–96, 137–59, 167, 175, 186, 225
Holocaust Celler, 141
Holocaust Martyrs' and Heroes' Remembrance Day, 138–39, 141, 144, 157, 173
Hong Kong, 233
Hungary, 114

immigrants, viii, x, 20, 100, 109, 112–20, 185–206
inequality, 44–45, 227
International Day of Working Women, 186
International Monetary Fund, 235
Internet, 242–44
Internet Zahav, 242
Iran, 111
Iraq, 10, 32, 114
Iraqi Jews, 178
Ireland, 32, 33, 57, 58
Irgun, 89
Islam, 34
Islamic countries, 2, 7, 10, 111, 176
Israel, x, xi, xi
Israel Aircraft Industries, 249
Israel Defence Forces (IDF), 1, 3, 17, 42, 85, 97, 116, 169, 215, 221, 249
Israel Democracy Institute, 124
Israeli Historiography, 1–27
Israeli, Raphael, 35
Israel Land Authority, 46
Israel Museum, 85
Israel Religious Action Center (IRAC), 118
Italy, 114, 240, 243

Jabotinsky, Ze'ev, 78
Japan, 32
Jerusalem, 50, 117–18, 240, 247
Jewish Agency, 120, 240
Jewish National Fund, 47
Jewishness, 167, 169, 170–72, 174–77, 193, 195–96
Jewish Theological Seminary, 118
Jews, ix, x, 17, 34, 36, 41–42, 46, 47, 55–56, 69–103, 225, 253
Jordan River, 26
Judaean Hills, 81, 85, 90
Judaism, 85, 109, 112, 115, 163, 167, 169–78, 187, 194
Judea, 102
Judenrat, 155, 158

Kach movement, 52
Kadish, Alon, 16
Kaganskaya, Maya, 191
Kahana, Rabbi, 52,
Kanovich, Grogorii, 191
Kaplan, Mordechai, 124
Karyon, 245
Kastner Trial, 89, 138
Katznelson, Berl, 71, 77–79
Katznelson, Itzhak, 79
Kavai Zahav, 242
Kedar, Mordechai, 35
kehilla, 121
Keinan, Alex, 80
Keinan, Amos, 84–85, 102
Kesse, Yona, 149

Kfar-al-Kassem, 46
Kfar Yona, 245
Khanin, Vladimir, 201
kibbutz, 10, 75–76, 96, 98, 117
Kibbutz Ha-Me'uhad, 75–78, 88–89
Kibbutz Lohamei Hageta'ot, 141–42, 144
Kibbutz Ma'agan Michael, 149
Kibbutz Yad Mordechai, 141
kiddush, 170
kiddush hashem, 79
Kiev, 190
Kimmerling, Baruch, 2, 7
Kiryat Shmonah, 245
Klein, Kerwin Lee, 4
Klein, Uri, 171
Knesset, 45, 47, 50, 52, 86, 124–25, 137–38, 140, 148–50, 154, 157, 186, 197–98, 200, 235, 241
Kol Bo Shalom, 244
Korczak, Ruzhka, 96
Korea, 32
Kosherovsky, Yulii, 198
Kovner, Abba, 96, 139, 143–44
Kristalnacht, 150
Ktav el Ha-No'ar Ha-Ivri, 80
Kubovy, Arich, 149, 159
Kulka, Dov, 142, 153
Kulturkampf, 2, 220
Kuper, Leo, 32
Kurzweil, Baruch, 82–83
Kuznetsov, Edward, 191, 197–98

Labor Government, 38
Labor movement, 78
Labor Party, viii, 198
Land day Strike, 37, 46
Landua, Jacob, 35
Lapid, Ron, 247
Latin American Jews, 110, 118
Latvia, 32
Lavi, Shlelomo, 75
Law for the Punishment of Nazis and Nazi Collaborators, 138
Law of Return, x, 50, 59, 124, 205
League of Nations, 39
Lebanon, 116
Lebanon war, 238
Lederhendler, Eli, x
Lev Hamifratz, 245
Levin, Rabbi Yitzak Meir, 137, 156
Levite, Lyova, 75–76, 79
Lev Mall, 245
Liberman, Avigdor, 198–99
Liebman, Charles, xi, 119
Lijphart, Arend, 32–33
Likrat, 83
Likud Party, viii, 198–99
Little Triangle, 31
Lod, 16
London, 233
London Ministore, 244
Lustick, Ian, 32, 35–36

Ma'agan Michael School, 151
Ma'ariv, 173, 236, 252
Macedonia, 58
Machon Schechter, 118
Mahanot Ha-Olim, 88
Maletz, David, 75
Mamlachtiyut, 217, 221–22, 225, 228
Mamon, 242
MAMRAM, 249
Mannheim, Karl, 77
Manor, Dalia, 176
Ma'of, 237
Mapai, 75, 77, 85, 89, 219
Mapam, 13, 84
Mapu, Abraham, 72
Masada, 15–16, 85
Masorti. *See* conservative
Massa Ha-Ptiha, 87
McDonald's, 247–48
Megged, Aharon, 6, 137
megillah, 173
Meir, Esther, 10
Meir, Golda, 26
melting pot, 7, 215–28
Mendel Mokher Seforim (Shalom Abromowitch), 72, 74, 79
Middle East, 234, 236
Migdal haemek, 245
military rule, 51
millets, 42, 80, 99
Ministry of the Interior, 48
mixed marriages, 42, 47

Mizrahi Jews, ix, xi, 7–11, 20, 112, 114, 165, 167–68, 170, 172, 174–75, 178, 196, 215, 219, 220, 223–24, 227
Mizrahi Party, 219
mizrahiut, 220
Mizug galuyot. *See* melting pot
Moda'i Yitzhak, 241
Modi'in, 117
Mofet Schools, 201
Moroccan Jews, 100, 178
Morocco, 9–10, 111, 114
Morris, Benny, 2–3, 16, 22
Moscow, 190, 193
multiculturalism, 41, 215–28
multinational corporations, 233
Munich, 97
Muslims, 31, 35, 41, 43, 150, 177, 253
mutual rapprochement thesis, 36

Nachman, Rabbi, 114
Nana, 242
NASDAQ, 251
Nasser, Abdul, 97
National Union, 198
Nazi Germany, 73
Nazis, 89, 150–51, 154–56, 186
Negev, 31
Netking, 242
New Historians. *See* Post-Zionists
New History, 1–27
New Outlook, 1
Newsweek, 251
New York, 233, 253
New York Stock Exchanges, 250–51
Nini, Yehuda, 10
Nora, Pierre, 22
North Africa, viii
Novokovitz, Sala, 137
Nudelman, Raphael, 191
Nukharan Jews, 188
Nurock, Mordechai, 156

October War. *See* Yom Kippur War
Ofer, Dalia, x
Ofira, 237
Ohana, David, 7, 10
Olam Ha-Zeh, 82, 89
Omer, 117
Ophir, Adi, 17, 24
Orhan, Nurit, 96
Orientalism, 24
Oriental music, 10
Ornan, Uzi, 99
ORT, 120
Orthodox, 117–19, 163–64, 166, 168–69, 173, 177–79, 197, 205
Oslo Accords, ix, 26, 38, 40, 46, 56
Oz, Amos, 11

Palestine, 22, 37, 39, 50, 73, 76, 79
Palestine Liberation Organization (PLO), 23, 38
Palestinian refugees, 13, 16, 37, 50, 98
Palestinians, xii, 10, 14, 17–18, 20, 22–23, 26, 31, 34, 37, 43, 44, 47, 49, 50, 57, 116
Palestinian state, 51, 55, 58–59
Palmah, 70, 82–83, 84–85, 96, 98, 221
Pappe, Ilan, 2, 16, 22
Paris, 233
Partnership 2000, 121
Passover, 170
peace process, 26, 38, 46
Peled, Matti, 80
Peled Eyal, 239
Pentagon, 253
Peretz, Isaac, 72, 73
philanthropy, 120–27
Philippines, 239
Piltz, Aryeh, 244
Pinsker, Leon, 70
Plotkin, Il'ya, 203
pluralism, 40, 43
Poland, 73, 78, 100, 112, 114, 124, 149–51
Polish Jewry, 78
Post-Zionists, ix, x, 1–6, 20–22, 223–26, 252
Project Renewal, 121
Purim, 173

Quebec, 233

Rabin, Yitzhak, 26, 38, 46, 53, 54, 101
Rabinowitz, Dan, 35
RAFAEL, 249

Ram, Uri, 2, 9
Ramat Gan, 242
Ramle, 16
Ratosh. *See* Shelah
Raz-Krakotzkin, Amnon, 69
Red Herring, 250, 251
Reform Judaism, 117, 179
Regev, Rabbi Uri, 118
Rekhess, Eli, 35
remembrance, 145–48
Remembrance of the Holocaust and Heroism Law, 140
revenge, 145–48
Rex, John, 32
Rimalt, Elimeleh, 86
Ringelblum, Emmanuel, 140
Rishon Letzion, 245, 247
Rome, 233
Rouhana, Nadim, 35
Rubina, Dina, 191
Rumania, 114
Russia, 100, 187, 190, 193–94, 203
Russian Jews, xi, 7, 12, 74, 100, 115–17, 166, 185–206, 215
Russian language, xi, 115, 123, 191, 192, 200–203
Rwanda, 32
Ryvkina, Rosalina, 195

Sabbath, 170, 172–73, 196, 202
Sabra, ix, x, 70, 77, 80, 83–90, 99, 216
Said, Edward, 24
Sali, Baba, 9
Samaria, 102
Satanovsky, Eugene, 195
Savir, Dalia, 151–52
Scandinavia, 32, 237
Schechter, Solomon, 124
Schein, Eliezer, 71
Schermerhorn, R. A., 32
Schudson, Michael, 4
Segev, Tom, 69
Sela, Avraham, 16
Sephardi. *See* Mizrahi
Serbia, 32
Shalem Institute, 12
Shalev, Mordechai, 83
Shalom Hartman Institute, 117
Shapira, Anita, x, 3, 18
Shapira, Avraham, 98
Sharansky, Anatolii, 191, 198–99
Sharett, Moshe, 18, 139, 144
Shas, 114–15, 178
Shdemot group, 96
Shelah, Uriel (Yonathan Ratosh), 79–85, 87, 96, 102
Sheleg, Yair, 163–64
Shinui Party, 197
Shizaf, Tzur, 239
Shlaim, Avi, 2, 16, 22
Shlonsky, Abraham, 81
Shneour, Zalman, 82
Sholem Aleichem (Sholem Rabinowitz), 72–73, 79, 100
Shopping malls, 244–46
shtetl, 75, 78–79, 81, 101
Shueftan, Dan, 35
Siah Lohamim, 98
Sinai Campaign, 13
Singapore, 233
Singer, Tsofit, 152–53
Six-Day War, xi, 13, 25, 37, 84, 97–99, 117, 165, 169, 171, 193, 249
Sklare, Marshall, 179
Skop, Barry, 247
Sky, 236
Slovakia, 33
Smith, M. G., 32
Smooha, Sammy, x, 33, 35–36
Soffer, Arnon, 35
Solomon Schechter Day Schools, 118
South Africa, 114
South African Jewry, 110, 127
Soviet Union, ix, xi, 7, 111, 156, 166, 186–87, 191, 193, 196–97, 199, 201, 233, 240, 249
Sri Lanka, 32, 57
Stalin, 190
State of Israel, 16, 18–20, 24, 31, 34–35, 37–38, 47, 50, 58, 69–70, 78, 82–84, 88, 90–91, 97, 99, 110, 112, 122, 124, 126–27, 139, 144–45, 149, 159, 164–66, 169, 177, 185, 190, 193, 199, 204–6, 217, 234, 249, 253
St. Petersburg, 190

St. Petersburg Club, 200, 204
Straits of Tiran, 97
St. Sylvester's night, 186
succah, 170
Succoth, 171
Sudan, 32
Suez Canal, 26
Sukenik, E. L., 85
Supreme Court, 40, 46, 55, 118
Switzerland, 32, 240

Tabenkin, Yitzak, 78
TALI schools, 118
Talmi, Emma, 157
Tamir, Shmuel, 89
Tammuz, Benjamin, 80, 85
Tapuz, 242
Tchernichowsky, Saul, 70, 73, 82
Technion, 249
Tel-Aviv, 117, 240, 242, 247
telecommunications, 240–42
telephones, 240–42
television, 171, 173, 235–37, 239
Tel Hai, 15–16
Tel Mond, 245
Teoria u-Vikoret, 11, 24, 25
Tiberias, 238
Tikkun, 2–3
TIM, 243
Tisha B'av, 173
Tokyo, 233
Top Hat Theatre, 203
Torah Sages Council, 115
Toronto, 233, 245
tourism, 237–39
Treblinka, 152
Trumpeldor, Joseph, 15–16
tsedakah, 121
Tsur, Muki, 97
Tunisia, 114
Tunisian Jews, 178
Turkey, 238
Turks, 150
Tzur, Yaron, 10

Ufaz, Gad, 90
Uganda, 73
Ukraine, 114, 187, 189–90
ultra-orthodox, 112
Ultra-Orthodox. *See* Haredi
UNESCO, 16, 27
UN forces, 97
Union of Immigrant Teachers, 201
United Europe, 233
United Nations, 53, 251
United States, 32, 51, 87, 97, 100–102, 110–11, 118, 122–23, 150, 173, 175, 178–79, 189, 217–18, 240, 247, 249, 250–51
UN November 1947 Resolution, 37, 39
Urbach, Ephraim, 86
Urian, Dan, 171

Vaadia, Moshe, 80
van den Berghe, Pierre, 32–33
Van Leer Institute, 11
Vesti, 191, 198, 202

Walla, 242
Waqf, 42
Warhaftig, Zerah, 156
War of Attrition, 15
War of Independence (1948 War), ix, 1–2, 13–15, 18, 22–23, 25, 70, 85, 88–90, 97–98, 149, 155
Warsaw Ghetto, 87, 155
Washington, 253
Weiss, Shevah, 150
Weizmann Institute, 249
welfare state, xi, 226
West Bank, 36, 43, 46, 51, 56
West Bank Settlers, 163–64
West Germany, 89, 138, 144, 145, 146
White, Hayden, 24
Wired, 250
Wisse, Ruth, 112
Wistrich, Robert, 15
Women's International Zionist Organization (WIZO), 86
World Trade Center, 253
World War I, 77, 150, 178
World War II, x, 77, 97, 100, 111–12, 138, 140, 179, 186, 188, 190

World Zionist Organization, (WZO), 124

Ya'ari, Menahem, 27
Yadgar, Yaacov, xi
Yadin, Yigal, 16, 85, 91
Yad Vashem, 138–41, 148–49, 153, 156–57
Yediot Aharanot, 173, 236, 239, 242–43, 246
Yemen, 114, 219
yeridah, 100–101
Yerushalmi, Yosef, 4
yeshiva, 115, 118, 127, 157
Yiddish, 72, 77–79, 112, 123, 219
Yiftachel, Oren, 33, 35–36
Yishuv, 73, 75, 110, 185, 221
Yisrael Ba'Aliyah, 198–99
Yisrael Betenu, 199
YIVO, 140
Yom Kippur, 170–71
Yom Kippur War, viii, 25–26, 99, 165, 168–69, 249
yordim, 101
Yugoslavia, 57

Zabar, Meier, 147
Zaremski, Laura, 167
Zerkalo, 203
Zertal, Idith, 19, 69
Zionism, vii, viii, x, xi, 2, 4, 10, 18, 20–22, 24, 34, 41, 43, 50, 69–70, 72, 74, 77–78, 82–83, 86, 101, 112, 118, 168, 169, 172, 177, 185–86, 216, 225–26, 252
Zionist Forum, 191
Zionist Movement, 15, 18, 37, 49, 50, 69, 124
Zionists, 16, 71, 109, 178, 226, 253
Zohar, Ezra, 80
Zohar, Uri, 172
Zorea, Naomi, 149
Zucker, Dedi, 150
Zuckerman, Moshe, 69
Zureik, Elia, 35, 36
Zvi, Beit, 69

About the Editor and Contributors

OZ ALMOG is a sociologist and social historian in the Land of Israel Studies Department at Haifa University. He is the author of *The Sabra: The Creation of the New Jew* (2000) and *Farewell to Srulik: The Transformation of Values in the Israeli Elite* (2004; in Hebrew).

MORDECHAI BAR-ON, who is presently a research fellow at the Yitzhak Ben-Zvi Memorial Institute, had previously served as the chief of education for the Israel Defense Forces and had at one time been a member of the Knesset (Israel's parliament). Among his many published works are *The Gates of Gaza: Israel's Road to Suez and Back 1955–1957* (1994) and *In Pursuit of Peace: A History of Israel's Peace Movement* (1996).

THEODORE H. FRIEDGUT is emeritus professor of Russian and Slavic studies at the Hebrew University of Jerusalem. His major works include *Political Participation in the USSR* (1979) and the two-volume *Iuzovka and Revolution* (1989 and 1994).

DANIEL GUTWEIN is a lecturer in modern Jewish history at the University of Haifa. His publications have concentrated in the fields of Jewish economic and social history and Jewish nationalism and socialism. More recently, he has investigated the interrelationship between collective memory and economic and social politics in Israel.

ELI LEDERHENDLER is an associate professor in the Harman Institute of Contemporary Jewry of the Hebrew University of Jerusalem. His recent works include *Jewish Responses to Modernity* (1997) and *New York Jews and the Decline of Urban Ethnicity, 1950–1970* (2001). The latter publication was awarded the 2001 Koret Foundation book prize for Jewish history.

The late CHARLES LIEBMAN was professor emeritus in the Department of Political Studies at Bar Ilan University. His numerous publications dealt with issues relating to Jewish identity in America and Israel. He was awarded the prestigious Israel Prize in political science. The chapter he coauthored in this volume represents one of his final works.

DALIA OFER holds the Max and Rita Haber Chair of Contemporary Jewry at the Hebrew University of Jerusalem. She has written extensively on the Holocaust in both Hebrew and English. Among her better-known English works are *Escaping the Holocaust* (1998) and her coedited volume *Women in the Holocaust* (1998).

ANITA SHAPIRA is a professor of modern and contemporary Jewish History at Tel Aviv University, with special interests in social and cultural history as well as issues relating to identity. She has published widely on the history of Zionism and the Jewish community in Palestine. Her best-known works include *Berl Katzenelson: A Biography of a Socialist Zionist* (1984) and *Land and Power: The Zionist Resort to Force, 1882–1984* (1992).

SAMMY SMOOHA is professor of sociology at the University of Haifa. A specialist in comparative ethnic relations, he has published widely on the internal divisions in Israel. His books include *Israel: Pluralism and Conflict* (1978), the two-volume *Arabs and Jews in Israel* (1989 and 1992), and *Autonomy for Arabs in Israel?* (1999).

YAACOV YADGAR teaches politics at the Department of Political Studies at Bar Ilan University. He has published several works on various aspects of Jewish Israeli collective identity, and is currently engaged in research on non-Orthodox Jewish identities in Israel.

CPSIA information can be obtained
at www.ICGtesting.com
Printed in the USA
LVHW022103080920
665373LV00004B/160

9 780275 976606